C++ from the Ground Up

Herbert Schildt

Osborne **McGraw-Hill**

Berkeley New York St. Louis San Francisco Auckland Bogotá Hamburg London Madrid Mexico City
Milan Montreal New Delhi Panama City Paris São Paulo Singapore Sydney Tokyo Toronto

Table of Contents

Osborne **McGraw-Hill**
2600 Tenth Street
Berkeley, California 94710
U.S.A.

For information on translations or book distributors outside of the U.S.A.,
please write to Osborne **McGraw-Hill** at the above address.

C++ from the Ground Up

90 DOC 9987

ISBN 0-07-881969-5

Publisher	**Computer Designer**
Lawrence Levitsky	Marcela V. Hancik
Acquisitions Editor	**Quality Control Specialist**
Jeff Pepper	Joe Scuderi
Project Editor	**Illustrator**
Nancy McLaughlin	Rhys Elliott
Technical Editor	**Interior Designer**
James Turley	Marla Shelasky
Proofreader	**Indexer**
Audrey Baer Johnson	Sheryl Schildt

Cover Design
Ted Mader Associates

Introduction

This book teaches you how to program in C++. No previous programming experience is required (although, of course, any prior background in programming will be helpful.) The book starts with the basics and concludes with C++'s most advanced features. Nothing is left out. By the time you finish this book, you will be an accomplished C++ programmer.

C++ represents the current state of the art as applied to computer programming languages. It is the language of choice of professional programmers worldwide. C++ combines power with flexibility, efficiency with elegance, and tradition with innovation. As you work your way through this book, you will see that every element of C++ exists for a reason. There is very little of the "bloat," or redundant features, that are so common in other programming languages. In fact, one of the most important aspects of C++ is its streamlined design.

One final point: Because it was designed for professional programming, C++ is not the easiest programming language to learn. It is, however, ***the best*** programming language to learn. Once you have mastered C++, you will have virtually complete control over the computer. C++ is, above all, the most powerful programming language ever invented!

How to Use This Book

The best way to learn any programming language, including C++, is by doing. Therefore, after you have read through a section, try the sample programs before moving on. Make sure that you understand why they do what they do. You should also experiment with the programs, changing one or two lines at a time and observing the results. The more you program, the better you will become at programming. But most of all, have fun with it.

If You're Using Windows

If your computer uses Windows, and if your goal is to write Windows-based programs, then you have chosen to learn the right language. C++ is completely at home with Windows programming. However, none of the programs in this book are Windows programs. Instead, they are console-based programs. The reason for this is easy to understand: Windows programs are, by their nature, large and complex. The overhead required to create just a skeletal Windows program is 50 to 70 lines of code. Windows programs that demonstrate the features of C++ would require hundreds of lines of code each. Put simply, Windows is not an appropriate environment in which to learn programming. However, you can still use a Windows-based compiler to compile the programs in this book. It is just that you will need to use the command-prompt (console) interface. (Your compiler manual will explain how to do this.)

Once you have mastered C++, you will be able to apply your knowledge to Windows programming. In fact, C++ allows the use of class libraries that can greatly simplify the development of Windows programs. Many of the Windows programs being created today are coded in C++.

Diskette Offer

There are many useful and interesting functions, classes, and programs contained in this book. If you're like me, you probably would like to use them, but hate typing code into the computer. When I key in routines from a book, it always seems that I type something wrong and spend hours trying to get the program to work. For this reason, I am offering the source code on diskette for all the functions and programs contained in this book for $24.95. Just fill in the order blank on the next page and mail it, along with your payment, to the address shown. Or, if you're in a hurry, just call (217) 586-4021 (the number of my consulting office) and place your order by telephone. (Visa and MasterCard accepted.) You can also order by FAX at (217) 586-4997.

Please send me _____ copies, at $24.95 each, of the programs in *C++ from the Ground Up* on an IBM-compatible diskette.

Foreign orders only: Checks must be drawn on a U.S. bank. Please add $5.00 shipping and handling.

_____
Name

_____
Address

_____ _____ _____
City   State   ZIP

_____
Telephone

Diskette size (check one): 5.25"_____   3.5"_____

Method of payment: Check _____   Visa _____   MC _____

Credit card number: _____

Expiration date: _____

Signature: _____

Send to:

Herbert Schildt
398 County Rd 2500 N
Mahomet, Il 61853

Phone: (217) 586-4021
FAX: (217) 586-4997

For Further Study

C++ from the Ground Up is your gateway into the other programming books written by Herbert Schildt. To learn more about C++, you will find these books especially helpful:

C++: The Complete Reference

Teach Yourself C++

If you want to learn more about C (which forms the foundation for C++), then the following titles will be of interest:

C: The Complete Reference

The Annotated ANSI C Standard

Teach Yourself C

If you want to program for Windows, we recommend the Osborne Windows Programming Series, co-authored by Herbert Schildt. You will find it invaluable when trying to understand the complexities of Windows. The series titles are:

Volume 1: Programming Fundamentals

Volume 2: General Purpose API Functions

Volume 3: Special Purpose API Functions

Finally, here are some other books about C and C++ written by Herbert Schildt that you will also find useful and interesting:

The Art of C

The Craft of C

Turbo C/C++: The Complete Reference

When you need solid answers fast, turn to Herbert Schildt, the recognized authority on programming.

Chapter 1

The Story of C++

C++ is the culmination of years spent in the pursuit of the perfect programming language. While it is certainly true that new and better languages will be developed in the future, C++ represents the current "state of the art." It is the quest for a better way to program that is the story of C++.

Before beginning your study of C++, it is important for you to know how C++ came about and what factors drove its creation. Once you understand the forces and reasons that led to the development of C++, its many unique features and attributes will make more sense.

The purpose of this chapter is to present a brief history of the C++ programming language, its origins, its relationship to its predecessor (C), its uses, and the programming philosophies that it supports. This chapter will also put C++ into perspective relative to other programming languages.

The Origins of C++

The story of C++ begins with C. The reason for this is simple: C++ is built upon the foundation of C. In fact, C++ is a superset of C. (Indeed, all C++ compilers can also be used to compile C programs!) Specifically, C++ is an expanded and enhanced version of C that embodies the philosophy of object-oriented programming (which is described later in this chapter). C++ also includes several other improvements to the C language. However, much of the spirit and flavor of C++ is inherited directly from C. To fully understand and appreciate C++, you need to understand the "how and why" behind C.

The Creation of C

The C language shook the computer world. Its impact should not be underestimated because it fundamentally changed the way programming was approached and thought about. C is considered by many to be the first modern "programmer's language." Prior to the invention of C, computer languages were generally designed either as academic exercises or by bureaucratic committees. C is different. C was designed, implemented and developed by real, working programmers, and it reflected the way they approached the job of programming. Its features were honed, tested, thought about and rethought by the people who actually used the language. The result of this process was a language that programmers liked to use. Indeed, C quickly attracted many followers who had a near religious zeal for it, and it found wide and rapid acceptance in the programmer community. In short, C is a language designed by and for programmers.

C was invented and first implemented by Dennis Ritchie on a DEC PDP-11 using the UNIX operating system. C is the result of a development process that started with an older language called BCPL. BCPL was developed by Martin Richards. BCPL influenced a language called B, which was invented by Ken Thompson and which led to the development of C in the 1970s.

For many years, the *de facto* standard for C was the one supplied with the UNIX version 5 operating system and described in *The C Programming Language* by Brian Kernighan and Dennis Ritchie (Prentice-Hall, 1978). With the advent of personal computers, a large number of C implementations were created and C grew in popularity. However, because no standard existed, there were discrepancies between implementations. To alter this situation, a committee was established in the beginning of the summer of 1983 to work on the creation of an ANSI (American National Standards Institute) standard that would define once and for all the C language. The final version of the standard was adopted in December of 1989, with the first copies becoming available in early 1990. ANSI standard C is the foundation upon which C++ is built.

1

It may seem hard to understand at first, but C is often called a "middle-level" computer language. As it is applied to C, middle-level does not have a negative connotation; it does not mean that C is less powerful, harder to use, or less developed than a "high-level" language, or that it is as difficult to use as assembly language. (Assembly language, or *assembler* as it is often called, is simply a symbolic representation of the actual machine code that a computer can execute.) C is thought of as a middle-level language because it combines elements of high-level languages, such as Pascal or Modula-2, with the functionality of assembler.

From a theoretical point of view, a high-level language attempts to give the programmer everything he or she could possibly want, already built into the language. A low-level language provides nothing other than access to the actual machine instructions. A middle-level language gives the programmer a concise set of tools and allows the programmer to develop higher level constructs on his or her own. A middle-level language offers the programmer built-in power, coupled with flexibility.

Being a middle-level language, C allows you to manipulate the bits, bytes, addresses, and ports which are the constituent components of the computer. That is, C does not attempt to buffer the hardware of the machine from your program, to any significant extent. For example, unlike many high-level languages, which can operate directly on strings of characters to perform a multitude of string manipulations, C can directly operate only on individual characters. Further, in most high-level languages there are built-in statements for reading and writing disk files. In C, all of these procedures are performed by calls to library routines that are not, technically, part of the language. This approach increases C's flexibility. Although all ANSI standard compilers supply functions capable of performing disk I/O, your programs can bypass them if they choose.

C allows—indeed, needs—the programmer to define routines for performing high-level operations. These routines are called *functions*, and they are very important to the C language. In fact, functions are the building blocks of both C and C++. You can easily tailor a library of functions to perform various tasks that are used by your program. In this sense, you can personalize C to fit your needs.

There is another aspect of C that you must understand, because it is also important to C++: C is a structured language. The most distinguishing feature of a structured language is that it uses blocks. A *block* is a set of statements that are logically connected. For example, imagine an IF statement that, if successful, will execute five discrete statements. If these statements can be grouped together and referenced as an indivisible unit, then they form a block.

A structured language allows a variety of programming possibilities. It supports the concept of subroutines with local variables. A *local variable* is simply a variable that is known only to the subroutine in which it is defined. A structured language also supports several loop constructs, such as **while**, **do-while** and **for**. The use of the **goto** statement, however, is either prohibited or discouraged, and is not the common form of program control in the same way that it is in traditional BASIC or FORTRAN. A structured language allows you to indent statements and does not require a strict field concept (as did early versions of FORTRAN).

Finally, and perhaps most importantly, C is a language that stays out of the way. The underlying philosophy of C is that the programmer, not the language, is in charge. Therefore, C will let you do virtually anything that you want, even if what you tell it to do is unorthodox, highly unusual, or suspicious. C gives you nearly complete control over the machine. Of course, with this power comes considerable responsibility, which you, the programmer, must shoulder.

Understanding the Need For C++

Given the preceding discussion of C, you might be wondering why C++ was invented. Since C is a successful and useful computer programming language, why was there a need for something else? The answer is complexity. Throughout the history of programming, the increasing complexity of programs has driven the need for better ways to manage that complexity. C++ is a response to that need. To better understand this correlation, consider the following.

Approaches to programming have changed dramatically since the invention of the computer. The primary reason for change has been to accommodate the increasing complexity of programs. For example, when computers were first invented, programming was done by toggling in the binary machine instructions, using the computer's front panel. As long as programs were just a few hundred instructions long, this approach worked. As programs grew, assembly language was invented so that programmers could deal with larger, increasingly complex programs by using symbolic representations of the machine instructions. As programs continued to grow, high-level languages were developed to give programmers more tools with which to handle the complexity.

The first widespread language was, of course, FORTRAN. While FORTRAN was a very impressive first step, it is hardly a language that encourages clear, easy-to-understand programs. The 1960s gave birth to structured programming. This is the method of programming encouraged by languages such as C. With structured languages it was, for the first time, possible to write moderately complex programs fairly easily. However, even with structured programming methods, once a project reaches a certain size its complexity exceeds what a programmer can manage. Today, many projects are near or at the point where the structured approach no longer works. To solve this problem, a new way to program has emerged. This method is called *object-oriented programming* (OOP for short). And as you will see, C++ is the object-oriented version of C.

In the final analysis, although C is one of the most liked and widely used professional programming languages in the world, there comes a time when its ability to handle complexity is reached. Once a program exceeds somewhere between 25,000 to 100,000 lines of code, it becomes so complex that it is difficult to grasp as a totality. The purpose of C++ is to allow this barrier to be broken and to help the programmer comprehend and manage larger, more complex programs.

C++ is Born

In response to the need to manage greater complexity, C++ was born. It was invented by Bjarne Stroustrup in 1980, at Bell Laboratories in Murray Hill, New Jersey. He initially called the new language "C with Classes." However, in 1983 the name was changed to C++.

C++ contains the entire C language. As stated earlier, C is the foundation upon which C++ is built. C++ includes all of C's features, attributes, and benefits. It also adheres to C's philosophy that the programmer, not the language, is in charge. At this point, it is critical to understand that the invention of C++ was not an attempt to create a new programming language. Instead, it was an enhancement to an already highly successful language.

Most of the additions that Stroustrup made to C were designed to support object-oriented programming. Stroustrup states that some of C++'s object-oriented features were inspired by another object-oriented language called Simula67. Therefore, C++ represents the blending of two powerful programming methods.

Since C++ was first invented, it has gone through three major revisions, once in 1985 and again in 1989. The third revision occurred when work began on the ANSI standard for C++. The first draft of the proposed standard was created on January 25, 1994. The ANSI C++ committee (of which I am a member) has kept virtually all of the features first defined by Stroustrup and has added several new ones, as well.

The standardization process is typically a slow one, and it will probably be years before the C++ standard is finally adopted. Therefore, keep in mind that C++ is still a "work in progress," and that some features are still being developed and added. However, the material presented in this book is stable.

It is applicable to all contemporary C++ compilers, and is in compliance with the currently proposed ANSI standard for C++. Therefore, you can learn with confidence.

When C++ was invented, Bjarne Stroustrup knew that it was important to maintain the original spirit of C, including its efficiency, flexibility, and philosophy, while at the same time adding support for object-oriented programming. Happily, his goal was accomplished. C++ still provides the programmer with the freedom and control of C, coupled with the power of objects. The object-oriented features in C++, to use Stroustrup's words, "allow programs to be structured for clarity, extensibility, and ease of maintenance without loss of efficiency."

Although C++ was initially designed to aid in the management of very large programs, it is in no way limited to this use. In fact, the object-oriented attributes of C++ can be effectively applied to virtually any programming task. It is not uncommon to see C++ used for projects such as editors, databases, personal file systems, and communication programs. Also, because C++ shares C's efficiency, much high-performance systems software is constructed using C++.

One important point to remember is this: Because C++ is a superset of C, once you can program in C++, you can also program in C! Thus, you will actually be learning two programming languages at the same time, with the same effort that you would use to learn only one.

What Is Object-Oriented Programming?

Since object-oriented programming was fundamental to the development of C++, it is important to define precisely what object-oriented programming is. Object-oriented programming has taken the best ideas of structured programming and combined them with several powerful, new concepts that encourage you to approach the task of programming in a new way. In general, when programming in an object-oriented fashion, you decompose a problem into subgroups of related parts that take into account both the code and the data related to each group. You organize these subgroups into a hierarchical structure. Finally, you translate these subgroups into self-contained units called objects.

All object-oriented programming languages have three things in common: encapsulation, polymorphism, and inheritance. Although we will examine them in detail later in this book, let's take a brief look at these concepts now.

Encapsulation

As you probably know, all programs are composed of two fundamental elements: program statements (code) and data. *Code* is that part of a program that performs actions, and *data* is the information affected by those actions. *Encapsulation* is a programming mechanism that binds together code and the data it manipulates, and that keeps both safe from outside interference and misuse.

In an object-oriented language, code and data may be bound together in such a way that a self-contained *black box* is created. Within the box are all necessary data and code. When code and data are linked together in this fashion, an *object* is created. In other words, an object is the device that supports encapsulation.

Within an object, code, data, or both may be *private* to that object or *public*. Private code or data is known to and accessible only by another part of the object. That is, private code or data may not be accessed by a piece of the program that exists outside the object. When code or data is public, other parts of your program may access it even though it is defined within an object. Typically, the public parts of an object are used to provide a controlled interface to the private parts of the object.

Polymorphism

Polymorphism (from the Greek, meaning "many forms") is the quality that allows one interface to be used for a general class of actions. The specific action is determined by the exact nature of the situation. A simple example of polymorphism is found in the steering wheel of an automobile. The steering wheel (i.e., the interface) is the same no matter what type of actual steering mechanism is used. That is, the steering wheel works the same whether your car has manual steering, power steering, or rack-and-pinion steering. Therefore, once you know how to operate the steering wheel, you can drive any type of car. The same principle can also apply to programming. For example, consider a stack (which is a first-in, last-out list.) You might have a program that requires three different types of stacks. One stack is used for integer values, one for floating point values, and one for characters. In this case, the algorithm that implements each stack is the same, even though the data being stored differs. In a non-object-oriented language, you would be required to create three different sets of stack routines, calling each set by different names, with each having its own interface. However, because of polymorphism, in C++ you can create one general set of stack routines (one interface) that works for all three specific situations. This way, once you know how to use one stack, you can use them all.

More generally, the concept of polymorphism is often expressed by the phrase "one interface, multiple methods." This means that it is possible to design a generic interface to a group of related activities. Polymorphism helps reduce complexity by allowing the same interface to be used to specify a general class of action. It is the compiler's job to select the *specific action* (i.e., method) as it applies to each situation. You, the programmer, don't need to do this selection manually. You need only remember and utilize the general interface.

The first object-oriented programming languages were interpreters, so polymorphism was, of course, supported at run time. However, C++ is a compiled language. Therefore, in C++, both run-time and compile-time polymorphism are supported.

Inheritance

Inheritance is the process by which one object can acquire the properties of another object. The reason this is important is that it supports the concept of hierarchical classification. If you think about it, most knowledge is made manageable by hierarchical (i.e., top-down) classifications. For example, a Red Delicious apple is part of the classification *apple,* which in turn is part of the *fruit* class, which is under the larger class *food.* That is, the *food* class possesses certain qualities (edible, nutritious, etc.) which also, logically, apply to its subclass, *fruit.* In addition to these qualities, the *fruit* class has specific characteristics (juicy, sweet, etc.) that distinguish it from other food. The *apple* class defines those qualities specific to an apple (grows on trees, not tropical, etc.). A Red Delicious apple would, in turn, inherit all the qualities of all preceding classes, and would define only those qualities that make it unique.

Without the use of hierarchies, each object would have to explicitly define all of its characteristics. However, using inheritance, an object need only define those qualities that make it unique within its class. It can inherit its general attributes from its parent. Thus, it is the inheritance mechanism which makes it possible for one object to be a specific instance of a more general case.

C++ Implements OOP

As you will see as you progress through this book, many of the features of C++ exist to provide support for encapsulation, polymorphism, and inheritance. Remember, however, that you can use C++ to write any type of program, using any type of approach. The fact that C++ supports object-oriented programming does not mean that you can only write object-oriented programs. As with its predecessor, C, one of C++'s strongest advantages is its flexibility.

What You Will Need

1

To use this book effectively, you will need a computer and a C++ compiler. The best way to learn is to try the examples yourself, experimenting with your own variations. There really is no substitute for hands-on experience.

If you are using a PC, then you have several C++ compilers to choose from. Just make sure that you use an up-to-date C++ compiler. The code in this book has been tested with both Borland C++ and Microsoft C++. However, it should work with virtually any contemporary C++ compiler.

Now that you know the story behind C++, it is time to start learning to use it. The next chapter introduces you to the C++ fundamentals.

Chapter

2

An Overview of C++

By far the hardest thing about learning a programming language is the fact that no element of it exists in isolation. Rather, the components of the language work in relationship with each other. This means that it is necessary for you to have a general idea about what constitutes a C++ program, including some basic control structures, operators, and functions, before moving on to examine the sample programs in later chapters, which have been developed to illustrate the various aspects of the language. With this goal in mind, this chapter provides a generhal overview of a C++ program, showing several simple examples. It does not go into too many details but, rather, concentrates on the general concepts common to any C++ program. It also introduces constructs used by almost all C++ programs. Most of the topics presented here are examined more closely in later chapters.

Since learning is best accomplished by doing, it is recommended that you work through the examples using your computer.

Your First C++ Program

Before getting into any theory, let's look at a simple C++ program. Enter and compile the following:

```
/* Program #1 - A first C++ program.

   Enter this program, then compile and run it.
*/


#include <iostream.h>

// main() is where program execution begins.
main()
{
  cout << "This is my first C++ program.";

  return 0;
}
```

Source code is the form of your program that you create. Object code is the form of your program that the computer executes.

When run, this program displays the following text on the screen:

This is my first C++ program.

Before we continue, it is necessary to define two terms. The first is *source code*. Source code is the version of your program that humans can read. The preceding listing is an example of source code. The executable version of your program is called *object code* or *executable code*. Object code is created by the compiler when it compiles your program.

A Line-by-Line Explanation

Let's examine each line in this program. First, the program begins with the lines

```
/* Program #1 - A first C++ program.

   Enter this program, then compile and run it.
*/
```

This is a *comment*. Like most other programming languages, C++ lets you enter a remark into a program's source code. The contents of a comment are ignored by the compiler. The purpose of a comment is to describe or explain the operation of a program to anyone reading its source code. In the case of

A comment is a remark that is embedded in your program.

this comment, it identifies the program. In more complex programs, you will use comments to help explain what each feature of the program is for and how it goes about doing its work. In other words, you can use comments to provide a "play-by-play" description of what your program does.

In C++, there are two types of comments. The one you've just seen is called a *multiline comment*. This type of comment begins with a /* (a slash followed by an asterisk). It ends only when a */ is encountered. Anything between these two comment symbols is completely ignored by the compiler. Multiline comments may be one or more lines long. The second type of comment is found a little further on in the program; we'll be discussing it shortly.

The next line of code looks like this:

```
#include <iostream.h>
```

The C++ language defines several files, called *header files,* which contain information that is either necessary or useful to your program. For this program, the file **iostream.h** is needed. (It is used to support the C++ I/O system.) This file is provided with your compiler. Later in this book you will learn more about header files and why they are important.

The next line in the program is

```
// main() is where program execution begins.
```

This line shows you the second type of comment available in C++: the *single-line comment.* Single-line comments begin with // and stop at the end of the line. Typically, C++ programmers use multiline comments when writing larger, more detailed commentaries, and single-line comments when short remarks are needed. However, this is a matter of personal style.

The next line, as the preceding comment indicates, is where program execution begins.

```
main()
```

main() is where a C++ program begins execution.

All C++ programs are composed of one or more functions. (Loosely speaking, a function is a subroutine.) Every C++ function must have a name, and the only function that any C++ program *must* include is the one shown here, called **main( ).** The **main( )** function is where program execution begins and (most commonly) ends. (Technically speaking, a C++ program begins with a call to **main( )** and, in most cases, ends when **main( )** returns.) The opening curly brace on the line that follows **main( )** marks the start of the **main( )** function's code.

The next line in the program is

```
cout << "This is my first C++ program.";
```

This is a console output statement. It causes the message **This is my first C++ program.** to be displayed on the screen. It accomplishes this by using the standard C++ output operator **<<**. The **<<** operator causes whatever expression is on its right side to be output to the device specified on its left side. **cout** is a predefined identifier that stands for console output and (most generally) refers to the computer's screen. Thus, this statement causes the message to be output to the screen. Notice that this statement ends with a semicolon. In fact, all C++ statements end with a semicolon.

The message "This is my first C++ program." is a *string*. In C++, a string is a sequence of characters enclosed between double quotes. As you will see, strings are used frequently in C++.

The next line in the program is

```
return 0;
```

This line terminates **main( )** and causes it to return the value 0 to the calling process (which is typically the operating system). For most operating systems, a return value of 0 signifies that the program is terminating normally. (Other values indicate that the program is terminating because of some error.) **return** is one of C++'s keywords, and it is used to return a value from a function. (**return** will be discussed in detail later in this book.) Technically, a return value from **main( )** is optional, but desirable. Generally, all of your programs should return 0 when they terminate normally (that is, without error).

The closing curly brace at the end of the program formally concludes the program. Although the brace is not actually part of the object code of the program, conceptually you can think of a C++ program ending when the closing curly brace of **main( )** is executed. In fact, if the **return** statement were not part of this sample program, the program would automatically end when the closing curly brace was encountered.

Handling Errors

If you have not yet done so, enter, compile, and run the preceding program. As you may know from your previous programming experience, it is quite easy to accidentally type something incorrectly when entering code into your computer. Fortunately, if you enter something incorrectly into your program, the compiler will report a *syntax error* message when it tries to compile it. Most C++ compilers attempt to make sense out of your source code no matter what you have written. For this reason, the error that is reported may not always reflect the actual cause of the problem. In the preceding program, for example, an accidental omission of the opening curly brace after the **main( )** function might cause some compilers to report the **cout** statement as the source of a syntax error. The point of this discussion is that when you receive syntax error messages, be prepared to look at the last few lines of code in your program in order to find the error.

Many C++ compilers report not only actual errors, but also warnings. The C++ language was designed to be very forgiving, and to allow virtually anything that is syntactically correct to be compiled. However, some things, even though syntactically correct, are highly suspicious. When the compiler encounters one of these situations it prints a warning. You, as the programmer, then decide whether its suspicions are justified or not. Frankly, some compilers are a bit too helpful and flag warnings on perfectly correct C++ statements. There are also compilers that allow you to turn on various options that report information about your program that you might like to know. Sometimes this information is reported in the form of a warning message even though there is nothing to be "warned" about. The programs in this book are in compliance with the proposed ANSI standard for C++, and when entered correctly, they will not generate any troublesome warning messages.

2

Tip: Although all C++ compilers report fatal syntax errors, most C++ compilers offer several levels of error (and warning) reporting. Generally, you can select the specific type of error reporting you want. For example, most compilers offer options that report such things as inefficient constructs or the use of obsolete features. For the examples in this book, you will want to use your compiler's default (or "normal") error reporting. However, you should examine your compiler's user manual to see what options you have at your disposal. Many compilers have sophisticated features that can help you spot subtle errors before they become big problems. Understanding your compiler's error reporting system is worth the time and effort that you spend.

A Second Simple Program

Beyond the general form of a program, perhaps no other construct is as important to a programming language as the assignment of a value to a variable. A *variable* is a named memory location that may be assigned a value. Further, the value of a variable may be changed one or more times during the execution of a program. That is, the content of a variable is changeable, not fixed.

The following program creates a variable called **value,** gives it the value 1023, and then displays the message **This program prints the value: 1023** on the screen.

```
// Program #2 - Using a variable

#include <iostream.h>

main()
{
  int value; // this declares a variable

  value = 1023; // this assigns 1023 to value

  cout << "This program prints the value: ";
  cout << value; // This displays 1023

  return 0;
}
```

This program introduces two new concepts. First, the statement

```
int value;  // this declares a variable
```

The type of a variable determines the values it may hold.

declares a variable called **value** of type integer. In C++, all variables must be declared before they are used. Further, the type of values that the variable can hold must also be specified. This is called the *type* of the variable. In this case, **value** may hold integer values. For most compilers, this means the whole number values between –32,768 and 32,767. In C++, to declare a variable to be of type integer, precede its name with the keyword **int.** Later, you will see that C++ supports a wide range of built-in variable types. (You can create your own data types, too.)

The second new feature is found in the next line of code:

```
value = 1023; // this assigns 1023 to value
```

As the comment suggests, this assigns the value 1023 to **value.** In C++, the assignment operator is the single equal sign. It copies the value on its right side into the variable on its left. After the assignment, the variable **value** will contain the number 1023.

The two **cout** statements display the output generated by the program. Notice how the following statement is used to display the value of **value**:

```
cout << value; // This displays 1023
```

In general, if you want to display the value of a variable, simply put it on the right side of << in a **cout** statement. In this specific case, because **value** contains the number 1023, it is this number that is displayed on the screen. Before moving on, you might want to try giving **value** other values and watching the results.

A More Practical Example

2

Your first two sample programs, while illustrating several important features of the C++ language, are not very useful. The next sample program actually performs a meaningful task: it converts gallons to liters. It also shows how to input information.

```
// This program converts gallons to liters.

#include <iostream.h>

main()
{
  int gallons, liters;

  cout << "Enter number of gallons: ";
  cin >> gallons; // this inputs from the user

  liters = gallons * 4; // convert to liters

  cout << "Liters: " << liters;

  return 0;
}
```

This program first displays a prompting message on the screen, and then waits for you to enter a whole number amount of gallons. (Remember, integer types cannot have fractional components.) The program then displays the approximate liter equivalent. There are actually 3.7854 liters in a gallon, but since integers are used in this example, the conversion is rounded to 4 liters per gallon. For example, if you enter 1 gallon, the program responds with the metric equivalent of 4 liters.

The first new thing you see in this program is that two variables are declared following the **int** keyword, in the form of a comma-separated list. In general, you can declare any number of variables of the same type by separating them with commas. (As an alternative, the program could have used multiple **int** statements to accomplish the same thing.)

The function uses this statement to actually input a value entered by the user:

```
cin >> gallons; // this inputs from the user
```

cin is another predefined identifier that is provided with your C++ compiler. It stands for *console input* (which generally means input from the keyboard). The input operator is the **>>** symbol. The value entered by the user (which must be an integer, in this case) is put into the variable that is on the right side of the **>>** (in this case, **gallons**).

There is one more new thing in this program. Examine this line:

```
cout << "Liters: " << liters;
```

It uses two output operators within the same output statement. Specifically, it outputs the string "Liters: " followed by the value of **liters**. In general, you can string together as many output operations as you like within one output statement. Just use a separate **<<** for each item.

A New Data Type

Although the gallons to liters program is fine for rough approximations, because it uses integers it leaves something to be desired when a more accurate answer is needed. As stated, integer data types cannot represent any fractional value. If you need fractions, then you must use a floating point data type. One of these is called **float**. Data of this type will typically be in the range 3.4E–38 to 3.4E+38. Operations on floating point numbers preserve any fractional part of the outcome and, hence, provide a more accurate conversion.

The following version of the conversion program uses floating point values.

```
/* This program converts gallons to liters using
   floating point numbers. */

#include <iostream.h>

main()
{
  float gallons, liters;

  cout << "Enter number of gallons: ";
  cin >> gallons; // this inputs from the user

  liters = gallons * 3.7854; // convert to liters

  cout << "Liters: " << liters;
```

```
    return 0;
}
```

There are two changes to this program from the previous version. First, **gallons** and **liters** are declared as **float**s. Second, the conversion coefficient is now specified as 3.7854, allowing a more accurate conversion. Whenever C++ encounters a number that contains a decimal point, it automatically knows that it is a floating point constant. One other point: Notice that the **cout** and **cin** statements are unchanged from the previous version of this program that used **int** variables. C++'s I/O system automatically adjusts to whatever type of data you give it.

Try the program at this time. Enter 1 gallon when prompted. The equivalent number of liters is now 3.7854.

A Quick Review

Before proceeding, let's review the most important things that you have learned:

1. All C++ programs must have a **main( )** function, and it is there that program execution begins.
2. All variables must be declared before they are used.
3. C++ supports a variety of data types, including integer and floating point.
4. The output operator is **<<**, and when used with **cout**, it causes information to be displayed on the screen.
5. The input operator is **>>**,and when used with **cin**, it reads information from the keyboard.
6. Program execution stops when the end of **main( )** is encountered (or the **return 0;** statement is executed).

Functions

Functions are the building blocks of a C++ program.

A C++ program is constructed from building blocks called *functions*. A function is a subroutine that contains one or more C++ statements and performs one or more tasks. In well-written C++ code, each function performs only one task.

Each function has a name and it is this name that is used to call the function. In general, you can give a function whatever name you please. However, remember that **main( )** is reserved for the function which begins execution of your program.

In C++, one function cannot be embedded within another function. Unlike Pascal, Modula-2, and some other programming languages which allow the nesting of functions, C++ considers all functions to be separate entities. (Of course, one function may call another.)

When denoting functions, this book has used and will continue to use a convention which has become common when writing about C++. A function will have parentheses after its name. For example, if a function's name is **getval**, then it will be written **getval( )** when its name is used in a sentence. This notation will help you distinguish variable names from function names in this book.

In your first programs, **main( )** was the only function. As stated earlier, **main( )** is the first function executed when your program begins to run, and it must be included in all C++ programs. There are two types of functions that will be used by your programs. The first type is written by you. **main( )** is an example of this type of function. The other type of function is implemented by the compiler and is found in the compiler's *standard library*. (The standard library is discussed shortly, but in general terms, it is a collection of predefined functions.) Programs that you write will generally contain a mix of functions that you create and those supplied by the compiler.

Since functions form the foundation of C++, let's take a closer look at them now.

A Program with Two Functions

The following program contains two functions: **main( )** and **myfunc( )**. Before running this program (or reading the description that follows), examine it closely and try to figure out exactly what it displays on the screen.

```
/* This program contains two functions: main()
   and myfunc().
*/
#include <iostream.h>

void myfunc(); // myfunc's protoype

main()
{
  cout << "In main()";
  myfunc(); // call myfunc()
  cout << "Back in main()";

  return 0;
}

void myfunc()
{
```

```
    cout << " Inside myfunc() ";
}
```

The program works like this. First, **main( )** begins, and it executes the first **cout** statement. Next, **main( )** calls **myfunc( )**. Notice how this is achieved: the function's name, **myfunc**, appears, followed by parentheses, and finally by a semicolon. A function call is a C++ statement and, therefore, must end with a semicolon. Next, **myfunc( )** executes its **cout** statement, and then returns to **main( )** at the line of code immediately following the call. Finally, **main( )** executes its second **cout** statement and then terminates. Hence, the output on the screen is this:

2

In main( ) Inside myfunc( ) Back in main( )

There is one other important statement in the preceding program:

```
void myfunc(); // myfunc's prototype
```

A prototype declares a function prior to its first use.

As the comment states, this is the *prototype* for **myfunc( )**. Although we will discuss prototypes in detail later in this book, a few words are necessary now. A function prototype declares the function prior to its definition. The prototype allows the compiler to know the function's return type, as well as the number and type of any parameters that the function may have. The compiler needs to know this information prior to the first time the function is called. This is why the prototype occurs before **main( )**.

As you can see, **myfunc( )** does not contain a **return** statement. The keyword **void**, which precedes both the prototype for **myfunc( )** and its definition, formally states that **myfunc( )** does not return a value. In C++, functions that don't return values are declared as **void**.

Function Arguments

An argument is a value passed to a function when it is called.

It is possible to pass one or more values to a function. A value passed to a function is called an *argument*. In the programs that you have studied so far, none of the functions take any arguments. Specifically, neither **main( )** nor **myfunc( )** in the preceding examples have an argument. However, functions in C++ can have anywhere from no arguments at all to many arguments. The upper limit is determined by the compiler you are using, but the proposed C++ standard specifies that a function must be able to take at least 256 arguments.

Here is a short program that uses one of C++'s standard library (i.e., built-in) functions, called **abs( )**, to display the absolute value of number. The **abs( )**

function takes one argument, converts it into its absolute value, and returns the result.

```
// Use the abs() function.
#include <iostream.h>
#include <stdlib.h> // required by abs()

main()
{
  cout << abs(-10);

  return 0;
}
```

Here, the value –10 is passed as an argument to **abs( )**. The **abs( )** function receives the argument that it is called with and returns its absolute value, which is 10 in this case. Although **abs( )** takes only one argument, other functions can have several. The key point here is that when a function requires an argument, it is passed by specifying it between the parentheses that follow the function's name.

The return value of **abs( )** is used by the **cout** statement to display the absolute value of –10 on the screen. The reason this works is that whenever a function is part of a larger expression, it is automatically called so that its return value can be obtained. In this case, the return value of **abs( )** becomes the value of the right side of the **<<** operator and is, therefore, displayed on the screen.

Notice one other thing about the preceding program: it also includes the header file **stdlib.h**. This is the header file required by **abs( )**. In general, whenever you use a library function, you must include its header file. The header file provides the prototype for the library function, among other things.

A parameter is a variable defined by a function that receives an argument.

When you create a function that takes one or more arguments, the variables that will receive those arguments must also be declared. These variables are called the *parameters* of the function. For example, the function shown next prints the product of the two integer arguments used in the call to the function.

```
void mul(int x, int y)
{
  cout << x * y << " ";
}
```

Each time **mul( )** is called, it will multiply the value passed to **x** by the value passed to **y**. Remember, however, that **x** and **y** are simply the operational variables that receive the values you use when calling the function.

Consider the following short program, which illustrates how to call **mul( )**:

```
// A simple program that demonstrates mul().

#include <iostream.h>

void mul(int x, int y); // mul()'s prototype

main()
{
  mul(10, 20);
  mul(5, 6);
  mul(8, 9);

  return 0;
}

void mul(int x, int y)
{
  cout << x * y << " ";
}
```

This program will print 200, 30, and 72 on the screen. When **mul()** is called, the C++ compiler copies the value of each argument into the matching parameter. That is, in the first call to **mul()**, 10 is copied into **x** and 20 is copied into **y**. In the second call, 5 is copied into **x** and 6 into **y**. In the third call, 8 is copied into **x** and 9 into **y**.

If you have never worked with a language that allows parameterized functions, then the preceding process may seem a bit strange. Don't worry; as you see more examples of C++ programs, the concept of arguments, parameters, and functions will become clear.

Remember: The term *argument* refers to the value that is used to call a function. The variable that receives the value of an argument is called a parameter. In fact, functions that take arguments are called parameterized functions.

In C++ functions, when there are two or more arguments, they are separated by commas. In this book, the term *argument list* will refer to comma-separated arguments. The argument list for **mul()** is x,y.

Functions Returning Values

Many of the C++ library functions that you will use return values. For example, the **abs()** function used earlier returned the absolute value of its argument. Also, functions you write may return values to the calling routine.

In C++, a function uses a **return** statement to return a value. The general form of **return** is

return *value*;

where *value* is the value being returned.

To illustrate the process of functions returning values, the foregoing program can be rewritten as follows. In this version, **mul( )** returns the product of its arguments. Notice that the placement of the function on the right side of an assignment statement assigns the return value to a variable.

```
// Returning a value.

#include <iostream.h>

mul(int x, int y); // mul()'s prototype

main()
{
  int answer;

  answer = mul(10, 11); // assign return value
  cout << "The answer is " <<  answer;

  return 0;
}

/* This function returns a value. */
mul(int x, int y)
{
  return x * y; // return product of x and y
}
```

In this example, **mul( )** returns the value of **x*y** using the **return** statement. This value is then assigned to **answer**. That is, the value returned by the **return** statement becomes **mul( )**'s value in the calling routine.

Since **mul( )** now returns a value, it is not preceded by the keyword **void**. (Remember, **void** is only used when a function does *not* return a value.) Just as there are different types of variables, there are also different types of return values. The return type of a function precedes its name in both its prototype and its definition. If no return type is specified, then the function is assumed to return an integer value. Thus, the type returned by **mul( )** is **int**, by default, since no other return type is specified. Keep in mind that you can also specify the integer return type explicitly, as shown here:

```
/* This function returns a value. */
int mul(int x, int y)
{
  return x * y; // return product of x and y
}
```

However, most C++ programmers don't bother to actually specify **int** since it can be used automatically.

It is possible to cause a function to return by using the **return** statement without any value attached to it, but this form of **return** can only be used with functions that have no return values and that are declared as **void**. Also, there can be more than one **return** in a function.

2

The main() Function

As you know, the **main( )** function is special because it is the first function called when your program executes. It signifies the beginning of your program. Unlike some programming languages that always begin execution at the "top" of the program, C++ begins every program with a call to the **main( )** function, no matter where that function is located in the program. (However, it is good form for **main( )** to be the first function in your program so that it can be easily found.)

There can only be one **main( )** in a program. If you try to include more than one, your program will not know where to begin execution. Actually, most compilers will catch this type of error and report it.

The General Form of C++ Functions

The preceding examples have shown some specific types of functions. However, all C++ functions share a common form, which is shown here:

```
return-type function-name(parameter list)
{
  .
  . body of the function
  .
}
```

Let's look closely at the different parts that make up a function.

The return type of a function is integer by default. But, as you will see later in this book, you can specify any return type you like. Keep in mind, however, that no function has to return a value. If it does not return a value, its return type is **void**. But if it does return a value, that value must be of a type that is compatible with the function's return type.

Every function must have a name. After the name is a parenthesized parameter list. The parameter list specifies the names and types of variables that will be passed information. If a function has no parameters, the parentheses are empty.

Next, braces surround the body of the function. The body of the function is composed of the C++ statements that define what the function does. The function terminates and returns to the calling procedure when the closing curly brace is reached, or when a **return** statement is encountered.

Some Output Options

Up to this point, there has been no occasion to advance output to the next line— that is, to execute a carriage return-linefeed sequence. However, the need for this will arise very soon. In C++, the carriage return-linefeed sequence is generated using the *newline* character. To put a newline character into a string, use this code: **\n** (a backslash followed by a lowercase n). To see an example of a carriage return-linefeed sequence, try the following program.

```
/* This program demonstrates the \n code, which
   generates a new line.
*/
#include <iostream.h>

main()
{
  cout << "one\n";
  cout << "two\n";
  cout << "three";
  cout << "four";

return 0;
}
```

This program produces the following output:

```
one
two
threefour
```

The newline character can be placed anywhere in the string, not just at the end. You might want to try experimenting with the newline character now, just to make sure you understand exactly what it does.

Two Simple Commands

So that the examples developed in the next few chapters will be meaningful to you, it is necessary for you to understand, in their simplest form, two C++ commands: the **if** and the **for**. In later chapters these commands will be explored completely.

2

The if Statement

The C++ **if** statement operates in much the same way that an IF statement operates in any other language. Its simplest form is

> if(*condition*) *statement*;

if selects between two paths of execution.

where *condition* is an expression that is evaluated to be either true or false. In C++, true is non-zero and false is zero. If the condition is true, then the statement will execute. If it is false, then the statement will not execute. The following fragment displays the phrase **10 is less than 11** on the screen.

```
if(10 < 11) cout << "10 is less than 11";
```

The comparison operators, such as < (less than) and >= (greater than or equal), are similar to those in other languages. However, in C++, the equality operator is ==. The following statement will not execute, because the condition of equality is false; that is, because 10 is not equal to 11, the statement will not display **hello** on the screen.

```
if(10==11) cout << "hello";
```

Of course, the operands inside an **if** statement need not be constants. They can also be variables, or even calls to functions.

The following program shows an example of the **if** statement. It prompts the user for two numbers, and displays a report if the first value is less than the second.

```
// This program illustrates the if statement.

#include <iostream.h>

main()
```

```
{
  int a, b;

  cout << "enter first number: ";
  cin >> a;
  cout << "enter second number: ";
  cin >> b;

  if(a < b) cout << "First number is less than second.";

  return 0;
}
```

The for Loop

The **for** loop is used to repeat a statement a specified number of times. The **for** loop can operate much like the FOR loop in other languages, including Pascal and BASIC. Its simplest form is

for(*initialization, condition, increment*) *statement*;

for is one of the loop statements used in C++.

Here, *initialization* sets the loop control variable to an initial value. *Condition* is an expression that is tested each time the loop repeats. As long as *condition* is true (non-zero), the loop keeps running. *Increment* is an expression that determines how the loop control variable is incremented each time the loop repeats successfully (that is, each time *condition* is evaluated to be true).

For example, the following program prints the numbers 1 through 100 on the screen.

```
// A program that illustrates the for loop.

#include <iostream.h>

main()
{
  int count;

  for(count=1; count<=100; count=count+1)
        cout << count << " ";

  return 0;
}
```

Figure 2-1 illustrates the execution of the **for** loop in this example. As you can see, **count** is initialized to 1. Each time the loop repeats, the condition **count<=100** is tested. If it is true, the value is output and **count** is

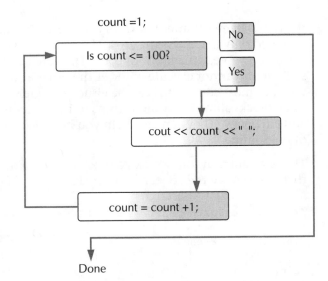

count =1;

Is count <= 100?

No

Yes

cout << count << " ";

count = count +1;

Done

2

How the **for**
loop works
Figure 2-1.

increased by one. When **count** reaches a value greater than 100, the
condition becomes false, and the loop stops running.

In professionally written C++ code, you will never see a statement like
count=count+1, because for this sort of statement, C++ supports a special
shorthand that looks like this: **count++**. The **++** is the *increment* operator.
It increases its operand by 1. The complement of **++** is **– –**, the *decrement*
operator. **– –** decreases its operand by 1. For example, the preceding **for**
statement will generally be written like this:

```
for(count=1; count<=100; count++)
  cout << count << " ";
```

This is the form that will be used throughout the rest of this book.

Blocks of Code

A block is
a logically
connected
unit of
statements.

Because C++ is a structured (as well as an object-oriented) language, it
supports the creation of blocks of code. A *block* is a logically connected
group of program statements that is treated as a unit. In C++, a code block
is created by placing a sequence of statements between opening and closing
curly braces. In this example,

```
if(x<10) {
  cout << "too low, try again";
  cin >> x;
}
```

the two statements after the **if** and between the curly braces are both executed only if **x** is less than 10. These two statements together with the braces represent a block of code. They are a logical unit: one of the statements cannot execute without the other also executing. In C++, the target of most commands can be either a single statement or a code block. Code blocks allow many algorithms to be implemented with greater clarity and efficiency. They can also help you better conceptualize the true nature of the routine.

The program that follows uses a block of code. Enter and run the program so that you can see the effect of the block.

```
// This program demonstrates a block of code.

#include <iostream.h>

main()
{
  int a, b;

  cout << "enter first number: ";
  cin >> a;
  cout << "enter second number: ";
  cin >> b;

  if(a < b) {
    cout << "First number is less than second.\n";
    cout << "Their difference is: " << b-a;
  }

  return 0;
}
```

This program prompts the user to enter two numbers from the keyboard. If the first number is less than the second number, then both **cout** statements are executed. Otherwise, both are skipped. At no time can just one of them execute.

Semicolons and Positioning

You may be wondering why so many statements are terminated with a semicolon. In C++, the semicolon is a statement *terminator*. That is, each individual statement must be ended with a semicolon. It indicates the end of one logical entity.

As you know, a block is a set of logically connected statements that are surrounded by opening and closing braces. A block is *not* terminated with a semicolon. Since a block is a group of statements, with a semicolon after each statement, it makes sense that a block is not terminated by a semicolon; instead, the end of the block is indicated by the closing brace. This is also the reason that there is no semicolon following the closing brace of a function.

C++ does not recognize the end of the line as a terminator. For this reason, it does not matter where on a line you put a statement. For example,

```
x = y;
y = y+1;
mul(x, y);
```

is the same as

```
x = y;   y = y+1;   mul(x, y);
```

to a C++ compiler.

2

Indentation Practices

You may have noticed in the previous examples that certain statements were indented. C++ is a free-form language, meaning that it does not matter where you place statements relative to each other on a line. However, over the years, a common and accepted indentation style has developed that allows for very readable programs. This book follows that style, and it is recommended that you do so as well. Using this style, you indent one level after each opening brace, and move back out one level after each closing brace. There are certain statements that encourage some additional indenting; these will be covered later.

C++ Keywords

There are 60 keywords currently defined for C++. These are shown in Table 2-1. Together with the formal C++ syntax, they form the C++ programming language. However, at the time of this writing, the keywords **bool, const_cast, dynamic_cast, false, mutable, namespace, reinterpret_cast, static_cast, true, typeid, using,** and **wchar_t** are in the process of being defined by the ANSI C++ standard committee, and are not implemented by any commonly available compiler. These keywords were not part of the original specification for C++ created by Bjarne Stroustrup. They are being added primarily to allow C++ to accommodate some special case situations, and they are subject to change or deletion. You

asm	dynamic_cast	new	template
auto	else	operator	this
bool	enum	private	throw
break	extern	protected	true
case	false	public	try
catch	float	register	typedef
char	for	reinterpret_cast	typeid
class	friend	return	union
const	goto	short	unsigned
const_cast	if	signed	using
continue	inline	sizeof	virtual
default	int	static	void
delete	long	static_cast	volatile
do	mutable	struct	wchar_t
double	namespace	switch	while

The Current
C++ Keywords
Table 2-1.

should also know that some older versions of C++ include the **overload** keyword, which is now obsolete. You will want to check your compiler user's manual to determine precisely what C++ keywords it supports.

Keep in mind that the case of the keywords is significant. C++ is a case-sensitive language, and it requires that all keywords be in lowercase. For example, **RETURN** will *not* be recognized as the keyword **return**.

Identifiers in C++

In C++ an identifier is a name assigned to a function, a variable, or any other user-defined item. Identifiers can be from one to several characters long. The first 1024 characters will be significant. Variable names may start with any letter of the alphabet, or with an underscore. Next may be either a letter, a digit, or an underscore. (The underscore can be used to enhance the readability of a variable name, as in **first_name**.) Uppercase and lowercase are different; that is, to C++, **count** and **COUNT** are separate names. Here are some examples of acceptable identifiers:

```
first    last    Addr1    top_of_file
name23   _temp    t    s23e3    MyVar
```

You cannot use any of the C++ keywords as identifier names. Also, you should not assign the name of any standard function, such as **abs**, to an identifier. Beyond these two restrictions, good programming practice dictates that you use identifier names that reflect the meaning or usage of the items being named.

The Standard C++ Library

The C++
standard
library
contains many
predefined
functions that
you can use in
your programs.

In the discussion of the sample programs earlier in this chapter, it was mentioned that **abs( )** is provided with your C++ compiler. **abs( )** is not part of the C++ language per se, yet you will find it included with every C++ compiler. This function, and many others, are found in the *standard library*. We will be making extensive use of library functions in the example programs throughout this book.

2

C++ defines a rather large set of functions that will be contained in the standard library. These functions are designed to perform many commonly needed tasks, including I/O operations, mathematical computations, and string handling. When you use a library function, the C++ compiler automatically links the object code for that function to the object code of your program.

Because the C++ standard library is so large, it already contains many of the functions that you will need to use in your programs. The library functions act as building blocks that you simply assemble. You should explore your compiler's library manual. You may be surprised at how varied the library functions are. If you write a function that you will use again and again, it too can be stored in a library. Some compilers will allow you to place your function in the standard library; others will require that you create an additional library. Either way, the code will be there for you to use over and over.

One last point: Every C++ compiler also contains a *class library*, which contains object-oriented functions. However, you will need to wait until you learn about classes and objects before you can make use of the class library.

Chapter

3

Introducing Variables, Constants, and Operators

Variables and constants are manipulated by operators to form expressions. This process is the basis of most programming. Unlike some other computer languages that take a simple (and limited) approach to these elements, C++ places a much greater value upon them. This chapter introduces these concepts as they relate to the C++ programming language.

The Basic Data Types

As you saw in Chapter 2, all variables in C++ must be declared prior to their use. This is necessary because the compiler must know what type of data a variable contains before it can properly compile any statement that uses the variable. In C++ there are five basic data types: character, integer, floating point, double floating point and, somewhat surprisingly, valueless. The keywords used to declare variables of these types are **char**, **int**, **float**, **double**, and **void**, respectively. Common sizes and ranges of each data type are shown in Table 3-1. (Remember, the sizes and ranges used by your compiler may vary slightly from those listed here.)

Note: The proposed ANSI C++ standard also defines two other basic types: **bool** and **wchar_t**. Values of type **bool** can hold only the values **true** and **false**. **wchar_t** is used to declare wide (16-bit) character types. These are special-use types and, at the time of this writing, no commonly available compiler currently supports them as built-in types. **bool** and **wchar_t** are discussed later in this book.

Variables of type **char** are used to hold 8-bit ASCII characters such as A, B, or C, or any other 8-bit quantity. To specify a character, you must enclose it between single quotes. Variables of type **int** can hold integer quantities that do not require fractional components. Variables of this type are often used for controlling loops and conditional statements. Variables of the types **float** and **double** are employed either when a fractional component is required or when your application requires large numbers. The difference between a **float** and a **double** variable is the magnitude of the largest (and smallest) number that each one can hold. As shown in Table 3-1, a **double** in C++ can store a number approximately ten times larger than a **float**. As you have seen, **void** is used to declare any function that does not return a value. Other purposes of **void** are discussed later in this book.

Common Sizes and Ranges of the Basic Types in C++
Table 3-1.

Type	Bit Width	Range
char	8	–128 to 127
int	16	–32,768 to 32,767
float	32	3.4E–38 to 3.4E+38
double	64	1.7E–308 to 1.7E+308
void	N/A	valueless

Declaration of Variables

The general form of a variable declaration statement is shown here:

   type variable_list;

Here, *type* must be a valid C++ data type and *variable_list* may consist of one or more identifier names separated by commas. Some declarations are shown here, for example:

```
int i, j, k;

char ch, chr;

float f, balance;

double d;
```

In C++, the name of a variable has nothing to do with its type.

The proposed ANSI C++ standard states that at least the first 1,024 characters of any identifier name (including variable names) will be significant. This means that if two variable names differ in at least one character within the first 1,024 characters, then the compiler will consider them to be different names.

There are three places where variables will be declared: inside functions, in the definition of function parameters, and outside of all functions. These variables are called *local variables, formal parameters,* and *global variables,* respectively. Although we will examine the importance of these three different types of variables in greater detail later in this book, let's take a brief look at these three categories of variables now.

Local Variables

Variables that are declared inside a function are local variables. They can be referenced only by statements that are inside the function in which the variables are declared. Local variables are not known to functions outside their own. Consider this example:

```
#include <iostream.h>

void func();

main()
{
```

3

```
  int x; // local to main()

  x = 10;
  func();
  cout << "\n";
  cout << x; // displays 10

  return 0;
}

void func()
{
  int x; // local to func()

  x = -199;
  cout << x; // displays -199
}
```

A local variable is known only to the function in which it is declared.

Here, the integer variable **x** is declared twice, once in **main( )** and once in **func( )**. The **x** in **main( )** has no bearing on, or relationship to, the **x** in **func( )**. Specifically, changes to the **x** inside **func( )** will not affect the **x** inside **main()**. Therefore, this program will print –199 and 10 on the screen.

In C++, local variables are created when the function is called and destroyed when the function is exited. Correspondingly, the storage for these local variables is created and destroyed in the same way. For these reasons, local variables do not maintain their values between function calls. (That is, the value of a local variable is lost each time its function returns.)

In some other C++ literature, a variable of this sort is called a *dynamic variable* or an *automatic variable*. However, this book will continue to use the term *local variable* because it is the more common term.

Formal Parameters

A formal parameter is a local variable that receives the value of an argument passed to a function.

As you saw in Chapter 2, if a function has arguments, then those arguments must be declared. These are called the formal parameters of the function. As shown in the following fragment, this declaration occurs after the function name, inside the parentheses.

```
func1(int first, int last, char ch)
{
    .
    .
    .
}
```

The **func1()** function has three arguments called **first**, **last**, and **ch**. You must tell C++ what type of variables these are by declaring them as shown above. Once this has been done, they receive information passed to the function. They may also be used inside the function as normal local variables. For example, you may make assignments to a function's formal parameters or use them in any allowable C++ expression. Even though these variables perform the special task of receiving the value of the arguments passed to the function, they can be used like any other local variable. Like other local variables, their value is lost once the function terminates.

Global Variables

You may be wondering how to make a variable and its data stay in existence throughout the entire execution of your program. You can do this in C++ by using global variables. Unlike local variables, *global variables* will hold their value throughout the lifetime of your program. You create global variables by declaring them outside of any function. A global variable can be accessed by any function. That is, a global variable is available for use throughout your entire program.

Global variables are known throughout your entire program.

In the following program, you can see that the variable **count** has been declared outside of all functions. Its declaration is before the **main( )** function. However, it could have been placed anywhere, as long as it was not in a function. Remember, though, that since you must declare a variable before you use it, it is best to declare global variables at the top of the program.

```
#include <iostream.h>

void func1();
void func2();

int count; // this is a global variable

main()
{
  int i; // this is a local variable

  for(i=0; i<10; i++) {
    count = i * 2;
    func1();
  }

  return 0;
}

void func1()
```

3

```
{
   cout << "count: " << count; // access global count
   cout << '\n'; // output a newline
   func2();
}

void func2()
{
   int count; // this is a local variable

   for(count=0; count<3; count++) cout << '.';
}
```

Looking closely at this program, it should be clear that although neither
main( ) nor **func1( )** has declared the variable **count**, both may use it. In
func2( ), however, a local variable called **count** is declared. When **func2( )**
references **count**, it will be referencing only its local variable, not the global
one. It is important to remember that if a global variable and a local variable
have the same name, all references to that variable name inside the function
in which the local variable is declared will refer to the local variable and
have no effect on the global variable.

Some Type Modifiers

Excepting type **void**, C++ allows the basic data types to have *modifiers*
preceding them. A modifier is used to alter the meaning of the base type so
that it more precisely fits the needs of various situations. The data type
modifiers are listed here:

    signed
    unsigned
    long
    short

The modifiers **signed, unsigned, long**, and **short** can be applied to
integer base types. In addition, **signed** and **unsigned** can be applied to
char, and **long** can be applied to **double**. Table 3-2 shows all allowed
combinations of the basic types and the type modifiers. The table also shows
the most common size and range for each type. You should check your
compiler's user manual for the actual range supported by your compiler.

Type	Bit Width	Common Range
char	8	−128 to 127
unsigned char	8	0 to 255
signed char	8	−128 to 127
int	16	−32,768 to 32,767
unsigned int	16	0 to 65,535
signed int	16	−32,768 to 32,767
short int	16	same as int
unsigned short int	16	same as unsigned int
signed short int	16	same as short int
long int	32	−2,147,483,648 to 2,147,483,647
signed long int	32	−2,147,483,648 to 2,147,483,647
unsigned long int	32	0 to 4,294,967,295
float	32	3.4E−38 to 3.4E+38
double	64	1.7E−308 to 1.7E+308
long double	80	3.4E−4932 to 1.1E+4932

All Possible Combinations of the Basic Types and Modifiers in C++, Along with Common Bit Lengths and Ranges
Table 3-2.

3

Although it is allowed, the use of **signed** on integers and characters is redundant because the default declarations assume a signed value.

The difference between signed and unsigned integers is in the way the high-order bit of the integer is interpreted. If a signed integer is specified, then the C++ compiler will generate code that assumes that the high-order bit of an integer is to be used as a *sign flag*. If the sign flag is 0, then the number is positive; if it is 1, then the number is negative. Negative numbers are represented using the *two's complement* approach. In this method, all bits in the number (except the sign flag) are reversed, and then 1 is added to this number. Finally, the sign flag is set to 1.

Signed integers are important for a great many algorithms, but they have only half the absolute magnitude of their unsigned brothers. For example, here is 32,767:

```
0 1 1 1 1 1 1 1   1 1 1 1 1 1 1 1
```

For a signed value, if the high order bit were set to 1, the number would then be interpreted as −1 (assuming the two's complement format). However, if you declared this to be an **unsigned int**, then when the high-order bit was set to 1, the number would become 65,535.

To understand the difference between the way that signed and unsigned integers are interpreted by C++, you should run this short program now:

```
#include <iostream.h>

/* This program shows the difference between
   signed and unsigned integers.
*/
main()
{
  int i; // a signed integer
  unsigned int j; // an unsigned integer

  j = 60000;
  i = j;
  cout << i << " " << j;

  return 0;
}
```

When this program is run, the output is **–5536 60000**. This is because the bit pattern that represents 60,000 as an unsigned integer is interpreted as –5,536 by a signed integer.

C++ allows a shorthand notation for declaring **unsigned**, **short**, or **long** integers. You can simply use the word **unsigned**, **short**, or **long**, without the **int**. The **int** is implied. For example, the following two statements both declare unsigned integer variables.

```
unsigned x;
unsigned int y;
```

Variables of type **char** can be used to hold values other than just the ASCII character set. A **char** variable can also be used as a "small" integer with the range –128 through 127 and can be used in place of an integer when the situation does not require larger numbers. For example, the following program uses a **char** variable to control the loop that prints the alphabet on the screen.

```
// This program prints the alphabet in reverse order.

#include <iostream.h>

main()
{
  char letter;
```

```
    for(letter = 'Z'; letter >= 'A'; letter--)
      cout << letter;

    return 0;
}
```

If the **for** loop seems weird to you, keep in mind that the character A is represented inside the computer as a number, and that the values from A to Z are sequential in ascending order.

Constants

In C++, constants refer to fixed values that cannot be altered by the program. For the most part, constants, and their usage, are so intuitive that they have been used in one form or another by all the preceding sample programs. However, the time has come to explain them formally.

3

C++ constants can be of any of the basic data types. The way each constant is represented depends upon its type. Character constants are enclosed between single quotes. For example 'a', and '%' are both character constants. As some of the examples thus far have shown, if you wish to assign a character to a variable of type **char**, you will use a statement similar to this one:

```
ch = 'Z';
```

Integer constants are specified as numbers without fractional components. For example, 10 and –100 are integer constants. Floating-point constants require the use of the decimal point followed by the number's fractional component. For example, 11.123 is a floating-point constant. C++ also allows you to use scientific notation for floating-point numbers.

There are two floating-point types: **float** and **double**. There are also several flavors of the basic types that can be generated with the type modifiers. The question is: How does the compiler determine the type of a constant? For example, is 123.23 a **float** or a **double**? The answer to this question has two parts. First, the C++ compiler automatically makes certain assumptions about constants and, second, you can explicitly specify the type of a constant, if you like.

By default, the C++ compiler fits a numeric constant into the smallest compatible data type that will hold it, beginning with **int**. Therefore, 10 is **int** by default, but 60,000 is **long**. Even though the value 10 could be fit into a character, the compiler will not do this because it means crossing type boundaries. The only exception to the smallest type rule is floating-point constants, which are assumed to be **double**. For virtually all programs you will write as a beginner the compiler defaults are perfectly adequate. However, it is possible to specify precisely the type of constant you want.

In cases where the default assumption that C++ makes about a numeric constant is not what you want, C++ allows you to specify the exact type of numeric constant by using a suffix. For floating-point types, if you follow the number with an F, the number is treated as a **float**. If you follow it with an L, the number becomes a **long double**. For integer types, the U suffix stands for **unsigned** and the L for **long**. (Both the U and the L must be used to specify an **unsigned long**.) Some examples are shown here:

Data Type	Examples of Constants
int	1 123 21000 –234
long int	35000L –34L
unsigned int	10000U 987U 40000U
unsigned long	12323UL 900000UL
float	123.23F 4.34e–3F
double	23.23 123123.33 –0.9876324
long double	1001.2L

Hexadecimal and Octal Constants

As you probably know, in programming it is sometimes easier to use a number system based on 8 or 16 instead of 10. The number system based on 8 is called *octal*, and it uses the digits 0 through 7. In octal the number 10 is the same as 8 in decimal. The base 16 number system is called *hexadecimal* and uses the digits 0 through 9 plus the letters A through F, which stand for 10, 11, 12, 13, 14, and 15. For example, the hexadecimal number 10 is 16 in decimal. Because of the frequency with which these two number systems are used, C++ allows you to specify integer constants in hexadecimal or octal instead of decimal. A hexadecimal constant must begin with 0x (a zero followed by an x). An octal constant begins with a zero. Here are some examples.

```
hex = 0xFF; // 255 in decimal
oct = 011; // 9 in decimal
```

String Constants

C++ supports one other type of constant in addition to those of the predefined data types: the string. A *string* is a set of characters enclosed by double quotes. For example, "this is a test" is a string. You have seen examples of strings in some of the **cout** statements in the preceding sample programs. Keep in mind one important fact: although C++ allows you to define string constants, it does not have a built-in string data type. Instead, as you will see a little later in this book, strings are supported in C++ as character arrays. (However, all C++ compilers provide library functions that support strings in one fashion or another.)

Caution: You must not confuse the strings with characters. A single character constant is enclosed by single quotes, as with 'a'. However, "a" is a string containing only one letter.

Backslash Character Constants

3

Enclosing character constants in single quotes works for most printing characters, but a few characters, such as the carriage return, pose a special problem when a text editor is used. In addition, certain other characters, such as the single and double quotes have special meaning in C++, so you cannot use them directly. For these reasons, C++ provides the special backslash character constants shown in Table 3-3.

The following sample program illustrates the use of backslash codes. When this program is run, it outputs a newline, a backslash, and a backspace.

```
#include <iostream.h>

main()
{
  cout << "\n\\b";

  return 0;
}
```

Variable Initializations

You can assign a value to a variable in C++ at the same time that it is declared by placing an equal sign and the value after the variable name. The general form of initialization is:

type variable_name = constant;

Some examples are:

```
char ch = 'a';
int first = 0;
float balance = 123.23F;
```

Code	Meaning
\b	backspace
\f	form feed
\n	newline
\r	carriage return
\t	horizontal tab
\"	double quote
\ '	single quote character
\0	null
\\	backslash
\v	vertical tab
\a	alert
\?	?
\N	octal constant (where *N* is an octal constant)
\xN	hexadecimal constant (where *N* is a hexadecimal constant)

Backslash
Codes
Table 3-3.

Although variables are frequently initialized by constants, you can initialize a variable using any valid C++ expression. As you will see, initialization plays an important role when you are working with objects.

Global variables are initialized only at the start of the program. Local variables are initialized each time the function in which they are declared is entered. All global variables are initialized to zero if no other initializer is specified. Local variables that are not initialized will have unknown values before the first assignment is made to them.

Here is a simple example of variable initialization. This program requests a number, and then it sums all the numbers between 1 and that number.

```
// An example using variable initialization.
#include <iostream.h>

void total(int x);

main()
{
  int t;

  total(5);
  total(6);
```

```
    cout << "enter a number: ";
    cin >> t;
    total(t);

    return 0;
}

void total(int x)
{
    int sum=0; // initialize sum
    int i, count;

    for(i=1; i<=x; i++) {
        sum = sum + i;
        for(count=0; count<10; count++) cout << '.';
        cout << "The current sum is " << sum << '\n';
    }
}
```

As you will see when you run this program, each time **total( )** is called, **sum** is initialized to zero.

Operators

C++ is rich in built-in operators. An *operator* is a symbol that tells the compiler to perform specific mathematical or logical manipulations. C++ has three general classes of operators: *arithmetic, relational* and *logical,* and *bitwise.* In addition, C++ has some special operators for particular tasks. This chapter will examine the arithmetic, relational, and logical operators, reserving the more advanced bitwise operators for later.

Arithmetic Operators

Table 3-4 lists the arithmetic operators allowed in C++. The operators +, −, *, and / all work the same way in C++ as they do in any other computer language (or algebra, for that matter). These can be applied to any built-in data type allowed by C++. When / is applied to an integer or a character, any remainder will be truncated; for example, 10/3 will equal 3 in integer division.

The modulus operator **%** also works in C++ the way that it does in other languages. Remember that the modulus operation yields the remainder of an

Operator	Action
–	subtraction, also unary minus
+	addition
*	multiplication
/	division
%	modulus
––	decrement
++	increment

Arithmetic
Operators
Table 3-4.

integer division. This means that the **%** cannot be used on type **float** or **double**. The following program illustrates its use.

```
#include <iostream.h>

main()
{
  int x, y;

  x = 10;
  y = 3;
  cout << x/y; // will display 3
  cout << "\n";
  cout << x%y; /* will display 1, the remainder of
                  the integer division */
  cout << "\n";

  x = 1;
  y = 2;
  cout << x/y << " " << x%y; // will display 0 1

  return 0;
}
```

The reason the last line prints a 0 and 1 is because 1/2 in integer division is 0 with a remainder of 1. Thus, 1%2 yields the remainder 1.

The unary minus, in effect, multiplies its single operand by –1. That is, any number preceded by a minus sign switches its sign.

Increment and Decrement

C++ has two operators not generally found in other computer languages. These are the increment and decrement operators, **++** and **––**. These operators were mentioned in passing in Chapter 2, when the **for** loop was introduced. The **++** operator adds 1 to its operand, and **––** subtracts 1.

Therefore,

```
x = x+1;
```

is the same as

```
++x;
```

and

```
x = x-1;
```

is the same as

```
--x;
```

Both the increment and decrement operators can either precede (prefix) or follow (postfix) the operand. For example:

```
x = x+1;
```

can be written as

```
++x; // prefix form
```

or as

```
x++; // postfix form
```

In the foregoing example, there is no difference whether the increment is applied as a prefix or a postfix. However, when an increment or decrement is used as part of a larger expression, there is an important difference. When an increment or decrement operator precedes its operand, C++ will perform the corresponding operation prior to obtaining the operand's value. If the operator follows its operand, then C++ will obtain the operand's value before incrementing or decrementing it. Consider the following:

```
x = 10;
y = ++x;
```

In this case, **y** will be set to 11. However, if the code is written as

```
x = 10;
y= x++;
```

then **y** will be set to 10. In both cases, **x** is still set to 11; the difference is when it happens. There are significant advantages in being able to control when the increment or decrement operation takes place.

Most C++ compilers write very fast, efficient object code for increment and decrement operations that is better than the code generated when the corresponding assignment statement is used. Therefore, it is a good idea to use increment and decrement operators when you can. The precedence of the arithmetic operators is shown here:

highest	++ --
	– (unary minus)
	* / %
lowest	+ –

Operators on the same precedence level are evaluated by the compiler from left to right. Of course, parentheses may be used to alter the order of evaluation. Parentheses are treated by C++ in the same way that they are by virtually all other computer languages: they force an operation, or a set of operations, to have a higher precedence level.

How C++ Got Its name

Now that you understand the full meaning behind the ++ operator, you can probably guess how C++ got its name. As you know, C++ is built upon the C language. In fact, C++ simply adds to the C language several enhancements, most of which support object-oriented programming. C++ represents an *incremental* improvement to C, and thus the addition of the ++ (which is, of course, the increment operator) to the name C is a fitting way to describe C++.

As mentioned in Chapter 1, Stroustrup initially named C++ "C with Classes." However, at the suggestion of Rick Mascitti, Stroustrup later changed the name to C++. While the new language was already destined for success, the adoption of the name C++ virtually guaranteed its place in history because it was a name that every C programmer would instantly recognize!

Relational and Logical Operators

In the terms *relational operator* and *logical operator*, *relational* refers to the relationships which values can have with one another, and *logical* refers to the ways these relationships can be connected together. Because the

Relational Operators	
Operator	**Meaning**
>	greater than
>=	greater than or equal to
<	less than
<=	less than or equal to
==	equal to
!=	not equal to

Logical Operators	
Operator	**Meaning**
&&	AND
||	OR
!	NOT

The Relational and Logical Operators in C++

Table 3-5.

3

relational and logical operators often work together, they will be discussed together here.

The key to using the relational and logical operators is the idea of *true versus false*. In C++, true is any value other than 0. False is 0. Thus, only expressions that evaluate to 0 are false. Any other value is true. As you learn more about C++, you will see that this concept of true and false makes certain algorithms much easier to write.

In C++, true is any non-zero value. False is zero.

The relational and logical operators are shown in Table 3-5. Notice that in C++, *not equal* is represented by **!=** and *equal* is represented by the double equal sign, **==**.

The logical operators are used to support the basic logical operations AND, OR, and NOT, according to the following truth table. The table uses 1 for true and 0 for false.

p	q	p AND q	p OR q	NOT p
0	0	0	0	1
0	1	0	1	1
1	1	1	1	0
1	0	0	1	0

Although C++ does not contain a built-in exclusive-OR (XOR) logical operator, it is easy to construct one. The XOR operation uses this truth table:

p	q	XOR
0	0	0
0	1	1
1	0	1
1	1	0

In words, the XOR operation produces a true result when one and only one operand is true. The following function uses the **&&** and | | operators to construct an XOR operation. The result is returned by the function.

```
xor(int a, int b)
{
  return (a || b) && !(a && b);
}
```

The following program uses this function. It displays the results of an AND, OR, and XOR on the values you enter.

```
// This program demonstrates the xor() function.
#include <iostream.h>

xor(int a, int b);

main()
{
  int p, q;

  cout << "enter P (0 or 1): ";
  cin >> p;
  cout << "enter Q (0 or 1): ";
  cin >> q;

  cout << "P AND Q: " << (p && q) << '\n';
  cout << "P OR Q: " << (p || q) << '\n';
  cout << "P XOR Q: " << xor(p, q) << '\n';

  return 0;
}

xor(int a, int b)
{
  return (a || b) && !(a && b);
}
```

Both the relational and logical operators are lower in precedence than the arithmetic operators. This means that an expression like 10 > 1+12 is evaluated as if it were written 10 > (1+12). The result is, of course, false. Also, the parentheses surrounding **p && q** and **p | | q** in the preceding program are necessary because the **&&** and | | operators are lower in precedence than the output operator.

You can link any number of relational operations together using logical operators. For example, this expression joins three relational operations:

```
var>15 | | !(10<count) && 3<=item
```

The following table shows the relative precedence of the relational and logical operators:

3

highest	!
	>>= <<=
	== !=
	&&
lowest	| |

All relational and logical expressions produce a result of either true or false. Generally, the value 1 is used for true and (of course) 0 is false. Therefore, the following program is not only correct, but will also display the number 1 on the screen.

```
#include <iostream.h>

main()
{
  int x;

  x = 100;
  cout << (x>10);

  return 0;
}
```

 Note: The proposed ANSI C++ standard states that the outcome of a relational or logical expression is a value of type **bool**, which can be either **true** or **false**. However, these values automatically convert into integers that are nonzero and zero, respectively.

Expressions

Operators, constants, and variables are the constituents of *expressions*. An expression in C++ is any valid combination of those pieces. You probably already know the general form of expressions from your other programming experience or from algebra. However, there are a few aspects of expressions that relate specifically to C++; these will be discussed now.

Type Conversion in Expressions

When constants and variables of different types are mixed in an expression, they are converted to the same type. The C++ compiler will convert all operands "up" to the type of the largest operand. This is done on an operation-by-operation basis. For example, if one operand is a **char** and the other an **int**, then the **char** is promoted to an integer. Or, if either operand is a **double**, the other operand is promoted to **double**. This means that conversions such as that from a **char** to a **double** are perfectly valid. Once a conversion has been applied, each pair of operands will be of the same type, and the result of each operation will be the same as the type of both operands.

For example, consider the type conversions that occur in Figure 3-1. First, the character **ch** is converted to an integer, and **f** is converted to **double**. Then the outcome of **ch/i** is converted to a **double** because **f*d** is a **double**. The final result is **double** because, by this time, both operands are **double**.

Casts

It is possible to force an expression to be of a specific type by using a construct called a *cast*. The general form of a cast is

   (*type*) *expression*

where *type* is a valid C++ data type. For example, if you wish to make sure the expression **x/2** is evaluated to type **float,** you can write

```
(float) x / 2
```

Casts are often considered operators. As an operator, a cast is unary and has the same precedence as any other unary operator.

```
char ch;
int i;
float f;
double d;
```

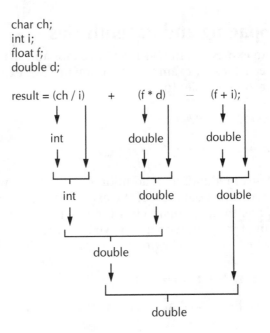

A type
conversion
example
Figure 3-1.

There are times when a cast can be very useful. For example, you may wish
to use an integer for loop control, but also perform computation on it that
requires a fractional part, as in the program shown here:

```cpp
#include <iostream.h>

main() // print i and i/2 with fractions
{
  int i;

  for(i=1; i<=100; ++i )
    cout << i << "/ 2 is: " << (float) i / 2 << '\n';

  return 0;
}
```

Without the cast **(float)** in this example, only an integer division would be
performed. The cast ensures that the fractional part of the answer will be
displayed on the screen.

Spacing and Parentheses

An expression in C++ may have tabs and spaces in it to make it more readable. For example, the following two expressions are the same, but the second is easier to read:

```
x=10/y*(127/x);
```

```
x = 10 / y * (127/x);
```

Use of redundant or additional parentheses will not cause errors or slow down the execution of the expression. You are encouraged to use parentheses to make clear the exact order of evaluation, both for yourself and for others who may have to figure out your program later. For example, which of the following two expressions is easier to read?

```
x = y/3-34*temp&127;
```

```
x = (y/3) - ((34*temp) & 127);
```

Chapter

4

Program Control
Statements

In this chapter you will learn about the statements that control a program's flow of execution. There are three specific categories of program control statements: *selection* statements, which include the **if** and the **switch**; *iteration* statements, which include the **for**, **while**, and **do-while** loops; and *jump* statements, which include **break**, **continue**, **return**, and **goto**. (However, a discussion of the **return** statement is deferred until later in this book.)

This chapter begins with a thorough examination of the **if** and **for** statements, to which you have already had a brief introduction. It then discusses the other program control statements.

The if Statement

Chapter 2 introduced the **if** statement. Now it is time to examine it in detail. The complete form of the **if** statement is

```
if(expression) statement;
else statement;
```

if selects between two paths of execution.

where the targets of the **if** and **else** are single statements. The **else** clause is optional. The targets of both the **if** and **else** can be blocks of statements. The general form of the **if** using blocks of statements is

```
if(expression)
{
  statement sequence
}
else
{
  statement sequence
}
```

If the conditional expression is true (i.e., anything other than 0), the target of the **if** will be executed; otherwise, if it exists, the target of the **else** will be executed. At no time will both of them be executed. The conditional expression controlling the **if** may be any type of valid C++ expression that produces a Boolean (i.e., true or false) result.

The following program demonstrates the **if** by playing a simple version of the "guess the magic number" game. The program generates a random number, prompts for your guess, and prints the message ** **Right** ** if you guess the magic number. This program also introduces another standard C++ library function, called **rand( )**, which returns a randomly selected unsigned integer value. It requires the header file called **stdlib.h**.

```
// Magic Number program.
#include <iostream.h>
#include <stdlib.h>

main()
{
  int magic;  // magic number
  int guess;  // user's guess

  magic = rand(); // get a random number
```

```
     cout << "Enter your guess: ";
     cin >> guess;

     if(guess == magic) cout << "** Right **";

     return 0;
}
```

This program uses the relational operator **==** to determine whether the guess matches the magic number. If it does, the message is printed on the screen.

Taking the Magic Number program further, the next version uses the **else** to print a message when the wrong number is picked.

```
// Magic Number program: 1st improvement.

#include <iostream.h>
#include <stdlib.h>

main()
{
  int magic;   // magic number
  int guess;   // user's guess

  magic = rand(); // get a random number

  cout << "Enter your guess: ";
  cin >> guess;

  if(guess == magic) cout << "** Right **";
  else cout << "...Sorry, you're wrong.";

  return 0;
}
```

4

The Conditional Expression

Sometimes newcomers to C++ are confused by the fact that any valid C++ expression can be used to control the **if**. That is, the type of expression need not be restricted to only those involving the relational and logical operators (as is the case in languages like BASIC or Pascal). All that is required is that the expression evaluate to either a zero or non-zero value. For example, this program reads two integers from the keyboard and displays the quotient. In order to avoid a divide-by-zero error, an **if** statement, controlled by the second number, is used.

```
// Divide the first number by the second.

#include <iostream.h>

main()
{
  int a, b;

  cout << "enter two numbers: ";
  cin >> a >> b;

  if(b) cout << a/b << '\n';
  else cout << "cannot divide by zero\n";

  return 0;
}
```

Notice that **b** (the divisor) is tested for zero using **if(b)**. This approach works because when **b** is zero, the condition controlling the **if** is false and the **else** executes. Otherwise, the condition is true (non-zero) and the division takes place. It is not necessary (and would be considered bad style by most C++ programmers) to write this **if** as shown here:

```
if(b == 0) cout << a/b << '\n';
```

This form of the statement is redundant and potentially inefficient.

Nested ifs

A *nested* **if** is an **if** statement that is the target of another **if** or **else**. Nested **if**s are very common in programming. The main thing to remember about nested **if**s in C++ is that an **else** statement always refers to the nearest **if** statement that is within the same block as the **else** and not already associated with an **else**. Here is an example:

```
if(i) {
  if(j) statement1;
  if(k) statement2; // this if
  else statement3; // is associated with this else
}
else statement4; // associated with if(i)
```

As the comments indicate, the final **else** is not associated with **if(j)** (even though it is the closest **if** without an **else**), because it is not in the same block. Rather, the final **else** is associated with **if(i)**. The inner **else** is associated with **if(k)** because that is the nearest **if**.

A nested
if is an **if**
statement
that is the
target of
either
another **if**
or an **else**.

C++ allows at least 256 levels of nesting. In practice, you will seldom need to nest **if** statements this deeply.

We can use a nested **if** to add a further improvement to the Magic Number program. This addition provides the player with feedback about a wrong guess.

```cpp
// Magic Number program: 2nd improvement.

#include <iostream.h>
#include <stdlib.h>

main()
{
  int magic;  // magic number
  int guess;  // user's guess

  magic = rand(); // get a random number

  cout << "Enter your guess: ";
  cin >> guess;

  if (guess == magic) {
    cout << "** Right **\n";
    cout << magic << " is the magic number\n";
  }
  else {
    cout << "...Sorry, you're wrong.";
    if(guess > magic) cout <<" Your guess is too high\n";
    else cout << " Your guess is too low\n";
  }

  return 0;
}
```

The if-else-if Ladder

A common programming construct that is based upon nested **if**s is the **if-else-if** *ladder*. It looks like this:

```
if(condition)
  statement;
else if(condition)
  statement;
else if(condition)
  statement;
    .
```

4

.
.

```
        else
            statement;
```

The conditional expressions are evaluated from the top downward. As soon as a true condition is found, the statement associated with it is executed, and the rest of the ladder is bypassed. If none of the conditions is true, then the final **else** statement will be executed. The final **else** often acts as a default condition; that is, if all other conditional tests fail, then the last **else** statement is performed. If there is no final **else** and all other conditions are false, then no action will take place.

The following program demonstrates the **if-else-if** ladder.

```
// Demonstrate an if-else-if ladder.
#include <iostream.h>

main()
{
  int x;

  for(x=0; x<6; x++) {
    if(x==1) cout << "x is one\n";
    else if(x==2) cout << "x is two\n";
    else if(x==3) cout << "x is three\n";
    else if(x==4) cout << "x is four\n";
    else cout << "x is not between 1 and 4\n";
  }

  return 0;
}
```

The program produces the following output:

```
x is not between 1 and 4
x is one
x is two
x is three
x is four
x is not between 1 and 4
```

As you can see, the default **else** is executed only if none of the preceding **if** statements succeed.

The for Loop

You were introduced to a simple form of the **for** loop in Chapter 2. You might be surprised just how powerful and flexible the **for** loop is. Let's begin by reviewing the basics, starting with the most traditional forms of the **for**.

The *for* is
C++'s most
versatile loop.

The general form of the **for** loop for repeating a single statement is:

   for(*initialization; expression; increment*) *statement;*

For repeating a block, the general form is:

   for(*initialization; expression; increment*)
   {
      statement sequence
   }

The *initialization* is usually an assignment statement that sets the initial value of the *loop control variable,* which acts as the counter that controls the loop. The *expression* is a conditional expression that determines whether or not the loop will repeat. The *increment* defines the amount by which the loop control variable will change each time the loop is repeated. Notice that these three major sections of the loop must be separated by semicolons. The **for** loop will continue to execute as long as the conditional expression tests true. Once the condition becomes false, the loop will exit, and program execution will resume on the statement following the **for** block.

4

The following program uses a **for** loop to print the square roots of the numbers between 1 and 99. Notice that in this example, the loop control variable is called **num**.

```
#include <iostream.h>
#include <math.h>

main()
{
  int num;
  double sq_root;

  for(num=1; num < 100; num++) {
    sq_root = sqrt((double) num);
    cout << num << " " << sq_root << '\n';
  }

  return 0;
}
```

This program introduces another of C++'s standard functions: **sqrt( )**. The **sqrt( )** function returns the square root of its argument. The argument must be of type **double**, and the function returns a value of type **double**. Notice that the header file **math.h** has been included. This file is needed to support the **sqrt( )** function.

Tip: In addition to **sqrt( )**, C++ supports an extensive set of mathematical library functions. For example, **sin( )**, **cos( )**, **tan( )**, **log( )**, **ceil( )**, and **floor( )** are a few. If mathematical programming is your interest, you will want to explore the C++ math functions. Remember, they all require the header file **math.h**.

The **for** loop can proceed in a positive or negative fashion, and it can increment the loop control variable by any amount. For example, the following program prints the numbers 100 to –100, in decrements of 5.

```
#include <iostream.h>

main()
{
  int i;

  for(i=100; i >= -100; i = i-5) cout << i << ' ';

  return 0;
}
```

An important point about **for** loops is that the conditional expression is always tested at the top of the loop. This means that the code inside the loop may not be executed at all if the condition is false to begin with. Here is an example:

```
for(count=10; count < 5; count++)
  cout << count; // this statement will not execute
```

This loop will never execute because its control variable, **count**, is greater than 5 when the loop is first entered. This makes the conditional expression, **count<5**, false from the outset; thus, not even one iteration of the loop will occur.

Some Variations on the for Loop

The **for** is one of the most versatile statements in the C++ language because it allows a wide range of variations from its traditional use. For example, multiple loop control variables can be used. Consider the following fragment of code:

```
for(x=0, y=10; x<=10; ++x, --y)
  cout << x << ' ' << y << '\n';
```

Here, commas separate the two initialization statements and the two increment expressions. This is necessary in order for the compiler to understand that there are two initialization and two increment statements. In C++, the comma is an operator that essentially means "do this and this." We will look at other uses for the comma operator later in this book. But its most common use is in the **for** loop. You can have any number of initialization and increment statements, but in practice, more than two or three make the **for** loop unwieldy.

The condition controlling the loop may be any valid C++ expression. It does not need to involve the loop control variable. In the next example, the loop continues to execute until the user presses a key at the keyboard. The example also introduces an important library function: **kbhit()**. This function returns false if no key has been pressed, or true if a key has been struck. It does not wait for a keypress, thus allowing the loop to continue execution. The **kbhit( )** function uses the header file **conio.h**.

4

```
#include <iostream.h>
#include <conio.h>

main()
{
  int i;

  // print numbers until a key is pressed
  for(i=0; !kbhit(); i++) cout << i << ' ';

  return 0;
}
```

Each time through the loop, **kbhit( )** is called. If a key has been pressed, then a true value is returned, which causes **!kbhit( )** to be false, so the loop stops. However, if no key has been pressed, **kbhit( )** returns false, and **!kbhit( )** is true, allowing the loop to continue.

Tip: The **kbhit( )** function is not part of the C++ standard library. This is because the C++ standard library defines only a minimum set of functions that all C++ compilers must have. **kbhit( )** is not included in this minimal set because not all environments can support keyboard interactivity. However, **kbhit( )** is supported by virtually all mainstream C++ compilers, although it might be called something slightly different. A compiler manufacturer is free—in fact, encouraged—to provide more library functions than are required to meet the minimum requirements of the standard C++ library. These extra functions are included so that you can fully access and utilize your programming environment. You should feel free to use all the functions supplied by your compiler.

Missing Pieces

Another aspect of the **for** loop that is different in C++ than in many computer languages is that pieces of the loop definition need not be there. For example, if you want to write a loop that runs until the number 123 is typed in at the keyboard, it could look like this:

```
#include <iostream.h>

main()
{
  int x;

  for(x=0; x != 123; ) {
    cout << "enter a number: ";
    cin >> x;
  }

  return 0;
}
```

The increment portion of the **for** definition is blank. This means that each time the loop repeats, **x** is tested to see whether it equals 123, but no further action takes place. If, however, you type 123 at the keyboard, the loop condition becomes false and the loop exits. The C++ **for** loop will not modify the loop control variable if no increment portion of the loop is present.

Another variation on the **for** is to move the initialization section outside of the loop, as shown in this fragment:

```
x = 0;

for( ; x<10; )
```

```
{
  cout << x << ' ';
  ++x;
}
```

Here, the initialization section has been left blank, and **x** is initialized before the loop is entered. Placing the initialization outside of the loop is generally done only when the initial value is derived through a complex process that does not lend itself to containment inside the **for** statement. Notice that in this example, the increment portion of the **for** is located inside the body of the loop.

The Infinite Loop

You can create an *infinite loop* (a loop that never terminates) using this **for** construct:

An infinite loop is a loop that never terminates.

```
for(;;)
{
  //...
}
```

4

This loop will run forever. Although there are some programming tasks, such as operating system command processors, that require an infinite loop, most "infinite loops" are really just loops with special termination requirements. Near the end of this chapter you will see how to halt a loop of this type. (Hint: it's done using the **break** statement.)

Time Delay Loops

Time delay loops are often used in programs. These are loops that have no other function than to kill time. Delay loops can be created by specifying an empty target statement. For example:

```
for(x=0; x<1000; x++) ;
```

This loop increments **x** one thousand times but does nothing else. The semicolon that terminates the line is necessary because the **for** expects a statement, which can be empty.

Before moving on, you might want to experiment with your own variations on the **for** loop. As you will find, it is a fascinating loop.

The switch Statement

Before looking at C++'s other loop constructs, let's examine its other selection statement: the **switch**. Although a series of nested **if** statements can perform multiway tests, for many situations a more efficient approach can be used. C++ has a built-in multiple branch decision statement called **switch**. It works like this: the value of an expression is successively tested against a list of integer or character constants. When a match is found, the statement sequence associated with that match is executed. The general form of the **switch** statement is:

switch is C++'s multiway decision statement.

```
switch(expression) {
    case constant1:
        statement sequence
        break;
    case constant2:
        statement sequence
        break;
    case constant3:
        statement sequence
        break;
          .
          .
          .
    default:
        statement sequence
}
```

break stops the execution of code within a **switch**.

The **switch** expression must evaluate to either a character or an integer value. (Floating point expressions, for example, are not allowed.) Frequently, the expression controlling the **switch** is simply a variable.

The **default** statements are executed if no **case** constant matches the **switch** expression.

The **default** statement sequence is performed if no matches are found. The **default** is optional; if it is not present, no action takes place if all matches fail. When a match is found, the statements associated with that **case** are executed until the **break** is encountered or, in the case of **default** or the last **case**, until the end of the **switch** is reached.

There are four important things to know about the **switch** statement:

♦ The **switch** differs from the **if** in that **switch** can test only for equality (i.e., for matches between the **switch** expression and the **case** constants), whereas the **if** conditional expression can be of any type.

- No two **case** constants in the same **switch** can have identical values. Of course, a **switch** statement enclosed by an outer switch may have **case** constants that are the same.

- A **switch** statement is usually more efficient than nested **if**s.

- The statement sequences associated with each **case** are *not* blocks. However, the entire **switch** statement *does* define a block. The importance of this will become apparent as you learn more about C++.

The proposed ANSI C++ standard specifies that a **switch** can have at least 16,384 **case** statements. In practice, you will want to limit the number of **case** statements you use to a much smaller total, for reasons of efficiency.

The following program demonstrates the **switch**. It creates a simple "help" system that describes the meaning of the **for**, **if**, and **switch** statements. It displays the help topics and then waits for the user to enter his or her choice. This choice is then used by the **switch** to display information about the requested topic. (You might find it fun to expand the information in this program. You can also add new topics as you learn about them.)

4

```
// Demonstrate the switch using a simple "help" program.
#include <iostream.h>

main()
{
  int ch;

  cout << "Help on:\n\n";
  cout << "1. for\n";
  cout << "2. if\n";
  cout << "3. switch\n\n";

  cout << "Enter choice: (1-3): ";
  cin >> ch;

  switch(ch) {
    case 1:
      cout << "for is C++'s most versatile loop.\n";
      break;
    case 2:
      cout << "if is C++'s conditional branch statement.\n";
      break;
    case 3:
      cout << "switch is C++'s multi-way branch statement.\n";
```

```
      break;
    default:
      cout << "You must enter a number between 1 and 3.\n";
  }

  return 0;
}
```

Technically, the **break** statement is optional, although most applications of the **switch** will use it. When encountered within the statement sequence of a **case**, the **break** statement causes program flow to exit from the entire **switch** statement and resume at the next statement outside the **switch**. However, if a **break** statement does not end the statement sequence associated with a **case**, then all the statements *at and below* the matching **case** will be executed until a **break** (or the end of the **switch**) is encountered.

For example, study the following program carefully. Can you figure out what it will display on the screen?

```
#include <iostream.h>

main()
{
  int i;

  for(i=0; i<5; i++) {
    switch(i) {
      case 0: cout << "less than 1\n";
      case 1: cout << "less than 2\n";
      case 2: cout << "less than 3\n";
      case 3: cout << "less than 4\n";
      case 4: cout << "less than 5\n";
    }
    cout << '\n';
  }

  return 0;
}
```

This program displays the following output:

```
less than 1
less than 2
```

```
less than 3
less than 4
less than 5

less than 2
less than 3
less than 4
less than 5

less than 3
less than 4
less than 5

less than 4
less than 5

less than 5
```

As this program illustrates, execution will continue into the next **case** if no **break** statement is present.

You can have empty **case**s, as shown in this example:

```
switch(i) {
  case 1:
  case 2:
  case 3: do_something();
    break;
  case 4: do_something_else();
    break;
```

In this fragment, if **i** has the value 1, 2, or 3, then **do_something( )** is called. If it is 4, then **do_something_else( )** is called. The "stacking" of **case**s, as shown in this example, is very common when several **case**s share common code.

Nested switch Statements

It is possible to have a **switch** as part of the statement sequence of an outer **switch**. Even if the **case** constants of the inner and outer **switch** contain common values, no conflicts will arise. For example, the following code fragment is perfectly acceptable:

```
switch(ch1) {
  case 'A': cout << "This A is part of outer switch";
    switch(ch2) {
      case 'A':
```

```
      cout << "This A is part of inner switch";
      break;
    case 'B': // ...
  }
  break;
case 'B': // ...
```

C++ specifies that at least 256 levels of nesting be allowed for **switch** statements. Frankly, few programs ever require anywhere near 256 levels of nesting.

The while Loop

while is another of C++'s loop statements.

The proposed ANSI C++'s loops is the **while.** The general form of the **while** loop is

    while(*expression*) *statement*;

where *statement* may be a single statement or a block of statements. The *expression* defines the condition that controls the loop and it may be any valid expression. The statement is performed while the condition is true. When the condition becomes false, program control passes to the line immediately following the loop.

The next program illustrates the **while** in a short but sometimes fascinating program. Virtually all PCs support an extended character set beyond that defined by ASCII. The extended characters, if they exist, often include special characters such as foreign language symbols and scientific notations. The ASCII characters use values that are less than 128 . The extended character set begins at 128 and continues to 255. This program prints all characters between 32 (which is a space) and 255. When you run this program, you will most likely see some very interesting characters!

```
/* This program displays all printable characters,
   including the extended character set, if one exists.
*/

#include <iostream.h>

main()
{
  unsigned char ch;

  ch = 32;
  while(ch) {
    cout << ch;
    ch++;
```

```
    }

    return 0;
}
```

Examine the loop expression in the preceding program. You might be
wondering why only **ch** is used to control the **while**. The answer is quite
easy. Since **ch** is an unsigned character, it can only hold the values 0 through
255. When it holds the value 255 and is then incremented, its value will
"wrap around" to zero. Therefore, the test for **ch** being zero serves as a
convenient stopping condition.

As with the **for** loop, the **while** checks the conditional expression at the
top of the loop, which means that the loop code may not execute at all. This
eliminates the need for performing a separate test before the loop. The
following program illustrates this characteristic of the **while** loop. It
displays a line of periods. The number of periods displayed is equal to the
value entered by the user. The program does not allow lines longer than 80
characters. The test for a permissible number of periods is performed inside
the loop's conditional expression, not outside of it.

```
#include <iostream.h>

main()
{
  int len;

  cout << "enter length (1 to 79): ";
  cin >> len;

  while(len>0 && len<80)  {
    cout << '.';
    len--;
  }

  return 0;
}
```

There need not be any statements at all in the body of the **while** loop. Here
is an example:

```
while(rand() != 100) ;
```

This loop iterates until the random number generated by **rand()** equals 100.

The do-while Loop

Unlike the **for** and the **while** loops, in which the condition is tested at the top of the loop, the **do-while** loop checks its condition at the bottom of the loop. This means that a **do-while** loop will always execute at least once. The general form of the **do-while** loop is:

The *do-while* is the only C++ loop that will always iterate at least once.

```
do {
    statements;
} while(expression);
```

Although the braces are not necessary when only one statement is present, they are often used to improve readability of the **do-while** construct, thus preventing confusion with the **while**. The **do-while** loop executes as long as the conditional expression is true.

The following program loops until the number 100 is entered.

```
#include <iostream.h>

main()
{
  int num;

  do {
      cout << "Enter a number (100 to stop): ";
      cin >> num;
  } while(num != 100);

  return 0;
}
```

Using a **do-while** loop, we can further improve the Magic Number program. This time, the program loops until you guess the number.

```
// Magic Number program: 3rd improvement.

#include <iostream.h>
#include <stdlib.h>

main()
{
  int magic; // magic number
  int guess; // user's guess

  magic = rand(); // get a random number

  do {
```

```
      cout << "Enter your guess: ";
      cin >> guess;
      if(guess == magic) {
        cout << "** Right ** ";
        cout << magic << " is the magic number.\n";
      }
      else {
        cout << "...Sorry, you're wrong.";
        if(guess > magic)
           cout << " Your guess is too high.\n";
        else cout << " Your guess is too low.\n";
      }
    } while(guess != magic);

    return 0;
}
```

Using continue

It is possible to force an early iteration of a loop, bypassing the loop's normal control structure. This is accomplished using **continue**. The **continue** statement forces the next iteration of the loop to take place, skipping any code between itself and the conditional expression that controls the loop. For example, the following program prints the even numbers between 0 and 100.

continue immediately causes the next iteration of a loop.

4

```
#include <iostream.h>

main()
{
  int x;

  for(x=0; x<=100; x++) {
    if(x%2) continue;
    cout << x << ' ';
  }

  return 0;
}
```

Only even numbers are printed, because an odd one will cause the loop to iterate early, bypassing the **cout** statement.

In **while** and **do-while** loops, a **continue** statement will cause control to go directly to the conditional expression and then continue the looping process. In the case of the **for**, the increment part of the loop is performed, then the conditional expression is executed, and then the loop continues.

Using break to Exit Loops

It is possible to force an immediate exit from a loop, bypassing the loop's conditional test, by using the **break** statement. When the **break** statement is encountered inside a loop, the loop is immediately terminated, and program control resumes at the next statement following the loop. Here is a simple example:

```cpp
#include <iostream.h>

main()
{
  int t;

  // Loops from 0 to 9, not to 100!
  for(t=0; t<100; t++) {
    if(t==10) break;
    cout << t << ' ';
  }

  return 0;
}
```

break causes immediate termination of a loop.

This program will print the numbers 0 through 9 on the screen before ending. It will not go to 100, because the **break** statement will cause it to terminate early.

The **break** statement is commonly used in loops in which a special condition can cause immediate termination. The following fragment contains an example of such a situation, where a keypress can stop the execution of the loop:

```cpp
for(i=0; i<1000; i++) {
  // do something
  if(kbhit()) break;
}
```

A **break** will cause an exit from only the innermost loop. Here is an example:

```cpp
#include <iostream.h>

main()
{
  int t, count;

  for(t=0; t<100; t++) {
    count = 1;
    for(;;) {
```

```
      cout << count << ' ';
      count++;
      if(count==10) break;
    }
    cout << '\n';
  }

  return 0;
}
```

This program will print the numbers 1 through 10 on the screen 100 times. Each time the **break** is encountered, control is passed back to the outer **for** loop.

Note: A **break** used in a **switch** statement will affect only that switch, and not any loop the **switch** happens to be in.

4

As you have seen, it is possible to create an infinite loop in C++ using the **for** statement. (You can also create infinite loops using the **while** and the **do-while**, but the **for** is the traditional method.) In order to exit from an infinite loop, you must use the **break** statement. Of course, you can also use **break** to terminate a non-infinite loop as well.

Nested Loops

As you have seen in some of the preceding examples, one loop can be nested inside of another. C++ allows at least 256 levels of nesting. Nested loops are used to solve a wide variety of programming problems. For example, the following program uses a nested **for** loop to find the prime numbers from 2 to 1000.

```
/* This program finds the prime numbers from
   2 to 1000.
*/

#include <iostream.h>

main()
{
  int i, j;

  for(i=2; i<1000; i++) {
    for(j=2; j <= i/2; j++)
```

```
      if(!(i%j)) break; // if factor found, not prime
    if(j>i/2) cout << i << " is prime\n";
  }

  return 0;
}
```

One way to determine whether a number is prime is to successively divide it by the numbers between 2 and the number one-half its value. (You can stop at the halfway point because, obviously, a number that is larger than one-half of another number cannot be a factor.) If any division is even, the number is not prime. However, if the loop completes, the number is, indeed, prime.

Using the goto Statement

goto is C++'s unconditional branch statement.

The **goto** statement fell out of favor with programmers many years ago because it encouraged the creation of "spaghetti code." However, it is still occasionally—and sometimes effectively—used. This book will not make a judgment regarding its validity as a form of program control. It should be stated, however, that there are no programming situations that require the use of the **goto** statement—it is not an item necessary for making the language complete. Rather, it is a convenience which, if used wisely, can be of benefit in certain programming situations. As such, the **goto** is not used in this book outside of this section. The chief concern most programmers have about the **goto** is its tendency to clutter a program and render it nearly unreadable. However, there are times when the use of the **goto** will actually clarify program flow rather than confuse it.

A label is an identifier followed by a colon.

The **goto** requires a label for operation. A *label* is a valid C++ identifier followed by a colon. Furthermore, the label must be in the same function as the **goto** that uses it. For example, a loop from 1 to 100 could be written using a **goto** and a label, as shown here:

```
x = 1;
  loop1:
    x++;
    if(x < 100) goto loop1;
```

One good use for the **goto** is to exit from a deeply nested routine. For example, consider the following code fragment:

```
for(...) {
  for(...) {
```

```
      while(...) {
        if(...) goto stop;
           .
           .
           .
      }
    }
  }
stop:
  cout << "error in program\n";
```

Eliminating the **goto** would force a number of additional tests to be performed. A simple **break** statement would not work here, because it would only cause the program to exit from the innermost loop.

   ip: You should use the **goto** sparingly, if at all. But if the code would otherwise be much more difficult to read, or if execution speed of the code is critical, then by all means use the **goto**.

4

Putting Together the Pieces

This next example shows the final version of the Magic Number game. It uses many of the concepts that were presented in this chapter, and you should be able to understand all of its elements before going on. The program allows you to generate a new number, to play the game, and to quit.

```
// Magic Number program: Final improvement.

#include <iostream.h>
#include <stdlib.h>

void play(int m);

main()
{
  int option;
  int magic;

  magic = rand();

  do {
    cout << "1. Get a new magic number\n";
    cout << "2. Play\n";
```

```
      cout << "3. Quit\n";
      do {
        cout << "Enter your choice: ";
        cin >> option;
      } while(option<1 || option>3);

      switch(option) {
        case  1:
          magic = rand();
          break;
        case 2:
          play(magic);
          break;
        case 3:
          cout << "Goodbye\n";
          break;
      }
    } while(option!=3);

    return 0;
}

// Play the game.
void play(int m)
{
    int t, x;

    for(t=0; t<100; t++) {
      cout << "Guess the number: ";
      cin >> x;
      if(x==m) {
        cout << "** Right **\n";
        return;
      }
      else
        if(x<m) cout << "Too low\n";
        else cout << "Too high\n";
    }
    cout << "You've used up all your guesses. Try again.\n";
}
```

Chapter 5

Arrays and Strings

This chapter discusses the array. An array is a collection of variables of the same type that are referred to by a common name. In C++, arrays may have from one to several dimensions, although the one-dimensional array is the most common. Arrays offer a convenient means of grouping together several related variables.

The array that you will probably use most often is the character array. Because there is no built-in string data type in C++, strings are represented as arrays of characters. As you will shortly see, this approach to strings allows greater power and flexibility than are available in languages which use a special string type.

One-dimensional Arrays

A one-dimensional array is a list of related variables. The general form of a one-dimensional array declaration is:

type var_name[size];

Here, *type* declares the base type of the array. The base type determines the data type of each element that comprises the array. *size* defines how many elements the array will hold. For example, the following declares an integer array named **sample** that is ten elements long.

```
int sample[10];
```

An index identifies a specific element within an array.

An individual element within an array is accessed by use of an index. An *index* describes the position of an element within an array. In C++, all arrays have zero as the index of their first element. Because **sample** has ten elements, it has index values of 0 through 9. You access an array element by indexing the array using the number of the element. To index an array, specify the number of the element you want, surrounded by square brackets. Thus, the first element in **sample** is **sample[0]**, and the last element is **sample[9]**. For example, the following program loads **sample** with the numbers 0 through 9.

```
#include <iostream.h>

main()
{
  int sample[10]; // this reserves 10 integer elements
  int t;

  // load the array
  for(t=0; t<10; ++t) sample[t]=t;

  // display the array
  for(t=0; t<10; ++t) cout << sample[t] << ' ';

  return 0;
}
```

In C++, all arrays consist of contiguous memory locations. (That is, all array elements reside next to each other in memory.) The lowest address corresponds to the first element, and the highest address to the last element. For example, after this fragment is run,

```
int i[7];
int j;

for(j=0; j<7; j++) i[j] = j;
```

i looks like this:

For a one-dimensional array, the total size of an array in bytes is computed as shown here:

   total bytes = number of bytes in type × number of elements

Arrays are common in programming because they let you deal easily with large numbers of related variables. For example, the following program creates an array of ten elements, assigns each element a random value, and then displays the minimum and the maximum value.

```cpp
#include <iostream.h>
#include <stdlib.h>

main( )
{
  int i, min_value, max_value;
  int list[10];

  for(i=0; i<10; i++) list[i] = rand();

  // find minimum value
  min_value = 32767;
  for(i=0; i<10; i++)
    if(min_value>list[i]) min_value = list[i];

  cout << "minimum value: " << min_value << '\n';

  // find maximum value
  max_value = 0;
  for(i=0; i<10; i++)
    if(max_value<list[i]) max_value = list[i];

  cout << "maximum value: " <<  max_value << '\n';
```

```
    return 0;
}
```

In C++, you cannot assign one array to another. For example, the following is illegal:

```
int a[10], b[10];

// ...

a = b; // error -- illegal
```

To transfer the contents of one array into another, you must assign each value individually.

No Bounds Checking

C++ performs no bounds checking on arrays; nothing stops you from overrunning the end of an array. If this happens during an assignment operation, you will be assigning values to some other variable's data, or even into a piece of the program's code. In other words, you can index an array of size *N* beyond *N* without causing any compile- or run-time error messages, even though doing so will probably cause your program to crash. As the programmer, it is your job both to ensure that all arrays are large enough to hold what the program will put in them, and to provide bounds checking whenever necessary.

For example, C++ will compile and run the following program even though the array **crash** is being overrun.

Caution: Do not try the following example. It will probably crash your system!

```
// An incorrect program.  Do Not Execute!

main()
{
  int crash[10], i;

  for(i=0; i<100; i++) crash[i]=i;

  return 1;
}
```

In this case, the loop will iterate 100 times, even though **crash** is only ten elements long! This causes important information to be overwritten, resulting in a program failure.

You might be wondering why C++ does not provide boundary checks on arrays. The answer is that C++ was designed to allow professional programmers to create the fastest, most efficient code possible. Towards this end, virtually no error checking is included because it slows (often dramatically) the execution of a program. Instead, C++ expects you, the programmer, to be responsible enough to prevent array overruns in the first place, and to add appropriate error checking on your own, as needed. Also, as you will learn later in this book, it is possible for you to define array types of your own that perform bounds checking, if your program actually requires this feature.

Sorting an Array

One common operation performed upon an array is to sort it. As you may know, there are a number of different sorting algorithms. There are the quick sort, the shaker sort, and the shell sort, to name just three. However, the best known, simplest, and easiest to understand sorting algorithm is called the bubble sort. While the bubble sort is not very efficient—in fact, its performance is unacceptable for sorting very large arrays—it may be used effectively for sorting small ones.

The bubble sort gets its name from the way it performs the sorting operation. It uses the repeated comparison and, if necessary, exchange of adjacent elements in the array. In this process, small values move toward one end and large ones toward the other end. The process is conceptually similar to bubbles finding their own level in a tank of water. The bubble sort operates by making several passes through the array, exchanging out-of-place elements when necessary. The number of passes required to ensure that the array is sorted is equal to one less than the number of elements in the array.

The following program sorts an array of integers that contains random values. If you carefully examine the sort, you will find its operation easy to understand.

5

```
// Using the bubble sort to order an array.
#include <iostream.h>
#include <stdlib.h>

main()
{
  int nums[10];
  int a, b, t;
  int size;

  size = 10; // number of elements to sort

  // give the array some random initial values
  for(t=0; t<size; t++) nums[t] = rand();

  // display original array
  cout << "Original array is: ";
  for(t=0; t<size; t++) cout << nums[t] << ' ';
  cout << '\n';

  // This is the bubble sort.
  for(a=1; a<size; a++)
    for(b=size-1; b>=a; b--) {
      if(nums[b-1] > nums[b]) { // if out of order
        // exchange elements
        t = nums[b-1];
        nums[b-1] = nums[b];
        nums[b] = t;
      }
    }
  // This is the end of the bubble sort.

  // display sorted array
  cout << "Sorted array is: ";
  for(t=0; t<size; t++) cout << nums[t] << ' ';

  return 0;
}
```

Although the bubble sort is good for small arrays, it is not efficient when used on larger ones. The best general-purpose sorting algorithm is the quick sort. The C++ standard library contains a function called **qsort()** that implements a version of the quick sort. However, you will need to know more about C++ before you can use it. Chapter 18 of this book discusses the **qsort( )** function in detail.

Strings

By far the most common use for one-dimensional arrays is to create character strings. In C++, a string is defined as a character array that is terminated by a null. A null is specified using '\0', and is zero. Because of the null terminator, it is necessary to declare a character array to be one character longer than the largest string that it will hold.

For example, if you wished to declare an array **str** that could hold a 10-character string, here is what you would write:

```
char str[11];
```

This would make room for the null at the end of the string.

A string is a null-terminated character array.

As you learned earlier in this book, although C++ does not have a string data type, it still allows string constants. A string constant is a list of characters enclosed in double quotes. Here are some examples:

"hello there"   "I like C++"

"#$%@@#$"   ""

The last string shown is "". This is called a *null string*. It contains only the null terminator, and no other characters. Null strings are useful because they represent the empty string.

5

It is not necessary to manually add the null onto the end of string constants; the C++ compiler does this for you automatically. Therefore, the string "Hello" will appear in memory like this:

Reading a String from the Keyboard

The easiest way to read a string entered from the keyboard is to make the array that will receive the string the target of a **cin** statement. For example, the following program reads a string entered by the user.

```
// Using cin to read a string from the keyboard.

#include <iostream.h>
main()
{
```

```
   char str[80];

   cout << "Enter a string: ";
   cin >> str; // read string from keyboard
   cout << "Here is your string: ";
   cout << str;

   return 0;
}
```

Although this program is technically correct, there is still a problem. To see what it is, run the program and try entering the string "This is a test". As you will see, when the program redisplays your string, it will show only the word "This", not the entire sentence. The reason for this is that the C++ I/O system stops reading a string when the first *whitespace* character is encountered. Whitespace characters include spaces, tabs, and newlines.

To solve the whitespace problem, you will need to use another of C++'s library functions, **gets( )**. The general form of a **gets( )** call is:

gets(*array-name*);

If you need your program to read a string, call **gets( )** with the name of the array, without any index, as its argument. Upon return from **gets( )**, the array will hold the string input from the keyboard. The **gets( )** function will continue to read characters until you enter a carriage return. The header file used by **gets( )** is **stdio.h**.

This version of the preceding program uses **gets( )** to allow the entry of strings containing spaces.

```
// Using gets() to read a string from the keyboard.

#include <iostream.h>
#include <stdio.h>

main( )
{
  char str[80];

  cout << "Enter a string: ";
  gets(str); // read a string from the keyboard
  cout << "Here is your string: ";
  cout << str;

  return 0;
}
```

Notice that in a **cout** statement, **str** can be used directly. For reasons that will be clear after you have read a few more chapters, the name of a character array that holds a string can be used any place that a string constant can be used.

Keep in mind that neither **cin** or **gets( )** performs any bounds checking on the array. Therefore, if the user enters a string longer than the size of the array, the array will be overwritten.

Note: In addition to **gets( )**, C++ also has some object-oriented functions that let you read strings from the keyboard. You will learn about them later in this book.

Some String Library Functions

C++ supports a wide range of string manipulation functions. The most common are:

```
strcpy( )
strcat( )
strlen( )
strcmp( )
```

5

The string functions all use the same header file, **string.h**. Let's take a look at these functions now.

strcpy

A call to **strcpy( )** takes this general form:

```
strcpy(to, from);
```

The **strcpy( )** function is used to copy the contents of the string *from* into *to*. Remember, the array that forms *to* must be large enough to hold the string contained in *from*. If it isn't, the *to* array will be overrun, which will probably crash your program.

The following program will copy "hello" into string **str**.

```
#include <iostream.h>
#include <string.h>

main( )
```

```
{
    char str[80];

    strcpy(str, "hello");
    cout << str;

    return 0;
}
```

strcat

A call to **strcat( )** takes this form.

strcat(*s1, s2*);

The **strcat( )** function appends *s2* to the end of *s1*; *s2* is unchanged. Both strings must be null-terminated, and the result is null-terminated. For example, the following program will print **hello there** on the screen.

```
#include <iostream.h>
#include <string.h>

main()
{
    char s1[20], s2[10];

    strcpy(s1, "hello");
    strcpy(s2, " there");
    strcat(s1, s2);
    cout << s1;

    return 0;
}
```

strcmp

A call to **strcmp()** takes this general form.

strcmp(*s1, s2*);

The **strcmp( )** function compares two strings and returns 0 if they are equal. If *s1* is greater than *s2* lexicographically (i.e., according to dictionary order), then a positive number is returned; if it is less than *s2*, a negative number is returned.

The **password( )** function, shown in the following program, is a password verification routine. It uses **strcmp( )** to check a user's input against a password.

```
#include <string.h>
#include <stdio.h>
#include <iostream.h>

int password();

main()
{
  if(password()) cout << "logged on\n";
  else cout << "access denied\n";

  return 0;
}

// Return true if password accepted; false otherwise.
password()
{
  char s[80];

  cout << "enter password: ";
  gets(s);

  if(strcmp(s, "password")) {  // strings differ
    cout << "invalid password\n";
    return 0; // return false
  }

  // strings compared the same
  return 1; // return true
}
```

The key to using **strcmp( )** is to remember that it returns false when the strings match. Therefore, you will need to use the **!** (NOT) operator if you wish something to occur when the strings are equal. For example, the following program continues to request input until the user types the word "quit".

```
#include <iostream.h>
#include <stdio.h>
#include <string.h>

main()
{
  char s[80];
```

```
for(;;) {
  cout << "Enter a string: ";
  gets(s);
  if(!strcmp("quit", s)) break;
}

return 0;
}
```

strlen

The general form of a call to **strlen( )** is

strlen(*s*);

where *s* is a string.

The **strlen( )** function returns the length of the string pointed to by *s*.

The following program will print the length of a string entered from the keyboard.

```
#include <iostream.h>
#include <stdio.h>
#include <string.h>

main()
{
  char str[80];

  cout << "Enter a string: ";

  gets(str);

  cout << "Length is: " <<  strlen(str);

  return 0;
}
```

If the user enters the string "Hi there", this program will display **8**. The null terminator is not counted by **strlen( )**.

When the following program is run, the string entered at the keyboard is printed in reverse. For example, "hello" will be displayed as **olleh**. Remember that strings are simply character arrays; thus each character can be referenced individually.

```
// Print a string backwards.
#include <iostream.h>
#include <stdio.h>
#include <string.h>

main()
{
  char str[80];
  int i;

  cout << "Enter a string: ";
  gets(str);

  for(i=strlen(str)-1; i>=0; i--) cout << str[i];

  return 0;
}
```

As a final example, the following program illustrates the use of all four string functions.

5

```
#include <stdio.h>
#include <string.h>
#include <iostream.h>

main()
{
  char s1[80], s2[80];

  cout << "enter two strings: ";

  gets(s1); gets(s2);

  cout << "lengths: " << strlen(s1);
  cout << ' ' << strlen(s2) << '\n';

  if(!strcmp(s1, s2))
    cout << "The strings are equal\n";
  else cout << "not equal\n";

  strcat(s1, s2);
  cout << s1 << '\n';
```

```
   strcpy(s1, s2);
   cout << s1 << " and " << s2 << ' ';
   cout << "are now the same\n";

   return 0;
}
```

If this program is run and the strings "hello" and "there" are entered, then
the output will be

    lengths: 5 5
    not equal
    hellothere
    there and there are now the same

It is important to remember that **strcmp( )** returns false if the strings are
equal. This is why you must use the **!** operator to reverse the condition, as
shown in the preceding example, if you are testing for equality.

Using the Null Terminator

The fact that all strings are null-terminated can often be used to simplify
various operations on strings. For example, look at how little code is required
to uppercase every character in a string:

```
// Convert a string to uppercase.
#include <iostream.h>
#include <string.h>
#include <ctype.h>

main()
{
  char str[80];
  int i;

  strcpy(str, "this is a test");

  for(i=0; str[i]; i++) str[i] = toupper(str[i]);

  cout << str;

  return 0;
}
```

This program will print **THIS IS A TEST**. It uses the library function **toupper( )**, which returns the uppercase equivalent of its character argument, to convert each character in the string. The **toupper( )** function uses the header file **ctype.h**.

Notice that the test condition of the **for** loop is simply the array indexed by the control variable. The reason this works is that a true value is any non-zero value. Remember, all character values are non-zero, but the null terminating the string is zero. Therefore, the loop runs until it encounters the null terminator, which causes **str[i]** to become zero. Since the null terminator marks the end of the string, the loop stops precisely where it is supposed to. As you progress, you will see many examples that use the null terminator in a similar fashion.

Tip: In addition to **toupper( )**, the C++ standard library contains several other character manipulation functions. For example, the complement to **toupper( )** is **tolower( )**, which returns the lowercase equivalent of its character argument. Other character functions include: **isalpha( )**, **isdigit( )**, **isspace( )**, and **ispunct( )**. These functions each take a character argument and determine the category of that argument. For example, **isalpha( )** returns true if its argument is a letter of the alphabet.

Two-dimensional Arrays

5

C++ allows multidimensional arrays. The simplest form of the multidimensional array is the two-dimensional array. A two-dimensional array is, in essence, a list of one-dimensional arrays. To declare a two-dimensional integer array **twod** of size 10,20 you would write

```
int twod[10][20];
```

Pay careful attention to the declaration. Unlike some other computer languages, which use commas to separate the array dimensions, C++ places each dimension in its own set of brackets.

Similarly, to access point 3,5 of array **twod**, you would use **twod[3][5]**. In the next example, a two-dimensional array is loaded with the numbers 1 through 12.

```
#include <iostream.h>

main()
{
  int t,i, num[3][4];
```

```
for(t=0; t<3; ++t) {
  for(i=0; i<4; ++i) {
    num[t][i] = (t*4)+i+1;
    cout << num[t][i] << ' ';
  }
  cout << '\n';
}

return 0;
}
```

In this example, **num[0][0]** will have the value 1, **num[0][1]** the value 2, **num[0][2]** the value 3, and so on. The value of **num[2][3]** will be 12. Conceptually, the array will look like that shown in Figure 5-1.

Two-dimensional arrays are stored in a row-column matrix, where the first index indicates the row and the second indicates the column. This means that when array elements are accessed in the order in which they are actually stored in memory, the rightmost index changes faster than the leftmost.

You should remember that storage for all array elements is determined at compile time. Also, the memory used to hold an array is required the entire time that the array is in existence. In the case of a two-dimensional array, you can use this formula to determine the number of bytes of memory that will be allocated:

bytes = row × column × number of bytes in type

Therefore, assuming two-byte integers, an integer array with dimensions 10,5 would have 10 × 5 × 2 (or 100) bytes allocated.

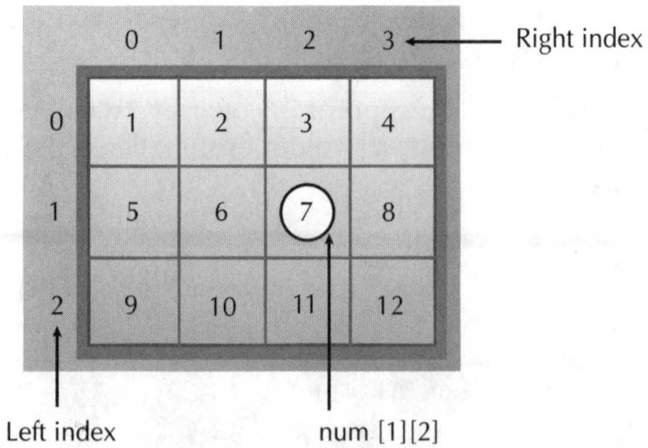

A conceptual view of the **num** array
Figure 5-1.

Multidimensional Arrays

C++ allows arrays with more than two dimensions. Here is the general form of a multidimensional array declaration:

type name[size1][size2]...[sizeN];

For example, the following declaration creates a 4 × 10 × 3 integer array.

```
int multidim[4][10][3];
```

Arrays of three or more dimensions are not often used, due to the amount of memory required to hold them. As stated before, storage for all array elements is allocated during the entire lifetime of an array. When multidimensional arrays are used, large amounts of memory are consumed. For example, a four-dimensional character array with dimensions 10,6,9,4 would require 10 × 6 × 9 × 4 (or 2,160) bytes. If each array dimension is increased by a factor of 10 each (that is, 100 × 60 × 90 × 40), then the memory required for the array increases to 21,600,000 bytes! As you can see, large multidimensional arrays may cause a shortage of memory for other parts of your program. Thus, a program with arrays of more than two or three dimensions may find itself quickly out of memory!

Array Initialization

5

C++ allows the initialization of arrays. The general form of array initialization is similar to that of other variables, as shown here:

type-specifier array_name[size] = {value-list};

The *value-list* is a comma-separated list of constants that are type-compatible with the base type of the array. The first constant will be placed in the first position of the array, the second constant in the second position, and so on. Notice that a semicolon follows the }.

In the following example, a 10-element integer array is initialized with the numbers 1 through 10.

```
int i[10] = {1, 2, 3, 4, 5, 6, 7, 8, 9, 10};
```

This means that **i[0]** will have the value 1, and **i[9]** will have the value 10.

Character arrays that will hold strings allow a shorthand initialization that takes this form:

char array_name[size] = "string";

For example, the following code fragment initializes **str** to the phrase "hello".

```
char str[6] = "hello";
```

This is the same as writing

```
char str[6] = {'h', 'e', 'l', 'l', 'o', '\0'};
```

Because strings in C++ must end with a null, you must make sure that the array you declare is long enough to include it. This is why **str** is 6 characters long in these examples, even though "hello" is only 5. When a string constant is used, the compiler automatically supplies the null terminator.

Multidimensional arrays are initialized in the same way as one-dimensional arrays. For example, the following program initializes an array called **sqrs** with the numbers 1 through 10 and their squares.

```
int sqrs[10][2] = {
  1, 1,
  2, 4,
  3, 9,
  4, 16,
  5, 25,
  6, 36,
  7, 49,
  8, 64,
  9, 81,
  10, 100
};
```

Examine figure 5-2 to see how the **sqrs** array appears in memory.

The following program uses the **sqrs( )** array to find the square of a number entered by the user. It first looks up the number in the array and then prints the corresponding square.

```
#include <iostream.h>

int sqrs[10][2] = {
  1, 1,
  2, 4,
  3, 9,
  4, 16,
  5, 25,
  6, 36,
  7, 49,
  8, 64,
```

```
     9, 81,
    10, 100
};

main()
{
  int i, j;

  cout << "Enter a number between 1 and 10: ";
  cin >> i;

  // look up i
  for(j=0; j<10; j++)
    if(sqrs[j][0]==i) break;
  cout << "The square of " << i << "is ";
  cout << sqrs[j][1];

  return 0;
}
```

Global arrays are initialized when the program begins. Local arrays are initialized each time the function that contains them is called, as shown here:

```
#include <iostream.h>
#include <string.h>

void f1();

main()
{
  f1();
  f1();

  return 0;
}

void f1()
{
  char s[80]="this is a test\n";

  cout << s;
  strcpy(s, "CHANGED"); // change s
  cout << s;
}
```

In this program, the array **s** is initialized each time **f1( )** is called. The fact that **s** is changed in the function does not affect its reinitialization upon subsequent calls. This means that **f1( )** prints **this is a test** every time it is entered.

5

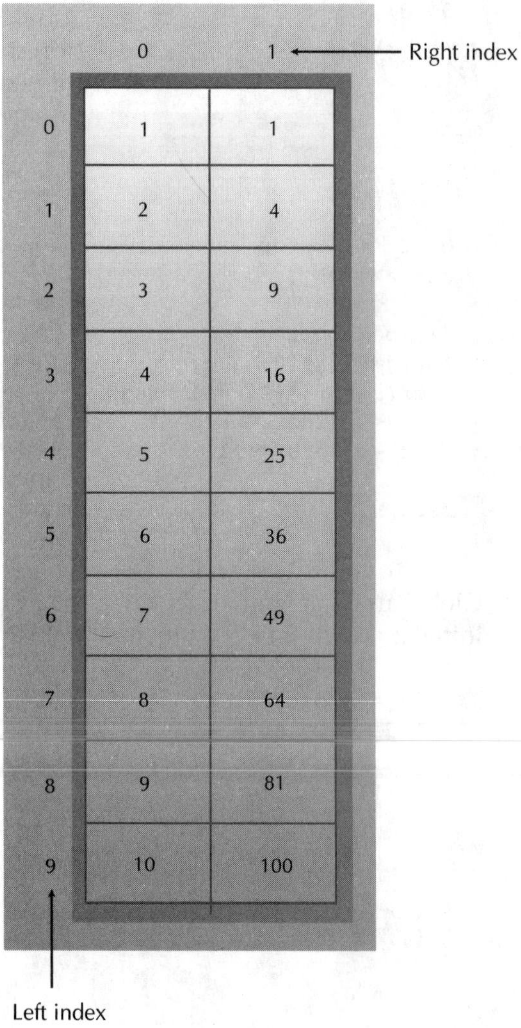

The initialized
sqrs array
Figure 5-2.

Unsized Array Initializations

Imagine that you are using array initialization to build a table of error
messages, as shown here:

```
char e1[14] = "Divide by 0\n";
char e2[23] = "End-of-File\n";
char e3[21] = "Access Denied\n";
```

As you might guess, it is very tedious to manually count the characters in
each message to determine the correct array dimension. It is possible to let

C++ automatically dimension the arrays in this example through the use of *unsized arrays*. If an array initialization statement does not specify the size of the array, then C++ will automatically create an array large enough to hold all the initializers present. When this approach is used, the message table becomes

```
char e1[] = "Divide by 0\n";
char e2[] = "End-of-File\n";
char e3[] = "Access Denied\n";
```

Besides being less tedious, the unsized array initialization method allows you to change any of the messages without fear of accidentally miscounting the characters in the message.

Unsized array initializations are not restricted to one-dimensional arrays. For a multidimensional array, you must specify all but the leftmost dimension so that C++ can index the array properly. Using unsized array initializations, you can build tables of varying lengths, with the compiler automatically allocating enough storage for them.

In the following example, **sqrs** is declared as an unsized array .

```
int sqrs[][2] = {
  1, 1,
  2, 4,
  3, 9,
  4, 16,
  5, 25,
  6, 36,
  7, 49,
  8, 64,
  9, 81,
  10, 100
};
```

5

The advantage to this declaration over the sized version is that the table may be lengthened or shortened without changing the array dimensions.

Arrays of Strings

A special form of a two-dimensional array is an array of strings. It is not uncommon in programming to use an array of strings. The input processor to a database, for instance, may verify user commands against a string array of valid commands. To create an array of strings, a two-dimensional character array is used, with the size of the left index determining the number of strings and the size of the right index specifying the maximum length of each string. For example, the following declares an array of 30 strings, each having a maximum length of 80 characters.

```
char str_array[30][80];
```

A string array is a two-dimensional array of characters.

Accessing an individual string is quite easy: you simply specify only the left index. For example, the following statement calls **gets( )** with the third string in **str_array**.

```
gets(str_array[2]);
```

To better understand how string arrays work, study the next short program, which accepts lines of text entered at the keyboard and redisplays them after a blank line is entered.

```
// Enter and display strings.
#include <iostream.h>
#include <stdio.h>

main()
{
  int t, i;
  char text[100][80];

  for(t=0; t<100; t++) {
    cout << t << ": ";
    gets(text[t]);
    if(!text[t][0]) break; // quit on blank line
  }

  // redisplay the strings
  for(i=0; i<t; i++)
    cout << text[i] << '\n';

  return 0;
}
```

Notice how the program checks for the entry of a blank line. The **gets( )** function returns a zero-length string if the only key you press is ENTER. This means that the first byte in that string will be the null character. A null value is always false, thus allowing the conditional expression to be true.

An Example Using String Arrays

Arrays of strings are commonly used for handling tables of information. One such application would be an employee database that stores the name, telephone number, hours worked per pay period, and hourly wage of each employee. To create such a program for a staff of ten employees, you would define these four arrays (the first two of which are string arrays):

```
char name[10][80];   // this array holds employee names
char phone[10][20];  // their phone numbers
float hours[10];     // hours worked per week
float wage[10];      // wage
```

To enter information about each employee, you could use a function like **enter( )**, as shown here:

```
// Enter information.
void enter()
{
  int i;
  char temp[80];

  for(i=0; i<10; i++) {
    cout << "enter name: ";
    gets(name[i]);
    cout << "enter phone number: ";
    gets(phone[i]);
    cout << "enter number of hours worked: ";
    cin >> hours[i];
    cout << "enter wage: ";
    cin >> wage[i];
  }
}
```

Once information has been entered, the database can report the data and calculate the amount of pay each employee is to receive, using the **report( )** function, as shown here:

```
// Display report.
void report()
{
  int i;

  for(i=0; i<10; i++) {
    cout << name[i] << ' ' << phone[i] << '\n';
    cout << "pay for the week: " << wage[i] * hours[i];
```

5

```
    cout << '\n';
  }
}
```

The entire employee database program is shown next. Pay special attention to how each array is accessed. This version of the employee database program is not particularly useful, because the information is lost when the program is terminated. Later in this book, however, you will learn how to store information in a disk file.

```
// A simple employee database program.

#include <stdio.h>
#include <iostream.h>
#include <stdlib.h>

char name[10][80];  // this array holds employee names
char phone[10][20]; // their phone numbers
float hours[10];    // hours worked per week
float wage[10];     // wage

int menu();
void enter(), report();

main()
{
  int choice;

  do {
    choice = menu(); // get selection
    switch(choice) {
      case 0: break;
      case 1: enter();
        break;
      case 2: report();
        break;
      default: cout << "try again\n\n";
    }
  } while(choice!=0);

  return 0;
}

// Return a user's selection.
menu()
{
  int choice;
```

```cpp
      cout << "0. Quit\n";
      cout << "1. Enter information\n";
      cout << "2. Report information\n";
      cout << "\nchoose one: ";
    cin >> choice;
    return choice;
}

// Enter information.
void enter()
{
  int i;
  char temp[80];

  for(i=0; i<10; i++) {
    cout << "enter name: ";
    gets(name[i]);
    cout << "enter phone number: ";
    gets(phone[i]);
    cout << "enter number of hours worked: ";
    cin >> hours[i];
    cout << "enter wage: ";
    cin >> wage[i];
  }
}

// Display report.
void report()
{
  int i;

  for(i=0; i<10; i++) {
    cout << name[i] << ' ' << phone[i] << '\n';
    cout << "pay for the week: " << wage[i] * hours[i];
    cout << '\n';
  }
}
```

5

Chapter

6

Pointers

Pointers are without a doubt one of the most important—and troublesome—aspects of C++. In fact, a large measure of C++'s power is derived from pointers. For example, they allow C++ to support such things as linked lists and dynamic memory allocation. They also provide one means by which a function can alter the contents of an argument. However, these and other uses of pointers will be discussed in subsequent chapters. In this chapter you will learn the basics about pointers, see how to manipulate them, and discover how to avoid some potential troubles.

In a few places in this chapter it is necessary to refer to the size of several of C++'s basic data types. For the sake of discussion, assume that characters are one byte in length, integers are two bytes long, **float**s are four bytes long, and **double**s have a length of eight bytes.

What Are Pointers?

A pointer is a variable that contains the address of another object.

A *pointer* is a variable that contains a memory address. Very often this address is the location of another variable. For example, if **x** contains the address of **y**, then **x** is said to "point to" **y**.

Pointer variables must be declared as such. The general form of a pointer variable declaration is:

   type *var-name;

Here, *type* is the pointer's base type; it must be a valid C++ type. *Var-name* is the name of the pointer variable. For example, to declare **p** to be a pointer to an integer, use this declaration:

```
int *p;
```

For a **float** pointer, use

```
float *p;
```

In general, in a declaration statement, preceding a variable name with an * causes that variable to become a pointer.

The base type of a pointer determines what type of data it will point to.

The type of data that a pointer will point to is determined by its *base type*. Here is an example:

```
int *ip; // pointer to integers

double *dp; // pointer to doubles
```

As the comments indicate, **ip** is a pointer to integers because its base type is **int**, and **dp** is a pointer to **double**s because its base type is **double**. As you will see, the base type is very important in pointer operations.

The Pointer Operators

There are two special operators that are used with pointers: * and **&**.

The **&** is a unary operator that returns the memory address of its operand. (Recall that a unary operator requires only one operand.) For example,

```
balptr = &balance;
```

puts into **balptr** the memory address of the variable **balance**. This address is the location of the variable in the computer's internal memory. It has *nothing* to do with the *value* of **balance**. The operation of **&** can be remembered as returning "the address of" the variable it precedes. Therefore, the above assignment statement could be verbalized as "**balptr** receives the address of **balance**." To better understand this assignment, assume that the variable **balance** is located at address 100. Then, after the assignment takes place, **balptr** has the value 100.

The second operator is *****, and it is the complement of **&**. It is a unary operator that returns the value of the variable located at the address specified by its operand. Continuing with the same example, if **balptr** contains the memory address of the variable **balance**, then

```
value = *balptr;
```

will place the value of **balance** into **value**. For example, if **balance** originally had the value 3,200, then **value** will have the value 3,200, because that is the value stored at location 100, the memory address that was assigned to **balptr**. The operation of ***** can be remembered as "at address". In this case, then, the statement could be read as "**value** receives the value at address **balptr**." Figure 6-1 depicts the actions of the two preceding statements.

The following program executes the sequence of operations shown in Figure 6-1.

```
#include <iostream.h>

main()
{
  int balance;
  int *balptr;
  int value;

  balance = 3200;
  balptr = &balance;
  value = *balptr;
  cout << "balance is: " << value << '\n';

  return 0;
}
```

6

It is unfortunate that the multiplication symbol and the "at address" symbol are the same. This fact sometimes confuses newcomers to the C++ language. These operators have no relationship to each other. Keep in mind that both **&** and ***** have a higher precedence than any of the arithmetic operators except the unary minus, with which they are equal.

The act of using a pointer is often called *indirection* because you are accessing one variable indirectly through another variable.

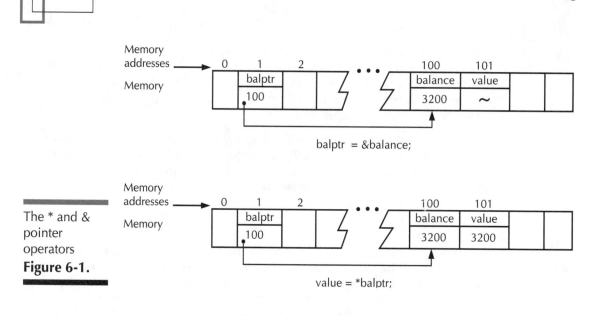

The * and &
pointer
operators
Figure 6-1.

The Base Type Is Important

In the preceding discussion, you saw that it was possible to assign **value** the value of **balance** indirectly through a pointer. At this point you may have thought of this important question: How does C++ know how many bytes to copy into **value** from the address pointed to by **balptr**? Or, more generally, how does the compiler transfer the proper number of bytes for any assignment using a pointer? The answer is that the base type of the pointer determines the type of data that the compiler assumes the pointer is pointing to. In this case, because **balptr** is an integer pointer, C++ copies two bytes of information into **value** from the address pointed to by **balptr**. However, if it had been a **double** pointer for example, then eight bytes would have been copied.

Your pointer variables must always point to the correct type of data. For example, when you declare a pointer to be of type **int**, the compiler assumes that anything it points to will be an integer variable. Generally, you won't need to worry about this because C++ will not allow you to assign one type of pointer to another unless the two types of pointers are compatible (i.e., essentially, the same).

For example, the following fragment is incorrect:

```
int *p;
float f;
// ...
p = &f; // ERROR
```

This fragment is invalid because you cannot assign a **float** pointer to an integer pointer. That is, **&f** generates a pointer to a **float**, but **p** is a pointer to an **int**. These two types are not compatible. (In fact, the compiler would flag an error at this point and not compile your program.)

Although two pointers must have compatible types in order for one to be assigned to another, you can override this restriction (at your own risk) using a cast. For example the following fragment is now technically correct:

```
int *p ;
float f;
// ...
p = (int *) &f; // Now technically OK
```

The cast to **int *** causes the **float** pointer to be converted to an integer pointer. However, to use a cast for this purpose is questionable. The reason is that the base type of a pointer determines how the compiler treats the data it points to. In this case, even though **p** is actually pointing to a floating-point value, the compiler still "thinks" that **p** is pointing to an integer (because **p** is an integer pointer).

To better understand why using a cast to assign one type of pointer to another is not usually a good idea, consider the following short program:

```
// This program will not work right.
#include <iostream.h>

main()
{
  float x, y;
  int *p;

  x = 123.23;
  p = (int *) &x; // use cast to assign float * to int *

  y = *p; // What will this do?
  cout << y; // What will this print?

  return 0;
}
```

6

As you can see, **p** (which is an integer pointer) has been assigned the address of **x** (which is a **float**). Thus, when **y** is assigned the value pointed to by **p**, **y** receives only two bytes of data (and not the four required for a **float** value), because **p** is an integer pointer. Therefore, the **cout** statement displays not 123.23, but a garbage value instead. (Try this program and observe the result.)

Assigning Values Through a Pointer

You can use a pointer on the right-hand side of an assignment statement to assign a value to the location pointed to by the pointer. Assuming that **p** is an integer pointer, this assigns the value 101 to the location pointed to by **p**.

```
*p = 101;
```

You can verbalize this assignment like this: "at the location pointed to by **p**, assign the value 101." To increment or decrement the value at the location pointed to by a pointer, you can use a statement like this:

```
(*p)++;
```

The parentheses are necessary because the * operator has lower precedence than the ++ operator.

The following program includes an assignment using a pointer. This program prints **100 101 100** on the screen.

```
#include <iostream.h>

main()
{
  int *p, num;

  p = &num;

  *p = 100;
  cout << num << ' ';
  (*p)++;
  cout << num << ' ';
  (*p)--;
  cout << num << '\n';

  return 0;
}
```

Pointer Expressions

Pointers can be used in most valid C++ expressions. However, some special rules apply. Remember also that you may need to surround some parts of a pointer expression with parentheses in order to ensure that the outcome is what you desire.

Pointer Arithmetic

There are only four arithmetic operators that can be used on pointers: **++, --, + and -**. To understand what occurs in pointer arithmetic, let **p1** be an integer pointer with a current value of 2,000 (that is, it contains the address 2,000). After the expression:

```
p1++;
```

The contents of **p1** will be 2,002, not 2,001! Each time **p1** is incremented, it will point to the *next integer*. The same is true of decrements. For example,

```
p1--;
```

will cause **p1** to have the value 1998, assuming that it previously was 2000. Here is why: Each time that a pointer is incremented, it will point to the memory location of the next element of its base type. Each time it is decremented it will point the location of the previous element of its base type.

In the case of character pointers, an increment or decrement will appear as "normal" arithmetic because characters are one byte long. However, every other type of pointer will increase or decrease by the length of its base type.

You are not limited to only increment and decrement operations. You can also add or subtract integers to or from pointers. The expression

```
p1 = p1 + 9;
```

makes **p1** point to the ninth element of **p1**'s base type, beyond the one it is currently pointing to.

While you cannot add pointers, you can subtract one pointer from another (provided they are both of the same base type). The remainder will be the number of elements of the base type that separate the two pointers.

Other than addition and subtraction of a pointer and an integer, or the subtraction of two pointers, no other arithmetic operations can be performed on pointers. For example, you cannot add or subtract **float** or **double** values to or from pointers.

6

To see the effects of pointer arithmetic, execute the next short program. It prints the actual physical addresses that an integer pointer (**i**) and a floating-point pointer (**f**) are pointing to. Observe how each changes, relative to its base type, each time the loop is repeated. (For most compilers, **i** will increase by 2s and **f** will increase by 4s.) Notice that when using a pointer in a **cout** statement, its address is automatically displayed in the addressing format applicable to the current processor and environment.

```
#include <iostream.h>

main()
{
  int *i, j[10];
  float *f, g[10];
  int x;

  i = j;
  f = g;

  for(x=0; x<10; x++)
    cout << i+x << ' ' << f+x << '\n';

  return 0;
}
```

Remember: All pointer arithmetic is performed relative to the base type of the pointer.

Pointer Comparisons

Pointers may be compared using the relational operators, such as **==**, **<**, and **>**. However, for the outcome of a pointer comparison to be meaningful, the two pointers normally must have some relationship to each other. For example, if **p1** and **p2** are pointers that point to two separate and unrelated variables, then any comparison between **p1** and **p2** is generally meaningless. (Unless you are just the curious type!) However, if **p1** and **p2** point to variables that are related to each other, such as elements of the same array, then **p1** and **p2** can be meaningfully compared. Later in this chapter you will see a sample program that compares two pointers.

Pointers and Arrays

In C++, there is a close relationship between pointers and arrays. In fact, frequently a pointer and an array are interchangeable. In this section, you will see how pointers and arrays relate.

To begin, consider this fragment:

```
char str[80];
char *p1;

p1 = str;
```

Here, **str** is an array of 80 characters and **p1** is a character pointer. However, it is the third line that is of interest. In this line **p1** is assigned the address of the first element in the **str** array. (That is, after the assignment, **p1** will point to **str[0]**.) Here's why: In C++, using the name of an array without an index generates a pointer to the first element in the array. Thus the assignment **p1 = str** assigns the address of **str[0]** to **p1**. This is a crucial point to understand: When an unindexed array name is used in an expression, it yields a pointer to the first element in the array.

Since, after the assignment, **p1** points to the beginning of **str**, you may use **p1** to access elements in the array. For example, if you wished to access the fifth element in **str** you could use

```
str[4]
```

or

```
*(p1+4)
```

6

Both statements will return the fifth element. Remember, array indices start at zero, so when **str** is indexed, a 4 used to access the fifth element. A 4 is also added to the pointer **p1** to get the fifth element, because **p1** currently points to the first element of **str**.

The parentheses surrounding **p1+4** are necessary because the * operation has a higher priority than the + operation. Without them, the expression would first find the value pointed to by **p1** (the first location in the array) and then add 4 to it.

Tip: Be sure to properly parenthesize a pointer expression. If you don't, an error will be hard to find later because your program will look correct. (If in doubt about whether to add parentheses or not, add them; it will do no harm.)

In effect, C++ allows two methods of accessing array elements: pointer arithmetic and array indexing. This is important because pointer arithmetic can sometimes be faster than array indexing—especially when you are accessing an array in strictly sequential order. Since speed is often a consideration in programming, the use of pointers to access array elements is very common in C++ programs. Also, you can sometimes write tighter code by using pointers instead of array indexing.

To get the flavor of the difference between using array indexing and pointer arithmetic, two versions of the same program will be shown next. The program extracts words, separated by spaces, from a string. For example, given "Hello Tom", the program would extract "Hello" and "Tom". Programmers typically refer to these extracted words as *tokens,* and the process of extracting tokens is generally called *tokenizing*. The program scans the input string, copying characters from the string into another array, called **token**, until a space is encountered. It then prints the token and repeats the process until the null at the end of the string is reached. For example, if you enter **This is a test.** the program displays the following:

```
This
is
a
test.
```

Here is the pointer version of the tokenizing program:

```
// Tokenizing program: pointer version.
#include <iostream.h>
#include <stdio.h>

main()
{
  char str[80];
  char token[80];
  char *p, *q;

  cout << "Enter a sentence: ";
  gets(str);
```

```
  p = str;

  // Read a token at a time from the string.
  while(*p) {
    q = token;  // set q pointing to start of token

    /* Read characters until either a space or the
       null terminator is encountered.
    */
    while(*p!=' ' && *p) {
      *q = *p;
      q++; p++;
    }
    if(*p) p++; // advance past the space
    *q = '\0'; // null terminate the token
    cout << token << '\n';
  }

  return 0;
}
```

Here is the array-indexing version:

```
// Tokenizing program: array-indexing version.
#include <iostream.h>
#include <stdio.h>

main()
{
  char str[80];
  char token[80];
  int i, j;

  cout << "Enter a sentence: ";
  gets(str);

  // Read a token at a time from the string.
  for(i=0; ; i++) {
    /* Read characters until either a space or the
       null terminator is encountered.
    */
    for(j=0; str[i]!=' ' && str[i]; j++, i++)
      token[j] = str[i];

    token[j] = '\0'; // null terminate the token
    cout << token << '\n';
```

```
  if(!str[i]) break;
}

return 0;
}
```

Because of the way some C++ compilers generate code, these two programs may not be equivalent in performance. Generally, it takes more machine instructions to index an array than it does to perform arithmetic on a pointer. Consequently, in professionally written C++ code it is common to see the pointer version used more frequently. However, as a beginning C++ programmer, feel free to use array indexing until you are comfortable with pointers.

Indexing a Pointer

As you have just seen, it is possible to access an array using pointer arithmetic. What you might find surprising is that the reverse is also true. In C++, it is possible to index a pointer as if it were an array. This further illustrates the close relationship between pointers and arrays. To see an example of indexing a pointer, try the following program. It prints **HELLO TOM** on the screen.

```
// Indexing a pointer like an array.

#include <iostream.h>
#include <ctype.h>

main()
{
  char str[20] = "hello tom";
  char *p;
  int i;

  p = str;

  for(i=0; p[i]; i++) p[i] = toupper(p[i]);
  cout << p; // display the string

  return 0;
}
```

In C++, the statement **p[t]** is functionally identical to ***(p+t)**.

Are Pointers and Arrays Interchangeable?

As the preceding few pages have shown, pointers and arrays are strongly related. In fact, pointers and arrays are interchangeable in many cases. For example, a pointer that points to the beginning of an array can access that array using either pointer arithmetic or array-style indexing. However, pointers and arrays are not completely interchangeable. For example, consider this fragment:

```
int num[10];
int i;

for(i=0; i<10; i++) {
  *num = i; // this is OK
  num++; // ERROR -- cannot modify num
}
```

Here, **num** is an array of integers. As the comments describe, while it is perfectly acceptable to apply the * operator to **num** (which is a pointer operation), it is illegal to modify **num**'s value. The reason for this is that **num** is a constant that points to the beginning of an array. Thus, you cannot increment it. More generally, while an array name without an index does generate a pointer to the beginning of an array, it cannot be changed.

Although an array name generates a pointer constant, it can still take part in pointer-style expressions, as long as it is not modified. For example, the following is a valid statement that assigns **num[3]** the value 100.

```
*(num+3) = 100; // This is OK because num is not changed
```

6

String Constants

You might be wondering how string constants, like the one in the fragment shown here, are handled by C++.

```
cout << strlen("C++ Compiler");
```

The answer is that when the compiler encounters a string constant, it stores it in the program's *string table* and generates a pointer to the string. Therefore, the following program is perfectly valid, and prints the phrase **Pointers are fun to use.** on the screen.

```
#include <iostream.h>

main()
{
  char *s;

  s = "Pointers are fun to use.\n";

  cout << s;

  return 0;
}
```

The string table is a table generated by the compiler. It holds the strings used by your program.

In this program, the characters that make up a string constant are stored in the string table, and **s** is assigned a pointer to the string in that table.

Since a pointer into your program's string table is generated automatically whenever a string constant is used, you might be tempted to use this fact to modify the contents of the string table. However, this is usually not a good idea because many C++ compilers create optimized tables in which one string constant may be used at two or more different places in your program. Thus, changing a string may cause undesired side effects.

A Comparison Example

Earlier you learned that it is legal to compare the value of one pointer to that of another. Now that you know more about how pointers and arrays are related, here is an example.

The following program uses two pointer variables: one initially pointing to the beginning of an array, and the other to the end of the array. As the user enters numbers, the array is filled sequentially from the beginning to the end. Each number entered into the array also causes the starting pointer to be incremented. To see if the array is full, the program simply compares the starting pointer with the ending pointer. If they are equal, the array has been filled. Once the array is full, the contents of the array are printed.

```
#include <iostream.h>

main()
{
  int num[10];
  int *start, *end;

  start = num;
  end = &num[9];
```

```
while(start!=end) {
  cout << "Enter a number: ";
  cin >> *start;
  start++;
}
start = num;  /* reset the starting pointer */
while(start!=end) {
  cout << *start << ' ';
  start++;
}

return 0;
}
```

Arrays of Pointers

Pointers can be arrayed like any other data type. For example, the declaration for an integer pointer array of size 10 is:

```
int *pi[10];
```

Here, **pi** is an array of 10 integer pointers.

To assign the address of an integer variable called **var** to the third element of the pointer array, you would write

```
int var;
```

```
pi[2] = &var;
```

Remember, you are working with an array of pointers. The only values that the array elements can hold are the addresses of integer variables. To find the value of **var**, you would write:

```
*pi[2]
```

Like other arrays, arrays of pointers can be initialized. A common use for initialized pointer arrays is to hold pointers to strings. For example, to create a function that will output a fortune, you can define a number of different messages in a pointer array, as shown here:

```
char *fortunes[] = {
  "Soon, you will come into some money.\n",
  "A new love will enter your life.\n",
  "You will live long and prosper.\n",
```

6

```
  "Now is a good time to invest for the future.\n",
  "A close friend will ask for a favor.\n"
};
```

Remember, C++ stores all string constants in the string table associated with your program, so the array need only store pointers to the strings. To print the second message, use a statement like this:

```
cout << fortunes[1];
```

An entire "fortune cookie" program is shown here. It uses **rand( )** to generate a random number. It then uses the modulus operator to obtain a number between 0 and 4, which it uses to index the array.

```
#include <iostream.h>
#include <stdlib.h>
#include <conio.h>

char *fortunes[] = {
  "Soon, you will come into some money.\n",
  "A new love will enter your life.\n",
  "You will live long and prosper.\n",
  "Now is a good time to invest for the future.\n",
  "A close friend will ask for a favor.\n"
};

main()
{
  int chance;

  cout << "To see your fortune, press a key: ";

  // randomize the random number generator
  while(!kbhit()) rand();

  cout << '\n';

  chance = rand();
  chance = chance % 5;
  cout << fortunes[chance];

  return 0;
}
```

Notice the **while** loop in the program, which calls **rand( )** repeatedly until a key is pressed. Because the **rand( )** function always generates the same sequence of random numbers, it is important to have some way for the program to start using this sequence at a random point. (Otherwise, the same fortune will be given each time the program is run.) This is achieved by repeated calls to **rand( )**. When the user presses a key, the loop stops at a random point in the sequence, and the fortune is displayed on the screen. Remember, **kbhit( )** is a common extension provided by many compilers, but it is not defined by C++. If your compiler does not support the **kbhit( )** function, then ask the user for an arbitrary number, and call **rand( )** that number of times.

The next example uses a two-dimensional array of pointers to create the skeleton of a program that displays a syntax reminder for the C++ keywords. This program initializes a list of string pointers. The first dimension points to a C++ keyword, the second to a short description of the keyword. The list is terminated by two null strings. These nulls are used to mark the end of the list. The user enters a keyword, and the program displays the description. As you can see, only a few keywords have been listed. The expansion of the list is left to you, as an exercise.

```cpp
// A simple C++ keyword synopsis program.

#include <iostream.h>
#include <string.h>
#include <stdio.h>

char *keyword[][2] = {
  "for", "for(initialization; condition; increment)",
  "if", "if(condition) ... else ...",
  "switch", "switch(value) { case-list }",
  "while", "while(condition) ...",
  // add the rest of the C++ keywords here
  "", ""   // terminate the list with nulls
};

main()
{
  char str[80];
  int i;

  cout << "Enter keyword: ";
  gets(str);
  for(i=0; keyword[i][0]; i++)
    if(!strcmp(keyword[i][0], str))
      cout << keyword[i][1];

  return 0;
}
```

6

The Null Pointer Convention

After a pointer is declared, but before it has been assigned, it will contain an arbitrary value. Should you try to use the pointer prior to giving it a value, you will probably crash not only your program, but perhaps even the operating system of your computer (a very nasty type of error!). While there is no sure way to avoid using an uninitialized pointer, C++ programmers have adopted a procedure that helps prevent some errors. By convention, if a pointer contains the null (zero) value, it is assumed to point to nothing. Thus, if all unused pointers are given the null value and you avoid the use of a null pointer, you can avoid the accidental misuse of an uninitialized pointer. This is a good practice to follow.

Any type of pointer can be initialized to null when it is declared. For example, the following initializes **p** to null.

```
float *p = '\0'; // p is now a null pointer
```

To check for a null pointer, use an **if** statement, like one of these:

```
if(p) // succeeds if p is not null

if(!p) // succeeds if p is null
```

If you follow the null pointer convention, you will avoid many problems when using pointers.

Pointers and the 8086 Family of Processors

If you are using C++ on a computer that uses one of the 8086 family of processors, then you have up to seven different ways to compile your program, each organizing the memory of the machine differently. Specifically, you can compile your programs for the tiny, small, medium, compact, large, and huge memory models. If your processor is an 80386, 80486, or better, and if your operating system supports it, you can also compile your program for the flat memory model. The reason for the different memory organizations is based on the 8086 family's use of a segmented architecture.

For somewhat complex reasons, the way the program is compiled can, in some cases, have an effect on how pointers behave and on what you can do with them. It is beyond the scope of this book to discuss 8086 segmented memory architecture, its memory models, or their effects on pointers, except to say that for most applications, the effect on pointer operations is not an issue. For example, all the programs in this book compile and operate correctly no matter what approach to memory is taken. As a beginner you do not have to worry about the differences in memory organization. However, you will want to check your compiler's user manual for details—especially if you will be using pointers for special purposes.

Multiple Indirection

A pointer to a pointer is a form of multiple indirection, or a chain of pointers. Consider Figure 6-2.

As you can see, in the case of a normal pointer, the value of the pointer is the address of a value. In the case of a pointer to a pointer, the first pointer contains the address of the second pointer, which points to the location that contains the desired value.

Multiple indirection can be carried on to whatever extent desired, but there are few cases where more than a pointer to a pointer is needed, or, indeed, even wise to use. Excessive indirection is difficult to follow and prone to conceptual errors.

6

A variable that is a pointer to a pointer must be declared as such. This is done by placing an additional asterisk in front of its name. For example, this declaration tells the compiler that **balance** is a pointer to a pointer of type **int**.

```
int **balance;
```

It is important to understand that **balance** is not a pointer to an integer, but rather a pointer to an **int** pointer.

When a target value is indirectly pointed to by a pointer to a pointer, accessing that value requires that the asterisk operator be applied twice, as is shown in this short example:

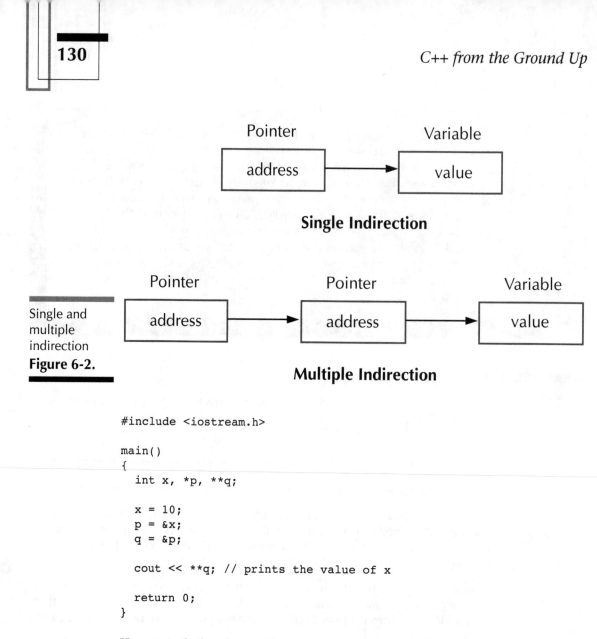

Single and
multiple
indirection
Figure 6-2.

```
#include <iostream.h>

main()
{
  int x, *p, **q;

  x = 10;
  p = &x;
  q = &p;

  cout << **q; // prints the value of x

  return 0;
}
```

Here, **p** is declared as a pointer to an integer, and **q** as a pointer to a pointer
to an integer. The **cout** statement will print the number 10 on the screen.

Problems with Pointers

Nothing will get you into more trouble than a "wild" pointer! Pointers are a
mixed blessing. They give you tremendous power and are useful for a number
of different operations. But, when a pointer accidentally contains the wrong
value, it can be the most difficult bug to track down in your program.

Bugs caused by bad pointers are hard to find because usually, the pointer
itself does not exhibit the problem. Instead, the problem shows itself only

indirectly, perhaps several steps after you have performed a pointer operation. For example, if a pointer accidentally points to the wrong data, then a pointer operation may alter this data, but the problem associated with this unintended alteration will not manifest itself until much later in the program's execution. This may lead you to look for the bug in the wrong place. By the time the problem is evident, there may be little or no indication that the pointer was the original cause of the problem. For this reason, pointer bugs have caused programmers to lose sleep time and time again.

Since pointer problems are so troublesome, let's look at some ways they can happen, and at how they can be avoided.

Uninitialized Pointers

The classic example of a pointer error is the *uninitialized pointer*. Consider this example:

```
// This program is wrong.
main(){
  int x, *p;

  x = 10;
  *p = x; // where does p point?

  return 0;
}
```

Here, **p** contains an unknown address because it has never been defined. You will have no way of knowing where the value of **x** has been written. When your program is very small, as it is here, the odds are that **p** will contain an address which is not in your code or data area. Most of the time, your program will seem to work fine. However, as your program grows, the probability of **p** pointing into either your program's code or data area increases. Eventually your program stops working. The solution is to always make sure that a pointer is pointing at something valid before it is used.

6

Invalid Pointer Comparisons

Comparisons between pointers that do not access the same array are generally invalid, and often cause errors. You can never know where your data will be placed in memory, or if it will always be in the same place, or whether every compiler will treat it in the same way. Therefore, making any comparisons between pointers to two different objects may yield unexpected results. Here is an example:

```
char s[80];
char y[80];
char *p1, *p2;

p1 = s;
p2 = y;
if(p1 < p2) . . .
```

This code is based on an invalid concept since C++ makes no guarantees about the placement of variables in memory. You should write your applications in such a way that they work no matter where data is located in memory.

A related error assumes that two back-to-back arrays can be indexed as one by simply incrementing a pointer across the array boundaries. For example:

```
int first[10];
int second[10];

int *p, t;

p = first;
for(t=0; t<20; ++t) {
  *p = t;
  p++;
}
```

The aim here is to initialize arrays **first** and **second** with the numbers 0 through 19, but the code is not reliable. Even though it may work with some compilers under certain circumstances, it assumes that both arrays will be placed back-to-back in memory with **first** first. However, C++ does not guarantee how variables will be located in memory.

Forgetting to Reset a Pointer

The following (incorrect) program inputs a string entered from the keyboard and then displays the ASCII code for each character in the string. (Notice that it uses a cast to cause the ASCII codes to be displayed.) However, this program has a serious bug.

```
// This program is wrong.

#include <iostream.h>
```

```
#include <stdio.h>
#include <string.h>

main()
{
  char s[80];
  char *p1;

  p1 = s;

  do {
    cout << "Enter a string: ";
    gets(s); // read a string
    // print the ASCII values of each character
    while(*p1) cout << (int) *p1++ << ' ';
    cout << '\n';
  } while(strcmp(s, "done"));

  return 0;
}
```

Can you find the error?

p1 is assigned the address of **s** once. This assignment is made outside of the loop. The first time through the loop, **p1** does point to the first character in **s**. However, the second time through, it continues on from where it left off, because it has not been reset to the start of the array **s**. This will eventually cause **s** to be overrun.

The proper way to write this program is shown here:

```
// This program is correct.

#include <iostream.h>
#include <stdio.h>
#include <string.h>

main()
{
  char s[80];
  char *p1;

  do {
    p1 = s; // reset p1 each time through the loop
```

6

```
    cout << "Enter a string: ";
    gets(s); // read a string
    // print the ASCII values of each character
    while(*p1) cout << (int) *p1++ << ' ';
    cout << '\n';
  } while(strcmp(s, "done"));

  return 0;
}
```

Here, each time the loop iterates, **p1** is set to the beginning of the string. You must know where your pointers are pointing at all times.

Chapter

7

Functions, Part One: The Fundamentals

This chapter begins an in-depth discussion of the function. (Chapter 8 continues this discussion.) Functions are the building blocks of C++, and a firm understanding of them is fundamental to becoming a successful C++ programmer. Aside from their brief introduction in Chapter 2, you have been using functions more or less intuitively. In this chapter you will study them in detail. Several topics mentioned in passing in earlier chapters are examined formally here, and several new issues relating to functions are introduced. This chapter also ties together a number of loose ends relating to functions. Topics include the scope rules of a function, recursive functions, some special properties of the **main( )** function, the **return** statement, and function prototypes.

Scope Rules of Functions

The *scope rules* of a language are the rules that govern how an object may be accessed by various parts of your program. In other words, the scope rules determine what code has access to a variable. The scope rules also determine the lifetime of a variable. As mentioned earlier in this book, there are three types of variables: local variables, formal parameters, and global variables. Let's look more closely at the scope rules at this time.

Local Variables

As you know, variables that are declared inside a function are called *local variables*. However, C++ supports a more subtle concept of the local variable than you have previously seen. In C++, variables can be localized to a block. That is, a variable can be declared inside any block of code, and is then local to it. (Remember, a block begins with an opening curly brace and ends with a closing curly brace.) In reality, variables local to a function are simply a special case of the more general concept.

A local variable can be referenced only by statements located in the block in which it is declared. Stated another way, local variables are not known outside their own code blocks. Thus, statements defined outside a block cannot access an object defined within it.

One of the most important things to understand about local variables is that they exist only while the block of code in which they are declared is executing. That is, a local variable is created upon entry into its block, and destroyed upon exit. Because a local variable is destroyed upon exit from its block, its value is lost.

As you know, the most common code block is the function. In C++, each function defines a block of code that begins with the function's opening curly brace and ends with its closing curly brace. A function's code and data are private to that function, and cannot be accessed by any statement in any other function except through a call to that function. (It is not possible, for instance, to use a **goto** statement to jump into the middle of another function.) The body of a function is hidden from the rest of the program and, unless it uses global variables, it can neither affect nor be affected by other parts of the program. Thus, the contents of one function are completely separate from the contents of another. Stated another way, the code and data that are defined within one function cannot interact with the code or data defined in another function, because the two functions have a different scope.

Because each function defines its own scope, the variables declared within one function have no effect on those declared in another—even if those variables share the same name. For example, consider the following program:

```
#include <iostream.h>
#include <stdio.h>
void f1();

main()
{
  char str[]="this is str in main()";

  cout << str << '\n';
  f1();
  cout << str << '\n';

  return 0;
}

void f1()
{
  char str[80];

  cout << "enter something: ";
  gets(str);
  cout << str << '\n';
}
```

A character array called **str** is declared twice here, once in **main( )** and once in **f1( )**. The **str** in **main( )** has no bearing on, or relationship to, the one in **f1( )**. The reason for this is that each **str** is known only to the block in which it is declared. To confirm this, try running the program. As you will see, even though **str** receives a string entered by the user inside **f1( )**, the contents of **str** in **main( )** remain unchanged.

The C++ language contains the keyword **auto**, which can be used to declare local variables. However, since all non-global variables are, by default, assumed to be **auto**, it is virtually never used. Hence, you will not see it used in any of the examples in this book. However, if you choose to use it, place it immediately before the variable's type, as shown here:

```
auto char ch;
```

It is common practice to declare all variables needed within a function at the beginning of that function's code block. This is done mainly so that anyone reading the code can easily determine what variables are used. However, the beginning of the function's block is not the only place where local variables can be declared. A local variable can be declared anywhere, within any block of code. A variable declared within a block is local to that block. This means that the variable does not exist until the block is entered, and is destroyed

7

when the block is exited. Furthermore, no code outside that block—including other code in the function—can access that variable.

To understand this, try the following program:

```
/* This program illustrates how variables can be
   local to a block.
*/

#include <stdio.h>
#include <iostream.h>
#include <string.h>

main()
{
  char str[80];
  int choice;

  cout << "(1) add numbers or ";
  cout << "(2) concatenate strings?: ";

  cin >> choice;
  if(choice == 1) {
    int a, b;  /* activate two integer vars */
    cout << "Enter two numbers: ";
    cin >> a >> b;
    cout << "Sum is " << a+b << '\n';
  }
  else {
    char s1[80], s2[80];  /* activate two strings */
    cout << "Enter two strings: ";
    gets(s1);
    gets(s2);
    strcat(s1, s2);
    cout << "Concatenation is " << s1 << '\n';
  }

  return 0;
}
```

This program either adds two numbers or concatenates two strings, depending on the user's choice. Notice the variable declarations for **a** and **b** in the **if** block, and those for **s1** and **s2** in the **else** block. These variables will come into existence only when their respective blocks are entered, and they will cease to exist when their blocks are left. If the user chooses to add numbers, then **a** and **b** are created. If the user wants to concatenate strings, **s1** and **s2** are created. Finally, none of these variables can be referenced from outside of its block—not even in other parts of the function. For example, if you try to compile the following (incorrect) version of the program, you will receive an error message.

```
/* This program is incorrect. */

#include <stdio.h>
#include <iostream.h>
#include <string.h>

main()
{
  char str[80];
  int choice;

  cout << "(1) add numbers or ";
  cout << "(2) concatenate strings?: ";

  cin >> choice;
  if(choice == 1) {
    int a, b;  /* activate two integer vars */
    cout << "Enter two numbers: ";
    cin >> a >> b;
    cout << "Sum is " << a+b << '\n';
  }
  else {
    char s1[80], s2[80];  /* activate two strings */
    cout << "Enter two strings: ";
    gets(s1);
    gets(s2);
    strcat(s1, s2);
    cout << "Concatenation is " << s1 << '\n';
  }

  a = 10; // *** ERROR *** a not known here!

  return 0;
}
```

7

In addition to restricting the variable's scope, another advantage of declaring a local variable within a conditional block is that memory for the variable will only be allocated if needed. This is because a local variable does not come into existence until the block in which it is declared is entered. Although this is not generally important in most computer environments in which plenty of RAM is available, it can matter when code is being produced for dedicated controllers (a controller for a microwave oven, for example), where RAM may be in very short supply.

Because local variables are created and destroyed with each entry and exit from the blocks in which they are declared, a local variable will not hold its value between activations of its block. This is especially important to remember in terms of a function call. When a function is called, its local variables are created, and upon its return, they are destroyed. This means that local variables cannot retain their values between calls. (There is one way around this restriction, however, which will be explained later in this book.)

Unless otherwise specified, storage for local variables is on the stack. The fact that the stack is a dynamic, changing region of memory explains why local variables cannot, in general, hold their values between function calls.

As mentioned earlier, although local variables are typically declared at the beginning of their block, they need not be. A local variable can be declared anywhere within a block as long as it is declared before it is used. For example, this is a perfectly valid program:

```
#include <iostream.h>

main()
{
  cout << "Enter a number: ";
  int a; // declare one variable
  cin >> a;

  cout << "Enter a second number: ";
  int b; // declare another variable
  cin >> b;

  cout << "Product: " << a*b << '\n';

  return 0;
}
```

In this example, **a** and **b** are not declared until just before they are needed. Frankly, most programmers declare all local variables at the beginning of the block that uses them, but this is a stylistic issue.

Formal Parameters

As you know, if a function uses arguments, then it must declare variables that will accept the values of those arguments. These variables are called the *formal parameters* of the function. Aside from receiving a function's arguments when that function is called, formal parameters behave like any other local variables inside the function. In essence, the scope of a parameter is local to its function.

You must make sure that the formal parameters you declare are of the same type as the arguments you will use to call the function. Also, even though these variables perform the special task of receiving the values of the arguments passed to the function, they can be used like any other local variable.

Global Variables

Global variables are, in many ways, the opposite of local variables. They are known throughout the entire program, can be used by any piece of code, and maintain their values during the entire execution of the program. Therefore, their scope extends to the entire program. You can create global variables by declaring them outside of any function. Because they are global, they can be accessed by any expression, regardless of which function the expression is located in.

When a global and a local variable share the same name, the local variable has precedence. Put differently, a local variable will mask a global variable of the same name. Thus, even though global variables can be accessed by any code in your program, this will only happen when no local variable's name overrides the global variable.

The following program demonstrates the use of global variables. As you can see, the variables **count** and **num_right** have been declared outside of all functions; they are, therefore, global. Common practice dictates that it is best to declare global variables near the top of the program. However, technically, they simply have to be declared before they are first used. This program is a simple addition drill. It first asks you how many problems you want. For each problem, the program calls **drill( )**, which generates two random numbers in the range 0 through 99. It prompts for and then checks your answer. You get three tries per problem. At the end, the program displays the number of answers you've gotten right.

Pay special attention to the global variables used in this program.

7

```
// A simple addition drill program.

#include <iostream.h>
#include <stdlib.h>
void drill();

int count;  // count and num_right are global.
int num_right;

main()
{
```

```
    cout << "How many practice problems: ";
    cin >> count;

    num_right = 0;
    do {
      drill();
      count--;
    } while(count);
    cout << "You got " << num_right << " right.\n";

    return 0;
}

void drill()
{
    int count;   /* This count is local and unrelated to
                    the global one.
                */
    int a, b, ans;

    // generate two numbers between 0 and 99
    a = rand() % 100;
    b = rand() % 100;

    // The user gets three tries to get it right.
    for(count=0; count<3; count++) {
      cout << "What is " << a << " + " << b << "? ";
      cin >> ans;
      if(ans==a+b) {
        cout << "Right\n";
        num_right++;
        return;
      }
    }
    cout << "You've used up all your tries\n";
    cout << "The answer is " << a+b << '\n';
}
```

Looking closely at this program, it should be clear that both **main( )** and **drill( )** access the global **num_right**. However, **count** is a little more complex. The reference to **count** in **main( )** is to the global **count**. However, **drill( )** has declared a local variable called **count**. When **drill( )** references **count**, it will be referencing only its local variable, not the global one. Remember that if, within a function, a global variable and a local variable have the same name, all references to that variable will refer to the local variable, not the global variable.

Storage for global variables is in a fixed region of memory set aside for this purpose by your program. Global variables are helpful when the same data is used by several functions in your program, or when a variable must hold its value throughout the duration of the program. You should avoid using unnecessary global variables, however, for three reasons:

♦ They take up memory the entire time your program is executing, not just when they are needed.

♦ Using a global where a local variable will do makes a function less general, because it relies on something that must be defined outside itself.

♦ Using a large number of global variables can lead to program errors because of unknown, and unwanted, side effects. A major problem in developing large programs is the accidental modification of a variable's value due to its use elsewhere in a program. This can happen in C++ if you use too many global variables in your programs.

Passing Pointers and Arrays

Up to now, the examples in this book have only passed single variables to functions. However, there will be times when you will want to use pointers and arrays as arguments. While passing these types of arguments is a straightforward process, some special issues need to be addressed.

Calling Functions with Pointers

C++ allows you to pass a pointer to a function. To do so, simply declare the parameter as a pointer type. Here is an example:

```
// Pass a pointer to a function
#include <iostream.h>

void f(int *j);

main()
```

7

```
{
  int i;
  int *p;

  p = &i; // p now points to i

  f(p);

  cout << i;  // i is now 100

  return 0;
}

void f(int *j)
{
  *j = 100; // var pointed to by j is assigned 100
}
```

Study this program carefully. As you can see, **f( )** takes one parameter: an integer pointer. Inside **main( )**, **p** is assigned the address of **i**. Next, **f( )** is called with **p** as an argument. When the pointer parameter **j** receives **p**, it then also points to **i** within **main( )**. Thus, the assignment

```
*j = 100;
```

causes **i** to be given the value 100. For the general case, **f( )** assigns 100 to whatever address it is called with.

In the preceding example, it is not actually necessary to use the pointer variable **p**. Instead, you can simply precede **i** with an **&** when **f( )** is called. (This, of course, will cause the address of **i** to be generated.) The revised program is shown here:

```
// Pass a pointer to a function
#include <iostream.h>

void f(int *j);

main()
{
  int i;

  f(&i);

  cout << i;

  return 0;
```

```
}

void f(int *j)
{
   *j = 100; // var pointed to by j is assigned 100
}
```

It is crucial that you understand one important point about passing pointers to functions: when you perform an operation within the function that uses the pointer, you are operating on the variable that is pointed to by that pointer. Thus, the function will be able to change the value of the object pointed to by the parameter.

Calling Functions with Arrays

When an array is an argument to a function, only the address of the first element of the array is passed, not a copy of the entire array. (Remember, in C++, an array name without any index is a pointer to the first element in the array.) This means that the parameter declaration must be of a compatible type. There are three ways to declare a parameter that is to receive an array pointer. First, it can be declared as an array of the same type and size as that used to call the function, as shown here:

```
#include <iostream.h>

void display(int num[10]);

main()   // print some numbers
{
   int t[10],i;

   for(i=0;  i<10;  ++i) t[i]=i;
   display(t);

   return 0;
}

void display(int num[10])
{
   int i;

   for(i=0;  i<10;  i++) cout << num[i] << ' ';
}
```

Even though the parameter **num** is declared to be an integer array of 10 elements, the C++ compiler will automatically convert it to an integer

7

pointer. This is necessary because no parameter can actually receive an entire array. Since only a pointer to the array will be passed, a pointer parameter must be there to receive it.

A second way to declare an array parameter is to specify it as an unsized array, as shown here:

```
void display(int num[])
{
  int i;

  for(i=0; i<10; i++) cout << num[i] << ' ';
}
```

Here, **num** is declared to be an integer array of unknown size. Since C++ provides no array boundary checks, the actual size of the array is irrelevant to the parameter (but not to the program, of course). This method of declaration is also automatically transformed into an integer pointer by the compiler.

The final way that **num** can be declared is as a pointer. This is the method most commonly used in professionally written C++ programs. Here is an example:

```
void display(int *num)
{
  int i;

  for(i=0; i<10; i++) cout << num[i] << ' ';
}
```

The reason it is possible to declare **num** as a pointer is that any pointer can be indexed using **[ ]**, as if it were an array. Recognize that all three methods of declaring an array parameter yield the same result: a pointer.

On the other hand, an array *element* used as an argument is treated like any other simple variable. For example, the preceding program could also be written without passing the entire array, as shown here:

```
#include <iostream.h>

void display(int num);

main() // print some numbers
```

```
{
  int t[10],i;

  for(i=0; i<10; ++i) t[i]=i;
  for(i=0; i<10; i++) display(t[i]);

  return 0;
}

void display(int num)
{
  cout << num << ' ';
}
```

As you can see, the parameter to **display( )** is of type **int**. It is not relevant that **display( )** is called using an array element, because only that one value of the array is used.

It is important to remember that when an array is used as a function argument, its address is passed to a function. This means that the code inside the function will be operating on, and potentially altering, the actual contents of the array used to call the function. For example, in the following program examine the function **cube( )**, which converts the value of each element in an array into its cube. To call **cube( )**, pass the address of the array as the first argument, and the size of the array as the second.

```
#include <iostream.h>

void cube(int *n, int num);

main()
{
  int i, nums[10];

  for(i=0; i<10; i++) nums[i] = i+1;
  cout << "Original contents: ";
  for(i=0; i<10; i++) cout << nums[i] << ' ';
  cout << '\n';

  cube(nums, 10); // compute cubes

  cout << "Altered contents: ";
  for(i=0; i<10; i++) cout << nums[i] << ' ';
```

7

```
  return 0;
}

void cube(int *n, int num)
{
  while(num) {
    *n = *n * *n * *n;
    num--;
    n++;
  }
}
```

After the call to **cube( )**, the contents of array **nums** in **main( )** will be cubes of its original values. That is, the values of the elements of **nums** have been modified by the statements within **cube( )**, because **n** points to **nums**.

Passing Strings

As you know, strings are simply character arrays that are null-terminated. Thus, when you pass a string to a function, only a pointer to the beginning of the string is actually passed. For example, consider the following program. It defines the function **stringupper( )**, which converts a string to uppercase.

```
// Pass a string to a function.
#include <iostream.h>
#include <string.h>
#include <ctype.h>

void stringupper(char *str);

main()
{
  char str[80];

  strcpy(str, "this is a test");

  stringupper(str);
  cout << str; // display uppercase string
  return 0;
}

void stringupper(char *str)
{
  while(*str) {
```

```
      *str = toupper(*str); // uppercase one char
      str++; // move on to next char
  }
}
```

Here is another example of passing a string to a function. As you learned in Chapter 5, the standard library function **strlen( )** returns the length of a string. To see one way of implementing this function, examine this program:

```
// A custom version of strlen().
#include <iostream.h>

int mystrlen(char *str);

main()
{
  cout << "Length of Hello There is: ";
  cout << mystrlen("Hello There");

  return 0;
}

// A custom version of strlen().
int mystrlen(char *str)
{
  int i;

  for(i=0; str[i]; i++) ; // find the end of the string

  return i;
}
```

On your own, you might want to try implementing the other string functions, such as **strcpy( )** or **strcat( )**. Doing so is a good way to test your understanding of arrays, strings, and pointers.

7

argc and argv: Arguments to main( )

Sometimes you will want to pass information into a program when you run it. This is generally accomplished by passing *command line arguments* to **main( )**. A command line argument is the information that follows the program's name on the command line of the operating system. For example, you might compile C++ programs from the command line by typing something like this,

A command
line argument
is information
specified on
the command
line after a
program's
name.

cpp *progname*

where *progname* is the program you wish compiled. The name of the
program is passed into the C++ compiler as a command line argument.

C++ defines two built-in, but optional, parameters to **main( )**. They are
argc and **argv**, and they receive the command line arguments. These are
the only parameters defined by C++ for **main( )**. However, other arguments
may be supported in your specific operating environment, so you will want
to check your compiler's user manual. Let's now look at **argc** and **argv**
more closely.

Note: Technically, the names of the command line parameters are
arbitrary—you can use any names you like. However, **argc** and **argv** have
been used by convention for several years, and it is best that you use these
names so that anyone reading your program can quickly identify them as
the command line parameters.

The **argc** parameter is an integer that holds the number of arguments on
the command line. It will always be at least 1, because the name of the
program qualifies as the first argument.

The **argv** parameter is a pointer to an array of character pointers. Each
pointer in the **argv** array points to a string containing a command line
argument. The program's name is pointed to by **argv[0]**; **argv[1]** will point
to the first argument, **argv[2]** to the second argument, and so on. All
command line arguments are passed to the program as strings, so numeric
arguments will have to be converted by your program into their proper
internal format.

It is important that you declare **argv** properly. The most common method is:

```
char *argv[];
```

You can access the individual arguments by indexing **argv**. The following
program demonstrates how to access the command line arguments. It
prints **hello** followed by your name, which must be the first command line
argument.

```
#include <iostream.h>

main(int argc, char *argv[])
{
  if(argc!=2) {
    cout << "You forgot to type your name.\n";
    return 1;
  }
  cout << "Hello " << argv[1] << '\n';

  return 0;
}
```

If you titled this program **name** and your name were Tom, then to run the program you would type **name Tom**. The output from the program would be **Hello Tom**. For example, if you were logged into drive A and running DOS, you would see

```
A>name Tom
 Hello Tom
A>
```

C++ does not stipulate the exact nature of a command line argument because host environments (operating systems) vary considerably on this point. However, the most common convention is as follows: Each command line argument must be separated by spaces or tabs. Often commas, semicolons, and the like are not valid argument separators. For example,

    one, two, and three

is made up of four strings, while

    one,two,and three

has two strings—the comma is not a legal separator.

If you need to pass a command line argument that does, in fact, contain spaces, then you must place it between quotes. For example, this will be treated as a single command line argument:

7

"this is one argument"

Keep in mind that the examples provided here apply to a wide variety of environments, but not necessarily to yours.

To access an individual character in one of the command strings, add a second index to **argv**. For example, the program below will display all the arguments it is called with, one character at a time on the screen.

```c
/* The program prints all command line arguments it is
   called with one character at a time. */
#include <iostream.h>

main(int argc, char *argv[])
{
  int t, i;

  for(t=0; t<argc; ++t) {
    i = 0;
    while(argv[t][i]) {
      cout << argv[t][i];
      ++i;
    }
    cout << ' ';
  }

  return 0;
}
```

Recall that the first index accesses the string and the second index accesses a character in the string.

Usually, you will use **argc** and **argv** to get initial options or values into your program. In C++, you can have as many command line arguments as the operating system will allow. For example, in DOS, a command line is limited to 128 characters or a maximum of 63 arguments. You normally use these arguments to indicate a filename or an option. Using command line arguments will give your program a professional appearance and facilitate the program's use in batch files.

Passing Numeric Command-line Arguments

As mentioned, when you pass numeric data as a command-line argument to a program, that data will be received in string form. Your program will need to convert it into the proper internal format using one of the standard library functions supported by C++. For example, the program shown next prints the sum of the two numbers that follow its name on the command line. The program uses the **atof( )** function to convert each argument into its internal representation. **atof( )** is another of C++'s standard library functions. It converts the string form of a number into a **double**.

```
/* This program displays the sum of the two numeric
   command line arguments.
*/

#include <iostream.h>
#include "stdlib.h"

main(int argc, char *argv[])
{

  double a, b;

  if(argc!=3) {
    cout << "Usage: add num num\n";
    return 1;
  }

  a = atof(argv[1]);
  b = atof(argv[2]);

  cout << a + b;

  return 0;
}
```

To add two numbers, use this type of command line (assuming the program is called *add*):

    add 100.2 231

7

Converting Numeric Strings to Numbers

The C++ standard library includes several functions that allow you to convert the string representation of a number into its internal format. These are **atoi( )**, **atol( )**, and **atof( )**, which convert a numeric string into an integer, a long integer, and a double floating-point value, respectively. These functions all require the header file **stdlib.h**. The following program illustrates their use:

```cpp
// Demonstrate atoi(), atol(), and atof().
#include <iostream.h>
#include <stdlib.h>

main()
{
  int i;
  long j;
  double k;

  i = atoi("100");
  j = atol("100000");
  k = atof("-0.123");

  cout << i << ' ' << j << ' ' << k;
  cout << '\n';

  return 0;
}
```

The string conversion functions are useful in a variety of programming situations, especially those that entail passing numeric data to a program through a command-line argument.

The return Statement

You have been using the **return** statement without much explanation since Chapter 2. As you know, the **return** statement performs two important operations: First, it will cause a function to immediately return to its calling routine. Second, it can be used to return a value. This section of the chapter presents some important issues related to both of these processes.

Returning from a Function

As you already know, a function returns to its calling routine in one of two situations: either when the function's closing curly brace is encountered or when a **return** statement is executed. The **return** statement can be used with or without an associated value. However, functions that are declared as returning a value (i.e., that have a non-**void** return type) must return a value. Only functions declared as **void** can use **return** without a value.

For **void** functions, the **return** statement is mostly used as a program control structure. For example, the function shown next will print the outcome of one number raised to a positive integer power. If the exponent is negative, the **return** statement causes the function to terminate before any attempt is made to compute the exponent. In this capacity, it acts as a control statement designed to prevent part of the function from executing.

```
void power(int base, int exp)
{
  int i;

  if(exp<0) return; /* Can't do negative exponents,
                       so return to calling routine
                       and bypass the rest of the
                       function. */

  i = 1;

  for( ; exp; exp--) i = base * i;
  cout << "The answer is: " << i;
}
```

A function may contain several **return** statements. As soon as one is encountered, the function returns. For example, this fragment is perfectly valid:

```
void f()
{
  // ...

  switch(c) {
    case 'a': return;
    case 'b': // ...
    case 'c': return;
  }
```

7

```
   if(count<100) return;
   // ...
}
```

Be aware, however, that having too many **return**s can muddy the operation of a routine and confuse its meaning. It is best to use multiple **return**s only when they help clarify a function.

Returning Values

Every function, unless it is of type **void**, returns a value. This value is explicitly specified by the **return** statement. This means that as long as a function is not declared to be **void**, it can be used as an operand in any valid C++ expression. Therefore, each of the following expressions is valid in C++:

```
x = power(y);
```

```
if(max(x, y)) > 100) cout << "greater";
```

```
switch(abs(x)) {
```

Although all non-**void** functions return values, you don't necessarily have to use the values for anything. A very common question regarding function return values is, "Don't I have to assign this value to some variable, since a value is being returned?" The answer is no. If there is no assignment specified, then the return value is simply discarded.

Examine the following program, which uses the standard library function **abs( )**.

```
#include <iostream.h>
#include <stdlib.h>

main()
{
  int i;

  i = abs(-10);     // line 1
  cout << abs(-23); // line 2
  abs(100);         // line 3

  return 0;
}
```

The **abs( )** function returns the absolute value of its integer argument. It uses the **stdlib.h** header file. In line 1, the return value of **abs( )** is assigned to **i**. In line 2, the return value is not actually assigned, but it is used by the **cout** statement. Finally, in line 3, the return value is lost, because it is neither assigned to another variable nor used as part of an expression.

If a non-**void** function returns because its closing curly brace is encountered, an undefined (i.e., unknown) value is returned. Because of a quirk in the formal C++ syntax, a non-**void** function need not actually execute a **return** statement. However, because the function is declared as returning a value, a value must be returned—even if it is just a garbage value. Generally, any non-**void** function that you create should return a value via an explicit **return** statement.

Just as a **void** function may have more than one **return** statement, so may a function that returns a value. For example, the **find_substr( )** function shown in the next program uses two **return** statements to simplify its operation. The function searches a string for a substring. It returns the index of the first matching substring, or if no match is found, it returns –1. For example, if the string is "I like C++" and the substring is "like", then the function returns 2 (which is the index of the "l" in like).

```cpp
#include <iostream.h>

int find_substr(char *sub, char *str);

main()
{
  int index;

  index = find_substr("three", "one two three four");

  cout << "Index of three is " << index; // index is 8

  return 0;
}

// Return index of substring or -1 if not found.
find_substr(char *sub, char *str)
{
  int t;
  char *p, *p2;

  for(t=0; str[t]; t++) {
    p = &str[t]; // reset pointers
```

7

```
    p2 = sub;
    while(*p2 && *p2==*p) { // check for substring
      p++;
      p2++;
    }

    /* If at end of p2 (i.e., substring), then
       a match has been found. */
    if(!*p2) return t; // return index of match
  }
  return -1; // no match found
}
```

A function can be declared to return any valid C++ data type (except that a function cannot return an array.) The method of declaration is similar to that used with variables: the type specifier precedes the function name. The type specifier tells the compiler what type of data will be returned by the function. This return type must be compatible with the type of data used in the **return** statement. If it isn't, a compile-time error will result.

void Functions

As you have seen, functions that don't return values may be declared **void**. This prevents their use in any expression and helps head off accidental misuse. In the following example, the function **print_vertical( )** prints its string argument vertically down the side of the screen. Since it returns no value, it is declared as **void**.

```
#include <iostream.h>

void print_vertical(char *str);

main(int argc, char *argv[])
{
  if(argc) print_vertical(argv[1]);

  return 0;
}

void print_vertical(char *str)
{
  while(*str)
    cout << *str++ << '\n';
}
```

Since **print_vertical( )** is declared as **void**, it cannot be used in an expression. For example, the following statement is wrong, and will not compile.

```
x = print_vertical("hello"); // ERROR
```

Tip: Early versions of the C language did not allow the **void** return type. Thus, in old C programs, functions that did not return values were simply allowed to default to type **int**. You may still encounter functions of this sort when updating older C programs to C++. If you do, simply convert them to **void** functions.

Functions that Return Pointers

Functions can return pointers. Pointers are returned like any other data type, and pose no special problem. However, because the pointer is one of C++'s more confusing features, a short discussion of pointer return types is warranted.

In order to return a pointer, a function must declare its return type to be a pointer. For example, here the return type of **f( )** is declared to be an integer pointer:

```
int *f();
```

If a function's return type is a pointer, then the value used in its **return** statement must also be a pointer. (As with all functions, the return value must be compatible with the return type.)

The following program demonstrates the use of a pointer return type. It reworks the **find_substr( )** function, shown earlier, so that it returns a pointer to the substring, rather than the index of the substring. If no match is found, a null pointer is returned.

```
#include <iostream.h>

char *get_substr(char *sub, char *str);

main()
{
  char *substr;

  substr = get_substr("three", "one two three four");
```

7

```
  cout << "substring found: " << substr;

  return 0;
}

// Return pointer to substring or null if not found.
char *get_substr(char *sub, char *str)
{
  int t;
  char *p, *p2, *start;

  for(t=0; str[t]; t++) {
    p = &str[t]; // reset pointers
    start = p;
    p2 = sub;
    while(*p2 && *p2==*p) { // check for substring
      p++;
      p2++;
    }

    /* If at end of p2 (i.e., substring), then
       a match has been found. */
    if(!*p2)
      return start; // return pointer to beginning of substring
  }
  return 0; // no match found
}
```

Many of the string-related library functions supported by C++ return
character pointers. For example, the **strcpy( )** function returns a pointer
to the first argument. Check your compiler's library reference for
other examples.

Function Prototypes

Until this point in the book, prototypes have been used without explanation
in the sample programs. Now it is time to explain them formally. In C++, all
functions must be declared before they are used. Typically, this is
accomplished by use of a function prototype. Prototypes specify three things
about a function:

♦ Its return type

♦ The type of its parameters

♦ The number of its parameters

Prototypes allow the compiler to perform three important operations:

♦ They tell the compiler what type of code to generate when a function is called. Different return types must be handled differently by the compiler.

♦ They allow C++ to find and report any illegal type conversions between the type of arguments used to call a function and the type definition of its parameters.

♦ They allow the compiler to detect differences between the number of arguments used to call a function and the number of parameters in the function.

The general form of a function prototype definition is as follows. It is the same as a function definition, except that no body is present.

> *type func-name(type parm_name1, type parm_name2,...,*
> *type parm_nameN);*

The use of parameter names in a prototype is optional. However, their use does let the compiler identify any type mismatches by name when an error occurs, so it is a good idea to include them.

To better understand the usefulness of function prototypes, consider the following program. If you try to compile it, an error message will be issued, because the program attempts to call **sqr_it( )** with an integer argument instead of the integer pointer required. (It is illegal to transform an integer into a pointer.)

```
/* This program uses a function prototype to
   enforce strong type checking.
*/

void sqr_it(int *i); // prototype

main()
{
```

7

```
   int x;

   x = 10;
   sqr_it(x); // type mismatch

   return 0;
}

void sqr_it(int *i)
{
   *i = *i * *i;
}
```

Tip: Although the C language accepts prototypes, it does not require them. This is because early versions of C did not accept full prototypes. If you are porting older C code to C++, you may need to fully prototype all functions before a program will compile.

Header Files: A Closer Look

Earlier in this book you were introduced to the standard C++ header files. You have learned that these files contain information needed by your programs. While this partial explanation is true, it does not tell the whole story. C++'s header files contain the prototypes for the functions in the standard library. (They also contain various values and definitions used by those functions.) Like functions that you write, the standard library functions must be prototyped before they are used. For this reason, any program that uses a library function must also include the header file containing the prototype of that function.

To find out which header file a library function requires, look in your compiler's library reference manual. Along with a description of each function, you will find the name of the header file that must be included in order to use that function.

Classic Versus Modern Function Parameter Declarations

If you have examined older C code, you may have noticed that the function parameter declarations look different. When C was first invented it used a fundamentally different method for the declaration of parameters. This older method, sometimes called the *classic form,* is outdated, but is still commonly found in older code. The declaration approach used by C++ (and newer C code) is called the *modern form.* Because you may need to work on older C programs, especially if you are updating them to C++, it is useful to understand the classic form of parameter declaration.

The classic function parameter declaration consists of two parts: a parameter list, which goes inside the parentheses that follow the function name, and the actual parameter declarations, which go between the closing parenthesis and the function's opening curly brace. For example, this modern declaration

```
float f(int a, int b, char ch)
{ ...
```

would look like this in its classic form:

```
float f(a, b, ch)
int a, b;
char ch;
{ ...
```

Notice that in classic form, more than one parameter can be in a list after the type name. To convert the classic form into the modern (C++-style) form, simply move the parameter declarations inside the function's parentheses.

7

Recursion

The last topic that we will examine in this chapter is *recursion*. Sometimes called *circular definition*, recursion is the process of defining something in terms of itself. As it relates to programming, recursion is the process of a function calling itself. A function that calls itself is said to be is *recursive*.

The classic example of recursion is the function **factr( )**, which computes the factorial of an integer. The factorial of a number *N* is the product of all the whole numbers between 1 and *N*. For example, 3 factorial is 1 x 2 x 3, or 6. Both **factr( )** and its iterative equivalent are shown here:

A recursive function is a function that calls itself.

```
#include <iostream.h>
int factr(int n);
int fact(int n);

main()
{
  // use recursive version
  cout << "4 factorial is " << factr(4);
  cout << '\n';

  // use iterative version
  cout << "4 factorial is " << fact(4);
  cout << '\n';

  return 0;
}

// Recursive version
factr(int n)
{
  int answer;

  if(n==1) return(1);
  answer = factr(n-1)*n;
  return(answer);
}

// Iterative version
fact(int n)
{
  int t, answer;
```

```
    answer = 1;
    for(t=1; t<=n; t++) answer = answer*(t);
    return(answer);
}
```

The operation of the nonrecursive version of **fact( )** should be clear. It uses a loop starting at 1 and progressively multiplies each number by the moving product.

The operation of the recursive **factr( )** is a little more complex. When **factr( )** is called with an argument of 1, the function returns 1; otherwise it returns the product of **factr(n–1)*n**. To evaluate this expression, **factr( )** is called with **n–1**. This happens until **n** equals 1 and the calls to the function begin returning. For example, when the factorial of 2 is calculated, the first call to **factr( )** will cause a second call to be made with the argument of 1. This call will return 1, which is then multiplied by 2 (the original **n** value). The answer is then 2. You might find it interesting to insert **cout** statements into **factr( )** that will show at what level each call is, and what the intermediate answers are.

When a function calls itself, new local variables and parameters are allocated storage on the stack, and the function code is executed with these new variables from the start. A recursive call does not make a new copy of the function; only the arguments are new. As each recursive call returns, the old local variables and parameters are removed from the stack, and execution resumes at the point of the function call inside the function. Recursive functions could be said to "telescope" out and back.

Keep in mind that most recursive routines do not significantly reduce code size. Also, the recursive versions of most routines may execute a bit more slowly than their iterative equivalents, due to the added overhead of the additional function calls. Too many recursive calls to a function may cause a stack overrun. Because storage for function parameters and local variables is on the stack, and each new call creates a new copy of these variables, it is possible that the stack will be exhausted. If this occurs, other data may be destroyed as well. However, you probably will not have to worry about any of this unless a recursive function runs wild.

7

The main advantage of recursive functions is that they can be used to create clearer and simpler versions of several algorithms than those produced with their iterative relatives. For example, the QuickSort sorting algorithm is quite difficult to implement in an iterative way. Also, some problems, especially those related to artificial intelligence, seem to lend themselves to recursive solutions. Finally, some people find it easier to think recursively rather than iteratively.

When writing a recursive function, you must include an **if** statement somewhere to force the function to return without execution of the recursive call. If you don't provide the **if** statement, then once you call the function, it will never return. This is a very common error. When developing programs with recursive functions, use **cout** statements liberally so that you can watch what is going on, and abort execution if you see that you have made a mistake.

Here is another example of a recursive function, called **reverse( )**. It prints its string argument backwards on the screen.

```
// Print a string backwards using recursion.
#include <iostream.h>

void reverse(char *s);

main()
{
  char str[] = "this is a test";

  reverse(str);

  return 0;
}

void reverse(char *s)
{
  if(*s)
    reverse(s+1);

  cout << *s;
}
```

The **reverse( )** function first checks to see if it is passed a pointer to the null terminating the string. If not, then **reverse( )** calls itself with a pointer to the next character in the string. When the null terminator is finally found, the calls begin unraveling, and the characters are displayed in reverse order.

Creating recursive functions is often difficult for beginners. Over time, however, you will grow more accustomed to using them.

Chapter

8

Functions, Part Two: References, Overloading, and Default Arguments

This chapter continues our examination of the function. Specifically, it discusses three of C++'s most important function-related topics: references, function overloading, and default arguments. These three features vastly expand the capabilities of a function. As you will see, a reference is an implicit pointer. Function overloading is the quality that allows one function to be implemented two or more different ways, each performing a separate task. Function overloading is one way that C++ supports polymorphism. Using a default argument, it is possible to specify a value for a parameter that will be automatically used when no corresponding argument is specified.

Since references are frequently applied to function parameters (it is the main reason for their existence), this chapter begins with a brief discussion of how arguments can be passed to functions.

Two Approaches to Argument Passing

Call-by-value passes the value of an argument to a function.

To understand the genesis of the reference, you must understand the theory behind argument passing. In general, there are two ways that a computer language can pass an argument to a subroutine. The first is called *call-by-value*. This method copies the *value* of an argument into the formal parameter of the subroutine. Therefore, changes made to the parameters of the subroutine have no effect on the arguments used to call it.

Call-by-reference passes the address of an argument to a function.

Call-by-reference is the second way a subroutine can be passed arguments. In this method, the *address* of an argument (not its value) is copied into the parameter. Inside the subroutine, this address is used to access the actual argument specified in the call. This means that changes made to the parameter will affect the argument used to call the subroutine.

How C++ Passes Arguments

By default, C++ uses the *call-by-value* method for passing arguments. This means that, in general, code inside a function cannot alter the arguments used to call the function. In this book, all of the programs up to this point have used the call-by-value method.

Consider this function:

```
#include <iostream.h>

int sqr_it(int x);

main()
{
  int t=10;

  cout << sqr_it(t) << ' ' << t;

  return 0;
}

sqr_it(int x)
{
  x = x*x;
  return x;
}
```

In this example, the value of the argument to **sqr_it( )**, 10, is copied into the parameter **x**. When the assignment **x = x*x** takes place, the only thing modified is the local variable **x**. The variable **t**, used to call **sqr_it( )**, will still have the value 10, and is unaffected by the operations inside the function. Hence, the output will be 100 10.

Remember: By default, a copy of an argument is passed into a function. What occurs inside the function will have no effect on the variable used in the call.

Using a Pointer to Create a Call-by-Reference

Even though C++'s default parameter-passing convention is call-by-value, it is possible to manually create a call-by-reference by passing the address of an argument (i.e., a pointer to the argument) to a function. It will then be possible to change the value of the argument outside of the function. You saw an example of this in the preceding chapter when the passing of pointers was discussed. As you know, pointers are passed to functions just like any other values. Of course, it is necessary to declare the parameters as pointer types.

To see how passing a pointer allows you to manually create a call-by-reference, examine this version of **swap( )**. It exchanges the values of the two variables pointed to by its arguments.

```
void swap(int *x, int *y)
{
  int temp;

  temp = *x; // save the value at address x
  *x = *y;   // put y into x
  *y = temp; // put x into y
}
```

The ***x** and the ***y** reference the variables pointed to by **x** and **y**, which are the addresses of the arguments used to call the function. Consequently, the contents of the variables used to call the function will be swapped.

Since **swap( )** expects to receive two pointers, you must remember to call **swap( )** with the *addresses* of the variables you wish to exchange. The correct method is shown in this program:

```
#include <iostream.h>

// Declare swap() using pointers.
```

8

```
void swap(int *x, int *y);

main()
{
  int i, j;

  i = 10;
  j = 20;

  cout << "initial values of i and j: ";
  cout << i << ' ' << j << '\n';
  swap(&j, &i); // call swap() with addresses of i and j
  cout << "swapped values of i and j: ";
  cout << i << ' ' << j << '\n';

  return 0;
}

// Exchange arguments.
void swap(int *x, int *y)
{
  int temp;

  temp = *x; // save the value at address x
  *x = *y;   // put y into x
  *y = temp; // put x into y
}
```

In this example, the variable **i** is assigned the value 10, and **j** the value 20.
Then **swap( )** is called with the addresses of **i** and **j**. The unary operator **&** is
used to produce the addresses of the variables. Therefore, the addresses of **i**
and **j**, not their values, are passed into the function **swap( )**.

Reference Parameters

While it is possible to achieve a call-by-reference manually by using the
pointer operators, this approach is rather clumsy. First, it compels you to
perform all operations through pointers. Second, it requires that you
remember to pass the addresses (rather than the values) of the arguments
when calling the function. Fortunately, in C++, it is possible to tell the
compiler to automatically use call-by-reference rather than call-by-value for
one or more parameters of a particular function. You can accomplish this
with a *reference parameter*. When you use a reference parameter, the address
(not the value) of an argument is automatically passed to the function.
Within the function, operations on the reference parameter are
automatically dereferenced, so there is no need to use the pointer operators.

A reference parameter automatically receives the address of its corresponding argument.

A reference parameter is declared by preceding the parameter name in the function's declaration with an **&**. Operations performed on a reference parameter affect the argument used to call the function, not the reference parameter itself.

To understand reference parameters, let's begin with a simple example. In the following, the function **f( )** takes one reference parameter of type **int**.

```
// Using a reference parameter.
#include <iostream.h>

void f(int &i);

main()
{
  int val = 1;

  cout << "Old value for val: " << val << '\n';

  f(val); // pass address of val to f()

  cout << "New value for val: " << val << '\n';

  return 0;
}

void f(int &i)
{
  i = 10; // this modifies calling argument
}
```

This program displays the following output:

    Old value for val: 1
    New value for val: 10

Pay special attention to the definition of **f( )**, shown here:

```
void f(int &i)
{
  i = 10; // this modifies calling argument
}
```

Notice the declaration of **i**. It is preceded by an **&,** which causes it to become a reference parameter. (This declaration is also used in the function's prototype.) Inside the function, the following statement

8

```
i = 10;
```

does *not* cause **i** to be given the value 10. Instead, it causes the variable *referenced* by **i** (in this case, **val**) to be assigned the value 10. Notice that this statement does not use the ***** pointer operator. When you use a reference parameter, the C++ compiler automatically knows that it is an address (i.e., a pointer) and dereferences it for you. In fact, using the ***** would be an error.

Since **i** has been declared as a reference parameter, the compiler will automatically pass **f( )** the *address* of any argument it is called with. Thus, in **main( )**, the statement

```
f(val);   // pass address of val to f()
```

passes the address of **val** (not its value) to **f( )**. There is no need to precede **val** with the **&** operator. (In fact, doing so would be an error.) Since **f( )** receives the address of **val** in the form of a reference, it may modify the value of **val**.

Tip: If you are familiar with the Pascal programming language, it may help you to know that a reference parameter in C++ is similar to a **VAR** parameter in Pascal.

To illustrate reference parameters in actual use—and to fully demonstrate their benefits—the **swap( )** function is rewritten using references in the following program. Look carefully at how **swap( )** is declared and called.

```
#include <iostream.h>

// Declare swap() using reference parameters.
void swap(int &x, int &y);

main()
{
  int i, j;

  i = 10;
  j = 20;
```

```
cout << "initial values of i and j: ";
cout << i << ' ' << j << '\n';
swap(j, i);
cout << "swapped values of i and j: ";
cout << i << ' ' << j << '\n';

return 0;
}

/* Here, swap() is defined as using call-by-reference,
   not call-by-value. Thus, it can exchange the two
   arguments it is called with.
*/
void swap(int &x, int &y)
{
  int temp;

  temp = x; // save the value at address x
  x = y;    // put y into x
  y = temp; // put x into y
}
```

Notice again, that by making **x** and **y** reference parameters, there is no need to use the **&** or the ***** operator. In fact, it would be an error to do so. Remember, the compiler automatically generates the addresses of the arguments used to call **swap( )**, and automatically dereferences **x** and **y**.

Let's review. When you create a reference parameter, that parameter automatically refers to (i.e., implicitly points to) the argument used to call the function. Further, there is no need to apply the **&** operator to an argument. Also, inside the function, the reference parameter is used directly; the ***** operator is not necessary or, in fact, correct. All operations involving the reference parameter automatically refer to the argument used in the call to the function.

Remember: When you assign a value to a reference, you are actually assigning that value to the variable that the reference is pointing to. In the case of function parameters, this will be the variable used in the call to the function.

8

Declaring Reference Parameters

When Bjarne Stroustrup wrote *The C++ Programming Language* (in which he first described C++) in 1986, he introduced a style of declaring reference parameters which some other programmers have adopted. In this approach, the **&** is associated with the type name rather than the variable name. For example, here is another way to write the prototype to **swap( )**:

```
void swap(int& x, int& y);
```

As you can see, the **&** is immediately adjacent to **int** and not to **x**.

Further, some programmers also specify pointers by associating the ***** with the type rather the variable, as shown here:

```
float* p;
```

These types of declarations reflect the desire by some programmers for C++ to contain a separate reference or pointer type. However, the trouble with associating the **&** or ***** with the type rather than the variable is that, according to the formal C++ syntax, neither the **&** nor the ***** is distributive over a list of variables and this can lead to confusing declarations. For example, the following declaration creates one, *not* two, integer pointers. In the following line, **b** is declared as an integer (not an integer pointer) because, as specified by the C++ syntax, when used in a declaration an ***** or an **&** is linked to the individual variable that it precedes, not to the type that it follows.

```
int* a, b;
```

It is important to understand that as far as the C++ compiler is concerned it doesn't matter whether you write **int *p** or **int* p**. Thus, if you prefer to associate the ***** or **&** with the type rather than the variable, feel free to do so. However, to avoid confusion, this book will continue to associate the ***** and the **&** with the variable name that each modifies, rather than the type name.

Tip: The C language does not support references. Thus, the only way to create a call-by-reference in C is to use pointers, as shown earlier in the first version of **swap( )**. When converting C code to C++, you will want to convert these types of parameters to references, where feasible.

Returning References

A function can return a reference. In C++ programming, there are several uses for reference return values. You will see some of these later in this book when you learn about operator overloading. However, reference return values have other important applications which you can use now.

When a function returns a reference, it returns an implicit pointer to its return value. This gives rise to a rather startling possibility: the function can be used on the left side of an assignment statement! For example, consider this simple program:

```cpp
// Returning a reference.
#include <iostream.h>

double &f();

double val = 100.0;

main()
{
  double newval;

  cout << f() << '\n'; // display val's value

  newval = f(); // assign value of val to newval
  cout << newval << '\n'; // display newval's value

  f() = 99.1; // change val's value
  cout << f() << '\n'; // display val's new value

  return 0;
}

double &f()
{
  return val; // return reference to val
}
```

The output of this program is shown here:

```
100
100
99.1
```

8

Let's examine this program closely. At the beginning, **f( )** is declared as returning a reference to a **double**, and the global variable **val** is initialized to 100. Next, the following statement displays the original value of **val**:

```
cout << f() << '\n'; // display val's value
```

When **f( )** is called, it returns a reference to **val**. Because **f( )** is declared as returning a reference, the line

```
return val; // return reference to val
```

automatically returns a reference to **val**. This reference is then used by the **cout** statement to display **val**'s value.

In the line

```
newval = f(); // assign value of val to newval
```

the reference to **val** returned by **f( )** is used to assign the value of **val** to **newval**.

The most interesting line in the program is shown here:

```
f() = 99.1; // change val's value
```

This statement causes the value of **val** to be changed to 99.1. Here is why: Since **f( )** returns a reference to **val**, this reference becomes the target of the assignment statement. Thus, the value of 99.1 is assigned to **val** indirectly, through the reference to it returned by **f( )**.

Here is another sample program that uses a reference return type:

```
#include <iostream.h>

double &change_it(int i); // return a reference

double vals[] = {1.1, 2.2, 3.3, 4.4, 5.5};

main()
{
  int i;

  cout << "Here are the original values: ";
  for(i=0; i<5; i++)
    cout << vals[i] << ' ';
  cout << '\n';
```

```
change_it(1) = 5298.234; // change 2nd element
change_it(3) = -98.8; // change 4th element

cout << "Here are the changed values: ";
for(i=0; i<5; i++)
  cout << vals[i] << ' ';
cout << '\n';

return 0;
}

double &change_it(int i)
{
  return vals[i]; // return a reference to the ith element
}
```

This program changes the values of the second and fourth elements in the **vals** array. The program displays the following output:

```
Here are the orginal values: 1.1 2.2 3.3 4.4 5.5
Here are the changed values: 1.1 5298.23 3.3 -98.8 5.5
```

Let's see how this is accomplished.

As you can see, **change_it( )** is declared as returning a reference to a **double**. Specifically, it returns a reference to the element of **vals** that is specified by its parameter **i**. The reference returned by **change_it( )** is then used in **main( )** to assign a value to that element.

When returning a reference, be careful that the object being referenced does not go out of scope. For example, consider this function:

```
// Error, cannot return reference to local var.
int &f()
{
  int i=10;
  return i;
}
```

In **f( )**, the local variable **i** will go out of scope when the function returns. Therefore, the reference to **i** returned by **f( )** will be undefined. Actually, most compilers will not compile **f( )** as written for precisely this reason. However, this type of problem can be created indirectly, so be careful which object you return a reference to.

8

Creating a Bounded Array

One good use for a reference return type is to create a bounded array. As you
know, in C++, there is no run-time boundary checking on array indexing.
This means that arrays can be overrun. That is, an array index may be
specified that exceeds the size of the array. However, it is possible to prevent
array overruns by creating a *bounded* or *safe array*. When a bounded array is
created, any out-of-bounds index is prevented from indexing the array.

The following program illustrates one way to create a bounded array.

```cpp
#include <iostream.h>

int &put(int i); // put value into the array
int get(int i); // obtain a value from the array

int vals[10];
int error = -1;

main()
{
  int i;

  put(0) = 10; // put values into the array
  put(1) = 20;
  put(9) = 30;

  cout << get(0) << ' ';
  cout << get(1) << ' ';
  cout << get(9) << ' ';

  // now, intentionally generate an error
  put(12) = 1; // Out of Bounds

  return 0;
}

// Put a value into the array.
int &put(int i)
{
  if(i>=0 && i<10)
    return vals[i]; // return a reference to the ith element
  else {
    cout << "Bounds Error!\n";
    return error; // return a reference to error
  }
}
```

```
// Get a value from the array.
int get(int i)
{
  if(i>=0 && i<10)
    return vals[i]; // return the value of the ith element
  else {
    cout << "Bounds Error!\n";
    return error; // return an error
  }
}
```

This program creates a safe array of ten integers. To put a value into the array, use the **put( )** function. To retrieve a value, call **get( )**. For both functions, the index of the desired element is specified as an argument. As the program shows, both **get( )** and **put( )** prevent an array overrun. Notice that **put( )** returns a reference to the specified element, and is thus used on the left side of an assignment statement.

While the approach to implementing a bounded array shown in this example is correct, an even better implementation is possible. As you will see when you learn about operator overloading later in this book, it is possible to create your own custom, bounded arrays that also use standard array notation.

Independent References

An independent reference is simply another name for some other variable.

Even though the reference is included in C++ primarily for supporting call-by-reference parameter passing and for use as a function return type, it is possible to declare a stand-alone reference variable. This is called an *independent reference*. It must be stated at the outset, however, that non-parameter reference variables are seldom used, because they tend to confuse and destructure your program. With these reservations in mind, we will take a short look at them here.

An independent reference must point to some object. Thus, an independent reference must be initialized when it is declared. Generally, this means that it will be assigned the address of a previously declared variable. Once this is done, the name of the reference variable can be used anywhere that the variable it references can be used. In fact, there is virtually no distinction between the two. For example, consider the program shown here:

```
#include <iostream.h>

main()
{
  int j, k;
  int &i = j; // independent reference
```

8

```
  j = 10;

  cout << j << " " << i; // outputs 10 10

  k = 121;
  i = k; // copies k's value into j
         // not k's address

  cout << "\n" << j;  // outputs 121

  return 0;
}
```

This program displays the following output:

```
10 10
121
```

The address pointed to by a reference variable is fixed; it cannot be changed. Thus, when the statement **i = k** is evaluated, it is **k**'s value that is copied into **j** (pointed to by **i**), not its address. For another example, **i++** does *not* cause **i** to point to a new address. Instead, **j** is increased by 1.

Remember: References are not pointers!

As stated earlier, it is generally not a good idea to use independent references, because they are not necessary and they tend to garble your code. Having two names for the same variable is an inherently confusing situation.

A Few Restrictions When Using References

There are some restrictions that apply to reference variables:

♦   You cannot reference a reference variable.

♦   You cannot create arrays of references.

♦   You cannot create a pointer to a reference. That is, you cannot apply the **&** operator to a reference.

♦   References are not allowed on bit-fields. (Bit-fields are discussed later in this book.)

Function Overloading

Function overloading is the mechanism that allows two related functions to share the same name.

In this section you will learn about one of C++'s most exciting features: function overloading. In C++, two or more functions can share the same name as long as their parameter declarations are different. In this situation, the functions that share the same name are said to be *overloaded,* and the process is referred to as *function overloading.* Function overloading is one way that C++ achieves polymorphism.

Let's begin with a short sample program:

```cpp
// Overload a function three times.
#include <iostream.h>

void f(int i); // integer parameter
void f(int i, int j); // two integer parameters
void f(double k); // one double parameter

main()
{
  f(10); // call f(int)

  f(10, 20); // call f(int, int)

  f(12.23); // call f(double)

  return 0;
}

void f(int i)
{
  cout << "In f(int), i is " << i << '\n';
}

void f(int i, int j)
{
  cout << "In f(int, int), i is " << i;
  cout << ", j is " << j << '\n';
}

void f(double k)
{
  cout << "In f(double), k is " << k << '\n';
}
```

This program produces the following output:

8

```
In   f(int),   i   is   10
In   f(int,   int),   i   is   10,   j   is   20
In   f(double),   k   is   12.23
```

As you can see, **f( )** is overloaded three times. The first version takes one integer parameter, the second version requires two integer parameters, and the third version has one **double** parameter. Because the parameter list for each version is different, the compiler is able to call the correct version of each function. In general, to overload a function, you simply declare different versions of it.

The compiler uses the type and/or number of arguments as its guide to determining which version of an overloaded function to call. Thus, overloaded functions must differ in the type and/or number of their parameters. While overloaded functions may have different return types, the return type alone is not sufficient to distinguish two versions of a function. (Return types do not provide sufficient information in all cases for the compiler to correctly decide which function to use.)

To better understand the benefit of function overloading, consider these three functions, which are located in the standard library: **abs( )**, **labs( )**, and **fabs( )**. These functions were first defined by the C language and, for compatibility, are also included in C++. The **abs( )** function returns the absolute value of an integer, **labs( )** returns the absolute value of a **long**, and **fabs( )** returns the absolute value of a **double**. In C (which does not support function overloading), three slightly different names must be used to represent these essentially similar tasks. This makes the situation more complex, conceptually, than it actually is. Even though the underlying concept of each function is the same, the programmer has three names to remember, not just one. However, in C++ it is possible to use just one name for all three functions, as illustrated in this example:

```
// Overloading abs().
#include <iostream.h>

// abs() is overloaded three ways.
int abs(int i);
double abs(double d);
long abs(long l);

main()
{
  cout << abs(-10) << "\n";

  cout << abs(-11.0) << "\n";

  cout << abs(-9L) << "\n";
```

```
    return 0;
}

int abs(int i)
{
  cout << "using integer abs()\n";

  if(i<0) return -i;
  else return i;
}

double abs(double d)
{
  cout << "using double abs()\n";

  if(d<0.0) return -d;
  else return d;
}

long abs(long l)
{
  cout << "using long abs()\n";

  if(l<0) return -l;
  else return l;
}
```

This program creates three similar but different functions called **abs**, each of which returns the absolute value of its argument. The compiler knows which function to use in each given situation because of the type of the argument. The value of overloading is that it allows related sets of functions to be accessed using a common name. Thus, the name **abs** represents the *general action* which is being performed. It is left to the compiler to choose the right *specific* version for a particular circumstance. You, the programmer, need only remember the general action being performed. Therefore, through the application of polymorphism, three things to remember have been reduced to one. Although this example is fairly simple, if you expand the concept, you can see how overloading can help you manage greater complexity.

When you overload a function, each version of that function can perform any activity you desire. That is, there is no rule stating that overloaded functions must relate to one another. However, from a stylistic point of view, function overloading implies a relationship. Thus, while you can use the same name to overload unrelated functions, you should not. For example, you could use the name **sqr( )** to create functions which return the *square* of an **int** and the *square root* of a **double**. These two operations are

8

fundamentally different, however, and applying function overloading in this manner defeats its original purpose. (In fact, programming in this manner is considered to be extremely bad style!) In practice, you should overload only closely related operations.

The overload Anachronism

When C++ was created, overloaded functions had to be explicitly declared as such with the **overload** keyword. Although it is no longer required, you may still find **overload** used in some older C++ programs. While most C++ compilers still accept its use, **overload** is outmoded.

The general form of **overload** is shown here,

overload *func-name*;

where *func-name* is the name of the function being overloaded. This statement must precede the overloaded declarations. (Generally, it is found near the top of the program.) For example, if the function **abs( )** is being overloaded, then this line will be included in the program:

```
overload abs;
```

If you encounter **overload** declarations when working with older programs, you can simply remove them; they are no longer needed. Because **overload** is an anachronism, you should avoid its use in new C++ programs. In fact, it is very likely that future versions of C++ will not accept it.

Default Function Arguments

The last function-related feature discussed in this chapter is the *default argument*. In C++, you can give a parameter a default value that is automatically used when no argument corresponding to that parameter is specified in a call to a function. Default arguments can be used to simplify calls to complex functions. Also, they can sometimes be used as a "shorthand" form of function overloading.

A default argument is specified in a manner syntactically similar to a variable initialization. Consider the following example, which declares **myfunc( )** as taking one **double** argument with a default value of 0.0, and one character argument with a default value of 'X'.

```
void myfunc(double num = 0.0, char ch = 'X')
{
   .
   .
   .
}
```

Now, **myfunc( )** can be called by one of the three methods shown here:

```
myfunc(198.234, 'A');  // pass explicit values

myfunc(10.1); // pass num a value, let ch default

myfunc();    // let both num and ch default
```

A default argument is a value that will automatically be passed to a function when no explicit argument is specified.

The first call passes the value 198.234 to **num** and 'A' to **ch**. The second automatically gives **num** the value 10.1 and allows **ch** to default to 'X'. Finally, the third call causes both **num** and **ch** to default.

One reason that default arguments are included in C++ is that they enable the programmer to manage greater complexity. In order to handle the widest variety of situations, quite frequently a function will contain more parameters than are required for its most common usage. Thus, when the default arguments apply, you need remember and specify only the arguments that are meaningful to the exact situation, not all those needed for the most general case.

A simple illustration of how useful a default function argument can be is shown by the **clrscr( )** function in the following program. The **clrscr( )** function clears the screen by outputting a series of linefeeds (not the most efficient way, but sufficient for this example!). Since a very common video mode displays 25 lines of text, the default argument of 25 is provided. However, since some terminals can display more or less than 25 lines (usually depending upon what type of video mode is used), you can override the default argument by specifying another one explicitly.

```
#include <iostream.h>

void clrscr(int size=25);

main()
{
  int i;
```

8

```
  for(i=0; i<30; i++ ) cout << i << '\n';
  clrscr( ); // clears 25 lines

  for(i=0; i<30; i++ ) cout << i << '\n';
  clrscr(10); // clears 10 lines

  return 0;
}

void clrscr(int size)
{
   for(; size; size--) cout << '\n';
}
```

As this program illustrates, when the default value is appropriate to the situation, no argument need be specified when calling **clrscr( )**. However, it is still possible to override the default and give **size** a different value.

Two important points to remember about creating a function that has default argument values is that the default values must be specified only once, and that this must happen the first time the function is declared within the file. In the preceding example, the default argument was specified in **clrscr( )**'s prototype. If you try to specify new (or even the same) default values in **clrscr( )**'s definition, the compiler will display an error message, and will not compile your program.

Even though default arguments cannot be redefined within a program, you can specify different default arguments for each version of an overloaded function; that is, different versions of the overloaded function can have different default arguments.

It is important to understand that all parameters that take default values must appear to the right of those that do not. For example, the following prototype is invalid:

```
// wrong!
void f(int a = 1, int b);
```

Once you've begun defining parameters that take default values, you cannot specify a non-defaulting parameter. That is, a declaration like the following is also wrong, and will not compile:

```
int myfunc(float f, char *str, int i=10, int j);
```

Since **i** has been given a default value, **j** must be given one too.

Default Arguments Versus Overloading

As mentioned at the beginning of this section, one application of default arguments is as a shorthand form of function overloading. To see why this is the case, imagine that you want to create two customized versions of the standard **strcat( )** function. One version will operate like **strcat( )** and concatenate the entire contents of one string to the end of another. The other version will take a third argument that specifies the number of characters to concatenate. That is, this version will only concatenate a specified number of characters from one string to the end of another.

Assuming that you call your customized functions **mystrcat( )**, they will have the following prototypes:

```
void mystrcat(char *s1, char *s2, int len);
void mystrcat(char *s1, char *s2);
```

The first version will copy **len** characters from **s2** to the end of **s1**. The second version will copy the entire string pointed to by **s2** onto the end of the string pointed to by **s1** and will operate like **strcat( )**.

While it would not be wrong to implement two versions of **mystrcat( )** to create the two versions that you desire, there is an easier way. Using a default argument, you can create only one version of **mystrcat( )** that performs both functions. The following program demonstrates this.

```
// A customized version of strcat().
#include <iostream.h>
#include <string.h>

void mystrcat(char *s1, char *s2, int len = 0);

main()
{
  char str1[80] = "This is a test";
  char str2[80] = "0123456789";

  mystrcat(str1, str2, 5); // concatenate 5 chars
  cout << str1 << '\n';

  strcpy(str1, "this is a test"); // reset str1

  mystrcat(str1, str2); // concatenate entire string
  cout << str1 << '\n';

  return 0;
}
```

8

```
// A custom version of strcat().
void mystrcat(char *s1, char *s2, int len)
{
  // find end of s1
  while(*s1) s1++;

  if(len==0) len = strlen(s2);

  while(*s2 && len) {
    *s1 = *s2; // copy chars
    s1++;
    s2++;
    len--;
  }

  *s1 = '\0'; // null terminate s1
}
```

Here, **mystrcat( )** concatenates up to **len** characters from the string pointed to by **s2** onto the end of the string pointed to by **s1**. However, if **len** is zero, as it will be when it is allowed to default, **mystrcat( )** concatenates the entire string pointed to by **s2** onto **s1**. (Thus, when **len** is zero, the function operates like the standard **strcat( )** function.) By using a default argument for **len**, it is possible to combine both operations into one function. As this example illustrates, default arguments sometimes provide a shorthand form of function overloading.

Using Default Arguments Correctly

Although default arguments can be a very powerful tool when used correctly, they can also be misused. The point of default arguments is to allow a function to perform its job in an efficient, easy-to-use manner while still allowing considerable flexibility. Towards this end, all default arguments should reflect the way a function is generally used, or a reasonable alternate usage. When there is no single value that is normally associated with a parameter, then there is no reason to declare a default argument. In fact, declaring default arguments when there is insufficient basis for doing so destructures your code, because they are liable to mislead and confuse anyone reading your program.

Function Overloading and Ambiguity

Before concluding this chapter, we must discuss a type of error unique to C++: *ambiguity*. It is possible to create a situation in which the compiler is unable to choose between two (or more) correctly overloaded functions.

Ambiguity results when the compiler cannot resolve the difference between two overloaded functions.

When this happens, the situation is said to be *ambiguous*. Ambiguous statements are errors, and programs containing ambiguity will not compile.

By far the main cause of ambiguity involves C++'s automatic type conversions. C++ automatically attempts to convert the type of the arguments used to call a function into the type of the parameters defined by the function. Here is an example:

```
int myfunc(double d);
   .
   .
   .
cout << myfunc('c');  // not an error, conversion applied
```

As the comment indicates, this is not an error, because C++ automatically converts the character **c** into its **double** equivalent. Actually, in C++, very few type conversions of this sort are disallowed. While automatic type conversions are convenient, however, they are also a prime cause of ambiguity. Consider the following program:

```
// Overloading ambiguity
#include <iostream.h>

float myfunc(float i);
double myfunc(double i);

main()
{
  // unambiguous, calls myfunc(double)
  cout << myfunc(10.1) << " ";

  // ambiguous
  cout << myfunc(10);

  return 0;
}

float myfunc(float i)
{
  return i;
}

double myfunc(double i)
{
  return -i;
}
```

8

Here, **myfunc( )** is overloaded so that it can take arguments of either type **float** or type **double**. In the unambiguous line, **myfunc(double)** is called because, unless explicitly specified as **float**, all floating point constants in C++ are automatically of type **double**. However, when **myfunc( )** is called using the integer 10, ambiguity is introduced because the compiler has no way of knowing whether it should be converted to a **float** or to a **double**. Both are valid conversions. This confusion causes an error message to be displayed and prevents the program from compiling.

The central issue illustrated by the preceding example is that it is not the overloading of **myfunc( )** relative to **double** and **float** that causes the ambiguity. Rather, the confusion is caused by the specific call to **myfunc( )** using an indeterminate type of argument. Put differently, it is not the overloading of **myfunc( )** that is in error, but the specific invocation.

Here is another example of ambiguity caused by the automatic type conversions in C++.

```
#include <iostream.h>

char myfunc(unsigned char ch);
char myfunc(char ch);

main()
{
  cout << myfunc('c');  // this calls myfunc(char)
  cout << myfunc(88) << " "; // ambiguous

  return 0;
}

char myfunc(unsigned char ch)
{
  return ch-1;
}


char myfunc(char ch)
{
  return ch+1;
}
```

In C++, **unsigned char** and **char** are *not* inherently ambiguous. (They are different types.) However, when **myfunc( )** is called with the integer 88, the compiler does not know which function to call. That is, should 88 be converted into a **char** or **unsigned char**? Both are valid conversions.

Another way you can cause ambiguity is by using default arguments in overloaded functions. To see how, examine this program:

```
#include <iostream.h>

int myfunc(int i);
int myfunc(int i, int j=1);

main()
{
  cout << myfunc(4, 5) << " "; // unambiguous
  cout << myfunc(10); // ambiguous

  return 0;
}

int myfunc(int i)
{
  return i;
}

int myfunc(int i, int j)
{
  return i*j;
}
```

Here, in the first call to **myfunc( )** two arguments are specified; therefore no ambiguity is introduced, and **myfunc(int i, int j)** is called. However, the second call to **myfunc( )** results in ambiguity, because the compiler does not know whether to call the version of **myfunc( )** that takes one argument, or to apply the default to the version that takes two arguments.

As you continue to write your own C++ programs, be prepared to encounter ambiguity errors. Unfortunately, until you become more experienced, you will find that they are fairly easy to create.

Chapter

9

More Data Types and Operators

Before we move on to the more advanced features of C++, now is a good time to return to data types and operators, and to tie together a few loose ends. In addition to the data types and operators that you have been using so far, C++ supports several other data types. Some of these consist of modifiers added to the types you already know about. Other data types include enumerations, **typedef**s, and the new **bool** type.

C++ also includes several additional operators that greatly expand its scope and ease of application to various programming tasks. These include the bitwise, shift, **?**, and **sizeof** operators. Also, two special operators, **new** and **delete**, are discussed in this chapter. These operators support C++'s dynamic memory allocation system.

Let's begin with the type modifiers used in C++.

The Access Modifiers

The access modifiers control how a variable can be accessed.

C++ has two type modifiers that are used to control the ways in which variables can be accessed or modified. These modifiers are **const** and **volatile**. Commonly called the *access modifiers*, they precede the base type and variable name.

Note: In the draft ANSI C++ standard, the formal name for the access modifiers is *cv-qualifiers*. You may find this name used in some C++ literature. However, most programmers use the term *access modifiers* instead.

const

Variables declared with the **const** modifier cannot have their values changed during the execution of your program. You may give a variable declared as **const** an initial value, however. For example,

```
const float version =  3.2;
```

creates a **float** variable called **version** that contains the value 3.2 and that may not be modified by your program. The variable can, however, be used in other types of expressions. A **const** variable will receive its value either from an explicit initialization or by some hardware-dependent means. Applying the **const** modifier to a variable's declaration ensures that the variable will not be modified by other parts of your program.

*The **const** modifier prevents a variable from being modified by your program.*

The **const** modifier has several important uses. Perhaps the most common is to create **const** pointer parameters. A **const** pointer parameter prevents the object pointed to by a pointer parameter from being modified by a function. That is, when a pointer parameter is preceded by **const**, no statement in the function can modify the variable pointed to by that parameter. For example, the **code( )** function in this short program shifts each letter in a message by one (so that an **A** becomes a **B**, and so forth), thus displaying the message in code. The use of **const** in the parameter declaration prevents the code inside the function from modifying the object pointed to by the parameter.

```
#include <iostream.h>

void code(const char *str);
```

```
main()
{
  code("this is a test");

  return 0;
}

void code(const char *str)
{
  while(*str) {
    cout << (char) (*str+1);
    str++;
  }
}
```

Since **str** is declared as being a **const** pointer, the function can make no
changes to the string pointed to by **str**. Notice that if **code( )** were written
as shown in the next example, an error would result, and the program would
not compile.

```
// This is wrong.
void code(const char *str)
{
  while(*str) {
    *str = *str + 1; // Error, can't modify
    cout << (char) *str;
    str++;
  }
}
```

const can also be used on reference parameters to prevent functions from
modifying the variables that they reference. For example, the following
program is incorrect because **f( )** attempts to modify the variable referenced
by **i**.

```
// const references cannot be modified.
#include <iostream.h>
void f(const int &i);

main()
{
  int k = 10;

  f(k);
  return 0;
}
```

9

```
void f(const int &i)
{
  i = 100; // Error; cannot modify a const reference.
  cout <<  i;
}
```

Another use for **const** is to provide verification that your program does not, in fact, modify a variable. Remember, a variable of type **const** can be modified by something outside your program. For example, a hardware device may set its value. By declaring a variable as **const**, you can prove that any changes to that variable occur because of external events.

Finally, **const** is used to create named constants. Often programs will require the same value for many different purposes. For example, several different arrays may be declared that must all be the same size. When such a "magic number" is needed, one good way to implement it is as a **const** variable. Then you can use the name of the variable instead of the value and, if that value needs to be changed, you will only need to change it in one place in your program. The following example gives you the flavor of this application of **const**:

```
#include <iostream.h>

const int size = 10;

main()
{
  int A1[size], A2[size], A3[size];

  // ...
}
```

In this example, if you need to use a new size for the arrays, you need only change the declaration of **size** and recompile your program. All three arrays will then automatically be resized.

volatile

The **volatile** modifier tells the compiler that a variable's value may be changed in ways not explicitly specified by the program. For example, the address of a global variable may be passed to an interrupt-driven clock routine that updates the variable with each tick of the clock. In this situation, the contents of the variable are altered without the use of any explicit assignment statements in the program. The reason the external alteration of a variable may be important is that a C++ compiler is permitted to automatically optimize certain expressions, on the assumption that the content of a variable is unchanged if it does not occur on the left side of an assignment statement. However, if factors beyond program control change the value of a variable, then problems can occur.

*The **volatile** modifier informs the compiler that a variable may be changed by factors outside of the program.*

For example, in the following fragment, assume that **clock** is being updated every tenth second by the computer's clock mechanism. However, since **clock** is not declared as **volatile**, the fragment will not always work properly. (Pay special attention to the lines labeled A and B.)

```
int clock, timer;
// ...
timer = clock;                              // line A
// ... do something
cout << "elapsed type is " << clock-timer; // line B
```

In this fragment, the value of **clock** is obtained when it is assigned to **timer** in line A. However, because **clock** is not declared as **volatile**, C++ is free to optimize the code in such a way that the value of **clock** is not reexamined in the **cout** statement in line B. (That is, the compiler simply reuses the value it obtained in line A.) However, if a clock tick occurs between lines A and B, then the value of **clock** will have changed, and line B will not produce the correct output.

To solve this problem, you must declare **clock** to be **volatile**, as shown here:

```
volatile int clock;
```

Now, **clock**'s value will be obtained each time it is referenced.

Although it seems strange at first thought, it is possible to use **const** and **volatile** together. For example, the following declaration is perfectly valid. It creates a **const** pointer to a **volatile** object.

```
const volatile unsigned char *port;
```

Storage Class Specifiers

There are five storage class specifiers supported by C++. They are:

The storage class specifiers determine how a variable is stored.

auto
extern
register
static
mutable

These are used to tell the compiler how a variable should be stored. The storage specifier precedes the rest of the variable declaration.

The **mutable** specifier applies only to **class** objects, which are discussed later in this book. Each of the other specifiers is examined here.

auto

The **auto** specifier declares a local variable. However, it is rarely (if ever) used, because local variables are **auto** by default. It is extremely rare to see this keyword used in a program.

extern

All the programs that you have worked with so far have been quite small. However, in reality, computer programs tend to be much larger. As a program file grows, the compilation time eventually becomes long enough to be annoying. When this happens, you should break your program into two or more separate files. Once you divide your program this way, small changes to one file will not require that the entire program be recompiled. The multiple file approach can yield a substantial time savings with large projects. The **extern** keyword helps support this approach. Let's see how.

In programs that consist of two or more files, each file must know the names and types of the global variables used by the program. However, you cannot simply declare copies of the global variables in each file. The reason for this is that in C++, your program can only include one copy of each global variable. Therefore, if you try to declare the global variables needed by your program in each file, you will have trouble. When the linker tries to link together the files, it will find the duplicated global variables, and will not link your program. The solution to this dilemma is to declare all of the global variables in one file and use extern declarations in the others, as shown in Figure 9-1.

```
File One                        File Two

int x, y;                       extern int x, y;

char ch;                        extern char ch;

main()                          func22()
{                               {
  // ...                          x = y/10;
}                               }

func1()                         func23()
{                               {
  x = 123;                        y = 10;
}                               }
```

Using global variables in separately compiled modules
Figure 9-1.

File One declares and defines **x**, **y**, and **ch**. In File Two, the global variable list is copied from File One, and the **extern** specifier is added to the declarations. The **extern** specifier allows a variable to be made known to a module, but does not actually create that variable. In other words, **extern** lets the compiler know what the types and names are for these global variables without actually creating storage for them again. When the linker links the two modules together, all references to the external variables are resolved.

*The **extern** specifier declares a variable, but does not allocate storage for it.*

While we haven't yet worried about the distinction between the declaration and the definition of a variable, it is important here. A *declaration* declares the name and type of a variable. A *definition* causes storage to be allocated for the variable. In most cases, variable declarations are also definitions. However, by preceding a variable name with the **extern** specifier, you can declare a variable without defining it.

There is one additional, rarely used application of **extern**. When the body of a function uses a global variable, the global variable may be declared as **extern** inside the function. (Frankly, however, it is rare to see this done.) The following program fragment shows the use of this option:

```
int first, last;  /* global definition of first
                     and last */


main()
{
  extern int first;  /* optional use of the
                        extern declaration */

  // ...
}
```

Here, **extern** simply tells the compiler that **first** inside **main( )**, refers to the global variable **first**. However, using **extern** this way is redundant, because whenever the compiler encounters a variable that has not been declared, the compiler automatically determines whether it matches any of the global variables. If it does, then the compiler will assume that the global variable is the variable being used.

static Variables

Variables of type **static** are permanent variables within their own function or file. They differ from global variables because they are not known outside their function or file. Because **static** affects local variables differently than it does global ones, local and global variables will be examined separately here.

static Local Variables

When the **static** modifier is applied to a local variable, permanent storage for the variable is allocated in much the same way that it is for a global variable. This allows a **static** variable to maintain its value between function calls. (That is, its value is not lost when the function returns, unlike the value of a normal local variable.) The key difference between a **static** local variable and a global variable is that the **static** local variable is known only to the block in which it is declared. Thus, a **static** local variable is, more or less, a global variable that has restricted scope.

To declare a **static** variable, precede its type with the word **static**. For example, this statement declares **count** as a static variable.

```
static int count;
```

A **static** variable may be given an initial value. For example, this statement gives **count** an initial value of 200.

```
static int count = 200;
```

Local **static** variables are initialized only once, when program execution begins, not each time the function in which they are declared is entered.

A ***static*** local
variable
maintains its
value between
function calls.

It is important to the creation of stand-alone functions that **static** local variables are available, because there are several types of routines that must preserve a value between calls. If **static** variables were not allowed, then globals would have to be used—opening the door to possible side effects.

To see an example of a **static** variable, try this program:

```
/* Compute a running average of numbers entered by
   the user.
*/
#include <iostream.h>

int r_avg(int i);

main()
{
  int num;

  do {
    cout << "enter numbers (-1 to quit): ";
    cin >> num;
    cout << "running average is: " << r_avg(num);
    cout << '\n';
  } while(num > -1);
```

```
    return 0;
}

int r_avg(int i)
{
  static int sum=0, count=0;

  sum = sum + i;

  count++;

  return sum / count;
}
```

Here, the local variables **sum** and **count** are both declared as **static** and initialized to 0. Remember, for **static** variables the initialization only occurs once—not each time the function is entered. The program uses **r_avg( )** to compute and report the current average of the numbers entered by the user. Because both **sum** and **count** are **static**, they will maintain their values between calls, causing the program to work properly. To prove to yourself that the **static** modifier is necessary, try removing it and running the program. As you can see, the program no longer works correctly, because the running total is lost each time **r_avg( )** returns.

static Global Variables

A **static** global variable is known only to the file in which the variable is declared.

When the **static** specifier is applied to a global variable, it instructs the compiler to create a global variable that is known only to the file in which the **static** global variable is declared. This means that even though the variable is global, other functions in other files may have no knowledge of it and cannot alter its contents directly; thus it is not subject to side effects. Therefore, for the few situations where a local **static** cannot do the job, you can create a small file that contains only the functions that need the global **static** variable, separately compile that file, and use it without fear of side effects.

To see an example of this, create the two files shown here:

```
// ---------------------- First File ----------------------

#include <iostream.h>

int r_avg(int i);
void reset();

main()
{
```

```
  int num;

  do {
    cout << "enter numbers (-1 to quit, -2 to reset): ";
    cin >> num;
    if(num==-2) {
      reset();
      continue;
    }
    cout << "running average is: " << r_avg(num);
    cout << '\n';
  } while(num != -1);

  return 0;
}

// --------------------- Second File ---------------------

static int sum=0, count=0;

int r_avg(int i)
{
  sum = sum + i;

  count++;

  return sum / count;
}

void reset()
{
  sum = 0;
  count = 0;
}
```

Compile and link the two files. In this version of the program, the variables **sum** and **count** are global **static**s that are restricted to the second file. Thus, they may be accessed by both **r_avg( )** and **reset( )** in the second file. This allows them to be reset so that a second set of numbers can be averaged. However, no functions outside the second file can access those variables. When you run this program, you can reset the average by entering –2. You should try this now. You might also try to access either **sum** or **count** from the first file. (You will receive an error message.)

To review: The name of a local **static** variable is known only to the function or block of code in which it is declared, and the name of a global **static** variable is known only to the file in which it resides. In essence, the **static** modifier allows variables to exist that are known to the functions that need them, thereby controlling and limiting the possibility of side effects. Variables of type **static** enable you, the programmer, to hide portions of your program from other portions. This can be a tremendous advantage when you are trying to manage a very large and complex program.

Register Variables

Perhaps the most common storage class specifier is **register**. The **register** modifier tells the compiler to store a variable in such a way that it can be accessed as quickly as possible. Typically, this means storing the variable either in a register of the CPU or in cache memory. As you probably know, accessing the registers of the CPU (or cache memory) is fundamentally faster than is accessing the main memory of the computer. Thus, a variable stored in a register will be accessed much more quickly than if that variable had been stored in RAM, for example. Because the speed by which variables can be accessed has a profound effect on the overall speed of your programs, the careful use of **register** is an important programming technique.

The **register** specifier requests that a variable be optimized for access speed.

Technically, **register** is only a request to the compiler, which the compiler is free to ignore. The reason for this is easy to understand: there is a finite number of registers (or fast-access memory), and these may differ from environment to environment. Thus, if the compiler runs out of fast access memory, it simply stores the variable normally. Generally, this causes no harm, but of course the **register** advantage is lost.

Since only a limited number of variables can actually be granted the fastest access, it is important to choose carefully those to which you apply the **register** modifier. (Only by choosing the right variables can you gain the greatest increase in performance.) In general, the more often a variable is accessed, the more benefit there will be to optimizing it as a **register** variable. For this reason, variables that control or are accessed within loops are good variables to declare as **register**. The following example uses a **register** variable of type **int** to control a loop. This function computes the result of m^e for integers.

```
int_pwr(register int m, register int e)
{
  register int temp;

  temp = 1;
  for( ;e ;e--) temp = temp * m;
  return temp;
}
```

9

The Origins of the register Modifier

The **register** modifier was first defined by the C language. It originally applied only to variables of type **int** and **char**. It caused variables of these types to be held in the register of the CPU rather than in memory, where normal variables are stored. This meant that operations on **register** variables could occur much faster than on variables stored in memory, because no memory access was required to determine or modify their values. (A memory access takes much longer than a register access.)

When C was standardized, however, a decision was made to expand the definition of **register**. According to the ANSI C standard, the **register** modifier may be applied to any type of data. It simply tells the compiler to make access to a **register** type as fast as possible. For situations involving characters and integers, this means putting them into a CPU register, so the traditional definition still holds. Since C++ is built upon ANSI standard C, it has also adopted the expanded definition of **register**.

In this example, **m** and **temp** are also declared as **register**, because they are used within the loop.

As stated, the exact number of **register** variables that will actually be optimized within any one function is determined by both the processor type and the specific implementation of C++ that you are using. You can generally count on at least two. You don't have to worry about declaring too many **register** variables, though, because C++ will automatically make register variables into non-register variables when the limit is reached. (This is done to ensure portability of C++ code across a broad line of processors.)

To show you the difference that register variables can make, the following program measures the execution time of two **for** loops that differ only in the type of variable that controls them. This program uses the **clock( )** function found in C++'s standard library. The **clock( )** function returns the number of system clock ticks that have elapsed since the program began running. It requires the header file **time.h**.

```
/* This program shows the difference a register variable
   can make to the speed of program execution.
*/

#include <iostream.h>
```

```
#include <time.h>

unsigned int i; // non-register
unsigned int delay;

main()
{
  register unsigned int j;
  long start, end;

  start = clock();
  for(delay=0; delay<10; delay++)
    for(i=0; i<64000; i++);
  end = clock();
  cout << "Number of clock ticks for non-register loop: ";
  cout << end-start << '\n';

  start = clock();
  for(delay=0; delay<10; delay++)
    for(j=0; j<64000; j++) ;
  end = clock();
  cout << "Number of clock ticks for register loop: ";
  cout << end-start << '\n';

  return 0;
}
```

When you run this program, you will find that the register-controlled loop executes in about half the time of the non-register-controlled loop.

Enumerations

In C++, you can define a list of named integer constants. Such a list is called an *enumeration*. These constants can then be used anywhere that an integer can. Enumerations are defined using the keyword **enum**, and this general format:

   enum *enum-type-name* { *enumeration list* } *variable-list;*

The enumeration list is a comma-separated list of names that represent the values a variable of the enumeration type can have. The variable list is optional because variables may be declared later using the enumeration type name. The following fragment defines an enumeration called **apple**, and two variables of type **apple** called **red** and **yellow**.

```
enum apple {Jonathan, Golden_Del, Red_Del, Winesap,
            Cortland, McIntosh} red, yellow;
```

9

Once you have defined an enumeration, you can declare additional variables of its type using its name. For example, this statement declares one variable, called **fruit**, of enumeration **apple**.

```
apple fruit;
```

The statement can also be written like this:

```
enum apple fruit;
```

*The **enum** keyword declares an enumeration.*

However, the use of **enum** here is redundant. In C (which also supports enumerations), this second form was required, so you may see it used in older programs.

Assuming the preceding declarations, the following types of statements are perfectly valid:

```
fruit = Winesap;
if(fruit==Red_Del) cout << "Red Delicious\n";
```

The key point to understand about an enumeration is that each of the symbols stands for an integer value. As such, they can be used in any integer expression. Unless initialized otherwise, the value of the first enumeration symbol is 0, the value of the second symbol is 1, and so forth. Therefore,

```
cout << Jonathan << ' ' << Cortland;
```

displays **0 4** on the screen.

It is possible to specify the value of one or more of the symbols by using an initializer. This is done by following the symbol with an equal sign and an integer value. Whenever an initializer is used, each symbol that appears after it is assigned a value 1 greater than the previous initialization value. For example, the following statement assigns the value of 10 to **Winesap**.

```
enum    apple {Jonathan, Golden_Del, Red_Del, Winesap=10,
               Cortland, McIntosh};
```

Now, the values of these symbols are as follows:

Jonathan	0
Golden_Del	1
Red_Del	2
Winesap	10
Cortland	11
McIntosh	12

One common, but erroneous, assumption sometimes made about enumerations is that the symbols can be input and output as a string. This is not the case. For example, the following code fragment will not perform as desired.

```
// This will not print "McIntosh" on the screen.

fruit = McIntosh;

cout << fruit;
```

Remember, the symbol **McIntosh** is simply a name for an integer; it is not a string. Thus, the preceding code will display the numeric value of **McIntosh**, not the string "McIntosh". Actually, to create code that inputs and outputs enumeration symbols as strings is quite tedious. For example, the following code is needed in order to display, in words, the kind of apple that **fruit** contains.

```
switch(fruit) {
  case Jonathan: cout << "Jonathan";
    break;
  case Golden_Del: cout << "Golden Delicious";
    break;
  case Red_Del: cout << "Red Delicious";
    break;
  case Winesap: cout << "Winesap";
    break;
  case Cortland: cout << "Cortland";
    break;
  case McIntosh: cout << "McIntosh";
    break;
}
```

Sometimes it is possible to declare an array of strings and use the enumeration value as an index in order to translate an enumeration value into its corresponding string. For example, the following program prints the names of the apples.

```
#include <iostream.h>

enum  apple {Jonathan, Golden_Del, Red_Del, Winesap,
             Cortland, McIntosh};

char name[][20] = {
  "Jonathan",
  "Golden Delicious",
  "Red Delicious",
```

9

```
    "Winesap",
    "Cortland",
    "McIntosh"
};

main()
{
  apple fruit;

  for(fruit=Jonathan; fruit<=McIntosh; fruit++)
    cout << name[fruit] << '\n';

  return 0;
}
```

Given the fact that enumeration values must be converted manually to their human-readable string values, they find their greatest use in routines that do not make such conversions. It is common to see an enumeration used to define a compiler's symbol table, for example.

bool

While not part of the original specification for C++, the ANSI C++ standards committee has added the **bool** data type to C++. **bool**, which is short for Boolean, may be used to create variables that can only hold two values: **true** and **false**. (Both **true** and **false** are also new keywords added by the ANSI C++ standards committee.) Variables of type **bool** may be used in conditional expressions, such as the **if**. At the time of this writing, no commonly available compilers support the **bool** data type, or **true** or **false**. (Of course, future compilers will.) As such, they will not be used extensively in this book. However, check your compiler user's manual to see if your compiler supports the **bool** data type.

typedef

C++ allows you to define new data type names with the **typedef** keyword. When you use **typedef**, you are not actually creating a new data type, but rather defining a new name for an existing type. This process can help make machine-dependent programs more portable; only the **typedef** statements have to be changed. It also can help you to self-document your code by allowing descriptive names for the standard data types. The general form of the **typedef** statement is

typedef *type name*;

where type is any valid data type and *name* is the new name for this type. The new name you define is in addition to, not a replacement for, the existing type name.

typedef lets you create a new name for an existing data type.

For example, you could create a new name for **float** using

```
typedef float balance;
```

This statement would tell the compiler to recognize **balance** as another name for **float**. Next, you could create a **float** variable using **balance**:

```
balance over_due;
```

Here, **over_due** is a floating point variable of type **balance**, which is another name for **float**.

More Operators

Earlier in this book, you learned about the more commonplace C++ operators. Unlike many computer languages, C++ provides several special operators that greatly increase its power and flexibility. These operators are the subject of the remainder of this chapter.

Bitwise Operators

The bitwise operators operate upon individual bits.

Since C++ is designed to allow full access to the computer's hardware, it was important that it have the ability to operate directly upon the bits within a byte or word. Towards this end, C++ contains the bitwise operators. *Bitwise operations* refer to the testing, setting, or shifting of the actual bits in a byte or word, which correspond to C++'s character and integer types. Bitwise operations may not be used on **float**, **double**, **long double**, **void** or other more complex data types. Bitwise operations are important in a wide variety of systems-level programming in which status information from a device must be interrogated or constructed. Table 9-1 lists the bitwise operators. Let's now look at each operator in turn.

Operator	Action
&	AND
|	OR
^	exclusive OR (XOR)
~	one's complement (NOT)
>>	shift right
<<	shift left

The Bitwise Operators
Table 9-1.

9

AND, OR, XOR, and NOT

The bitwise AND, OR, and one's complement (NOT) are governed by the same truth table as their logical equivalents, except that they work on a bit-by-bit level. The exclusive OR (XOR) operates according to the following truth table:

p	q	p ^ q
0	0	0
1	0	1
1	1	0
0	1	1

As the table indicates, the outcome of an XOR is true only if exactly one of the operands is true; it is false otherwise.

In terms of its most common usage, you can think of the bitwise AND as a way to turn bits off. That is, any bit that is 0 in either operand will cause the corresponding bit in the outcome to be set to 0. For example,

```
      1 1 0 1  0 0 1 1
      1 0 1 0  1 0 1 0
  &   --------------------
      1 0 0 0  0 0 1 0
```

The following program reads characters from the keyboard and turns any lowercase letter into uppercase by resetting the sixth bit to 0. As the ASCII character set is defined, the lowercase letters are the same as the uppercase ones except that that they are greater in value by exactly 32. Hence, to uppercase a lowercase letter, you need to turn off the sixth bit, as this program illustrates.

```cpp
#include <iostream.h>

main()
{
  char ch;

  do {
    cin >> ch;

    // This statement turns off the 6th bit.
    ch = ch & 223;

    cout << ch;
```

```
  } while(ch!='Q');

  return 0;
}
```

The value 223 used in the AND statement is the decimal representation of 1101 1111. Hence, the AND operation leaves all bits in **ch** unchanged except for the sixth one, which is set to zero.

The AND operator is also useful when you want to determine whether a bit is on or off. For example, this statement checks to see if bit 4 in **status** is set.

```
if(status & 8) cout << "bit 4 is on";
```

The reason 8 is used is that in binary it is represented as 0000 1000. That is, the number 8 translated into binary has only the fourth bit set. Therefore, the **if** statement can succeed only when bit 4 of **status** is also on. An interesting use of this procedure is the **disp_binary( )** function, shown next. It displays, in binary format, the bit pattern of its argument. You will use **disp_binary( )** later in this chapter to examine the effects of other bitwise operations.

```
// Display the bits within a byte.
void disp_binary(unsigned u)
{
  register int t;

  for(t=128; t>0; t = t/2)
    if(u & t) cout << "1 ";
    else cout << "0 ";
  cout << "\n";
}
```

The **disp_binary( )** function works by successively testing each bit in the byte, using the bitwise AND, to determine if it is on or off. If the bit is on, the digit **1** is displayed; otherwise **0** is displayed.

The bitwise OR, as the reverse of AND, can be used to turn bits on. Any bit that is set to 1 in either operand will cause the corresponding bit in the variable to be set to 1. For example,

```
        1 1 0 1  0 0 1 1
        1 0 1 0  1 0 1 0
  |     -------------------
        1 1 1 1  1 0 1 1
```

We can make use of the OR to change the uppercasing program used earlier into a lowercasing program, as shown here:

9

```
#include <iostream.h>

main()
{
  char ch;

  do {
    cin >> ch;

    /* This lowercases the letter by turning
       on bit 6.
    */
    ch = ch | 32;

    cout << ch;
  } while(ch != 'q');

  return 0;
}
```

When the sixth bit is set, each uppercase letter is transformed into its lowercase equivalent.

An exclusive OR, usually abbreviated XOR, will set a bit on if, and only if, the bits being compared are different, as illustrated here:

```
        0 1 1 1 1 1 1 1
        1 0 1 1 1 0 0 1
    ^   -----------------------
        1 1 0 0 0 1 1 0
```

The unary 1's complement (NOT) operator reverses the state of all the bits of the operand. For example, if some integer called **A** has the bit pattern 1001 0110, then ~**A** produces a result with the bit pattern 0110 1001.

The following program demonstrates the NOT operator by displaying a number and its complement in binary, using the **disp_binary( )** function developed earlier.

```
#include <iostream.h>

void disp_binary(unsigned u);

main()
{
  unsigned u;
```

```
   cout << "enter a number: ";
   cin >> u;

   cout << "Here's the number in binary: ";
   disp_binary(u);

   cout << "Here's the complement of the number: ";
   disp_binary(~u);

   return 0;
}

// Display the bits within a byte.
void disp_binary(unsigned u)
{
  register int t;

  for(t=128; t>0; t = t/2)
    if(u & t) cout << "1 ";
    else cout << "0 ";
  cout << "\n";
}
```

In general, **&**, **|**, **^,** and ~apply their operations directly to each bit in the
variable individually. For this reason, and others, bitwise operations are not
usually used in conditional statements the way the relational and logical
operators are. For example if *x* equals 7, then *x* && 8 evaluates to true,
whereas *x* & 8 evaluates to false.

Remember: A relational or logical operator always produces a result
that is either true or false, whereas the similar bitwise operator can produce
any arbitrary value in accordance with the specific operation.

The Shift Operators

The shift operators, **>>** and **<<**, move all bits in a variable to the right or left
as specified. The general form of the right-shift operator is

variable >> num-bits

and the left-shift operator is

variable << num-bits

The value of *num-bits* determines how many bit places the bits are shifted. Each left-shift causes all bits within the specified variable to be shifted left one position and a zero bit to be brought in on the right. Each right-shift shifts all bits to the right one position, and brings in a zero on the left. However, if the variable is a signed integer containing a negative value, then (most commonly), each right-shift brings in a 1 on the left. Remember, a shift is not a rotation. That is, the bits shifted off of one end do not come back around to the other.

The shift operators only work with integral types, such as characters, integers, and long integers. They cannot be applied to floating-point values, for example.

Bit shift operations can be very useful for decoding external device input, like D/A converters, and reading status information. The bitwise shift operators can also be used to perform very fast multiplication and division of integers. A shift left will effectively multiply a number by 2, and a shift right will divide it by 2.

The following program illustrates the effects of the shift operators.

The shift operators shift the bits within an integral value.

```
// Example of bitshifting.

#include <iostream.h>

void disp_binary(unsigned u);

main()
{
  int i=1, t;

  for(t=0; t<8; t++) {
    disp_binary(i);
    i = i << 1;
  }

  cout << "\n";

  for(t=0; t<8; t++) {
    i = i >> 1;
    disp_binary(i);
  }

  return 0;
}

// Display the bits within a byte.
```

```
void disp_binary(unsigned u)
{
  register int t;

  for(t=128; t>0; t=t/2)
    if(u & t) cout << "1 ";
    else cout << "0 ";
  cout << "\n";
}
```

This program produces the following output:

```
0 0 0 0 0 0 0 1
0 0 0 0 0 0 1 0
0 0 0 0 0 1 0 0
0 0 0 0 1 0 0 0
0 0 0 1 0 0 0 0
0 0 1 0 0 0 0 0
0 1 0 0 0 0 0 0
1 0 0 0 0 0 0 0
1 0 0 0 0 0 0 0
0 1 0 0 0 0 0 0
0 0 1 0 0 0 0 0
0 0 0 1 0 0 0 0
0 0 0 0 1 0 0 0
0 0 0 0 0 1 0 0
0 0 0 0 0 0 1 0
0 0 0 0 0 0 0 1
```

The ? Operator

One of C++'s most fascinating operators is the **?**. The **?** operator can be used to replace **if-else** statements of this general form:

> if (*condition*)
>   *expression*;
> else
>   *expression*;

The targets of the **if** and the **else** must be single expressions. They cannot be another C++ statement, for example.

The **?** is called a *ternary operator* because it requires three operands. It takes the general form

> *Exp1* ? *Exp2* : *Exp3*;

where *Exp1, Exp2* and *Exp3* are expressions. Notice the use and placement of the colon.

The value of a **?** expression is determined like this: *Exp1* is evaluated. If it is true, then *Exp2* is evaluated and becomes the value of the entire **?** expression. If *Exp1* is false, then *Exp3* is evaluated and its value becomes the value of the expression. Consider this example:

```
while(something) {
  done = count>0 ? 0 : 1;
  // ...
  if(done) break;
}
```

Here, **done** will be assigned the value 0 until **count** is less than or equal to 0. The same code written using the **if-else** structure would look like this:

```
while(something) {
  if(count>0) done = 0;
  else done = 1;
  // ...
  if(done) break;
}
```

Here's an example of the **?** operator in action. This program divides two numbers, but will not allow a division by zero.

```
/* This program uses the ? operator to prevent
   a division by zero. */

#include <iostream.h>

int div_zero();

main()
{
  int i, j, result;

  cout << "Enter dividend and divisor: ";
  cin >> i >> j;

  // This statement prevents a divide by zero error.
  result = j ? i/j : div_zero();

  cout << "Result: " << result;
```

```
  return 0;
}

int div_zero()
{
  cout << "Cannot divide by zero.\n";
  return 0;
}
```

C++ Shorthand

C++ has a special shorthand that simplifies the coding of a certain type of assignment statement. For example

```
x = x+10;
```

can be written, in C++ shorthand, as

```
x += 10;
```

The operator pair **+=** tells the compiler to assign to **x** the value of **x** plus 10.

This shorthand will work for all the binary operators in C++ (that is, those that require two operands). The general form of the shorthand is

   var op = expression;

For another example,

```
x = x-100;
```

is the same as

```
x -= 100;
```

You will see shorthand notation used widely in professionally written C++ programs, so you should become familiar with it.

The Comma Operator

Another interesting C++ operator is the comma. You have seen some examples of the comma operator in the **for** loop, where it has been used to allow multiple initialization or incrementation statements. However, the comma can be used as a part of any expression. It strings together several

9

expressions. The value of a comma-separated list of expressions is the value of the right-most expression. The values of the other expressions will be discarded. This means that the expression on the right side will become the value of the total comma-separated expression. For example,

```
var = (count=19, incr=10, count+1);
```

first assigns **count** the value 19, then assigns **incr** the value 10, and finally assigns **var** the value produced by the entire comma expression, 20. The parentheses are necessary because the comma operator has a lower precedence than the assignment operator.

To actually see the effects of the comma operator, try running the following program:

```
#include <iostream.h>

main()
{
  int i, j;

  j = 10;

  i = (j++, j+100, 999+j);

  cout << i;

  return 0;
}
```

This program prints 1010 on the screen. Here is why: **j** starts with the value 10. **j** is then incremented to 11. Next, **j** is added to 100. Finally, **j** (still containing 11) is added to 999, which yields the result 1010.

Essentially, the comma's effect is to cause a sequence of operations to be performed. When it is used on the right side of an assignment statement, the value assigned is the value of the last expression in the comma-separated list. You can, in some ways, think of the comma operator as having the same meaning that the word "and" has in English when used in the phrase "do this and this and this."

Multiple Assignments

C++ allows a very convenient method of assigning many variables the same value: using multiple assignments in a single statement. For example, this fragment assigns **count**, **incr**, and **index** the value 10.

```
count = incr = index = 10;
```

In professionally written programs, you will often see variables assigned a common value using this format.

Using sizeof

Sometimes it is helpful to know the size, in bytes, of a type of data. Since the sizes of C++'s built-in types can differ between computing environments, knowing the size of a variable in all situations can be difficult. To solve this problem, C++ includes the **sizeof** compile-time operator, which has these general forms:

sizeof is a compile-time operator that obtains the size of a type or variable.

    sizeof (*type*)

    sizeof *var_name*

The first version returns the size of the specified data type, and the second returns the size of the specified variable. As you can see, if you want to know the size of a data type, such as **int**, you must enclose the type name in parentheses. If you want to know the name of a variable, no parentheses are needed, although you can use them if you desire.

To see how **sizeof** works, try the following short program. For many environments, it displays the values 1, 2, 4, and 8.

```
// Demonstrate sizeof.
#include <iostream.h>

main()
{
  char ch;
  int i;

  cout << sizeof ch << ' '; // size of char
  cout << sizeof i << ' ';  // size of int
  cout << sizeof (float) << ' '; // size of float
  cout << sizeof (double) << ' '; // size of double

  return 0;
}
```

As mentioned earlier, **sizeof** is a compile-time operator. All information necessary for computing the size of a variable or data type is known during compilation.

9

You may apply **sizeof** to any data type. For example, when it is applied to an array, it returns the number of bytes used by the array. Consider this fragment:

```
int nums[4];

cout << sizeof nums; // displays 8
```

Assuming 2-byte integers, this fragment displays the value 8 (i.e., 2 bytes times 4 elements).

sizeof primarily helps you to generate portable code that depends upon the size of the C++ data types. Remember, since the sizes of types in C++ are defined by the implementation, it is bad style to make assumptions about their sizes in code that you write.

Dynamic Allocation Using new and delete

There are two primary ways in which a C++ program can store information in the main memory of the computer. The first is through the use of variables. The storage provided by variables is fixed at compile time, and cannot be altered during the execution of a program. The second way information can be stored is through the use of C++'s dynamic allocation system. In this method, storage for data is allocated as needed from the free memory area that lies between your program (and its permanent storage area) and the stack. This region is called the *heap*. (Figure 9-2 shows conceptually how a C++ program appears in memory.)

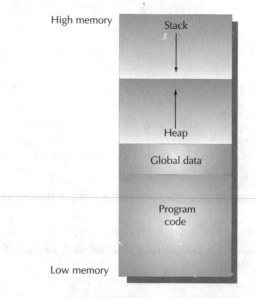

A conceptual view of memory usage in a C++ program
Figure 9-2.

High memory

Stack

Heap

Global data

Program code

Low memory

Dynamic
allocation
is the means
by which a
program
can obtain
memory
during its
execution.

Dynamically allocated storage is determined at run time. Thus, dynamic allocation makes it possible for your program to create variables that it needs during its execution. It can create as many or as few variables as required, depending upon the situation.

Memory to satisfy a dynamic allocation request is taken from the heap. As you might guess, it is possible, under fairly extreme cases, for free memory to become exhausted. Therefore, while dynamic allocation offers greater flexibility, it, too, is finite.

Dynamic allocation is typically used to support such data structures as linked lists, binary trees, and sparse arrays. (These topics are beyond the scope of this book.) However, you are free to use dynamic allocation wherever you determine it to be of value. Because real-world applications of dynamic allocation tend to be large and complex, only the mechanics of using it with C++ are discussed here. However, other uses for dynamic allocation can be found in any book on data structures.

C++ contains two operators, **new** and **delete**, that perform the functions of allocating and freeing memory. Their general forms are shown here:

pointer_var = new *var_type*;

delete *pointer_var*;

Here, *pointer_var* is a pointer of type *var_type*. The **new** operator allocates sufficient memory to hold a value of type *var_type* and returns a pointer to it. Any valid data type can be allocated using **new**. The **delete** operator frees the memory pointed to by *pointer_var*. Once freed, this memory can be reallocated to different purposes by a subsequent **new** allocation request.

new allocates
dynamic
memory.

Since the heap is finite, it can become exhausted. If there is not enough free memory available in the heap to fill a memory request, then the request fails, and **new** returns a null pointer. Therefore, you must always check the pointer produced by **new** before using it.

delete frees
previously
allocated
dynamic
memory.

Because of the way dynamic allocation is managed, you must only use **delete** with a pointer to memory that has been allocated using **new**. Using **delete** with any other type of address will cause serious problems.

Here is a simple example illustrating the use of **new** and **delete**.

```
#include <iostream.h>

main()
{
  int *p;
```

9

```
p = new int; // allocate memory for int
if(!p) {
  cout << "allocation failure\n";
  return 1;
}

*p = 20; // assign that memory the value 20
cout << *p; // prove that it works by displaying value

delete p; // free the memory

return 0;
}
```

This program assigns to **p** an address in the heap that is large enough to hold an integer. It then assigns that memory the value 20 and displays the contents of the memory on the screen. Finally, it frees the dynamically allocated memory.

Initializing Dynamically Allocated Memory

You can initialize dynamically allocated memory using the **new** operator. To do this, specify the initial value, inside parentheses, after the type name. For example, the following program uses initialization to give the memory pointed to by **p** the value 99.

```
#include <iostream.h>

main()
{
  int *p;

  p = new int (99);  // initialize with 99
  if(!p) {
    cout << "allocation failure\n";
    return 1;
  }

  cout << *p;

  delete p;

  return 0;
}
```

Allocating Arrays

You can allocate arrays using **new**. This is the general form used to allocate a singly dimensioned array:

pointer_var = new *var_type* [*size*];

Here, *size* specifies the number of elements in the array.

To free a dynamically allocated array, use this form of **delete**:

delete [ ] *pointer_var*;

Here, *pointer_var* is the address obtained when the array was allocated. The square brackets tell C++ that a dynamically allocated array is being deleted, and it automatically frees all the memory allocated to the array.

Tip: Older C++ compilers may require that you specify the size of the array being deleted. Older versions of C++ required this form of **delete** for freeing an array:

delete [*size*] *pointer_var*;

Here, *size* is the number of elements in the array. The modern specification for C++ no longer requires that the size of the array be specified.

The following program allocates space for a 10-element array of **float**s, assigns the array the values 100 to 109, and displays the contents of the array on the screen.

```
#include <iostream.h>

main()
{
  float *p;
  int i;

  p = new float [10]; // get a 10-element array
  if(!p) {
    cout << "allocation failure\n";
    return 1;
  }

  // assign the values 100 through 109
```

```
for(i=0; i<10; i++) p[i] = 100.00 + i;

// display the contents of the array
for(i=0; i<10; i++)  cout << p[i] << " ";

delete [] p; // delete the entire array

return 0;
}
```

There is one important point to remember about allocating an array: you cannot initialize it.

C's Approach to Dynamic Allocation: malloc( ) and free( )

The C language does not contain the **new** or the **delete** operator. Instead, C uses library functions to allocate and free memory. For compatibility, C++ still provides support for C's dynamic allocation system. It is still quite common to find the C-like dynamic allocation system used in both C and C++ programs, so the following discussion will explain how it works.

At the core of C's allocation system are the functions **malloc( )** and **free( )**. The **malloc( )** function allocates memory, and the **free( )** function releases it. That is, each time a **malloc( )** memory request is made, a portion of the remaining free memory is allocated. Each time a **free( )** memory release call is made, memory is returned to the system. Any program that uses these functions should include the header file **stdlib.h**.

The **malloc( )** function has this prototype:

```
void *malloc(size_t num_bytes);
```

Here, *num_bytes* is the number of bytes of memory you wish to allocate. (**size_t** is a defined type that is (more or less) an **unsigned** integer.) The **malloc( )** function returns a pointer of type **void**. You must use a type cast to convert this pointer into the type of pointer needed by your program. After a successful call, **malloc( )**) will return a pointer to the first byte of the region of memory allocated from the heap. If there is not enough available memory to satisfy the **malloc( )** request, an allocation failure occurs, and **malloc( )** returns a null.

The **free( )** function is the opposite of **malloc( )** in that it returns previously allocated memory to the system. Once the memory has been released, it may be reused by a subsequent call to **malloc( )**. The function **free( )** has this prototype:

```
void free(void *ptr);
```

Here, *ptr* is a pointer to memory previously allocated using **malloc( )**. You must never call **free( )** with an invalid argument; this would cause the free list to be destroyed.

The following short program allocates storage for several types of variables.

```
#include <iostream.h>
#include <stdlib.h>

main()
{
  int *i;
  float *j;

  i = (int *) malloc(sizeof(int));
  if(!i) {
    cout << "allocation failure";
    return 1;
  }

  j = (float *) malloc(sizeof(float));
  if(!j) {
    cout << "allocation failure";
    return 1;
  }

  *i= 10;
  *j = 100.123;

  cout << *i << ' ' << *j;

  // free the memory
  free(i);
  free(j);

  return 0;
}
```

While **malloc( )** and **free( )** are fully capable dynamic allocation functions, there are several reasons why C++ defines its own approach to dynamic allocation. First, **new** automatically computes the size of the type being allocated. You don't have to make use of the **sizeof** operator, so you save some effort. More importantly, automatic computation prevents the wrong amount of memory from being allocated. The second advantage to the C++ approach is that **new** automatically returns the correct pointer type—you don't need to use a type cast. Third, using **new**, you can initialize the object being allocated. Finally, as you will see later in this book, you can create your own, customized versions of **new** and **delete**.

One last point: Because of possible incompatibilities, you should not mix **malloc( )** and **free( )** with **new** and **delete** in the same program.

Precedence Summary

Table 9-2 lists the precedence, from highest to lowest, of all C++ operators. Most operators associate from left to right. The unary operators, the assignment operators, and the **?** operator associate from right to left. Note that the table includes a few operators that you have not yet learned about; most of these are used in object-oriented programming.

Highest	( ) [ ] –> :: .
	! ~ ++ –– – + (type cast) * &
	sizeof new delete typeid
	.* –>*
	* / %
	+ –
	<< >>
	< <= > >=
	== !=
	&
	^
	¦
	&&
	¦ ¦
	?
	= += –= *= /= etc.
Lowest	,

Precedence
of the C++
Operators
Table 9-2.

Chapter 10

Structures and Unions

C++ supports three compound (or *aggregate*) data types: the structure, the union, and the class. This chapter discusses the structure and the union. (A discussion of the class is deferred until the following chapter.) Although they fill different needs, both the structure and the union provide a convenient means of managing groups of related variables. Another important aspect of structures and unions is that when you create one, you are also creating a new programmer-defined data type. As you will see, providing you the ability to create your own data types is a powerful feature of C++.

In C++, structures and unions have both object-oriented and non-object-oriented attributes. However, this chapter discusses only their non-object-oriented features. (Their object-oriented qualities are discussed later in this book.) The reason for this is clear: Before you can apply the object-oriented features of structures or unions, you need to thoroughly understand their fundamentals. Only after you have mastered the basics will you be ready to move on to object-oriented programming.

Let's begin our discussion with structures.

Structures

In C++, a *structure* is a collection of variables that are referenced under one name, providing a convenient means of keeping related information together. Structures are called *aggregate data types* because they consist of several different, yet logically connected, variables.

A structure is a group of related variables.

Before a structure object can be created, the form of the structure must be defined. This is accomplished by means of a structure declaration. The structure declaration determines what type of variables the structure contains. The variables that comprise the structure are called *members* of the structure. (Structure members are also commonly referred to as *elements* or *fields*.)

A structure member is a variable that is part of a structure.

Generally, all members of the structure will be logically related to each other. For example, structures are typically used to hold information such as mailing addresses, compiler symbol tables, library card catalog entries, and the like. Of course, the relationship between the members of a structure is purely subjective and determined by you. The compiler doesn't know (or care).

Let's begin our examination of structures with an example. Specifically, let's define a structure that can hold the information relating to a company's inventory. An inventory record typically consists of several pieces of information, such as the item name, cost, and number on hand, so a structure is a good way to manage this information. The following code fragment declares a structure that defines the item name, cost and retail price, number on hand, and resupply time for maintaining an inventory. The keyword **struct** tells the compiler that a structure declaration is beginning.

```
struct inv_type {
  char item[40]; // name of item
  double cost;   // cost
  double retail; // retail price
  int on_hand;   // amount on hand
  int lead_time; // number of days before resupply
};
```

Notice that the declaration is terminated by a semicolon. This is because a structure declaration is a statement. The type name of the structure is **inv_type**. As such, **inv_type** identifies this particular data structure and is its type specifier.

A structure's name is its data type specifier.

In the preceding declaration, no variable has actually been created. Only the form of the data has been defined. To declare an actual variable (i.e., a physical object) with this structure, you would write something like this:

```
inv_type inv_var;
```

This declares a structure variable of type **inv_type** called **inv_var**. Remember, when you define a structure, you are defining a new data type. It is not until you declare a variable of that type that one actually exists.

C++ will automatically allocate sufficient memory to accommodate all the members of a structure. Figure 10-1 shows how **inv_var** would appear in memory (assuming 8-byte **double**s and 2-byte **int**s).

You can also declare one or more variables at the same time that you define a structure, as shown here:

```
struct inv_type {
  char item[40]; // name of item
  double cost;   // cost
  double retail; // retail price
  int on_hand;   // amount on hand
  int lead_time; // number of days before resupply
} inv_varA, inv_varB, inv_varC;
```

This fragment defines a structure type called **inv_type** and declares variables **inv_varA**, **inv_varB**, and **inv_varC** of that type.

If you only need one structure variable, then it is not necessary to include the name of the structure type. Consider this example:

```
struct  {
  char item[40]; // name of item
  double cost;   // cost
  double retail; // retail price
  int on_hand;   // amount on hand
  int lead_time; // number of days before resupply
} temp;
```

item	*40 bytes*
cost	*8 bytes*
retail	*8 bytes*
on_hand	*2 bytes*
lead_time	*2 bytes*

inv_var

The **inv_var** structure as it appears in memory

Figure 10-1.

This fragment declares one variable named **temp** as defined by the structure preceding it.

The general form of a structure declaration is shown here:

struct *struct-type-name* {

    type element_name1;
    type element_name2;
    type element_name3;
    .
    .
    .
    type element_nameN;
} *structure-variables;*

Accessing Structure Members

Individual structure members are accessed through the use of a period (generally called the "dot" operator). For example, the following code will assign the value 10.39 to the **cost** field of the structure variable **inv_var** declared earlier.

```
inv_var.cost = 10.39;
```

The structure variable name, followed by a period and the member name, refers to that member. All structure elements are accessed in the same way. The general form is:

    structure_varname.member_name

Therefore, to print **cost** on the screen, you could write

```
cout << inv_var.cost;
```

In the same fashion, the character array **inv_var.item** can be used to call **gets( )**, as shown here:

```
gets(inv_var.item);
```

This will pass a character pointer to the beginning of the element **item**.

If you wish to access the individual elements of the array **inv_var.item**, you can index **item**. For example, you can print the contents of **inv_var.item** one character at a time by using this code:

```
int t;

for(t=0; inv_var.item[t]; t++)
  cout << inv_var.item[t];
```

Arrays of Structures

Structures may be arrayed. (In fact, arrayed structures are quite common.) To declare an array of structures, you must first define a structure, then declare an array of its type. For example, to declare a 100-element array of structures of type **inv_type** (defined earlier), you would write

```
inv_type invtry[100];
```

To access a specific structure, you must index the structure name. For example, to print the **on_hand** member of the third structure, you would write

```
cout << invtry[2].on_hand;
```

Like all array variables, arrays of structures begin their indexing at zero.

A Simple Inventory Example

To help illustrate how structures and arrays of structures are used, a simple inventory management program will be developed that uses an array of structures to hold the inventory information. The functions in this program interact with structures and their elements to illustrate structure usage. The inventory will be held in the array called **invtry**, as shown here:

```
const int SIZE = 100;

struct inv_type {
  char item[40]; // name of item
  double cost;    // cost
  double retail; // retail price
  int on_hand;    // amount on hand
  int lead_time; // number of days before resupply
}invtry[SIZE];
```

The size of the array is arbitrary. Feel free to change it if you desire. Notice that the array dimension is specified using a **const** variable. Since the size of the array will be used at several places in the full program, using a **const** variable for this value is a good idea. This is common practice in professionally written C++ code.

The program will provide these three options:

♦ the entry of inventory information

♦ the display of the inventory

♦ modification of any specific item

The first function needed for the program is **main( )**, which is shown here:

```
main()
{
  char choice;

  init_list();

  for(;;) {
    choice = menu();
    switch(choice) {
      case 'e': enter();
        break;
      case 'd': display();
        break;
      case 'u': update();
        break;
      case 'q': return 0;
    }
  }
}
```

The **main( )** function begins by calling **init_list( )**, which initializes the structure array. It then enters a loop that displays the menu and processes the user's selection.

The **init_list( )** function is shown here:

```
// Initialize the inv_type_info array.
void init_list()
{
  int t;

  // a zero length name signifies empty
  for(t=0; t<SIZE; t++) *invtry[t].item = '\0';
}
```

The **init_list( )** function prepares the structure array for use by putting a null character into the first byte of the **item** field. The program assumes that a structure variable is not in use if the **item** field is empty.

The **menu_select( )** function, shown here, displays the options and returns the user's selection:

```
// Get a menu selection.
menu()
{
  char ch;

  cout << '\n';
  do {
    cout << "(E)nter\n";
    cout << "(D)isplay\n";
    cout << "(U)pdate\n";
    cout << "(Q)uit\n\n";
    cout << "choose one: ";
    cin >> ch;
  } while(!strchr("eduq", tolower(ch)));
  return tolower(ch);
}
```

The user selects an option by entering the specified letter. For example, to display the inventory list, press **D**.

The **menu( )** function makes use of another of C++'s library functions, **strchr( )**, which has this prototype:

   char *strchr(const char *str, char ch);

This function searches the string pointed to by *str* for an occurrence of the character in *ch*. If the character is found, a pointer to that character is returned. This is by definition a true value. However, if no match is found, a null is returned, which is by definition false. It is used in this program to see whether the user entered a valid menu selection.

The **enter( )** function sets up the call to **input( )**, which prompts the user for information. Both functions are shown here:

```
// Enter items into the list.
void enter()
{
  int i;

  // find the first free structure
```

```
  for(i=0; i<SIZE; i++)
    if(!*invtry[i].item) break;

  // i will equal SIZE if the list is full
  if(i==SIZE) {
    cout << "List full\n";
    return;
  }

  input(i);
}

// Input the information.
void input(int i)
{
  char str[80];

  // enter the information
  cout << "Item: ";
  cin >> invtry[i].item;

  cout << "Cost: ";
  cin >> invtry[i].cost;

  cout << "Retail price: ";
  cin >> invtry[i].retail;

  cout << "On hand: ";
  cin >> invtry[i].on_hand;

  cout << "Lead time to resupply (in days): ";
  cin >> invtry[i].lead_time;
}
```

The **enter( )** function first finds an empty structure. To do this, **enter( )** starts with the first element in **invtry** and advances through the array, checking the **item** field. If it finds an **item** field that is null, it knows that that structure is unused. If the routine reaches the end of the array without finding a free structure, then the loop control variable **i** will be equal to the size of the array. If the array is full, then the message **List full** is printed on the screen. The actual entry of the data is performed by **input( )**. The reason this code is not part of **enter( )** is that **input( )** is also used by the **update( )** function, which you will see next.

Since, like most things in life, inventory information changes, the inventory program lets you change the information about the individual items. This is accomplished with a call to the **update( )** function, as shown here:

```
// Modify an existing item.
void update()
{
  int i;
  char name[80];

  cout << "Enter item: ";
  cin >> name;

  for(i=0; i<SIZE; i++)
    if(!strcmp(name, invtry[i].item)) break;

  if(i==SIZE) {
    cout << "Item not found\n";
    return;
  }

  cout << "Enter new information.\n";
  input(i);
}
```

This function prompts the user for the name of the item to be changed. It then looks in the list to see if the item is there. If it is, **input( )** is called, and the new information can be entered.

The final function used by the program is **display( )**. It prints the entire inventory list on the screen. The **display( )** function is shown here:

```
// Display the list.
void display()
{
  int t;

  for(t=0; t<SIZE; t++) {
    if(*invtry[t].item) {
      cout << invtry[t].item << '\n';
      cout << "Cost: $" << invtry[t].cost;
      cout << "\nRetail: $";
      cout << invtry[t].retail << '\n';
      cout << "On hand: " << invtry[t].on_hand;
      cout << "\nResupply time: ";
      cout << invtry[t].lead_time << " days\n\n";
    }
  }
}
```

The complete inventory program is shown next. If you have any doubts about your understanding of structures, you should enter this program into your computer and study its execution. Make some changes and watch the effects they have. You should also try to expand the program by adding functions that search the list for a specific inventory item, remove an item from the list, or reset the inventory list.

```cpp
/* A simple inventory program that uses an array
   of structures. */

#include <iostream.h>
#include <ctype.h>
#include <string.h>
#include <stdlib.h>

const int SIZE = 100;

struct inv_type {
  char item[40]; // name of item
  double cost;   // cost
  double retail; // retail price
  int on_hand;   // amount on hand
  int lead_time; // number of days before resupply
} invtry[SIZE];

void enter(), init_list(), display();
void update(), input(int i);
int menu();

main()
{
  char choice;

  init_list();

  for(;;) {
    choice = menu();
    switch(choice) {
      case 'e': enter();
        break;
      case 'd': display();
        break;
      case 'u': update();
        break;
      case 'q': return 0;
    }
  }
}
```

```
// Initialize the inv_type_info array.
void init_list()
{
  int t;

  // a zero length name signifies empty
  for(t=0; t<SIZE; t++) *invtry[t].item = '\0';
}

// Get a menu selection.
menu()
{
  char ch;

  cout << '\n';
  do {
    cout << "(E)nter\n";
    cout << "(D)isplay\n";
    cout << "(U)pdate\n";
    cout << "(Q)uit\n\n";
    cout << "choose one: ";
    cin >> ch;
  } while(!strchr("eduq", tolower(ch)));
  return tolower(ch);
}

// Enter items into the list.
void enter()
{
  int i;

  // find the first free structure
  for(i=0; i<SIZE; i++)
    if(!*invtry[i].item) break;

  // i will equal SIZE if the list is full
  if(i==SIZE) {
    cout << "List full\n";
    return;
  }

  input(i);
}

// Input the information.
void input(int i)
{
  char str[80];
```

```
  // enter the information
  cout << "Item: ";
  cin >> invtry[i].item;

  cout << "Cost: ";
  cin >> invtry[i].cost;

  cout << "Retail price: ";
  cin >> invtry[i].retail;

  cout << "On hand: ";
  cin >> invtry[i].on_hand;

  cout << "Lead time to resupply (in days): ";
  cin >> invtry[i].lead_time;
}

// Modify an existing item.
void update()
{
  int i;
  char name[80];

  cout << "Enter item: ";
  cin >> name;

  for(i=0; i<SIZE; i++)
    if(!strcmp(name, invtry[i].item)) break;

  if(i==SIZE) {
    cout << "Item not found\n";
    return;
  }

  cout << "Enter new information.\n";
  input(i);
}

// Display the list.
void display()
{
  int t;

  for(t=0; t<SIZE; t++) {
    if(*invtry[t].item) {
      cout << invtry[t].item << '\n';
      cout << "Cost: $" << invtry[t].cost;
```

```
      cout << "\nRetail: $";
      cout << invtry[t].retail << '\n';
      cout << "On hand: " << invtry[t].on_hand;
      cout << "\nResupply time: ";
      cout << invtry[t].lead_time << " days\n\n";
    }
  }
}
```

Passing Structures to Functions

When a structure is used as an argument to a function, the entire structure is passed using the standard call-by-value parameter passing mechanism. This, of course, means that any changes made to the contents of the structure inside the function to which it is passed do not affect the structure used as an argument. However, be aware that passing large structures can incur significant overhead. (As a general rule, the more data passed to a function, the longer it takes.)

When using a structure as a parameter, remember that the type of the argument must match the type of the parameter. For example, the following program declares a structure called **sample**, and then a function called **f1( )** that takes a parameter of type **sample**.

```
// Pass a structure to a function.
#include <iostream.h>

// define a structure type
struct sample {
  int a, b;
  char ch;
} ;

void f1(sample parm);

main()
{
  struct sample arg; // declare arg

  arg.a = 1000;

  f1(arg);

  return 0;
}

void f1(sample parm)
```

```
{
  cout << parm.a;
}
```

If the structure type of a parameter is different from that of its argument, a compile time error will result.

Assigning Structures

You can assign the contents of one structure to another as long as both structures are of the same type. For example, the following program assigns the value of **svar1** to **svar2**.

```
// Demonstrate structure assignments.
#include <iostream.h>

struct stype {
  int a, b;
};

main()
{
  stype svar1, svar2;

  svar1.a = svar1.b = 10;
  svar2.a = svar2.b = 20;

  cout << "Structures before assignment.\n";
  cout << "svar1: " << svar1.a << ' ' << svar1.b;
  cout << '\n';
  cout << "svar2: " << svar2.a << ' ' << svar2.b;
  cout << "\n\n";

  svar2 = svar1; // assign structures

  cout << "Structures after assignment.\n";
  cout << "svar1: " << svar1.a << ' ' << svar1.b;
  cout << '\n';
  cout << "svar2: " << svar2.a << ' ' << svar2.b;

  return 0;
}
```

This program displays the following output:

```
Structures before assignment.
svar1: 10 10
```

svar2: 20 20

Structures after assignment.
svar1: 10 10
svar2: 10 10

In C++, each new structure declaration defines a new type. Therefore, even if two structures are physically the same, if they have different type names they will be considered different by the compiler and, thus, cannot be assigned to one another. Consider the following fragment, which is not valid, and will not compile.

```
struct stype1 {
  int a, b;
};

struct stype2 {
  int a, b;
};

stype1 svar1;
stype2 svar2;

svar2 = svar1; // ERROR - type mismatch
```

Even though **stype1** and **stype2** are physically the same, they are separate types as far as the compiler is concerned.

Remember: One structure can be assigned to another only if both are of the same type.

Pointers to Structures and the Arrow Operator

C++ allows pointers to structures in the same way that it allows pointers to any other type of variable. However, there are some special aspects to using structure pointers that you must be aware of.

You declare a structure pointer as you would any other pointer variable, by putting an ***** in front of a structure variable's name. For example, assuming the previously defined structure **inv_type**, the following statement declares **inv_pointer** to be a pointer to data of that type.

```
inv_type *inv_pointer;
```

To find the address of a structure variable, you must place the **&** operator before the structure variable's name. For example, given the following fragment,

```
struct bal {
  float balance;
  char name[80];
} person;

bal *p; // declare a structure pointer
```

then

```
p = &person;
```

puts the address of **person** into the pointer **p**.

The arrow operator (–>) accesses the members of a structure through a pointer.

The members of a structure can be accessed through a pointer to the structure. However, you cannot use the dot operator for this purpose. Instead, you must use the **–>** operator. For example, this fragment accesses **balance** through **p**.

```
p->balance
```

The **–>** is called the *arrow* operator by most C++ programmers. It is formed by using the minus sign followed by a greater than sign.

One important use of a structure pointer is as a function parameter. Because of the overhead that occurs when a large structure is passed to a function, many times only a pointer to a structure is passed. (Passing a pointer is always faster than passing a large structure.)

Remember: To access members of a structure, use the dot operator. To access members of a structure through a pointer, use the arrow operator.

An Example Using Structure Pointers

An interesting use of structure pointers can be found in C++'s time and date functions. These functions obtain the current system time and date. The time and date functions require the header file **time.h**. This header supplies two data types needed by the time and date functions. The first type is **time_t**. It is capable of representing the system time and date as a long integer. This is referred to as the *calendar time*. The second type is a structure called **tm**, that holds the individual elements of the date and time. This is called the *broken-down time*. The **tm** structure is defined as shown here:

```
struct tm {
  int tm_sec;   /* seconds, 0-59 */
  int tm_min;   /* minutes, 0-59 */
  int tm_hour;  /* hours, 0-23 */
  int tm_mday;  /* day of the month, 1-31 */
  int tm_mon;   /* months since Jan, 0-11 */
  int tm_year;  /* years from 1900 */
  int tm_wday;  /* days since Sunday, 0-6 */
  int tm_yday;  /* days since Jan 1, 0-365 */
  int tm_isdst; /* Daylight Saving Time indicator */
};
```

The value of **tm_isdst** will be positive if daylight saving time is in effect, 0 if it is not in effect, and negative if there is no information available.

The foundation for C++'s time and date functions is **time( )**, which has this prototype:

time_t time(time_t *curtime);

The **time( )** function returns the current calendar time. It can be called either with a null pointer or with a pointer to a variable of type **time_t**. If the latter is used, then the variable pointed to by *curtime* will also be assigned the current calendar time.

To convert the calendar time into broken-down time, use **localtime( )**, which has this prototype:

struct tm *localtime(const time_t *curtime);

The **localtime( )** function returns a pointer to the broken-down form of *curtime* in the form of a **tm** structure. The time is represented in local time. The *curtime* value is generally obtained through a call to **time( )**.

The structure used by **localtime( )** to hold the broken-down time is internally allocated by the **localtime( )** function and is overwritten each time the function is called. If you wish to save the contents of the structure, you must copy it elsewhere.

The following program demonstrates the use of **time( )** and **localtime( )** by displaying the current system time.

```
// This program displays the current system time.

#include <iostream.h>
#include <time.h>

main()
{
  struct tm *ptr;
  time_t lt;

  lt = time('\0');

  ptr = localtime(&lt);

  cout << ptr->tm_hour << ':' << ptr->tm_min;
  cout << ':' << ptr->tm_sec;

  return 0;
}
```

Although your programs can use the broken-down form of the time and date (as illustrated in the preceding example), the easiest way to generate a time and date string is to use **asctime( )**, whose prototype is shown here:

    char *asctime(const struct tm *ptr);

The **asctime( )** function returns a pointer to a string, which is the conversion of the information stored in the structure pointed to by *ptr*. This string has the following form:

    day month date hours:minutes:seconds year\n\0

The structure pointer passed to **asctime( )** is the one obtained from **localtime( )**.

The memory used by **asctime( )** to hold the formatted output string is an internally allocated character array, and is overwritten each time the function is called. If you wish to save the contents of the string, you must copy it elsewhere.

The following program uses **asctime( )** to print the system time and date on the screen.

```
// This program displays the current system time.

#include <iostream.h>
#include <time.h>

main()
{
  struct tm *ptr;
  time_t lt;

  lt = time('\0');

  ptr = localtime(&lt);
  cout << asctime(ptr);

  return 0;
}
```

C++ contains several other time and date functions; to learn about these, you will want to check the manuals that came with your compiler.

References to Structures

Structures can be referenced. Specifically, a function can have a reference to a structure as a parameter or as a return type. When accessing members using a structure reference, use the dot operator. (The arrow operator is explicitly reserved for accessing members through a pointer.)

The following program shows how a structure can be used as a reference parameter.

```
#include <iostream.h>
struct mystruct {
  int a;
  int b;
};

mystruct &f(mystruct &var);

main()
{
  mystruct x, y;
  x.a = 10; x.b = 20;
```

```
  cout << "Original x.a and x.b: ";
  cout << x.a << ' ' << x.b << '\n';

  y = f(x);

  cout << "Modified x.a and x.b: ";
  cout << x.a << ' ' << x.b << '\n';
  cout << "Modified y.a and y.b: ";
  cout << y.a << ' ' << y.b << '\n';

  return 0;
}

mystruct &f(mystruct &var)
{
  var.a = var.a * var.a;
  var.b = var.b / var.b;
  return var;
}
```

Since there is significant overhead incurred when passing a structure to a function or when returning a structure, many C++ programmers use references when performing these tasks.

Arrays and Structures Within Structures

A structure member can be of any valid data type, including such complex types as arrays and other structures. However, since this is an area that often causes confusion, a close examination is warranted.

A structure member that is an array is treated as you might expect from the earlier examples. Consider this structure:

```
struct stype {
  int nums[10][10]; // 10 x 10 array of ints
  float b;
} var;
```

To reference integer 3,7 in **nums** of **var** of structure **stype**, you would write

```
var.nums[3][7]
```

As this example shows, when an array is a member of a structure, it is the array name that is indexed—not the structure name.

When a structure is an element of another structure, it is called a *nested* structure. In the following example, the structure **addr** is nested inside **emp**.

```
struct addr {
  char name[40];
  char street[40];
  char city[40];
  char zip[10];
}

struct emp {
  addr address;
  float wage;
} worker;
```

Here, structure **emp** has been defined as having two members. The first member is the structure of type **addr** that will contain an employee's address. The second is **wage**, which holds the employee's wage. The following code fragment will assign the ZIP code 98765 to the **zip** field of **address** of **worker**.

```
worker.address.zip = 98765;
```

As you can see, the members of each structure are referenced left to right, from the outermost to the innermost.

A structure may also contain a pointer to a structure as a member. In fact, it is perfectly valid for a structure to contain a member that is a pointer to itself. For example, in the following structure, **sptr** is declared as a pointer to a structure of type **mystruct**, which is the structure being declared.

```
struct mystruct {
  int a;
  char str[80];
  mystruct *sptr; // pointer to mystruct objects
};
```

Structures containing pointers to themselves are quite common when various data structures, such as linked lists, are created. As you progress in C++, you will frequently see applications that make use of this feature.

C Structures Versus C++ Structures

C++ structures are derived from C structures. Thus, any C structure is also a valid C++ structure. There are two important differences, however. First, as you will see in the next chapter, C++ structures have some unique attributes that allow them to support object-oriented programming. Second, in C a structure does *not* actually define a new data type. A C++ structure does. As you know, when you define a structure in C++, you are defining a new type (which is the name of the structure). This new type can be used to declare variables, function return types, and the like. However, in C, the name of a structure is called its *tag*. The tag, by itself, is not a type name.

To understand the difference, consider the following C code fragment:

```
struct C_struct {
  int a;
  int b;
}

// declare a C_struct variable
struct C_struct svar:
```

Notice that the structure definition is exactly the same as it is in C++. However, look closely at the declaration of the structure variable **svar**. Its declaration also starts with the keyword **struct**. In C, after you have defined a structure, you must still use the keyword **struct** in conjunction with the structure's tag (in this case, **C_struct**) to specify a complete data type.

If you will be converting older C programs to C++, you won't need to worry about the differences between C and C++ structures, because C++ still accepts the C-like declarations. The preceding code fragment, for instance, would compile correctly as part of a C++ program. It is just that the redundant use of **struct** in the declaration of **svar** is unnecessary in C++.

Bit-Fields

Unlike many other computer languages, C++ has a built-in method for accessing a single bit within a byte. Bit access is achieved through the use of a *bit-field*. Bit-fields can be useful for a number of reasons: first, if storage is limited, you can store several Boolean (true/false) values in one byte; second, certain device interfaces transmit information encoded into bits within one byte; and third, certain encryption routines need to access the bits within a byte. All of these functions can be performed using the bitwise operators, as you saw in the previous chapter; however, a bit-field can add more structure and readability to your program. It might also make your code more portable.

A bit-field is a
bit-based
structure
member.

The method that C++ uses to access bits is based on the structure. A bit-field is really just a special type of structure that defines how long, in bits, each element is to be. The general form of a bit-field definition is:

```
struct struc-type-name {
  type name1 : length;
  type name2 : length;
     .
     .
     .
  type nameN : length;
}
```

A bit-field must be declared as either **int**, **unsigned**, or **signed**. Bit-fields of length 1 should be declared as **unsigned**, because a single bit cannot have a sign.

Bit-fields are commonly used for analyzing the input from a hardware device. For example, the status port of a serial communications adapter might return a status byte organized like this:

Bit	Meaning When Set
0	Change in clear-to-send line
1	Change in data-set-ready
2	Trailing edge detected
3	Change in receive line
4	Clear-to-send
5	Data-set-ready
6	Telephone ringing
7	Received signal

You can use the following bit-field to represent the information in a status byte.

```
struct status_type {
  unsigned delta_cts: 1;
```

```
    unsigned delta_dsr: 1;
    unsigned tr_edge:   1;
    unsigned delta_rec: 1;
    unsigned cts:       1;
    unsigned dsr:       1;
    unsigned ring:      1;
    unsigned rec_line:  1;
} status;
```

You might use a routine similar to that shown next for enabling a program to determine when it can send or receive data.

```
status = get_port_status();

if(status.cts) cout << "clear to send";
if(status.dsr) cout << "data ready";
```

To assign a value to a bit-field, simply use the same form that you would for any other type of structure element. For example, the following statement clears the **ring** field.

```
status.ring = 0;
```

As you can see from these examples, each bit-field is accessed using the dot operator. However, if the structure is accessed through a pointer, you must use the –> operator.

You do not have to name each bit-field. This makes it easy to reach the bit you want, passing up those that are unused. For example, if you only care about the **cts** and **dsr** bits, you could declare the **status_type** structure like this:

```
struct status_type {
  unsigned : 4;
  unsigned cts: 1;
  unsigned dsr: 1;
} status;
```

Notice here that the bits after **dsr** do not need to be mentioned at all.

Bit-field variables have certain restrictions. You cannot take the address of a bit-field variable or reference a bit-field. Bit-field variables cannot be arrayed. They cannot be declared as **static**. You cannot know, from machine to machine, whether the fields will run from right to left or from left to right; this implies that any code using bit-fields may have some machine dependencies. Other restrictions may be imposed by various specific implementations of C++, so check the user manual for your compiler.

It is valid to mix normal structure members with bit-field elements. Here is an example:

```
struct emp {
  struct addr address;
  float pay;
  unsigned lay_off: 1; // lay off or active
  unsigned hourly: 1: // hourly pay or wage
  unsigned deductions: 3: // IRS deductions
};
```

This structure defines an employee record that uses only one byte to hold three pieces of information: the employee's status, whether or not the employee is salaried, and the number of deductions. Without the use of the bit-field, this information would require three bytes.

The next section presents a program that uses a bit-field to display the ASCII character codes in binary.

Unions

In C++, a union is a memory location that is shared by two or more different variables. The union definition is similar to that of a structure, as shown in this example:

```
union utype {
  int i;
  char ch;
} ;
```

*The **union** keyword begins a union declaration.*

Be clear on one point: It is not possible to have this union hold *both* an integer and a character at the same time, because **i** and **ch** overlay each other. (Of course, your program is free to treat the information in the union as an integer or a character at any time.) As you can see, a union is declared using the **union** keyword.

As with structures, a union declaration does not define any variables. You may declare a variable either by placing its name at the end of the definition, or by using a separate declaration statement. To declare a union variable called **u_var** of type **utype** using the definition just given, you would write

```
utype u_var;
```

In **u_var**, both integer **i** and character **ch** share the same memory location. (Of course, **i** occupies two bytes and **ch** uses only one.) Figure 10-2 illustrates how **i** and **ch** share the same address.

When a union is declared, the compiler will automatically allocate enough storage to hold the largest variable type in the union.

To access a union element, use the same syntax that you would use for structures: the dot and arrow operators. If you are operating on the union directly (or through a reference), use the dot operator. If the union variable is accessed through a pointer, use the arrow operator. For example, to assign the letter 'A' to element **ch** of **u_var**, you would write the following:

```
u_var.ch = 'A';
```

In the next example, a pointer to **u_var** is passed to a function. Inside the function, **i** is assigned the value 10 through the pointer.

```
func1(&u_var);

// ...

void func1(utype *un)
{
  un->i = 10; /* Assign 10 to u_var using
                  a pointer. */
}
```

Using a union can help you produce portable code. Because the compiler keeps track of the actual sizes of the variables that make up the union, no machine dependencies are produced. You need not worry about the size of an integer, character, **float**, or whatever.

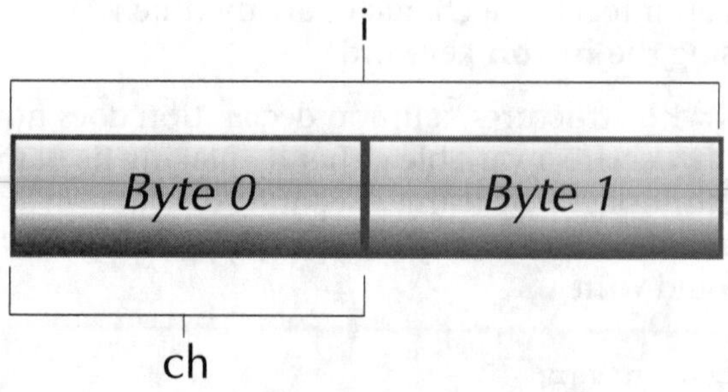

i and **ch** both utilize the union **u_var**
Figure 10-2.

Because unions allow your program to manipulate data in more than one way, they are used frequently when certain unusual type conversions are needed. For example, the following program uses a union to exchange the two bytes that comprise an integer. It uses the **disp_binary( )** function, as developed in Chapter 9, to display the contents of the integer. (This program assumes two-byte integers.)

10

```cpp
// Use a union to exchange the bytes within an integer.
#include <iostream.h>
void disp_binary(unsigned u);

union swap_bytes {
  int num;
  char ch[2];
};

main()
{
  swap_bytes sb;
  char temp;

  sb.num = 15;  // binary: 0000 0000 0000 1111

  cout << "Original bytes:  ";
  disp_binary(sb.ch[1]);
  cout << "  ";
  disp_binary(sb.ch[0]);
  cout << "\n\n";


  // exchange the bytes
  temp = sb.ch[0];
  sb.ch[0] = sb.ch[1];
  sb.ch[1] = temp;

  cout << "Exchanged bytes: ";
  disp_binary(sb.ch[1]);
  cout << "  ";
  disp_binary(sb.ch[0]);
  cout << "\n\n";

  return 0;
}

// Display the bits within a byte.
void disp_binary(unsigned u)
```

```
{
  register int t;

  for(t=128; t>0; t=t/2)
    if(u & t) cout << "1 ";
    else cout << "0 ";
}
```

The output from this program is shown here:

Original bytes: 0 0 0 0 0 0 0 0 0 0 0 0 1 1 1 1

Exchanged bytes: 0 0 0 0 1 1 1 1 0 0 0 0 0 0 0 0

In the program, 15 is assigned to the integer variable **sb.num**. However, the two bytes that form that integer are exchanged using the two-character array **ch**. This causes the high- and low-order bytes of **num** to be swapped. It is the fact that both **num** and **ch** share the same memory location that makes this operation possible.

Another use for a union is shown in the following program, which combines unions with bit-fields to display the ASCII code, in binary, generated when you press a key. This program also shows an alternative method for displaying the individual bits that make up a byte. The union allows the value of the key to be assigned to a character variable while the bit-field is used to display the individual bits. You should study this program to make sure that you fully understand its operation.

```
// Display the ASCII code in binary for characters.

#include <iostream.h>
#include <conio.h>

// a bit field that will be decoded
struct byte {
  unsigned a : 1;
  unsigned b : 1;
  unsigned c : 1;
  unsigned d : 1;
  unsigned e : 1;
  unsigned f : 1;
  unsigned g : 1;
  unsigned h : 1;
};

union bits {
  char ch;
```

```
    struct byte bit;
} ascii ;

void disp_bits(bits b);

main()
{
  do {
    cin >> ascii.ch;
    cout << ": ";
    disp_bits(ascii);
  } while(ascii.ch!='q'); // quit if q typed

  return 0;
}

// Display the bit pattern for each character.
void disp_bits(bits b)
{
  if(b.bit.h) cout << "1 ";
    else cout << "0 ";
  if(b.bit.g) cout << "1 ";
    else cout << "0 ";
  if(b.bit.f) cout << "1 ";
    else cout << "0 ";
  if(b.bit.e) cout << "1 ";
    else cout << "0 ";
  if(b.bit.d) cout << "1 ";
    else cout << "0 ";
  if(b.bit.c) cout << "1 ";
    else cout << "0 ";
  if(b.bit.b) cout << "1 ";
    else cout << "0 ";
  if(b.bit.a) cout << "1 ";
    else cout << "0 ";
  cout << "\n";
}
```

A sample run of the program is shown here:

```
a:   0 1 1 0 0 0 0 1
b:   0 1 1 0 0 0 1 0
c:   0 1 1 0 0 0 1 1
d:   0 1 1 0 0 1 0 0
e:   0 1 1 0 0 1 0 1
```

```
f:    0 1 1 0 0 1 1 0
g:    0 1 1 0 0 1 1 1
h:    0 1 1 0 1 0 0 0
i:    0 1 1 0 1 0 0 1
j:    0 1 1 0 1 0 1 0
k:    0 1 1 0 1 0 1 1
l:    0 1 1 0 1 1 0 0
m:    0 1 1 0 1 1 0 1
n:    0 1 1 0 1 1 1 0
o:    0 1 1 0 1 1 1 1
p:    0 1 1 1 0 0 0 0
q:    0 1 1 1 0 0 0 1
```

Tip: Because a union causes two or more variables to share the same memory location, unions provide a good way for your program to store and access information that may contain differing data types, depending upon the situation. If you think about it, unions provide low-level support for the principle of polymorphism. That is, a union provides a single interface to several different types of data, thus embodying the concept of "one interface, multiple methods" in its simplest form.

Anonymous Unions

There is a special type of union in C++ called an *anonymous union*. An anonymous union does not have a type name, and no variables can be declared of this sort of union. Instead, an anonymous union tells the compiler that its members will share the same memory location. However, in all other respects, the members act, and are treated, like normal variables. That is, the member variables are accessed directly, without the dot operator syntax.

Consider this example:

```
// Demonstrate an anonymous union
#include <iostream.h>

main()
{
  // this is an anonymous union
```

10

```
union {
  int count;
  char ch[2];
};

// Here, refer to union members directly
ch[0] = 'X';
ch[1] = 'Y';
cout << "union as chars: " << ch[0] << ch[1] << '\n';
cout << "union as integer: " << count << '\n';

  return 0;
}
```

This program displays the following output. (22872 is the integer produced by putting X and Y into its low- and high-order bytes, respectively.)

```
union as chars: XY
union as integer: 22872
```

As you can see, both **count** and **ch** are accessed as if they were normal variables, and not part of a union. Even though they are declared as being part of an anonymous union, their names are at the same scope level as any other local variable declared at the same point. In fact, a member of an anonymous union cannot have the same name as any other variable known to its scope.

An anonymous union declares local variables that share the same memory.

The anonymous union provides a way for you to tell the compiler that you want two or more variables to share the same memory location. Aside from this special attribute, members of an anonymous union behave like other variables.

Using sizeof to Ensure Portability

You have seen that structures and unions can be used to create variables of varying sizes, and that the actual sizes of these variables can change from machine to machine. Also, sometimes the compiler will pad a structure or union so that it aligns on an even word or on a paragraph boundary. (A paragraph is 16 bytes.) When you need to determine the size, in bytes, of a structure or union, use the **sizeof** operator. Do not try to manually add up the sizes of the individual members. Because of padding, or other machine dependencies, the size of a structure or union may be larger than the sum of the sizes of its individual members.

One other point: A union will always be large enough to hold its largest member. Consider this example:

```
union x {
  char ch;
  int i;
  float f;
} u_var;
```

Here, the **sizeof u_var** will be 4 (assuming four-byte **float**s). At run time, it does not matter what **u_var** is *actually* holding; all that matters is the size of the largest variable it can hold, because the union must be as large as its largest element.

Moving On to Object-Oriented Programming

This is the last chapter that describes those attributes of C++ that are not explicitly object-oriented. Beginning with the next chapter, features that support OOP will be examined. To understand and apply the object-oriented features of C++ requires a thorough understanding of the material in this and the preceding nine chapters. For this reason, you might want to take some time to quickly review. Specifically, make sure that you are comfortable with pointers, structures, functions, and function overloading.

Chapter

11

Introducing the Class

This chapter introduces the *class*. The class is the foundation of C++'s support for object-oriented programming, and is at the core of many of its more advanced features. The class provides the mechanism by which objects are created. Thus, the class is C++'s basic unit of encapsulation.

Class Fundamentals

A class defines a new data type, which can be used to create objects. A class is created using the keyword **class**. When you define a class, you will define both the data and the code that operates upon that data. That is, a class will have both code and data members.

A class declaration is syntactically similar to a structure. Let's begin with an example. The following class defines a type called **queue**, which will be used to implement a queue. (A queue is a first-in, first-out list.)

```
// This creates the class queue.
class queue {
  int q[100];
  int sloc, rloc;
public:
  void init();
  void qput(int i);
  int qget();
};
```

Let's look closely at this class declaration.

A class can contain private as well as public members. By default, all items defined in a class are private. For example, the variables **q**, **sloc**, and **rloc** are private. This means that they can only be accessed by other members of the **queue** class, and not by any other part of your program. This is one way encapsulation is achieved—you can tightly control access to certain items of data by keeping them private. Although there are none in this example, you can also define private functions, which can only be called by other members of the class.

To make parts of a class public (i.e., accessible to other parts of your program) you must declare them after the **public** keyword. All variables or functions defined after the **public** specifier are accessible by all other functions in your program. Typically, your program will access the private parts of a class through its public functions. Notice that the **public** keyword is followed by a colon.

The functions **init( )**, **qput( )** and **qget( )** are called *member functions*. Keep in mind that an object forms a bond between code and data. A member function has access to the private parts of the class of which it is a member. Thus, **init( )**, **qput( )**, and **qget( )** have access to **q**, **sloc**, and **rloc**. To create a member function, specify its prototype within the class declaration.

Once you have defined a class, you can create an object of that type using the class name. A class name becomes a new data type specifier. For example, the following statement creates two objects called **Q1** and **Q2** of type **queue**.

```
queue Q1, Q2;
```

When an object of a class is created, it will have its own copy of the data members that comprise the class. This means that **Q1** and **Q2** will each have their own, separate copies of **q**, **sloc**, and **rloc**. Thus, the data associated with **Q1** is distinct and separate from the data associated with **Q2**.

11

You may also create objects when the class is defined by putting their names after the closing curly brace, in exactly the same way as you would with a structure.

Let's review: In C++, a **class** creates a new data type that can be used to create objects. Specifically, a class creates a logical framework that defines a relationship between its members. When you declare a variable of a class, you are creating an object. An object has physical existence, and is a specific instance of a class. (That is, an object occupies memory space, but a type definition does not.) Further, each object of a class has its own copy of the data defined within that class.

The general form of a **class** declaration is:

```
class class-name {
    private data and functions
public:
    public data and functions
} object-list;
```

Of course, the object list may be empty.

Inside the declaration of **queue**, prototypes for the member functions are used. Because the member functions are prototyped within the class definition, they need not be prototyped elsewhere.

To implement a function that is a member of a class, you must tell the compiler which class the function belongs to by qualifying the function name with the class name. For example, here is one way to code the **qput( )** function:

```
void queue::qput(int i)
{
  if(sloc==100) {
    cout << "Queue is full";
    return;
```

```
  }
  sloc++;
  q[sloc] = i;
}
```

The **::** is called the *scope resolution operator*. Essentially, it tells the compiler that this version of **qput( )** belongs to the **queue** class. Or, put differently, **::** states that this **qput( )** is in **queue**'s scope. Several different classes can use the same function names. The compiler knows which function belongs to which class because of the scope resolution operator and the class name.

The scope resolution operator (::) qualifies a member name with its class.

Member functions can only be invoked relative to an object. To call a member function from a part of your program that is not part of the class, you must use the object's name and the dot operator. For example, this calls **init( )** for object **ob1**.

```
queue ob1, ob2;

ob1.init();
```

The invocation **ob1.init( )** causes **init( )** to operate on **ob1**'s copy of the data. Keep in mind that **ob1** and **ob2** are two separate objects. This means, for example, that initializing **ob1** does not cause **ob2** to also be initialized. The only relationship **ob1** has with **ob2** is that it is an object of the same type.

When one member function calls another member function, it can do so directly, without using the dot operator. In this case, the compiler already knows which object is being operated upon. It is only when a member function is called by code that does not belong to the class that the object name and the dot operator must be used.

The program shown here puts together all the pieces and missing details, and illustrates the **queue** class.

```
#include <iostream.h>

// This creates the class queue.
class queue {
  int q[100];
  int sloc, rloc;
public:
  void init();
  void qput(int i);
  int qget();
};
```

```
// Initialize the queue.
void queue::init()
{
  rloc = sloc = 0;
}

// Put an integer into the queue.
void queue::qput(int i)
{
  if(sloc==100) {
    cout << "Queue is full";
    return;
  }
  sloc++;
  q[sloc] = i;
}

// Get an integer from the queue.
int queue::qget()
{
  if(rloc == sloc) {
    cout << "Queue underflow";
    return 0;
  }
  rloc++;
  return q[rloc];
}

main()
{
  queue a, b;   // create two queue objects

  a.init();
  b.init();

  a.qput(10);
  b.qput(19);

  a.qput(20);
  b.qput(1);

  cout << "Contents of queue a: ";
  cout << a.qget() << " ";
  cout << a.qget() << "\n";

  cout << "Contents of queue b: ";
  cout << b.qget() << " ";
  cout << b.qget() << "\n";
```

```
   return 0;
}
```

This program displays the following output:

    Contents of queue a: 10 20
    Contents of queue b: 19 1

Keep in mind that the private members of an object are accessible only by functions that are members of that object. For example, a statement like

```
a.rloc = 0;
```

could not be included in the **main( )** function of the program.

A Closer Look at Class Member Access

How to access class members is the cause of considerable confusion for beginners. For this reason, let's take a closer look at it here. Consider the following simple class:

```
// Demonstrate class member access.
#include <iostream.h>

class myclass {
  int a; // private data
public:
  int b; // public data
  void setab(int i); // public functions
  int geta();
  void reset();
};

void myclass::setab(int i)
{
  a = i; // refer directly to a and b here
  b = i*i;
}

int myclass::geta()
{
  return a; // refer directly to a here.
}

void myclass::reset()
```

```
{
  // call setab() directly
  setab(0); // the object is already known
}

main()
{
  myclass ob;

  ob.setab(5); // set ob.a and ob.b
  cout << "ob after setab(5): ";
  cout << ob.geta() << ' ';
  cout << ob.b; // may access b because it is public
  cout << '\n';

  ob.b = 20; // again, may access b because it is public
  cout << "ob after ob.b=20: ";
  cout << ob.geta() << ' ';
  cout << ob.b;
  cout << '\n';

  ob.reset();
  cout << "ob after ob.reset(): ";
  cout << ob.geta() << ' ';
  cout << ob.b;
  cout << '\n';

  return 0;
}
```

11

This program produces the following output:

```
ob after setab(5): 5 25
ob after ob.b=20: 5 20
ob after ob.reset( ): 0 0
```

Let's look carefully at how each of the members of **myclass** is accessed.
First, examine the way that **setab( )** is coded. Because it is a member
function, it can refer to **a** and **b** directly, without explicit reference to an
object, and without the use of the dot operator. The reason for this is easy to
understand if you think about it. A member function is always invoked
relative to an object. Once this invocation has occurred, the object is known.
Thus, within a member function, there is no need to specify the object a
second time. Therefore, references to **a** and **b** will apply to the invoking
object's copy of these variables.

Second, notice that **a** is a private variable of **myclass**, but **b** is public. This means that **b** can be accessed by code outside of **myclass**. This is demonstrated within **main( )**, when **b** is assigned the value 20.

Finally, examine **reset( )**. Since **reset( )** is a member function, it can also directly refer to other members of the class without use of the dot operator or object. (In this case, it calls **setab( )**.) Again, because the object is already known (since it was used to call **reset( )**), there is no need to specify it again.

The key point to understand is this: when a member of a class is referred to outside of its class, it must be qualified with its object. However, member functions can refer to other members of the class directly.

Note: Don't worry if you are still a little unsure about how class members are accessed. A bit of uneasiness about this issue is common at first. As you read on and study more examples, member access will become clear.

Constructors and Destructors

It is very common for some part of an object to require initialization before it can be used. For example, consider the **queue** class, which was developed earlier in this chapter. Before the queue could be used, the variables **rloc** and **sloc** had to be set to zero. This was performed using the function **init( )**. Because the requirement for initialization is so common, C++ allows objects to initialize themselves when they are created. This automatic initialization is performed through the use of a *constructor* function.

A constructor is a function that is called when an object is created.

A constructor function is a special function that is a member of the class and has the same name as that class. For example, here is how the **queue** class looks when converted to use a constructor function for initialization.

```
// This creates the class queue.
class queue {
  int q[100];
  int sloc, rloc;
public:
  queue();  // constructor
  void qput(int i);
  int qget();
};
```

Notice that the constructor **queue( )** has no return type. In C++, constructor functions do return values and, therefore, have no return type. (Not even **void** may be specified.)

The **queue( )** function is coded as follows:

```
// This is the constructor function.
queue::queue()
{
  sloc = rloc = 0;
  cout << "Queue Initialized\n";
}
```

Keep in mind that the message **Queue Initialized** is output as a way to illustrate the constructor. In actual practice, most constructor functions would not print a message.

An object's constructor is called when the object is created. This means that it is called when the object's declaration is executed. For global objects, the constructor is called when the program begins execution, prior to the call to **main( )**. For local objects, the constructor is called each time the object declaration is encountered.

A destructor is the function that is called when an object is destroyed.

The complement of the constructor is the *destructor*. In many circumstances, an object will need to perform some action or series of actions when it is destroyed. Local objects are created when their block is entered, and destroyed when the block is left. Global objects are destroyed when the program terminates. There are many reasons why a destructor function may be needed. For example, an object may need to deallocate memory that it had previously allocated. In C++, it is the destructor function that handles deactivation. The destructor has the same name as the constructor, but preceded by a ~. Like constructors, destructors do not have return types.

Here is the **queue** class that contains constructor and destructor functions. (Keep in mind that the **queue** class does not require a destructor, so the one shown here is just for illustration.)

```
// This creates the class queue.
class queue {
  int q[100];
  int sloc, rloc;
public:
  queue();  // constructor
  ~queue(); // destructor
  void qput(int i);
  int qget();
};

// This is the constructor function.
queue::queue()
{
  sloc = rloc = 0;
  cout << "Queue initialized\n";
```

11

```
}

// This is the destructor function.
queue::~queue()
{
  cout << "Queue destroyed\n";
}
```

To show you how constructors and destructors work, here is a new version of the queue program:

```
#include <iostream.h>

// This creates the class queue.
class queue {
  int q[100];
  int sloc, rloc;
public:
  queue();   // constructor
  ~queue(); // destructor
  void qput(int i);
  int qget();
};

// This is the constructor function.
queue::queue()
{
  sloc = rloc = 0;
  cout << "Queue initialized\n";
}

// This is the destructor function.
queue::~queue()
{
  cout << "Queue destroyed\n";
}

// Put an integer into the queue.
void queue::qput(int i)
{
  if(sloc==100) {
    cout << "Queue is full";
    return;
  }
  sloc++;
  q[sloc] = i;
}
```

```
// Get an integer from the queue.
int queue::qget()
{
  if(rloc == sloc) {
    cout << "Queue Underflow";
    return 0;
  }
  rloc++;
  return q[rloc];
}

main()
{
  queue a, b;   // create two queue objects

  a.qput(10);
  b.qput(19);

  a.qput(20);
  b.qput(1);

  cout << a.qget() << " ";
  cout << a.qget() << " ";
  cout << b.qget() << " ";
  cout << b.qget() << "\n";

  return 0;
}
```

This program displays the following output:

Queue initialized
Queue initialized
10 20 19 1
Queue destroyed
Queue destroyed

Parameterized Constructors

A constructor function can have parameters. This allows you to give member variables program-defined initial values when an object is created. You do this by passing arguments to an object's constructor function. The next example will enhance the **queue** class to accept an argument which will act as the queue's ID number. First, **queue** is changed to look like this:

```
// This creates the class queue.
class queue {
```

```
   int q[100];
   int sloc, rloc;
   int who; // holds the queue's ID number
public:
   queue(int id);  // parameterized constructor
   ~queue(); // destructor
   void qput(int i);
   int qget();
};
```

The variable **who** is used to hold an ID number that will identify the queue. Its actual value will be determined by what is passed to the constructor function in **id** when a variable of type **queue** is created. The **queue( )** constructor function looks like this:

```
// This is the constructor function.
queue::queue(int id)
{
   sloc = rloc = 0;
   who = id;
   cout << "Queue " << who << " initialized\n";
}
```

To pass an argument to the constructor function, you must associate the value or values being passed with an object when it is being declared. C++ supports two ways to accomplish this. The first method is illustrated here:

```
queue a = queue(101);
```

This declaration creates a queue called **a** and passes the value 101 to it. However, this form is seldom used, because the second method, sometimes called the *shorthand* method, is shorter and more to the point. In the shorthand method, the argument or arguments must follow the object's name and be enclosed between parentheses. For example, this statement accomplishes the same thing as the previous declaration.

```
queue a(101);
```

Since the shorthand method is used by virtually all C++ programmers, this book will use the shorthand form exclusively. The general form of passing arguments to constructor functions is:

    class-type var(arg-list);

Here, *arg-list* is a comma-separated list of arguments that are passed to the constructor.

Note: Technically, there is a small difference between the two initialization forms, which you will learn about later in this book. However, this difference does not affect the programs in this chapter, or most programs that you will write.

11

The following version of the queue program demonstrates a parameterized constructor function.

```cpp
#include <iostream.h>

// This creates the class queue.
class queue {
  int q[100];
  int sloc, rloc;
  int who; // holds the queue's ID number
public:
  queue(int id);  // parameterized constructor
  ~queue(); // destructor
  void qput(int i);
  int qget();
};

// This is the constructor function.
queue::queue(int id)
{
  sloc = rloc = 0;
  who = id;
  cout << "Queue " << who << " initialized\n";
}

// This is the destructor function.
queue::~queue()
{
  cout << "Queue " << who << " destroyed\n";
}

// Put an integer into the queue.
void queue::qput(int i)
{
  if(sloc==100) {
    cout << "Queue is full";
    return;
  }
```

```
  sloc++;
  q[sloc] = i;
}

// Get an integer from the queue.
int queue::qget()
{
  if(rloc == sloc) {
    cout << "Queue underflow";
    return 0;
  }
  rloc++;
  return q[rloc];
}

main()
{
  queue a(1), b(2);  // create two queue objects

  a.qput(10);
  b.qput(19);

  a.qput(20);
  b.qput(1);

  cout << a.qget() << " ";
  cout << a.qget() << " ";
  cout << b.qget() << " ";
  cout << b.qget() << "\n";

  return 0;
}
```

This program produces the following output:

```
Queue 1 initialized
Queue 2 initialized
10 20 19 1
Queue 2 destroyed
Queue 1 destroyed
```

As you can see by looking at **main( )**, the queue associated with **a** is given the ID number 1, and the queue associated with **b** is given the number 2.

Although the **queue** example passes only a single argument when an object is created, it is, of course, possible to pass several. In the following example, objects of type **widget** are passed two values.

```
include <iostream.h>

class widget {
  int i;
  int j;
public:
  widget(int a, int b);
  void put_widget();
} ;

widget::widget(int a, int b)
{
  i = a;
  j = b;
}

void widget::put_widget()
{
  cout << i << " " << j << "\n";
}

main()
{
  widget x(10, 20), y(0, 0);

  x.put_widget();
  y.put_widget();

  return 0;
}
```

This program displays

```
10 20
0 0
```

Tip: Unlike constructor functions, destructor functions cannot have parameters. The reason for this is easy to understand: There is no means by which to pass arguments to an object that is being destroyed. Although the situation is rare, if your object needs access to some run-time-defined data when its destructor is called, you will need to create a public member variable for this purpose. Then, just prior to the object's destruction, you will need to access that variable.

Classes and Structures Are Related

As mentioned in the preceding chapter, in C++ the structure also has object-oriented capabilities. In fact, classes and structures are closely related. With one exception, they are interchangeable because the structure can also include data and the code that manipulates that data in just the same way that a class can. The only difference between a C++ structure and a class is that, by default, the members of a class are private while the members of a structure are public. Aside from this distinction, structures and classes perform exactly the same function. In fact, according to the formal C++ syntax, a structure declaration actually creates a class type.

Here is an example of a structure that uses its class-like features.

```cpp
#include <iostream.h>

struct cl {
  int get_i(); // these are public
  void put_i(int j); // by default
private:
  int i;
};

int cl::get_i()
{
  return i;
}

void cl::put_i(int j)
{
  i = j;
}

main()
{
  cl s;

  s.put_i(10);
  cout << s.get_i();

  return 0;
}
```

The *private* keyword is used to declare the private members of a class.

This simple program defines a structure type called **cl**, in which **get_i( )** and **put_i( )** are public and **i** is private. Notice that **struct**s use the keyword **private** to introduce the private elements of the structure.

The following program shows an equivalent program which uses a **class** instead of a **struct**.

11

```
#include <iostream.h>

class cl {
   int i; // private by default
public:
   int get_i();
   void put_i(int j);
};

int cl::get_i()
{
   return i;
}

void cl::put_i(int j)
{
   i = j;
}

main()
{
   cl s;

   s.put_i(10);
   cout << s.get_i();

   return 0;
}
```

For the most part, C++ programmers will use a class to define the form of an object, and use a **struct** in its more traditional role. However, from time to time you will see C++ code that uses the expanded abilities of structures.

Structures Versus Classes

On the surface, there is seeming redundancy in the fact that both structures and classes have virtually identical capabilities. Many newcomers to C++ wonder why this apparent duplication exists. In fact, it is not uncommon to hear the suggestion that either the keyword **class** or **struct** is unnecessary.

The answer to this line of reasoning is rooted in C++'s derivation from C, and the desire to keep C++ upwardly compatible with C. As C++ is currently defined, a standard C structure is also a completely valid C++ structure. In C, which has no concept of public or private structure members, all structure members are public by default. This is why members of C++ structures are public (rather than private) by default. Since the **class** construct is expressly designed to support encapsulation, it makes sense that its members are private by default. Thus, to avoid incompatibility with C on this issue, the structure default could not be altered, so a new keyword was added. However, in the long term, there is a more important reason for the separation of structures and classes. Because **class** is an entity syntactically separate from **struct**, the definition of a class is free to evolve in ways that may not be syntactically compatible with C-like structures. Since the two are separated, the future direction of C++ will not be encumbered by concerns of compatibility with C-like structures.

Before leaving this topic, one important note must be mentioned: At this point in the development of C++, a structure defines a class type. Thus, a structure *is* a class. This is not expected to change in the near future and, in fact, was intentional on the part of Bjarne Stroustrup. He believed that if structures and classes were made more or less equivalent, the transition from C to C++ would be eased. It seems that history has proven him correct.

Unions and Classes Are Related

The fact that structures and classes are related is not too surprising; however, you might be surprised to learn that unions are also related to classes. As far as C++ is concerned, a union is essentially a class in which all elements are stored in the same location. (A union also defines a class type.) A union can contain constructor and destructor functions as well as member functions. Of course, members of a union are public, not private, by default.

Here is a program that uses a union to display the characters that comprise the low and high order bytes of an integer (assuming two-byte integers).

```cpp
#include <iostream.h>

union u_type {
  u_type(int a);  // public by default
  void showchars();
  int i;
  char ch[2];
};

// constructor
u_type::u_type(int a)
{
  i = a;
}

// Show the characters that comprise an int.
void u_type::showchars()
{
  cout << ch[0] << " ";
  cout << ch[1] << "\n";
}

main()
{
  u_type u(1000);

  u.showchars();

  return 0;
}
```

Like the structure, the C++ union is derived from its C forerunner. However, in C++ it has the expanded capabilities of the class. But just because C++ gives unions greater power and flexibility does not mean that you have to use it. In cases where you simply need a traditional-style union, you are free to use one in that manner. However, in cases where you can encapsulate a union along with the routines that manipulate it, you will be adding considerable structure to your program by doing so.

Inline Functions

Before we continue exploring the class, a small, but important digression is in order. Although it does not pertain specifically to object-oriented programming, one very useful feature of C++, called an *inline function*, is frequently used in class definitions. An inline function is a function that is expanded in line at the point at which it is invoked, instead of actually being called. There are two ways to create an inline function. The first is to use the **inline** modifier. For example, to create an inline function called **f** which returns an **int** and takes no parameters, you declare it like this:

```
inline int f()
{
   // ...
}
```

The **inline** modifier precedes all other aspects of a function's declaration.

An inline function is a small function whose code is expanded in line rather than called.

The reason for inline functions is efficiency. Every time a function is called, a series of instructions must be executed, both to set up the function call, including pushing any arguments onto the stack, and to return from the function. In some cases, many CPU cycles are used to perform these procedures. However, when a function is expanded in line, no such overhead exists, and the overall speed of your program will increase. Even so, in cases where the inline function is large, the overall size of your program will also increase. For this reason, the best inline functions are those that are very small. Larger functions should be left as normal functions.

The following program demonstrates **inline**.

```
#include <iostream.h>

class cl {
  int i; // private by default
public:
  int get_i();
  void put_i(int j);
} ;

inline int cl::get_i()
{
  return i;
}

inline void cl::put_i(int j)
{
  i = j;
}

main()
{
```

```
    cl s;

    s.put_i(10);
    cout << s.get_i();

    return 0;
}
```

If you compile this version of the program, save its object code, and then compile it again with the **inline** specifier removed, you will see that the inline version is several bytes smaller.

It is important to understand that technically, **inline** is a *request*, not a *command*, that the compiler generate inline code. There are various situations that might prevent the compiler from complying with the request. Here are some examples:

♦ Some compilers will not generate inline code if a function contains a loop, a **switch** or a **goto**.

♦ Often, you cannot have inline recursive functions.

♦ Inline functions that contain **static** variables are frequently disallowed.

Remember: Inline restrictions are implementation-dependent, so you must check your compiler's user manual to find out about any restrictions that may apply in your situation.

Creating Inline Functions Inside a Class

There is another way to create an inline function. This is accomplished by defining the code to a member function *inside* a class definition. Any function that is defined inside a class definition is automatically made into an inline function. It is not necessary to precede its declaration with the keyword **inline**. For example, the preceding program can be rewritten as shown here:

```
#include <iostream.h>

class cl {
  int i; // private by default
public:
  // automatic inline functions
  int get_i() { return i; }
  void put_i(int j) { i = j; }
} ;
```

11

```
main()
{
  cl s;

  s.put_i(10);
  cout << s.get_i();

  return 0;
}
```

Notice the way the function code is arranged. For very short functions, this arrangement reflects common C++ style. However, there is no reason that you could not write them as shown here:

```
class cl {
  int i; // private by default
public:
  // inline functions
  int get_i()
  {
    return i;
  }

  void put_i(int j)
  {
    i = j;
  }
};
```

Generally, short functions like those illustrated in this example are defined inside the class declaration. This convention will be followed by the rest of the C++ examples in this book.

Tip: Defining short member functions inside their class definitions is very common in C++ programming. The reason for this is not necessarily because of the automatic inlining feature, but because it is very convenient. In fact, it is quite rare to see short member functions defined outside their class in professionally written C++ code.

Arrays of Objects

You can create arrays of objects in the same way that you create arrays of any other data type. For example, the following program establishes a class called **display** that holds information about the various display monitors that can be attached to a PC. Specifically, it contains the number of colors that can be displayed, and the type of video adapter being used. Inside **main( )**, an array of three **display** objects is created, and the objects that comprise the elements of the array are accessed using the normal indexing procedure.

```cpp
// An example of arrays of objects

#include <iostream.h>

enum disp_type {mono, cga, ega, vga};

class display {
  int colors;   // number of colors
  enum disp_type dt; // display type
public:
  void set_colors(int num) {colors = num;}
  int get_colors() {return colors;}
  void set_type(enum disp_type t) {dt = t;}
  enum disp_type get_type() {return dt;}
};

char names[4][5] = {
  "mono",
  "cga",
  "ega",
  "vga"
} ;

main()
{
  display monitors[3];
  register int i;

  monitors[0].set_type(mono);
  monitors[0].set_colors(1);

  monitors[1].set_type(cga);
  monitors[1].set_colors(4);

  monitors[2].set_type(vga);
  monitors[2].set_colors(16);

  for(i=0; i<3; i++) {
    cout << names[monitors[i].get_type()] << " ";
    cout << "has " << monitors[i].get_colors();
    cout << " colors" << "\n";
  }
```

```
  return 0;
}
```

This program produces the following output:

```
mono has 1 colors
cga has 4 colors
vga has 16 colors
```

Notice how the two-dimensional character array **names** is used to convert between an enumerated value and its equivalent character string. In all enumerations that do not contain explicit initializations, the first constant has the value 0, the second 1, and so on. Therefore, the value returned by **get_type( )** can be used to index the **names** array, causing the appropriate name to be printed.

Multidimensional arrays of objects are indexed in precisely the same way as arrays of other types of data.

Pointers to Objects

As you know, you can access a structure directly, or through a pointer to that structure. In like fashion, you can access an object either directly (as has been the case in all preceding examples), or by using a pointer to that object.

To access an element of an object when using the actual object itself, use the dot operator. To access a specific element of an object when using a pointer to the object, you must use the arrow operator. (The use of the dot and arrow operators for objects parallels their use for structures and unions.)

To declare an object pointer, you use the same declaration syntax that you would use for any other type of data. The next program creates a simple class called **P_example**, defines an object of that class called **ob**, and defines a pointer to an object of type **P_example** called **p**. It then illustrates how to access **ob** directly, and how to use a pointer to access it indirectly.

```
// A simple example using an object pointer.

#include <iostream.h>

class P_example {
  int num;
public:
  void set_num(int val) {num = val;}
  void show_num();
};
```

```
void P_example::show_num()
{
  cout << num << "\n";
}

main()
{
  P_example ob, *p; // declare an object and pointer to it

  ob.set_num(1); // access ob directly

  ob.show_num();

  p = &ob; // assign p the address of ob
  p->show_num();   // access ob using pointer

  return 0;
}
```

Notice that the address of **ob** is obtained using the **&** (address of) operator in the same way that the address is obtained for any type of variable.

As you know, when a pointer is incremented or decremented, it is increased or decreased in such a way that it will always point to the next element of its base type. The same thing occurs when a pointer to an object is incremented or decremented: the next object is pointed to. To illustrate this, the preceding program has been modified here so that **ob** is a two-element array of type **P_example**. Notice how **p** is incremented and decremented to access the two elements in the array.

```
// Incrementing an object pointer
#include <iostream.h>

class P_example {
  int num;
public:
  void set_num(int val) {num = val;}
  void show_num();
};

void P_example::show_num()
{
  cout << num << "\n";
}

main()
{
```

```
P_example ob[2], *p;

ob[0].set_num(10);   // access objects directly
ob[1].set_num(20);

p = &ob[0];  // obtain pointer to first element
p->show_num(); // show value of ob[0] using pointer

p++;   // advance to next object
p->show_num(); // show value of ob[1] using pointer

p--;   // retreat to previous object
p->show_num(); // again show value of ob[0]

return 0;
}
```

The output from this program is **10, 20, 10**.

As you will see later in this book, object pointers play an important role in one of C++'s most important concepts: polymorphism.

Object References

Objects can be referenced in the same way as any other data type. There are no special restrictions or instructions that apply. However, as you will see in the next chapter, the use of object references does help to solve some special problems that you can encounter when using classes.

Chapter

12

A Closer Look at Classes

This chapter continues our discussion of the class. Specifically, it discusses friend functions, overloading constructor functions, passing objects to functions, and returning objects. It also examines a special type of constructor, called the copy constructor, that can solve a problem associated with certain classes. The chapter concludes with a description of the **this** keyword.

Friend Functions

It is possible to allow a non-member function access to the private members of a class by declaring it as a *friend* of the class. To make a function a friend of a class, you include its prototype in the **public** section of a class declaration and begin it with the **friend** keyword. For example, in this fragment **frnd( )** is declared to be a friend of the class **cl**.

```
class cl {
  // ...
public:
  friend void frnd(cl ob);
  // ...
};
```

The **friend** keyword is used to give a non-member function access to the private members of a class.

As you can see, the keyword **friend** precedes the rest of the prototype. A function may be a friend of more than one class.

Here is a short example that uses a friend function to access the private members of **myclass**.

```
#include "iostream.h"

class myclass {
  int a, b;
public:
  myclass(int i, int j) { a=i; b=j; }
  friend int sum(myclass x);
};

// Note: sum() is not a member function of any class.
int sum(myclass x)
{
  /* Because sum() is a friend of myclass, it can
     directly access a and b. */

  return x.a + x.b;
}

main()
{
  myclass n(3, 4);

  cout << sum(n);

  return 0;
}
```

In this example, the **sum( )** function is not a member of **myclass**. However, it still has full access to the private members of **myclass**. Specifically, it can access **x.a** and **x.b**. Notice also that **sum( )** is called normally—that is, not in conjunction with an object and the dot operator. Since it is not a member function, it does not need to be qualified with an object's name. (In fact, it *cannot* be qualified with an object.)

While there is nothing gained by making **sum( )** a friend rather than a member function of **myclass**, there are some circumstances in which friend functions are quite valuable. First, friends can be useful for overloading certain types of operators. Second, friend functions simplify the creation of some types of I/O functions. Both of these uses are discussed later in this book.

The third reason that friend functions may be desirable is that, in some cases, two or more classes may contain members that are interrelated relative to other parts of your program. For example, imagine two different classes that each display a pop-up message on the screen when some sort of error condition occurs. Other parts of your program designed to write to the screen will need to know whether the pop-up message is active so that no message is accidentally overwritten. It is possible to create a member function in each class that returns a value indicating whether a message is active or not; however, checking this condition involves additional overhead (i.e., two function calls, not just one). If the status of the pop-up message needs to be checked frequently, the additional overhead may not be acceptable. However, by using a friend function, it is possible to directly check the status of each object by calling only one function that has access to both classes. In situations like this, a friend function allows you to generate more efficient code. The following program illustrates this concept.

12

```
#include <iostream.h>

const int IDLE=0;
const int INUSE=1;

class C2;  // forward reference

class C1 {
  int status;  // IDLE if off, INUSE if on screen
  // ...
public:
  void set_status(int state);
  friend int idle(C1 a, C2 b);
};
```

```
class C2 {
  int status; // IDLE if off, INUSE if on screen
  // ...
public:
  void set_status(int state);
  friend int idle(C1 a, C2 b);
};

void C1::set_status(int state)
{
  status = state;
}

void C2::set_status(int state)
{
  status = state;
}

int idle(C1 a, C2 b)
{
  if(a.status || b.status) return 0;
  else return 1;
}

main()
{
  C1 x;
  C2 y;

  x.set_status(IDLE);
  y.set_status(IDLE);

  if(idle(x, y)) cout << "Screen Can Be Used\n";
  else cout << "Pop-up In Use\n";

  x.set_status(INUSE);

  if(idle(x, y)) cout << "Screen Can Be Used\n";
  else cout << "Pop-up In Use\n";

  return 0;
}
```

A forward reference declares a class type name prior to the definition of the class.

Notice that this program uses a *forward reference* for the class **C2**. This is necessary because the declaration of **idle( )** inside **C1** references **C2** before it is declared. To create a forward reference to a class, simply use the form shown in this program.

A friend of one class may be a member of another. For example, here is the preceding program rewritten so that **idle( )** is a member of **C1**. Notice the use of the scope resolution operator when declaring **idle( )** to be a friend of **C2**.

```cpp
#include <iostream.h>

const int IDLE=0;
const int INUSE=1;

class C2;  // forward reference

class C1 {
  int status;  // IDLE if off, INUSE if on screen
  // ...
public:
  void set_status(int state);
  int idle(C2 b);  // now a member of C1
};

class C2 {
  int status;  // IDLE if off, INUSE if on screen
  // ...
public:
  void set_status(int state);
  friend int C1::idle(C2 b);
};

void C1::set_status(int state)
{
  status = state;
}

void C2::set_status(int state)
{
  status = state;
}

// idle() is member of C1, but friend of C2
int C1::idle(C2 b)
{
  if(status || b.status) return 0;
  else return 1;
}

main()
{
```

12

```
  C1 x;
  C2 y;

  x.set_status(IDLE);
  y.set_status(IDLE);

  if(x.idle(y)) cout << "Screen Can Be Used\n";
  else cout << "Pop-up In Use\n";

  x.set_status(INUSE);

  if(x.idle(y)) cout << "Screen Can Be Used\n";
  else cout << "Pop-up In Use\n";

  return 0;
}
```

Since **idle( )** is a member of **C1**, it can access the **status** variable of objects of type **C1** directly. Thus only objects of type **C2** need be passed to **idle( )**.

Overloading Constructor Functions

Although they perform a unique service, constructor functions are not much different from other types of functions and they too can be overloaded. To overload a class's constructor function, simply declare the various forms it will take and define each action relative to these forms. For example, the following program declares a class called **timer** which acts as a countdown timer (such as a darkroom timer). When an object of type **timer** is created it is given an initial time value. When the **run( )** function is called, the timer counts down to zero and then rings the bell. In this example, the constructor has been overloaded to allow the time to be specified in seconds as either an integer or a string, or in minutes and seconds by specifying two integers. This program makes use of the standard library function **clock( )**, which returns the number of system clock ticks since the program began running. Dividing this value by **CLOCKS_PER_SEC** converts the return value of **clock( )** into seconds. Both the prototype for **clock( )** and the definition of **CLOCKS_PER_SEC** are found in the header file **time.h**.

```
#include <iostream.h>
#include <stdlib.h>
#include <time.h>

class timer{
  int seconds;
```

```
public:
  // seconds specified as a string
  timer(char *t) { seconds = atoi(t); }

  // seconds specified as integer
  timer(int t) { seconds = t; }

  // time specified in minutes and seconds
  timer(int min, int sec) { seconds = min*60 + sec; }

  void run();
} ;

void timer::run()
{
  clock_t t1, t2;

  t1 = t2 = clock()/CLOCKS_PER_SEC;
  while(seconds) {
    if(t1/CLOCKS_PER_SEC+1
              <= (t2=clock())/CLOCKS_PER_SEC) {
      seconds--;
      t1 = t2;
    }
  }
  cout << "\a"; // ring the bell
}

main()
{
  timer a(10), b("20"), c(1, 10);

  a.run(); // count 10 seconds
  b.run(); // count 20 seconds
  c.run(); // count 1 minute, 10 seconds

  return 0;
}
```

12

As you can see, when **a, b**, and **c** are created inside **main( )**, they are given initial values using the three different methods supported by the overloaded constructor functions. Each approach causes the appropriate constructor to be utilized, thus properly initializing all three variables.

In the preceding program, you may see little value in overloading a constructor function, because it is not difficult to simply decide on a single way of specifying the time. However, if you were creating a library of classes for someone else to use, then you might want to supply constructors for the most common forms of initialization, thereby allowing the programmer to utilize the most appropriate form for his or her program. Also, as you will shortly see, there is one C++ attribute that makes overloaded constructors quite valuable.

Dynamic Initialization

In C++, both local and global variables can be initialized at run time. This process is sometimes referred to as *dynamic initialization*. So far, most initializations that you have seen in this book have used constants. However, under dynamic initialization, a variable can be initialized at run time using any C++ expression valid at the time the variable is declared. This means that you can initialize a variable using other variables and/or function calls so long as the overall expression has meaning when the declaration is encountered. For example, the following are all perfectly valid variable initializations in C++.

```
int n = strlen(str);

double arc = sin(theta);

float d = 1.02 * count / deltax;
```

Applying Dynamic Initialization to Constructors

Like simple variables, objects can be initialized dynamically when they are created. This feature allows you to create exactly the type of object you need, using information that is known only at run time. To illustrate how dynamic initialization works, let's rework the timer program from the previous section.

Recall that in the first example of the timer program, there is little to be gained by overloading the **timer( )** constructor, because all objects of its type are initialized using constants. However, in cases when an object will be initialized at run time, there may be significant advantages to providing a variety of initialization formats. This allows you, the programmer, the flexibility of using the constructor that most closely matches the format of the data available at the moment.

For example, in the following version of the timer program, dynamic initialization is used to construct two objects, **b** and **c,** at run time.

```
#include <iostream.h>
#include <stdlib.h>
#include <time.h>
```

```
class timer{
  int seconds;
public:
  // seconds specified as a string
  timer(char *t) { seconds = atoi(t); }

  // seconds specified as integer
  timer(int t) { seconds = t; }

  // time specified in minutes and seconds
  timer(int min, int sec) { seconds = min*60 + sec; }

  void run();
} ;

void timer::run()
{
  clock_t t1, t2;

  t1 = t2 = clock()/CLOCKS_PER_SEC;
  while(seconds) {
    if(t1/CLOCKS_PER_SEC+1
          <= (t2=clock())/CLOCKS_PER_SEC) {
      seconds--;
      t1 = t2;
    }
  }
  cout << "\a"; // ring the bell
}

main()
{
  timer a(10);

  a.run();

  cout << "Enter number of seconds: ";
  char str[80];
  cin >> str;
  timer b(str);  // initialize at run time
  b.run();

  cout << "Enter minutes and seconds: ";
  int min, sec;
  cin >> min >> sec;
  timer c(min, sec);  // initialize at run time
  c.run();
```

12

```
   return 0;
}
```

As you can see, object **a** is constructed using an integer constant. However, objects **b** and **c** are constructed using information entered by the user. For **b**, since the user enters a string, it makes sense that **timer( )** is overloaded to accept it. In similar fashion, object **c** is also constructed at run time from user-input information. In this case, since the time is entered as minutes and seconds, it is logical to use this format for constructing object **c**. As the example shows, having a variety of initialization formats keeps you from having to perform any unnecessary conversions when initializing an object.

The point of overloading constructor functions is to help programmers handle greater complexity by allowing objects to be constructed in the most natural manner relative to their specific use. Since there are three common methods of passing timing values to an object, it makes sense that **timer( )** be overloaded to accept each method. However, overloading **timer( )** to accept days or nanoseconds is probably not a good idea. Littering your code with constructors to handle seldom-used contingencies has a destabilizing influence on your program.

Remember: You must decide what constitutes valid constructor overloading and what is frivolous.

Assigning Objects

If both objects are of the same type (that is, both are objects of the same class), then one object may be assigned to another. (It is not sufficient for the two classes to simply be physically similar—their type names must be the same.) By default, when one object is assigned to another, a bitwise copy of the first object's data is copied to the second. The following program demonstrates object assignment.

```
// Demonstrate object assignment.
#include <iostream.h>

class myclass {
  int a, b;
public:
  void setab(int i, int j) { a = i, b = j; }
```

```
      void showab();
};

void myclass::showab()
{
   cout << "a is " << a << '\n';
   cout << "b is " << b << '\n';
}

main()
{
   myclass ob1, ob2;

   ob1.setab(10, 20);
   ob2.setab(0, 0);
   cout << "ob1 before assignment: \n";
   ob1.showab();
   cout << "ob2 before assignment: \n";
   ob2.showab();
   cout << '\n';

   ob2 = ob1; // assign ob1 to ob2

   cout << "ob1 after assignment: \n";
   ob1.showab();
   cout << "ob2 after assignment: \n";
   ob2.showab();

   return 0;
}
```

This program displays the following output:

```
   ob1 before assignment:
   a is 10
   b is 20
   ob2 before assignment:
   a is 0
   b is 0

   ob1 after assignment:
   a is 10
   b is 20
   ob2 after assignment:
   a is 10
   b is 20
```

Recall that by default, all data from one object is assigned to the other using a bit-by-bit copy. (That is, an exact duplicate is created.) However, as you will see later, it is possible to overload the assignment operator so that customized assignment operations can be defined.

Remember: Assignment of one object to another simply makes the data in those objects identical. The two objects are still completely separate. Thus, a subsequent modification of one object's data has no effect on that of the other.

Passing Objects to Functions

An object can be passed to a function in the same way as any other data type. Objects are passed to functions using the normal C++ call-by-value parameter passing convention. This means that a *copy* of the object, not the actual object itself, is passed to the function. Therefore, any changes made to the object inside the function do not affect the object used as the argument to the function. The following program illustrates this point.

```
#include <iostream.h>

class OBJ {
  int i;
public:
  void set_i(int x) { i = x; }
  void out_i() { cout << i << " "; }
};

void f(OBJ x)
{
  x.out_i();   // outputs 10
  x.set_i(100);   // this affects only local copy
  x.out_i();   // outputs 100
}

main()
{
  OBJ o;

  o.set_i(10);
  f(o);
  o.out_i();   // still outputs 10, value of i unchanged

  return 0;
}
```

As the comments indicate, the modification of **x** within **f( )** has no effect on object **o** inside **main( )**.

Constructors, Destructors, and Passing Objects

Although passing simple objects as arguments to functions is a straightforward procedure, some rather unexpected events occur when you pass an object that has a constructor and destructor. To understand why, consider this short program:

```
// Constructors, destructors, and passing objects
#include <iostream.h>

class myclass {
  int val;
public:
  myclass(int i) { val = i; cout << "Constructing\n"; }
  ~myclass() { cout << "Destructing\n"; }
  int getval() { return val; }
};

void display(myclass ob)
{
  cout << ob.getval() << '\n';
}

main()
{
  myclass a(10);

  display(a);

  return 0;
}
```

This program produces the following, unexpected output:

```
Constructing
10
Destructing
Destructing
```

As you can see, there is one call to the constructor function (as expected), but there are *two* calls to the destructor. Let's see why this is the case.

When an object is passed to a function, a copy of that object is made (and this copy becomes the parameter in the function). This means that a new object comes into existence. Also, when the function terminates, the copy of the argument (i.e., the parameter) is destroyed. This raises two fundamental questions: First, is the object's constructor called when the copy is made? Second, is the object's destructor called when the copy is destroyed? The answers may, at first, surprise you.

When a copy of an argument is made during a function call, the constructor function is *not* called. The reason for this is simple to understand if you think about it. Since the constructor function is generally used to initialize some aspect of an object, it must not be called to make a copy of an already existing object that is being passed to a function. Such a call would alter the contents of the object. When passing an object to a function, you want to use the current state of the object, not its initial state.

However, when the function terminates and the copy is destroyed, the destructor function *is* called. This is because the object might perform some operation that must be undone when it goes out of scope. For example, the copy may allocate memory that must be released.

To summarize: When a copy of an object is created to be used as an argument to a function, the constructor function is not called. However, when the copy is destroyed (usually by going out of scope when the function returns), the destructor function is called.

A Potential Problem When Passing Objects

Even though objects are passed to functions by means of the normal call-by-value parameter passing mechanism which, in theory, protects and insulates the calling argument, it is still possible for a side effect to occur that may affect, or even damage, the object used as an argument. For example, if an object used as an argument allocates dynamic memory and frees that memory when it is destroyed, then its local copy inside the function will free the same memory when its destructor is called. This will leave the original object damaged and effectively useless. Consider this sample program:

```
// Demonstrate a problem when passing objects.
#include <iostream.h>
#include <stdlib.h>

class myclass {
   int *p;
public:
   myclass(int i);
   ~myclass();
```

```
    int getval() { return *p; }
};

myclass::myclass(int i)
{
  cout << "Allocating p\n";
  p = new int;
  if(!p) {
    cout << "Allocation failure";
    exit(1); // exit program if out of memory
  }

  *p = i;
}

myclass::~myclass()
{
  cout << "Freeing p\n";
  delete p;
}

// This will cause a problem.
void display(myclass ob)
{
  cout << ob.getval() << '\n';
}

main()
{
  myclass a(10);

  display(a);

  return 0;
}
```

12

This program displays the following output:

> Allocating p
> 10
> Freeing p
> Freeing p
> Null pointer assignment

As the **Null pointer assignment** message suggests, this program contains a fundamental error. Here is why: When **a** is constructed within **main( )**, memory is allocated and assigned to **a.p**. When **a** is passed to **display( )**, **a** is copied into the parameter **ob**. This means that both **a** and **ob** will have the same value for **p**. That is, both objects will have their copies of **p** pointing to the same dynamically allocated memory. When **display( )** terminates, **ob** is destroyed, and its destructor is called. This causes **ob.p** to be freed. However, the memory freed by **ob.p** is the same memory that is still in use by **a.p**! This is, in itself, a serious bug.

However, things get even worse. When the program ends, **a** is destroyed, and its dynamically allocated memory is freed a second time. The problem is that freeing dynamically allocated memory a second time generally destroys the dynamic allocation system and usually causes a fatal error, as evidenced by the system-generated error message **Null pointer assignment**. (Depending on your compiler, you may not see this message, but the error will still have occurred.)

The exit( ) function

If you look closely at the programs in this chapter that use **new** to allocate memory, you will see that the **exit( )** function is called if an allocation request fails. The **exit( )** function is part of the C++ standard library, and it causes the immediate termination of any program that calls it. It is typically used to halt a program when a fatal error has occurred that renders further execution of the program meaningless or harmful. Since an allocation failure (usually caused by insufficient dynamic memory being available) is a fatal (and potentially harmful) error, the programs use **exit( )** to stop the program.

The **exit( )** function has the following prototype:

    void exit(int *status*);

Since **exit( )** causes immediate termination of the program, it does not return, and consequently it does not have a return value. However, the value of *status* is returned as an exit code to the calling process. By convention, a return value 0 indicates successful termination. Any other value indicates that your program terminated because of some sort of error.

You must include **stdlib.h** in any program that calls **exit( ).**

As you might guess, one way around the problem of a parameter's destructor function destroying data needed by the calling argument is to pass either a pointer or a reference, instead of the object itself. When either a pointer to an object or a reference to an object is passed, no copy is made; thus, no destructor is called when the function returns. For example, here is one way to correct the preceding program.

```cpp
// One solution to the problem of passing objects.
#include <iostream.h>
#include <stdlib.h>

class myclass {
   int *p;
public:
   myclass(int i);
   ~myclass();
   int getval() { return *p; }
};

myclass::myclass(int i)
{
   cout << "Allocating p\n";
   p = new int;
   if(!p) {
     cout << "Allocation failure";
     exit(1); // exit program if out of memory
   }

   *p = i;
}

myclass::~myclass()
{
   cout << "Freeing p\n";
   delete p;
}

/* This will NOT cause a problem.

   Because ob is now passed by reference, no
   copy of the calling argument is made and thus,
   no object goes out-of-scope when display()
   terminates.
*/
void display(myclass &ob)
{
   cout << ob.getval() << '\n';
}
```

12

```
main()
{
  myclass a(10);

  display(a);

  return 0;
}
```

Passing an object by reference is an excellent approach when the situation allows it, but it cannot be used in all cases. Fortunately, a more general solution is provided by C++. This solution is called a *copy constructor*. A copy constructor lets you define precisely how a copy of an object is made, allowing you to avoid the type of problem just described. However, before discussing the copy constructor, let's look at another, related situation that can also benefit from a copy constructor.

Returning Objects

Just as objects can be passed to functions, so functions can return objects. To return an object in this way, first declare the function as returning a class type. Second, return an object of that type using the normal **return** statement.

Here is an example of a function that returns an object:

```
// Returning an object
#include <iostream.h>
#include <string.h>

class sample {
  char s[80];
public:
  void show() { cout << s << "\n"; }
  void set(char *str) { strcpy(s, str); }
};

// Return an object of type sample
sample input()
{
  char instr[80];
  sample str;

  cout << "Enter a string: ";
  cin >> instr;
```

```
    str.set(instr);

    return str;
}

main()
{
  sample ob;

  // assign returned object to ob
  ob = input();
  ob.show();

  return 0;
}
```

In this example, **input( )** creates a local object called **str** and then reads a string from the keyboard. This string is copied into **str.s,** and then **str** is returned by the function. This object is then assigned to **ob** inside **main( )** after it is returned by **input( )**.

A Potential Problem When Returning Objects

There is one important point to understand about returning objects from functions: When an object is returned by a function, a temporary object is automatically created, which holds the return value. It is this object that is actually returned by the function. After the value has been returned, this object is destroyed. The destruction of this temporary object may cause unexpected side effects in some situations. For example, if the object returned by the function has a destructor that frees dynamically allocated memory, that memory will be freed even though the object that is assigned the return value is still using it. Consider the following incorrect version of the preceding program.

```
// An error generated by returning an object.
#include <iostream.h>
#include <string.h>
#include <stdlib.h>

class sample {
  char *s;
public:
  sample() { s = '\0'; }
  ~sample() { if(s) delete s; cout << "Freeing s\n"; }
  void show() { cout << s << "\n"; }
```

12

```
  void set(char *str);
};

// Load a string.
void sample::set(char *str)
{
  s = new char[strlen(str)+1];
  if(!s) {
    cout << "Allocation error\n";
    exit(1); // exit program if out of memory
  }

  strcpy(s, str);
}

// Return an object of type sample.
sample input()
{
  char instr[80];
  sample str;

  cout << "Enter a string: ";
  cin >> instr;

  str.set(instr);
  return str;
}

main()
{
  sample ob;

  // assign returned object to ob
  ob = input();  // This causes an error!!!!
  ob.show();

  return 0;
}
```

The output from this program is shown here:

    Enter a string: Hello
    Freeing s
    Freeing s
    Hello
    Freeing s
    Null pointer assignment

Notice that **sample**'s destructor function is called three times. First, it is called when the local object **str** goes out of scope upon the return of **input( )**. The second time **~sample( )** is called is when the temporary object returned by **input( )** is destroyed. Remember, when an object is returned from a function, an invisible (to you) temporary object is automatically generated which holds the return value. In this case, the object is simply a copy of **str**, which is the return value of the function. Therefore, after the function has returned, the temporary object's destructor is executed. Finally, the destructor for object **ob**, inside **main( )**, is called when the program terminates. The trouble is that in this situation, the first time the destructor executes, the memory allocated to hold the string input by **input( )** is freed. Thus, not only do the other two calls to **sample**'s destructor try to free an already released piece of dynamic memory, they also destroy the dynamic allocation system in the process, as evidenced by the run-time message **Null pointer assignment**. (Depending upon your compiler, you may or may not see this message if you try this program.)

12

The key point to be understood from this example is that when an object is returned from a function, the temporary object being used to effect the return will have its destructor function called. Thus, you should avoid returning objects in which this situation can be harmful. One solution is to return either a pointer or a reference. However, this is not always feasible. Another way to solve this problem involves the use of a copy constructor and, in some cases, an overloaded assignment operator. (The copy constructor is discussed next, but a complete solution to this problem will have to wait until later in this book, when we examine the process of overloading operators.)

Creating and Using a Copy Constructor

One of the more important forms of an overloaded constructor is the copy constructor. As earlier examples have shown, problems can occur when an object is passed to or returned from a function. As you will learn in this section, one way to avoid these problems is to define a copy constructor, which is a special type of overloaded constructor function.

To begin, let's restate the problem that a copy constructor is designed to solve. When an object is passed to a function, a bitwise (i.e., exact) copy of that object is made and given to the function parameter that receives the object. However, there are cases in which this identical copy is not desirable. For example, if the object contains a pointer to allocated memory, then the copy will point to the *same* memory as does the original object. Therefore, if the copy makes a change to the contents of this memory, it will be changed for the original object, too! Furthermore, when the function terminates, the copy will be destroyed, thus causing its destructor to be called. This may also have undesired effects on the original object.

A similar situation occurs when an object is returned by a function. Commonly, the compiler will generate a temporary object that holds a copy of the value returned by the function. (This is done automatically, and is beyond your control.) This temporary object goes out of scope once the value is returned to the calling routine, causing the temporary object's destructor to be called. However, if the destructor destroys something needed by the calling routine (such as dynamically allocated memory), trouble will follow.

At the core of these problems is the creation of a bitwise copy of the object. To prevent them, you need to define precisely what occurs when a copy of an object is made so that you can avoid undesired side effects. The way you accomplish this is by creating a copy constructor. By defining a copy constructor, you can fully specify exactly what occurs when a copy of an object is made.

Before we explore the use of the copy constructor, it is important for you to understand that C++ defines two distinct types of situations in which the value of one object is given to another. The first situation is assignment. The second situation is initialization, which can occur three ways:

The copy constructor is called when one object initializes another.

◆ When an object is used to initialize another in a declaration statement

◆ When an object is passed as a parameter to a function

◆ When a temporary object is created for use as a return value by a function

The copy constructor applies only to initializations. It does not apply to assignments.

By default, when an initialization occurs, the compiler will automatically provide a bitwise copy. (In other words, C++ automatically provides a default copy constructor that simply duplicates the object.) However, it is possible to define a copy constructor that specifies precisely how one object will initialize another. Once defined, the copy constructor is called whenever an object is used to initialize another.

Remember: Copy constructors do not affect assignment operations.

All copy constructors have this general form:

classname (const *classname* &*obj*) {
  // body of constructor
  }

Here, *obj* is a reference to an object that is being used to initialize another object. For example, assuming a class called **myclass**, and **y** as an object of type **myclass**, then the following statements would invoke the **myclass** copy constructor.

```
myclass x = y; // y explicitly initializing x
func1(y); // y passed as a parameter
y = func2(); // y receiving a returned object
```

In the first two cases, a reference to **y** would be passed to the copy constructor. In the third, a reference to the object returned by **func2( )** would be passed to the copy constructor.

To fully explore the value of copy constructors, let's see how they impact each of the three situations to which they apply.

Copy Constructors and Parameters

As you have seen, when an object is passed to a function as an argument, a copy of that object is made. If a copy constructor exists, the copy constructor is called to make the copy. Here is a program that uses a copy constructor to properly handle objects of type **myclass** when they are passed to a function. (This is a corrected version of the incorrect program shown earlier in this chapter.)

```
// Use a copy constructor to construct a parameter.
#include <iostream.h>
#include <stdlib.h>

class myclass {
  int *p;
public:
  myclass(int i);
  myclass(const myclass &ob);
  ~myclass();
  int getval() { return *p; }
};

// Copy constructor
myclass::myclass(const myclass &obj)
```

```
{
  p = new int;
  if(!p) {
    cout << "Allocation error";
    exit(1); // exit program if out of memory
  }

  *p = *obj.p; // copy value
  cout << "Copy constructor called.\n";
}

myclass::myclass(int i)
{
  cout << "Allocating p\n";
  p = new int;
  if(!p) {
    cout << "Allocation failure";
    exit(1); // exit program if out of memory
  }

  *p = i;
}

myclass::~myclass()
{
  cout << "Freeing p\n";
  delete p;
}

// This function takes one object parameter.
void display(myclass ob)
{
  cout << ob.getval() << '\n';
}

main()
{
  myclass a(10);

  display(a);

  return 0;
}
```

This program displays the following output:

```
Allocating p
Copy constructor called.
10
Freeing p
Freeing p
```

Here is what occurs when the program is run: When **a** is created inside **main( )**, the normal constructor allocates memory and assigns the address of that memory to **a.p**. Next, **a** is passed to **ob** of **display( )**. When this occurs, the copy constructor is called, and a copy of **a** is created. The copy constructor allocates memory for the copy, and a pointer to that memory is assigned to the copy's **p**. In this way, the areas of memory pointed to by **a** and **ob** are separate and distinct. That is, **ob.p** and **a.p** do not point to the same memory. (If the copy constructor had not been created, then the default bitwise copy would have caused **a.p** and **ob.p** to point to the same memory.)

12

When **display( )** returns, **ob** goes out of scope. This causes its destructor to be called, which frees the memory pointed to by **ob.p**. Finally, when **main( )** returns, **a** goes out of scope, causing its destructor to free **a.p**. As you can see, the use of the copy constructor has eliminated the destructive side effects associated with passing an object to a function.

Copy Constructors and Initializations

Recall that a copy constructor is also invoked when one object is used to initialize another. Examine this sample program:

```cpp
#include <iostream.h>
#include <stdlib.h>

class myclass {
  int *p;
public:
  myclass(int i);
  myclass(const myclass &ob);
  ~myclass();
  int getval() { return *p; }
};

// Copy constructor
myclass::myclass(const myclass &ob)
{
  p = new int;
```

```
  if(!p) {
    cout << "Allocation failure";
    exit(1); // exit program if out of memory
  }

  *p = *ob.p; // copy value
  cout << "Copy constructor allocating p.\n";
}

// Normal constructor
myclass::myclass(int i)
{
  cout << "Normal constructor allocating p\n";
  p = new int;
  if(!p) {
    cout << "Allocation failure";
    exit(1); // exit program if out of memory
  }

  *p = i;
}

myclass::~myclass()
{
  cout << "Freeing p\n";
  delete p;
}

main()
{
  myclass a(10); // calls normal constructor

  myclass b = a; // calls copy constructor

  return 0;
}
```

This program displays the following output:

    Normal constructor allocating p
    Copy constructor allocating p.
    Freeing p
    Freeing p

As you can see, the normal constructor is called for object **a**. However, when **a** is used to initialize **b**, the copy constructor is invoked. The use of the copy constructor ensures that **b** will allocate its own memory. Without the copy constructor, **b** would simply be an exact copy of **a**, and **a.p** would point to the same memory as **b.p**.

Keep in mind that the copy constructor is called only for initializations. For example, the following sequence does *not* call the copy constructor defined in the preceding program.

```
myclass a(2), b(3);
// ...
b = a;
```

In this case, **b = a** performs the assignment operation, not a copy operation.

Using Copy Constructors When an Object Is Returned

12

The copy constructor is also invoked when a temporary object is created as the result of a function returning an object. Consider this short program:

```
/* Copy constructor is called when a temporary object
   is created as a function return value.
*/
#include <iostream.h>

class myclass {
public:
  myclass() { cout << "Normal constructor\n"; }
  myclass(const myclass &obj) { cout << "Copy constructor\n"; }
};

myclass f()
{
  myclass ob; // invoke normal constructor

  return ob; // implicitly invoke copy constructor
}

main()
{
  myclass a; // invoke normal constructor

  a = f(); // invoke copy constructor

  return 0;
}
```

This program displays the following output:

```
Normal constructor
Normal constructor
Copy constructor
```

Here, the normal constructor is called twice: once when **a** is created inside **main( )**, and once when **ob** is created inside **f( )**. The copy constructor is called when the temporary object is generated as a return value from **f( )**.

Although copy constructors may seem a bit esoteric at this point, virtually every real-word class will require one, due to the side effects that often result from the default bitwise copy.

The this Keyword

Each time a member function is invoked, it is automatically passed a pointer, called **this**, to the object that has invoked it. The **this** pointer is an *implicit* parameter to all member functions. Therefore, inside a member function, **this** may be used to refer to the invoking object.

this is a pointer to the object that invokes a member function.

As you know, a member function can directly access the private data of its class. For example, given this class,

```
class cl {
  int i;
  .
  .
  .
};
```

the following statement can be used to assign **i** the value 10

```
i = 10;
```

In actuality, the preceding statement is shorthand for this one:

```
this->i = 10;
```

To see how the **this** pointer works, examine the following short program:

```
#include <iostream.h>

class cl {
  int i;
```

```
public:
  void load_i(int val) { this->i = val; } // same as i = val
  int get_i() { return this->i; } // same as return i
} ;

main()
{
  cl o;

  o.load_i(100);
  cout << o.get_i();

  return 0;
}
```

12

This program displays the number **100**.

The preceding example is, in fact, trivial—no one would actually use the **this** pointer in this way. Soon, however, you will see why the **this** pointer is important to C++ programming.

Tip: Friend functions do not have a **this** pointer, because friends are not members of a class. Only member functions have a **this** pointer.

Chapter

13

Operator Overloading

In C++, operators can be overloaded relative to class types that you define. As you will see, the principal advantage to overloading operators is that it allows you to seamlessly integrate new data types into your programming environment.

Operator overloading allows you to define the meaning of an operator for a particular class. For example, a class that defines a linked list might use the + operator to add an object to the list. A class that implements a stack might use the + to push an object onto the stack. Another class might use the + operator in an entirely different way. When an operator is overloaded, none of its original meaning is lost. It is simply that a new operation, relative to a specific class, is defined. Therefore, overloading the + to handle a linked list, for example, does not cause its meaning relative to integers (i.e., addition) to be changed.

Operator overloading is closely related to function overloading. To overload an operator, you must define what the operation means relative to the class to which it is applied. To do this you create an **operator** function, which defines the action of the operator. The general form of an **operator** function is:

> *type classname*::operator#(*arg-list*)
> {
>   *operation relative to the class*
> }

Here, the operator that you are overloading is substituted for the #, and *type* is the type of value returned by the specified operation. Although it can be of any type you choose, the return value is often of the same type as the class for which the operator is being overloaded. This correlation facilitates the use of the overloaded operator in compound expressions. The specific nature of *arg-list* is determined by several factors, as you will soon see.

*Operators are overloaded using an **operator** function.*

Operator functions are usually members or friends of the class for which they are being used. (An overloaded operator function can be a stand-alone function, but this is seldom practical.) Although very similar, there are some differences between the way a member operator function is overloaded and the way a friend operator function is overloaded. This chapter begins with a discussion of overloading using member functions. Later, you will see how to overload friend operator functions.

Operator Overloading Using Member Functions

To see how operator overloading works, let's start with a simple example. The following program creates a class called **three_d**, which maintains the coordinates of an object in three-dimensional space. This program overloads the + and the = operators relative to the **three_d** class. Examine it closely:

```
#include <iostream.h>

class three_d {
  int x, y, z; // 3-D coordinates
public:
  three_d() { x = y = z = 0; }
  three_d(int i, int j, int k) {x = i; y = j; z = k; }
  three_d operator+(three_d t);
  three_d operator=(three_d t);
  void show() ;
};
```

```
// Overload +.
three_d three_d::operator+(three_d t)
{
  three_d temp;

  temp.x = x+t.x;
  temp.y = y+t.y;
  temp.z = z+t.z;
  return temp;
}

// Overload assignment.
three_d three_d::operator=(three_d t)
{
  x = t.x;
  y = t.y;
  z = t.z;
  return *this;
}

// Show X, Y, Z coordinates.
void three_d::show()
{
  cout << x << ", ";
  cout << y << ", ";
  cout << z << "\n";
}

main()
{
  three_d a(1, 2, 3), b(10, 10, 10), c;

  a.show();
  b.show();

  c = a+b;   // now add a and b together
  c.show();

  c = a+b+c; // add a, b and c together
  c.show();

  c = b = a;   // demonstrate multiple assignment
  c.show();
  b.show();

  return 0;
}
```

This program produces the following output:

```
1, 2, 3
10, 10, 10
11, 12, 13
22, 24, 26
1, 2, 3
1, 2, 3
```

As you examined the program, you may have been surprised to see that both operator functions have only one parameter each, even though they overload binary operations. The reason for this apparent contradiction is that when a binary operator is overloaded using a member function, only one argument is explicitly passed to it. The other argument is implicitly passed using the **this** pointer. Thus, in the line

```
temp.x = x + t.x;
```

the **x** refers to **this–>x**, which is the **x** associated with the object that invokes the operator function. In all cases, it is the object on the left side of an operation that causes the call to the operator function. The object on the right side is passed to the function.

In general, when you use a member function, no parameters are used when overloading a unary operator, and only one parameter is required when overloading a binary operator. (You cannot overload the ternary **?** operator.) In either case, the object that invokes the operator function is implicitly passed via the **this** pointer.

To understand how operator overloading works, let's examine the preceding program carefully, beginning with the overloaded operator **+**. When two objects of type **three_d** are operated on by the **+** operator, the magnitudes of their respective coordinates are added together, as shown in the **operator+( )**. Notice, however, that this function does not modify the value of either operand. Instead, an object of type **three_d**, which contains the result of the operation, is returned by the function. To understand why the **+** operation does not change the contents of either object, think about the standard arithmetic **+** operation as applied like this: 10 + 12. The outcome of this operation is 22, but neither 10 nor 12 is changed by it. Although there is no rule that prevents an overloaded operator from altering the value of one of its operands, it is best for the actions of an overloaded operator to be consistent with its original meaning.

Notice that **operator+( )** returns an object of type **three_d**. Although the function could have returned any valid C++ type, the fact that it returns a **three_d** object allows the + operator to be used in compound expressions, such as **a+b+c**. Here, **a+b** generates a result that is of type **three_d**. This value can then be added to **c**. Had any other type of value been generated by **a+b**, such an expression would not work.

In contrast with the + operator, the assignment operator does, indeed, cause one of its arguments to be modified. (This is, after all, the very essence of assignment.) Since the **operator=( )** function is called by the object that occurs on the left side of the assignment, it is this object that is modified by the assignment operation. Most often, the return value of an overloaded assignment operator is the object on the left, after the assignment has been made. (This is in keeping with the traditional action of the = operator.) For example, to allow statements like

```
a = b = c = d;
```

it is necessary for **operator=( )** to return the object pointed to by **this**, which will be the object that occurs on the left side of the assignment statement. This allows a string of assignments to be made. The assignment operation is one of the most important uses of the **this** pointer.

13

Remember: When a member function is used for overloading a binary operator, the object on the left side of the operator invokes the operator function, and is passed to it implicitly. The object on the right is passed as a parameter to the operator function.

Using Member Functions to Overload Unary Operators

You may also overload unary operators, such as **++**, **– –**, or the unary **–**. As stated earlier, when a unary operator is overloaded by means of a member function, no object is explicitly passed to the operator function. Instead, the operation is performed on the object that generates the call to the function through the implicitly passed **this** pointer. For example, here is an expanded version of the previous example program. This version defines the increment operation for objects of type **three_d**.

```
#include <iostream.h>

class three_d {
  int x, y, z; // 3-D coordinates
public:
  three_d() { x = y = z = 0; }
  three_d(int i, int j, int k) {x = i; y = j; z = k; }
  three_d operator+(three_d op2);  // op1 is implied
  three_d operator=(three_d op2);  // op1 is implied
  three_d operator++(); // prefix version of ++

  void show() ;
} ;

// Overload +.
three_d three_d::operator+(three_d op2)
{
  three_d temp;

  temp.x = x+op2.x;  // these are integer additions
  temp.y = y+op2.y;  // and the + retains is original
  temp.z = z+op2.z;  // meaning relative to them
  return temp;
}

// Overload assignment.
three_d three_d::operator=(three_d op2)
{
  x = op2.x; // these are integer assignments
  y = op2.y; // and the = retains its original
  z = op2.z; // meaning relative to them
  return *this;
}

// Overload the prefix version of ++.
three_d three_d::operator++()
{
  x++;
  y++;
  z++;
  return *this;
}

// Show X, Y, Z coordinates.
void three_d::show()
{
  cout << x << ", ";
  cout << y << ", ";
```

```
    cout << z << "\n";
}

main()
{
  three_d a(1, 2, 3), b(10, 10, 10), c;
  a.show();
  b.show();

  c = a+b;   // now add a and b together
  c.show();

  c = a+b+c; // add a, b and c together
  c.show();

  c = b = a;   // demonstrate multiple assignment
  c.show();
  b.show();

  ++c;   // increment c
  c.show();

  return 0;
}
```

13

As you can see, **operator++( )** increments each coordinate in the object and returns the modified object. Again, this is in keeping with the traditional meaning of the **++** operator.

As you know, the **++** and **– –** have both a prefix and a postfix form. For example, both

```
++O;
```

and

```
O++;
```

are valid uses of the increment operator. As the comments in the preceding program state, the **operator++( )** function defines the prefix form of **++** relative to the **three_d** class. However, it is possible to overload the postfix form as well. The prototype for the postfix form of the **++** operator relative to the **three_d** class is shown here:

```
three_d three_d::operator++(int notused);
```

The parameter **notused** is not used by the function, and should be ignored. This parameter is simply a way for the compiler to distinguish between the prefix and postfix forms of the increment and decrement operators. (This same approach can be used to overload the postfix increment or decrement relative to any class.)

Here is one way to implement a postfix version of **++** relative to the **three_d** class.

```
// Overload the postfix version of ++.
three_d three_d::operator++(int notused)
{
  three_d temp = *this;
  x++;
  y++;
  z++;
  return temp;
}
```

Notice that this function saves the current state of the operand using the statement

```
three_d temp = *this;
```

and then returns **temp**. Keep in mind that the traditional meaning of a postfix increment is to first obtain the value of the operand, and then increment the operand. Therefore, it is necessary to save the current state of the operand and return its original value, before it is incremented, rather than its modified value.

The following version of our original program implements both forms of the **++** operator.

```
// Demonstrate prefix and postfix ++.
#include <iostream.h>

class three_d {
  int x, y, z; // 3-D coordinates
public:
  three_d() { x = y = z = 0; }
  three_d(int i, int j, int k) {x = i; y = j; z = k; }
```

```
    three_d operator+(three_d op2);   // op1 is implied
    three_d operator=(three_d op2);   // op1 is implied
    three_d operator++(); // prefix version of ++
    three_d operator++(int notused); // postfix version of ++

    void show() ;
};

// Overload +.
three_d three_d::operator+(three_d op2)
{
  three_d temp;

  temp.x = x+op2.x;   // these are integer additions
  temp.y = y+op2.y;   // and the + retains its original
  temp.z = z+op2.z;   // meaning relative to them
  return temp;
}

// Overload assignment.
three_d three_d::operator=(three_d op2)
{
  x = op2.x; // these are integer assignments
  y = op2.y; // and the = retains its original
  z = op2.z; // meaning relative to them
  return *this;
}

// Overload the prefix version of ++.
three_d three_d::operator++()
{
  x++;
  y++;
  z++;
  return *this;
}

// Overload the postfix version of ++.
three_d three_d::operator++(int notused)
{
  three_d temp = *this;
  x++;
  y++;
```

13

```
    z++;
    return temp;
}

// Show X, Y, Z coordinates.
void three_d::show( )
{
  cout << x << ", ";
  cout << y << ", ";
  cout << z << "\n";
}

main()
{
  three_d a(1, 2, 3), b(10, 10, 10), c;
  a.show();
  b.show();

  c = a+b;  // now add a and b together
  c.show();

  c = a+b+c; // add a, b and c together
  c.show();

  c = b = a;  // demonstrate multiple assignment
  c.show();
  b.show();

  ++c;  // prefix increment
  c.show();

  c++; // postfix increment
  c.show();

  a = ++c; // a receives c's value after increment
  a.show(); // a and c
  c.show(); // are the same


  a = c++; // a receives c's value prior to increment
  a.show(); // a and c
  c.show(); // now differ
```

```
    return 0;
}
```

Remember that if the **++** precedes its operand, the **operator++( )** is called. If it follows its operand, the **operator++(int notused)** function is called.

Tip: Old versions of C++ did not distinguish between the prefix and postfix forms of the increment or decrement operators. For these old versions, the prefix form of the operator function was called for both uses of the operator. When working on older C++ code, be aware of this possibility.

The action of an overloaded operator as applied to the class for which it is defined need not bear any relationship to that operator's default usage, as applied to C++'s built-in types. For example, the **<<** and **>>** operators, as applied to **cout** and **cin**, have little in common with the same operators applied to integer types. However, for the purposes of the structure and readability of your code, an overloaded operator should reflect, when possible, the spirit of the operator's original use. For example, the **+** relative to **three_d** is conceptually similar to the **+** relative to integer types. There would be little benefit in defining the **+** operator relative to some class in such a way that it acts more the way you would expect the **| |** operator, for instance, to perform. The central concept here is that while you can give an overloaded operator any meaning you like, for clarity it is best when its new meaning is related to its original meaning.

There are some restrictions to overloading operators. First, you cannot alter the precedence of any operator. Second, you cannot alter the number of operands required by the operator, although your operator function could choose to ignore an operand. Except for the **=**, overloaded operators are inherited by any derived classes. (Inheritance is discussed in the next chapter.) Finally, operator functions cannot have default arguments.

The only operators that you cannot overload are shown here:

. :: .* ?

The **.*** is a special purpose operator discussed later in this book.

13

Order Matters

When overloading binary operators, remember that in many cases, the order of the operands does make a difference. For example, while A + B is commutative, A – B is not. (That is, A – B is not the same as B – A!) Therefore, when implementing overloaded versions of the non-commutative operators, you must remember which operand is on the left and which is on the right. For example, in this fragment subtraction is overloaded relative to the **three_d** class.

```
// Overload subtraction.
three_d three_d::operator-(three_d t)
{
  three_d temp;

  temp.x = x - t.x;
  temp.y = y - t.y;
  temp.z = z - t.z;
  return temp;
}
```

Remember, it is the operand on the left that invokes the operator function. The operand on the right is passed explicitly.

Friend Operator Functions

It is possible for an operator function to be a friend of a class rather than a member. The only operators that cannot be overloaded using friend functions are =, ( ), [ ], and–>. As you learned earlier, friend functions do not have a **this** pointer. Therefore, when a friend is used to overload an operator, both operands are passed explicitly when a binary operator is overloaded, and a single operand is passed when a unary operator is overloaded.

Friend binary operator functions have two parameters. Friend unary operator functions have one parameter.

For example, in the following program a friend is used instead of a member function to overload the + operation.

```
#include <iostream.h>

class three_d {
```

```
      int x, y, z; // 3-D coordinates
  public:
    three_d() { x = y = z = 0; }
    three_d(int i, int j, int k) { x = i; y = j; z = k;}
    friend three_d operator+(three_d op1, three_d op2);
    three_d operator=(three_d op2);   // op1 is implied

    void show() ;
  } ;

  // This is now a friend function.
  three_d operator+(three_d op1, three_d op2)
  {
    three_d temp;

    temp.x = op1.x + op2.x;   // these are integer additions
    temp.y = op1.y + op2.y;   // and the + retains its original
    temp.z = op1.z+ op2.z;    // meaning relative to them
    return temp;
  }

  // Overload assignment.
  three_d three_d::operator=(three_d op2)
  {
    x = op2.x; // these are integer assignments
    y = op2.y; // and the = retains its original
    z = op2.z; // meaning relative to them
    return *this;
  }

  // Show X, Y, Z coordinates.
  void three_d::show()
  {
    cout << x << ", ";
    cout << y << ", ";
    cout << z << "\n";
  }

  main()
  {
    three_d a(1, 2, 3), b(10, 10, 10), c;

    a.show();
    b.show();

    c = a+b;   // now add a and b together
    c.show();
```

13

```
c = a+b+c; // add a, b and c together
c.show();

c = b = a;  // demonstrate multiple assignment
c.show();
b.show();

return 0;
}
```

As you can see by looking at **operator+( )**, now both operands are passed to it. The left operand is passed in **op1**, and the right operand in **op2**.

In many cases, there is no benefit to using a friend function instead of a member function when overloading an operator. However, there is one situation in which you must use a friend function. As you know, a pointer to the object that invokes a member operator function is passed in **this**. In the case of a binary operator, the object on the left invokes the function. This is fine, provided that the object on the left defines the specified operation. For example, assuming some object called **O**, which has assignment and addition defined for it, then this is a perfectly valid statement:

```
O = O + 10; // will work
```

Since the object **O** is on the left of the + operator, it invokes its overloaded operator function, which (presumably) is capable of adding an integer value to some element of **O**. However, this statement won't work:

```
O = 10 + O; // won't work
```

The problem with this statement is that the object on the left of the **+** operator is an integer, a built-in type for which no operation involving an integer and an object of **O**'s type is defined.

The problem of having a built-in type on the left side of an operation can be eliminated if the **+** is overloaded using two friend functions. In this case, the operator function is explicitly passed both arguments, and it is invoked like any other overloaded function, based upon the types of its arguments. One version of the + operator function handles *object + integer*, and the other handles *integer + object*. Overloading the **+** (or any other binary operator) using a friend allows a built-in type to occur on the left or right side of the operator. The following sample program shows you how to accomplish this.

```
#include <iostream.h>

class CL {
```

```
      public:
        int count;
        CL operator=(CL obj);
        friend CL operator+(CL ob, int i);
        friend CL operator+(int i, CL ob);
    };

    CL CL::operator=(CL obj)
    {
      count = obj.count;
      return *this;
    }

    // This handles ob + int.
    CL operator+(CL ob, int i)
    {
      CL temp;

      temp.count = ob.count + i;
      return temp;
    }

    // This handles int + ob.
    CL operator+(int i, CL ob)
    {
      CL temp;

      temp.count = ob.count + i;
      return temp;
    }

    main()
    {
      CL O;

      O.count = 10;
      cout << O.count << " "; // outputs 10

      O = 10 + O; // add object to integer
      cout << O.count << " "; // outputs 20

      O = O + 12; // add integer to object
      cout << O.count;        // outputs 32

      return 0;
    }
```

As you can see, the **operator+( )** function is overloaded twice, to accommodate the two ways in which an integer and an object of type **CL** can occur in the addition operation.

Using a Friend to Overload a Unary Operator

You can also overload a unary operator by using a friend function. However, doing so requires a little extra effort. To begin, think back to the original version of the overloaded **++** operator relative to the **three_d** class that was implemented as a member function. It is shown here for your convenience.

```
// Overload the prefix form of ++.
three_d three_d::operator++()
{
  x++;
  y++;
  z++;
  return *this;
}
```

As you know, every member function has, as an implicit argument, a pointer to the object that invokes it, which is referenced inside the member function by the keyword **this**. For this reason, when a unary operator is overloaded by use of a member function, no argument is explicitly declared. The only argument needed in this situation is the implicit pointer to the object that has activated the call to that overloaded operator function. Since **this** is a pointer to the object, any changes made to the object's private data will affect the object that invoked the operator function.

Unlike member functions, a friend function does not receive a **this** pointer, and therefore cannot reference the object that invoked it. Instead, a friend operator function is passed its operand explicitly. For this reason, trying to create a friend **operator++( )** function as shown here will not work.

```
// THIS WILL NOT WORK
three_d operator++(three_d op1)
{
  op1.x++;
  op1.y++;
  op1.z++;
  return op1;
}
```

This function will not work because only a *copy* of the object that activated the call to **operator++( )** is passed to the function in parameter **op1**. Thus, the changes inside **operator++( )** will not affect the calling object.

Using a friend function when overloading a unary **++** or **– –** requires that the object be passed to the function as a reference parameter. In this way the function can modify the object.

When a friend is used for overloading the increment or decrement operators, the prefix form takes one parameter (which is the operand). The postfix form takes two parameters. The second is an integer, which is not used.

Here is the entire **three_d** program, which uses a friend **operator++( )** function. Notice that both the prefix and postfix forms are overloaded.

```
// This program uses friend operator++() functions.
#include <iostream.h>

class three_d {
  int x, y, z; // 3-D coordinates
public:
  three_d() { x = y = z = 0; }
  three_d(int i, int j, int k) {x = i; y = j; z = k; }
  friend three_d operator+(three_d op1, three_d op2);
  three_d operator=(three_d op2);   // op1 is implied
  // use a reference to overload the ++
  friend three_d operator++(three_d &op1);
  friend three_d operator++(three_d &op1, int notused);

  void show() ;
} ;

// This is now a friend function.
three_d operator+(three_d op1, three_d op2)
{
  three_d temp;

  temp.x = op1.x + op2.x;  // these are integer additions
  temp.y = op1.y + op2.y;  // and the + retains its original
  temp.z = op1.z + op2.z;  // meaning relative to them
  return temp;
}

// Overload the =.
three_d three_d::operator=(three_d op2)
{
  x = op2.x; // these are integer assignments
  y = op2.y; // and the = retains its original
  z = op2.z; // meaning relative to them
  return *this;
}

/* Overload prefix ++ using a friend function.
   This requires the use of a reference parameter. */
three_d operator++(three_d &op1)
{
```

```
  op1.x++;
  op1.y++;
  op1.z++;
  return op1;
}

/* Overload postfix ++ using a friend function.
   This requires the use of a reference parameter. */
three_d operator++(three_d &op1, int notused)
{
  three_d temp = op1;
  op1.x++;
  op1.y++;
  op1.z++;
  return temp;
}

// Show X, Y, Z coordinates.
void three_d::show()
{
  cout << x << ", ";
  cout << y << ", ";
  cout << z << "\n";
}

main()
{
  three_d a(1, 2, 3), b(10, 10, 10), c;

  a.show();
  b.show();

  c = a+b;   // now add a and b together
  c.show();

  c = a+b+c; // add a, b and c together
  c.show();

  c = b = a;   // demonstrate multiple assignment
  c.show();
  b.show();

  ++c;   // prefix increment
  c.show();

  c++; // postfix increment
  c.show();

  a = ++c; // a receives c's value after increment
```

```
  a.show( ); // a and c
  c.show( ); // are the same

  a = c++; // a receives c's value prior to increment
  a.show( ); // a and c
  c.show( ); // now differ

  return 0;
}
```

Overloading the Relational Operators

Overloading a relational operator, such as **==** or **<**, is a straightforward process. However, there is one small distinction. As you know, an overloaded operator function usually returns an object of the class for which it is overloaded. However, an overloaded relational operator typically returns a true or false value. This is in keeping with the normal usage of relational operators, and allows the overloaded relational operators to be used in conditional expressions.

To show you how an overloaded relational operator can be implemented, the following function overloads the **==** relative to the **three_d** class.

```
// Overload ==.
int three_d::operator==(three_d t)
{
  if((x == t.x) && (y == t.y) && (z == t.z))
    return 1;
  else
    return 0;
}
```

Once **operator==( )** has been implemented, the following fragment is perfectly valid.

```
three_d a, b;

// ...

if(a == b) cout << "a equals b\n";
else cout << "a does not equal b\n";
```

As an exercise, try implementing all of the relational operators relative to the **three_d** class.

13

Remember: In general, you should use member functions to implement overloaded operators. Friend functions are used in C++ mostly to handle certain special-case situations.

A Closer Look at the Assignment Operator

In the preceding chapter, a potential problem associated with functions returning objects was discussed. Recall that when an object is returned by a function, the compiler creates a temporary object that becomes the return value. After the value has been returned, this object goes out of scope and is destroyed. Thus, its destructor is called. However, there can be cases in which the execution of the temporary object's destructor destroys something needed by the program. For example, assume that an object's destructor frees dynamically allocated memory. If this type of object is used as a return value that is assigned to another object using the default bitwise copy, then the temporary object's destructor frees dynamically allocated memory that will still be needed by the object that receives the value.

To understand this problem, review the following (incorrect) program from the previous chapter, shown here for your convenience.

```
// An error generated by returning an object.
#include <iostream.h>
#include <string.h>
#include <stdlib.h>

class sample {
  char *s;
public:
  sample() { s = '\0'; }
  ~sample( ) { if(s) delete s; cout << "Freeing s\n"; }
  void show() { cout << s << "\n"; }
  void set(char *str);
};

// Load a string.
void sample::set(char *str)
{
  s = new char[strlen(str)+1];
  if(!s) {
    cout << "Allocation error\n";
    exit(1); // exit program if out of memory
  }
```

```
   strcpy(s, str);
}

// Return an object of type sample.
sample input( )
{
  char instr[80];
  sample str;

  cout << "Enter a string: ";
  cin >> instr;

  str.set(instr);
  return str;
}

main()
{
  sample ob;

  // assign returned object to ob
  ob = input();   // This causes an error!!!!
  ob.show();

  return 0;
}
```

The output from this program is shown here:

    Enter a string: Hello
    Freeing s
    Freeing s
    Hello
    Freeing s
    Null pointer assignment

Recall that the message **Null pointer assignment** is a run-time error message displayed when the dynamic allocation system is destroyed.

There are actually two problems with this program. First, as you saw in Chapter 12, when **input( )** returns **str**, the compiler automatically generates a temporary object, places a bitwise copy of **str** into that temporary, and returns the temporary as the function's return value. After the return, both the temporary and **str** go out of scope, and are destroyed. Since both the temporary object's **s** and **str.s** point to the same dynamically allocated memory, both free the same memory when they are destroyed. This is the cause of the first error.

The second error in the program occurs because the default assignment also performs a bitwise copy. In this case, the temporary returned by **input( )** is copied into **ob**. This also causes **ob.s** to point to the same memory that the temporary object's **s** points to. However, this memory has already been released (twice!). Thus, **ob.s** is pointing to freed memory and, most likely, the dynamic allocation system has been damaged. Further, when the program ends, **ob.s** is released, causing the memory to be freed a third time. This most certainly destroys the allocation system.

The solution to these problems requires the use of a copy constructor and an overloaded assignment operator. The copy constructor ensures that a copy of an object will have its own memory, and the overloaded assignment operator ensures that the object on the left side of an assignment will use its own memory.

The following corrected program shows how such a solution can be accomplished.

```
// This program is now fixed.
#include <iostream.h>
#include <string.h>
#include <stdlib.h>

class sample {
  char *s;
public:
  sample() { s = '\0'; }
  sample(const sample &ob); // copy constructor
  ~sample( ) { if(s) delete s; cout << "Freeing s\n"; }
  void show() { cout << s << "\n"; }
  void set(char *str);
  sample operator=(sample &ob); // overload assignment
};

// Load a string.
void sample::set(char *str)
{
  s = new char[strlen(str)+1];
  if(!s) {
    cout << "Allocation error\n";
    exit(1); // exit program if out of memory
  }

  strcpy(s, str);
}

// Copy constructor
```

```
sample::sample(const sample &ob)
{
  s = new char[strlen(ob.s)+1];
  if(!s) {
    cout << "Allocation error\n";
    exit(1); // exit program if out of memory
  }
  strcpy(s, ob.s);
}

// Overload assignment operator
sample sample::operator=(sample &ob)
{
  /* If the target string is not large enough
     then allocate a new string. */
  if(strlen(ob.s) > strlen(s)) {
    delete s;
    s = new char[strlen(ob.s)+1];
    if(!s) {
      cout << "Allocation error\n";
      exit(1); // exit program if out of memory
    }
  }
  strcpy(s, ob.s);
  return *this;
}

// Return an object of type sample.
sample input()
{
  char instr[80];
  sample str;

  cout << "Enter a string: ";
  cin >> instr;

  str.set(instr);
  return str;
}

main()
{
  sample ob;

  // assign returned object to ob
  ob = input();  // This is now OK
  ob.show();
```

```
    return 0;
}
```

This program now displays the following output (assuming that you enter "Hello" when prompted):

```
Enter a string: Hello
Freeing s
Freeing s
Freeing s
Hello
Freeing s
```

As you can see, the program now runs properly.

You should be able to understand why each **Freeing s** message is printed. (Hint: one of them is caused by the **delete** statement inside the **operator=( )** function.)

Overloading new and delete

new and *delete* are overloaded as unary operators.

Because **new** and **delete** are operators, they too can be overloaded. One reason you might want to do this is that you want to use some special allocation method. For example, you may want to create allocation routines that automatically begin using a disk file as virtual memory when the heap has been exhausted. Whatever the reason, it is a simple matter to overload these operators.

The skeletons for the functions that overload **new** and **delete** are shown here:

```
// Allocate an object.
void *operator new(size_t size)
{
  // Perform allocation.
  return pointer_to_memory;
}

// Delete an object.
void operator delete(void *p)
{
  // Free memory pointed to by p.
}
```

The type **size_t** is a defined type capable of containing the largest single piece of memory that can be allocated. (**size_t** is essentially an unsigned integer.) The parameter **size** will contain the number of bytes needed to hold the object being allocated. The overloaded **new** function must return a pointer to the memory that it allocates, or zero if an allocation error occurs. Beyond these constraints, the overloaded **new** function can do anything else you require. When you allocate an object using **new** (whether your own version or not), the object's constructor is automatically called.

The **delete** function receives a pointer to the region of memory to be freed. It then releases the previously allocated memory back to the system. When an object is deleted, its destructor function is automatically called.

To allocate and free arrays of objects, you must use these forms of **new** and **delete**:

```
// Allocate an array of objects.
void *operator new[](size_t size)
{
  // Perform allocation.
  return pointer_to_memory;
}

// Delete an array of objects.
void operator delete[](void *p)
{
  /* Free memory pointed to by p.
     Destructor for each element automatically
     called.
  */
}
```

When an array is allocated, each object's constructor is automatically called. When an array is freed, each object's destructor is automatically called. You do not have to provide explicit code to accomplish these actions.

The **new** and **delete** operators are generally overloaded relative to a class. For the sake of simplicity, in the example that follows, no new allocation scheme will be used. Instead, the overloaded functions will simply invoke the C-based allocation functions **malloc( )** and **free( )**. (In your own application, you are, of course, free to implement any alternative allocation scheme you like.)

To overload the **new** and **delete** operators relative to a class, simply make the overloaded operator functions class members. In the following sample program, the **new** and **delete** operators are overloaded relative to the **three_d** class. Both are overloaded to allow objects and arrays of objects to be allocated and freed.

```
// Demonstrate overloaded new and delete.
#include <iostream.h>
#include <stdlib.h>

class three_d {
  int x, y, z; // 3-D coordinates
public:
  three_d() {
    x = y = z = 0;
    cout << "Constructing 0, 0, 0\n";
  }
  three_d(int i, int j, int k) {
    x = i; y = j; z = k;
    cout << "Constructing " << i << ", ";
    cout << j << ", " << k;
    cout << '\n';
  }
  ~three_d( ) { cout << "Destructing\n"; }
  void *operator new(size_t size);
  void *operator new[](size_t size);
  void operator delete(void *p);
  void operator delete[](void *p);
  void show() ;
};

// new overloaded relative to three_d.
void *three_d::operator new(size_t size)
{
  cout << "Allocating three_d object.\n";
  return malloc(size);
}
// new overloaded relative to arrays of three_d.
void *three_d::operator new[](size_t size)
{
  cout << "Allocating array of three_d objects.\n";
  return malloc(size);
}

// delete overloaded relative to three_d.
void three_d::operator delete(void *p)
{
  cout << "Deleting three_d object.\n";
  free(p);
}

// delete overloaded relative to arrays of three_d.
void three_d::operator delete[ ](void *p)
{
```

```
  cout << "Deleting array of three_d objects.\n";
  free(p);
}

// Show X, Y, Z coordinates.
void three_d::show( )
{
  cout << x << ", ";
  cout << y << ", ";
  cout << z << "\n";
}

main()
{
  three_d *p1, *p2;

  p1 = new three_d[3]; // allocate array
  p2 = new three_d(5, 6, 7); // allocate object

  p1[1].show();
  p2->show();

  delete [] p1; // delete array
  delete p2; // delete object

  return 0;
}
```

13

The output produced by this program is shown here.

```
Allocating array of three_d objects.
Constructing 0, 0, 0
Constructing 0, 0, 0
Constructing 0, 0, 0
Allocating three_d object.
Constructing 5, 6, 7
0, 0, 0
5, 6, 7
Destructing
Destructing
Destructing
Deleting array of three_d objects.
Destructing
Deleting three_d object.
```

The first three **Constructing** messages are caused by the allocation of the three-element array. As stated, when an array is allocated, each element's constructor is automatically called. The last **Constructing** message is caused by the allocation of a single object. The first three **Destructing** messages are caused by the deletion of the three-element array. Each element's destructor is automatically called. No special action is required on your part. The last **Destructing** message is caused by the deletion of the single object.

It is important to understand that when **new** and **delete** are overloaded relative to a specific class, the use of these operators on any other type of data causes the original **new** or **delete** to be employed. The overloaded operators are only applied to the types for which they are defined. This means that if you add the following line to **main( )**, the default **new** will be executed.

```
int *f = new int; // uses default new
```

Overloading [ ]

The last operator that we will overload is the **[ ]** array subscripting operator. In C++, the **[ ]** is considered a binary operator when it is overloaded. The **[ ]** can only be overloaded relative to a class, and only by a member function. Therefore, the general form of a member **operator[ ]( )** function is:

```
type class-name::operator[ ](int index)
{
  // ...
}
```

The [ ] is overloaded as a binary operator.

Technically, the parameter does not have to be of type **int**, but **operator[ ]( )** functions are typically used to provide array subscripting, so an integer value is generally used.

Given an object called **O**, this expression

```
O[3]
```

translates into this call to the **operator[ ]( )** function:

```
operator[](3)
```

That is, the value of the expression within the subscripting operator is passed to the **operator[ ]( )** function in its explicit parameter. The **this** pointer will point to **O**, the object that generated the call.

In the following program, **atype** declares an array of three integers. Its constructor function initializes each member of the array. The overloaded

operator[ ]( ) function returns the value of the element specified by its parameter.

```
#include <iostream.h>

const int SIZE = 3;

class atype {
  int a[SIZE];
public:
  atype() {
    register int i;

    for(i=0; i<SIZE; i++) a[i] = i;
  }
  int operator[](int i) {return a[i];}
};

main()
{
  atype ob;

  cout << ob[2];   // displays 2

  return 0;
}
```

The initialization of the array **a** by the constructor in this program, and in the following programs, is for the sake of illustration only. It is not required.

It is possible to design the **operator[ ]( )** function in such a way that the **[ ]** can be used on both the left and right sides of an assignment statement. To do this, simply specify that the return value of **operator[ ]( )** be a reference. This change is illustrated in the following program:

```
#include <iostream.h>

const int SIZE = 3;

class atype {
  int a[SIZE];
public:
  atype() {
    register int i;

    for(i=0; i<SIZE; i++) a[i] = i;
  }
```

```
     int &operator[](int i) {return a[i];}
};

main()
{
  atype ob;

  cout << ob[2];   // displays 2
  cout << " ";

  ob[2] = 25;   // [] on left of =

  cout << ob[2];   // now displays 25

  return 0;
}
```

Because **operator[ ]( )** now returns a reference to the array element indexed by **i**, it can now be used on the left side of an assignment statement to modify an element of the array. (Of course, it can still be used on the right side as well.)

One advantage of being able to overload the **[ ]** operator is that it provides a means of implementing safe array indexing. As you know, in C++, it is possible to overrun (or underrun) an array boundary at run time without generating a run-time error message. However, if you create a class that contains the array, and allow access to that array only through the overloaded **[ ]** subscripting operator, then you can intercept an out-of-range index. For example, the program shown next adds a range check to the preceding program, and proves that it works.

```
// A safe array example.
#include <iostream.h>
#include "stdlib.h"

const int SIZE = 3;

class atype {
  int a[SIZE];
public:
  atype() {
    register int i;

    for(i=0; i<SIZE; i++) a[i] = i;
  }
```

```
    int &operator[](int i);
};

// Provide range checking for atype.
int &atype::operator[](int i)
{
  if(i<0 || i> SIZE-1) {
    cout << "\nIndex value of ";
    cout << i << " is out-of-bounds.\n";
    exit(1);
  }
  return a[i];
}

main()
{
  atype ob;

  cout << ob[2];   // displays 2
  cout << " ";

  ob[2] = 25;   // [] appears on left

  cout << ob[2];   // displays 25

  ob[3] = 44; // generates runtime error, 3 out-of-range
  return 0;
}
```

In this program, when the statement

```
ob[3] = 44;
```

executes, the boundary error is intercepted by **operator[ ]( )**, and the program is terminated before any damage can be done.

Overloading Other Operators

Except for the –> and the ( ) operators, the other C++ operators are overloaded in the same way as those shown in the preceding examples. The –> and the ( ) are special operators which are seldom overloaded, and which are beyond the scope of this book. However, the interested reader is directed to my book *C++: The Complete Reference*, (Osborne/McGraw-Hill, 1991) for examples of overloading these two operators.

13

Another Example of Operator Overloading

To close this chapter, we'll develop another example of operator overloading that implements a string type and defines several operations relative to that type. Even though C++'s approach to strings—implemented as character arrays rather than as a type unto themselves—is both efficient and flexible, to beginners it can still lack the conceptual clarity of the way strings are implemented in languages such as BASIC. However, with C++ it is possible to combine the best of both worlds by defining a string class, along with operations which relate to that class.

Note: Several C++ compilers supply a string class. In fact, the draft ANSI C++ standard defines a string class. However, you are also free to implement your own. The following discussion gives you an idea about how such a class might be implemented.

To begin, the following class declares the type **str_type**.

```
#include <iostream.h>
#include <string.h>

class str_type {
  char string[80];
public:
  str_type(char *str = "\0") { strcpy(string, str); }

  str_type operator+(str_type str); // concatenate
  str_type operator=(str_type str); // assign

  // output the string
  void show_str() { cout << string; }
};
```

As you can see, **str_type** declares one private string. For the sake of this example, no string can be longer than 80 bytes. (A real-world string class would allocate strings dynamically, and would not have this restriction.) The class has one constructor function, which can be used to initialize the array **string** with a specific value or to assign it a null string in the absence of any initializer. The class also declares two overloaded operators, which will perform concatenation and assignment. Finally, it declares the function **show_str( )**, which will output **string** to the screen. The overloaded operator functions are shown here:

```
// Concatenate two strings.
str_type str_type::operator+(str_type str) {
```

```
  str_type temp;

  strcpy(temp.string, string);
  strcat(temp.string, str.string);
  return temp;
}

// Assign one string to another.
str_type str_type::operator=(str_type str) {
  strcpy(string, str.string);
  return *this;
}
```

Given these definitions, the following **main( )** illustrates their use:

```
main()
{
  str_type a("Hello "), b("There"), c;

  c = a + b;

  c.show_str();

  return 0;
}
```

This program outputs **Hello There** on the screen. It first concatenates **a** with **b**, and then assigns the resulting value to **c**.

Keep in mind that both the = and the + are defined only for objects of type **str_type**. For example, the following statement is invalid because it tries to assign object **a** a normal C++ string.

```
a = "this is currently wrong";
```

However, the **str_type** class can be enhanced to allow such a statement, as you will see next.

To expand the types of operations supported by the **str_type** class so that you can assign normal C++ strings to **str_type** objects or concatenate a C++ string with a **str_type** object, you will need to overload the + and = operations a second time. First, the class declaration must be changed, as shown here:

```
class str_type {
  char string[80];
public:
```

13

```
    str_type(char *str = "\0") { strcpy(string, str); }

    str_type operator+(str_type str); // concatenate objects
    str_type operator+(char *str); /* concatenate object with
                                      a string */

    str_type operator=(str_type str); /* assign object to
                                          object */
    char *operator=(char *str); // assign string to object

    void show_str() { cout << string; }
};
```

Next, the overloaded **operator+( )** and **operator=( )** are implemented, as
shown here:

```
// Assign a string to an object
str_type str_type::operator=(char *str)
{
  str_type temp;

  strcpy(string, str);
  strcpy(temp.string, string);
  return temp;
}

// Add a string to an object
str_type str_type::operator+(char *str)
{
  str_type temp;

  strcpy(temp.string, string);
  strcat(temp.string, str);
  return temp;
}
```

Look carefully at these functions. Notice that the right-side argument is not
an object of type **str_type**, but simply a pointer to a null-terminated
character array—that is, a normal C++ string. However, both functions
return an object of type **str_type**. Although the functions could, in theory,
return some other type, it makes the most sense to return an object, since
the targets of these operations are also objects. The advantage to defining a
string operation that accepts a normal C++ string as the right-side operand is
that it allows you to write certain statements in a natural way. For example,
these are now valid statements:

```
str_type a, b, c;
a = "hi there"; // assign a string to an object

c = a + " George"; // concatenate an object with a string
```

The following program incorporates the additional meanings of the + and = operators:

```
// Expanding the string type.
#include <iostream.h>
#include <string.h>

class str_type {
  char string[80];
public:
  str_type(char *str = "\0") { strcpy(string, str); }

  str_type operator+(str_type str);
  str_type operator+(char *str);

  str_type operator=(str_type str);
  str_type operator=(char *str);

  void show_str() { cout << string; }
} ;

str_type str_type::operator+(str_type str) {
  str_type temp;

  strcpy(temp.string, string);
  strcat(temp.string, str.string);
  return temp;
}

str_type str_type::operator=(str_type str) {
  strcpy(string, str.string);
  return *this;
}

str_type str_type::operator=(char *str)
{
  str_type temp;

  strcpy(string, str);
  strcpy(temp.string, string);
```

```
   return temp;
}

str_type str_type::operator+(char *str)
{
  str_type temp;

  strcpy(temp.string, string);
  strcat(temp.string, str);
  return temp;
}

main()
{
  str_type a("Hello "), b("There"), c;

  c = a + b;

  c.show_str();
  cout << "\n";

  a = "to program in because";
  a.show_str();
  cout << "\n";

  b = c = "C++ is fun";

  c = c+" "+a+" "+b;
  c.show_str();

  return 0;
}
```

This program displays this on the screen:

    Hello There
    to program in because
    C++ is fun to program in because C++ is fun

Before continuing, you should make sure that you understand how this output is created. Also, on your own, try creating other string operations. For example, you might try defining the – so that it performs a substring deletion. For example, if object **A**'s string is "This is a test" and object **B**'s string is "is", then **A–B** yields "th a test". In this case, all occurrences of the substring are removed from the original string.

T ip: You will want to experiment with operator overloading relative to classes that you create. As the examples in this chapter have shown, you can use operator overloading to add new data types to your programming environment. Without a doubt, this is one of C++'s most powerful features.

13

Chapter

14

Inheritance

Inheritance is one of the cornerstones of OOP because it allows the creation of hierarchical classifications. With inheritance, it is possible to create a general class that defines traits common to a set of related items. This class may then be inherited by other, more specific classes, each adding only those things which are unique to the inheriting class.

In standard C++ terminology, a class that is inherited is referred to as a *base class*. The class that does the inheriting is called the *derived class*. Further, a derived class can be used as a base class for another derived class. In this way, a multilayered class hierarchy can be achieved.

Before discussing the theory of inheritance and the details of its use, let's begin with an example.

Introducing Inheritance

A base class is inherited by a derived class.

C++ supports inheritance by allowing one class to incorporate another class into its declaration. The following class, called **road_vehicle**, defines very broadly vehicles that travel on the road. It stores the number of wheels a vehicle has and the number of passengers it can carry.

```
class road_vehicle {
  int wheels;
  int passengers;
public:
  void set_wheels(int num) { wheels = num; }
  int get_wheels() { return wheels; }
  void set_pass(int num) { passengers = num; }
  int get_pass() { return passengers; }
};
```

We can use this broad definition of a road vehicle to help define specific objects. For example, the fragment shown here declares a class called **truck** using **road_vehicle**.

```
class truck : public road_vehicle {
  int cargo;
public:
  void set_cargo(int size) { cargo = size; }
  int get_cargo() { return cargo; }
  void show();
};
```

Because **truck** inherits **road_vehicle**, **truck** includes all of **road_vehicle** and adds **cargo** to it, along with the supporting member functions.

Notice how **road_vehicle** is inherited. The general form for inheritance is shown here:

> class *derived-class* : *access base-class* {
>   *body of new class*
> }

Here, *access* is optional. However, if present, it must be either **public**, **private**, or **protected**. You will learn more about these options later in this chapter. For now, all inherited classes will use **public**. Using **public** means that all the public members of the base class will also be public members of the derived class. Therefore, in the preceding example, members of **truck** have access to the public member functions of **road_vehicle**, just as if they had been declared inside **truck**. However, **truck** *does not* have access to the private members of **road_vehicle**. For example, **truck** does not have access to **wheels**.

Here is a program that uses inheritance to create two subclasses of **road_vehicle**. One is **truck** and the other is **automobile**.

```
#include <iostream.h>

class road_vehicle {
  int wheels;
  int passengers;
public:
  void set_wheels(int num) { wheels = num; }
  int get_wheels() { return wheels; }
  void set_pass(int num) { passengers = num; }
  int get_pass() { return passengers; }
};

class truck : public road_vehicle {
  int cargo;
public:
  void set_cargo(int size) { cargo = size; }
  int get_cargo() { return cargo; }
  void show();
};

enum type {car, van, wagon};

class automobile : public road_vehicle {
  enum type car_type;
public:
  void set_type(type t) { car_type = t; }
  enum type get_type() { return car_type; }
  void show();
};

void truck::show()
{
  cout << "wheels: " << get_wheels() << "\n";
  cout << "passengers: " << get_pass() << "\n";
  cout << "cargo capacity in cubic feet: " << cargo << "\n";
}

void automobile::show()
{
```

14

```
    cout << "wheels: " << get_wheels() << "\n";
    cout << "passengers: " << get_pass() << "\n";
    cout << "type: ";
    switch(get_type()) {
      case van: cout << "van\n";
        break;
      case car: cout << "car\n";
        break;
      case wagon: cout << "wagon\n";
    }
}

main()
{
  truck t1, t2;
  automobile c;

  t1.set_wheels(18);
  t1.set_pass(2);
  t1.set_cargo(3200);

  t2.set_wheels(6);
  t2.set_pass(3);
  t2.set_cargo(1200);

  t1.show();
  t2.show();

  c.set_wheels(4);
  c.set_pass(6);
  c.set_type(van);

  c.show();

  return 0;
}
```

The output from this program is shown here:

```
wheels: 18
passengers: 2
cargo capacity in cubic feet: 3200
wheels: 6
passengers: 3
cargo capacity in cubic feet: 1200
wheels: 4
passengers: 6
type: van
```

As this program shows, the major advantage of inheritance is that it lets you create a base classification that can be incorporated into more specific ones. In this way, each derived class can precisely tailor its own classification.

One other point: Notice that both **truck** and **automobile** include a member function called **show( )**, which displays information about each object. This illustrates another aspect of polymorphism. Since each **show( )** is linked with it own class, the compiler can easily tell which one to call in any circumstance.

Now that you understand the basic procedure by which one class inherits another, let's examine inheritance in detail.

Base Class Access Control

When a base class is inherited as public, public members of the base class become public members of the derived class.

When one class inherits another, the members of the base class become members of the derived class. The access status of the base class members inside the derived class is determined by the access specifier used for inheriting the base class. The base class access specifier must be **public**, **private**, or **protected**. If the access specifier is not used, then it is **private** by default if the derived class is a **class**. If the derived class is a **struct**, then **public** is the default in the absence of an explicit access specifier. Let's examine the ramifications of using **public** or **private** access. (The **protected** specifier is described in the next section.)

When a base class is inherited as **public**, all public members of the base class become public members of the derived class. In all cases, the private elements of the base class remain private to that class, and are not accessible by members of the derived class. For example, in the following program, objects of type **derived** can directly access the public members of **base**.

14

```
#include <iostream.h>

class base {
  int i, j;
public:
  void set(int a, int b) {i=a; j=b;}
  void show() { cout << i << " " << j << "\n";}
};

class derived : public base {
  int k;
public:
  derived(int x) {k=x;}
  void showk() {cout << k << "\n";}
};
```

```
main()
{
  derived ob(3);

  ob.set(1, 2); // access member of base
  ob.show();  // access member of base

  ob.showk(); // uses member of derived class

  return 0;
}
```

The opposite of public inheritance is private inheritance. When the base class is inherited as **private**, then all public members of the base class become private members of the derived class. For example, the program shown next will not compile, because both **set( )** and **show( )** are now private members of **derived**, and thus cannot be called from **main( )**.

```
// This program won't compile.
#include <iostream.h>

class base {
  int i, j;
public:
  void set(int a, int b) {i=a; j=b;}
  void show() { cout << i << " " << j << "\n";}
};

// Public elements of base are private in derived.
class derived : private base {
  int k;
public:
  derived(int x) {k=x;}
  void showk() {cout << k << "\n";}
};

main()
{
  derived ob(3);

  ob.set(1, 2); // error, can't access set()
  ob.show(); // error, can't access show()

  return 0;
}
```

The key point to remember is that when a base class is inherited as **private**, public members of the base class become private members of the derived class. This means that they are still accessible by members of the derived class, but cannot be accessed by other parts of your program.

Using protected Members

When a base class is inherited as private, public members of the base class become private members of the derived class.

In addition to public and private, a class member can be declared as **protected**. Further, a base class can be inherited as protected. Both of these actions are accomplished using the **protected** access specifier. The **protected** keyword is included in C++ to provide greater flexibility for the inheritance mechanism. In this section, you will see why.

When a member of a class is declared as **protected**, that member is not accessible to other, non-member elements of the program. With one important exception, access to a protected member is the same as access to a private member; it can only be accessed by other members of the class of which it is a part. The sole exception to this is when a protected member is inherited. In this case, a protected member differs substantially from a private one.

As you know, a private member of a base class is not accessible by any other part of your program—including any derived class. However, protected members behave differently. When a base class is inherited as public, protected members in the base class become protected members of the derived class, and are accessible to the derived class. Therefore, by using **protected**, you can create class members that are private to their class, but that can still be inherited and accessed by a derived class.

The **protected** access specifier declares protected members or inherits a protected class.

Consider this sample program:

```
#include <iostream.h>

class base {
protected:
  int i, j; // private to base, but accessible to derived
public:
  void set(int a, int b) {i=a; j=b;}
  void show() { cout << i << " " << j << "\n";}
};

class derived : public base {
  int k;
public:
  // derived may access base's i and j
```

14

```
  void setk() {k=i*j;}

  void showk() {cout << k << "\n";}
};

main()
{
  derived ob;

  ob.set(2, 3);   // OK, known to derived
  ob.show(); // OK, known to derived

  ob.setk();
  ob.showk();
  return 0;
}
```

Here, because **base** is inherited by **derived** as public and because **i** and **j** are declared as protected, **derived**'s function **setk( )** may access them. If **i** and **j** were declared as private by **base**, then **derived** would not have access to them, and the program would not compile.

Remember: The **protected** specifier allows you to create a class member that is accessible within a class hierarchy, but is otherwise private.

When a derived class is used as a base class for another derived class, then any protected member of the initial base class that is inherited (as public) by the first derived class can be inherited again, as a protected member, by a second derived class. For example, the following program is correct, and **derived2** does, indeed, have access to **i** and **j**.

```
#include <iostream.h>

class base {
protected:
  int i, j;
public:
  void set(int a, int b) {i=a; j=b;}
```

```
  void show() { cout << i << " " << j << "\n";}
};

// i and j inherited as protected.
class derived1 : public base {
  int k;
public:
  void setk() {k = i*j;} // legal
  void showk() {cout << k << "\n";}
};

// i and j inherited indirectly through derived1.
class derived2 : public derived1 {
  int m;
public:
  void setm() {m = i-j;} // legal
  void showm() {cout << m << "\n";}
};

main()
{
  derived1 ob1;
  derived2 ob2;

  ob1.set(2, 3);
  ob1.show();
  ob1.setk();
  ob1.showk();

  ob2.set(3, 4);
  ob2.show();
  ob2.setk();
  ob2.setm();
  ob2.showk();
  ob2.showm();

  return 0;
}
```

When a base class is inherited as private, protected members of the base class become private members of the derived class. Therefore, in the preceding example, if **base** were inherited as private, then all members of **base** would become private members of **derived1**, meaning that they would not be accessible to **derived2**. (However, **i** and **j** would still be accessible to **derived1**.) This situation is illustrated by the following program, which is in error (and won't compile). The comments describe each error.

```cpp
// This program won't compile.

#include <iostream.h>

class base {
protected:
  int i, j;
public:
  void set(int a, int b) {i=a; j=b;}
  void show() { cout << i << " " << j << "\n";}
};

// Now, all elements of base are private in derived1.
class derived1 : private base {
  int k;
public:
  // This is legal because i and j are private to derived1.
  void setk() {k = i*j;}   // OK
  void showk() {cout << k << "\n";}
};

// Access to i, j, set(), and show() not inherited.
class derived2 : public derived1 {
  int m;
public:
  // Illegal because i and j are private to derived1.
  void setm() {m = i-j;}   // error
  void showm() {cout << m << "\n";}
};

main()
{
  derived1 ob1;
  derived2 ob2;

  ob1.set(1, 2);  // error, can't use set()
  ob1.show();  // error, can't use show()

  ob2.set(3, 4);  // error, can't use set()
```

```
  ob2.show();  // error, can't use show()

  return 0;
}
```

Even though **base** is inherited as private by **derived1**, **derived1** still has access to the public and protected elements of **base**. However, it cannot pass this privilege along. This is the reason that **protected** is part of the C++ language. It provides a means of protecting certain members from being modified by non-member functions, but allows them to be inherited.

The **protected** specifier can also be used with structures. It cannot be used with a union, however, because a union cannot inherit another class or be inherited. (Some compilers will accept its use in a union declaration, but since unions cannot participate in inheritance, **protected** is the same as **private** in this context.)

The **protected** access specifier may occur anywhere in a class declaration, although typically it occurs after the (default) private members are declared, and before the public members. Thus, the most common full form of a class declaration is:

class *class-name* {
  private members
protected:
  protected members
public:
  public members
};

Of course, the protected category is optional.

Using protected for Inheritance of a Base Class

In addition to specifying protected status for members of a class, the keyword **protected** can also be used to inherit a base class. When a base class is inherited as protected, all public and protected members of the base class become protected members of the derived class. Here is an example:

```
// Demonstrate inheriting a protected base class.
#include <iostream.h>
class base {
```

14

```
    int i;
protected:
    int j;
public:
    int k;
    void seti(int a) { i = a; }
    int geti() { return i; }
};

// Inherit base as protected.
class derived : protected base {
public:
    void setj(int a) { j = a; } // j is protected here
    void setk(int a) { k = a; } // k is also protected
    int getj() { return j; }
    int getk() { return k; }
};

main()
{
    derived ob;

    /* This next line is illegal because seti() is
       a protected member of derived, which makes it
       inaccessible outside of derived. */
//  ob.seti(10);

//  cout << ob.geti(); // illegal -- geti() is protected
//  ob.k = 10; // also illegal because k is protected

    // these next statements are OK
    ob.setk(10);
    cout << ob.getk() << ' ';
    ob.setj(12);
    cout << ob.getj() << ' ';

    return 0;
}
```

As you can see by reading the comments in this program, although **derived** has access to **k**, **j**, **seti( )**, and **geti( )** in **base**, they are **protected** members of **derived**. This means that they cannot be accessed by code outside of **base** or **derived**. Thus, inside **main( )**, references to these members are illegal.

Reviewing public, protected, and private

Since the access rights as defined by **public**, **protected**, and **private** are fundamental to C++ programming, let's review their meanings.

When a class member is declared as **public**, it can be accessed by any other part of a program. When a member is declared as **private**, it can only be accessed by members of its class. Further, derived classes do not have access to private base class members. When a member is declared as **protected**, it can only be accessed by members of its class. However, derived classes also have access to protected base class members. Thus, **protected** allows a member to be inherited, but to remain private within a class hierarchy.

When a base class is inherited by use of **public**, its public members become public members of the derived class, and its protected members become protected members of the derived class.

When a base class is inherited by use of **protected**, its public and protected members become protected members of the derived class.

When a base class is inherited by use of **private**, its public and protected members become private members of the derived class.

In all cases, private members of a base class remain private to that base class, and are not inherited.

As you become more familiar with C++, the meanings of **public**, **protected**, and **private** will become second nature. For now, if you are unsure about precisely what effect an access specifier has, write a short sample program as an experiment and observe the results.

14

Inheriting Multiple Base Classes

It is possible for a derived class to inherit two or more base classes. For example, in this short program, **derived** inherits both **base1** and **base2**.

```
// An example of multiple base classes.
#include <iostream.h>

class base1 {
protected:
  int x;
public:
  void showx() {cout << x << "\n";}
};

class base2 {
protected:
  int y;
public:
  void showy() {cout << y << "\n";}
};

// Inherit multiple base classes.
class derived: public base1, public base2 {
public:
  void set(int i, int j) {x=i; y=j;}
};

main()
{
  derived ob;

  ob.set(10, 20); // provided by derived
  ob.showx();  // from base1
  ob.showy();  // from base2

  return 0;
}
```

As this example illustrates, to cause more than one base class to be inherited, you must use a comma-separated list. Further, be sure to use an access specifier for each base class inherited.

Constructors, Destructors, and Inheritance

There are two important questions that arise relative to constructors and destructors when inheritance is involved. First, when are base class and derived class constructor and destructor functions called? Second, how can parameters be passed to base class constructor functions? This section answers these questions.

When Constructor and Destructor Functions Are Executed

It is possible for a base class, a derived class, or both to contain constructor and/or destructor functions. It is important to understand the order in which these functions are executed when an object of a derived class comes into existence and when it goes out of existence. To begin, examine this short program:

```cpp
#include <iostream.h>

class base {
public:
  base() {cout << "Constructing base\n";}
  ~base() {cout << "Destructing base\n";}
};

class derived: public base {
public:
  derived() {cout << "Constructing derived\n";}
  ~derived() {cout << "Destructing derived\n";}
};

main()
{
  derived ob;

  // do nothing but construct and destruct ob

  return 0;
}
```

As the comment in **main( )** indicates, this program simply constructs and then destroys an object called **ob**, which is of class **derived**. When executed, this program displays:

```
Constructing base
Constructing derived
Destructing derived
Destructing base
```

As you can see, the constructor of the **base** is executed, followed by the constructor of **derived**. Next (since **ob** is immediately destroyed in this program), the destructor of **derived** is called, followed by that of **base**.

14

The results of the foregoing experiment can be generalized as follows. When an object of a derived class is created, if the base class contains a constructor it will be called first, followed by the constructor of the derived class. When a derived object is destroyed, its destructor is called first, followed by that of the base class, if it exists. Put differently, constructor functions are executed in the order of their derivation. Destructor functions are executed in reverse order of derivation.

Constructors are called in order of derivation. Destructors are called in reverse order.

If you think about it, it makes sense that constructor functions are executed in order of derivation. Because a base class has no knowledge of any derived class, any initialization it needs to perform is separate from, and possibly prerequisite to, any initialization performed by the derived class. Therefore, it must be executed first.

Likewise, it is quite sensible that destructors be executed in reverse order of derivation. Since the base class underlies a derived class, the destruction of the base class implies the destruction of the derived class. Therefore, the derived destructor must be called before the object is fully destroyed.

In the case of a large class hierarchy (i.e., where a derived class becomes the base class for another derived class), the general rule applies: Constructors are called in order of derivation, destructors in reverse order. For example, this program

```
#include <iostream.h>

class base {
public:
  base() {cout << "Constructing base\n";}
  ~base() {cout << "Destructing base\n";}
};

class derived1 : public base {
public:
  derived1() {cout << "Constructing derived1\n";}
  ~derived1() {cout << "Destructing derived1\n";}
};

class derived2: public derived1 {
public:
  derived2() {cout << "Constructing derived2\n";}
  ~derived2() {cout << "Destructing derived2\n";}
};
```

```
main()
{
  derived2 ob;

  // construct and destruct ob

  return 0;
}
```

displays this output:

Constructing base
Constructing derived1
Constructing derived2
Destructing derived2
Destructing derived1
Destructing base

The same general rule applies in situations involving multiple base classes. For example, this program

```
#include <iostream.h>

class base1 {
public:
  base1() {cout << "Constructing base1\n";}
  ~base1() {cout << "Destructing base1\n";}
};

class base2 {
public:
  base2() {cout << "Constructing base2\n";}
  ~base2() {cout << "Destructing base2\n";}
};

class derived: public base1, public base2 {
public:
  derived() {cout << "Constructing derived\n";}
  ~derived() {cout << "Destructing derived\n";}
};

main()
{
  derived ob;
```

14

```
   // construct and destruct ob

   return 0;
}
```

produces this output:

```
Constructing base1
Constructing base2
Constructing derived
Destructing derived
Destructing base2
Destructing base1
```

As you can see, constructors are called in order of derivation—left to right—as specified in **derived**'s inheritance list. Destructors are called in reverse order—right to left. This means that if **base2** were specified before **base1** in **derived**'s list, as shown here:

```
class derived: public base2, public base1 {
```

then the output of the preceding program would look like this:

```
Constructing base2
Constructing base1
Constructing derived
Destructing derived
Destructing base1
Destructing base2
```

Passing Parameters to Base Class Constructors

So far, none of the preceding examples have included constructor functions requiring arguments. In cases where only the constructor of the derived class requires one or more arguments, you simply use the standard parameterized constructor syntax. However, how do you pass arguments to a constructor function in a base class? The answer is to use an expanded form of the derived class's constructor declaration, which passes arguments along to one or more base class constructors. The general form of this expanded declaration is shown here:

derived-constructor(arg-list) : base1(arg-list),
base2(arg-list),

$$
\vdots
$$

baseN(arg-list);

```
{
    body of derived constructor
}
```

Here, *base1* through *baseN* are the names of the base classes inherited by the derived class. Notice that a colon separates the constructor function declaration of the derived class from the base classes, and that the base classes are separated from each other by commas, in the case of multiple base classes.

Consider this sample program:

```
#include <iostream.h>

class base {
protected:
  int i;
public:
  base(int x) {i=x; cout << "Constructing base\n";}
  ~base() {cout << "Destructing base\n";}
};

class derived: public base {
  int j;
public:
  // derived uses x; y is passed along to base.
  derived(int x, int y): base(y)
    {j=x; cout << "Constructing derived\n";}

  ~derived() {cout << "Destructing derived\n";}
  void show() {cout << i << " " << j << "\n";}
};

main()
{
  derived ob(3, 4);

  ob.show();   // displays 4 3

  return 0;
}
```

14

Here, **derived**'s constructor is declared as taking two parameters, **x** and **y**. However, **derived( )** uses only **x**; **y** is passed along to **base( )**. In general, the constructor of the derived class must declare the parameter(s) that the class requires, as well as any required by the base class. As the preceding example illustrates, any parameters required by the base class are passed to it in the base class's argument list, specified after the colon.

Here is a sample program that uses multiple base classes:

```
#include <iostream.h>

class base1 {
protected:
  int i;
public:
  base1(int x) {i=x; cout << "Constructing base1\n";}
  ~base1() {cout << "Destructing base1\n";}
};

class base2 {
protected:
  int k;
public:
  base2(int x) {k=x; cout << "Constructing base2\n";}
  ~base2() {cout << "Destructing base2\n";}
};

class derived: public base1, public base2 {
  int j;
public:
  derived(int x, int y, int z): base1(y), base2(z)
    {j=x; cout << "Constructing derived\n";}

  ~derived() {cout << "Destructing derived\n";}
  void show() {cout << i << " " << j << " " << k << "\n";}
};

main()
{
  derived ob(3, 4, 5);

  ob.show();  // displays 4 3 5
```

```
   return 0;
}
```

It is important to understand that arguments to a base class constructor
are passed via arguments to the derived class's constructor. Therefore,
even if a derived class's constructor does not use any arguments, it still
must declare one or more if the base class takes one or more arguments.
In this situation, the arguments passed to the derived class are simply
passed along to the base. For example, in the following program, the
constructor of **derived** takes no arguments, but **base1( )** and **base2( )**
do.

```cpp
#include <iostream.h>

class base1 {
protected:
  int i;
public:
  base1(int x) {i=x; cout << "Constructing base1\n";}
  ~base1() {cout << "Destructing base1\n";}
};

class base2 {
protected:
  int k;
public:
  base2(int x) {k=x; cout << "Constructing base2\n";}
  ~base2() {cout << "Destructing base2\n";}
};

class derived: public base1, public base2 {
public:
  /* Derived constructor uses no parameters,
     but still must be declared as taking them to
     pass them along to base classes.
  */
  derived(int x, int y): base1(x), base2(y)
    {cout << "Constructing derived\n";}

  ~derived() {cout << "Destructing derived\n";}
  void show() {cout << i << " " << k << "\n";}
```

14

```
};

main()
{
  derived ob(3, 4);

  ob.show();  // displays 3 4

  return 0;
}
```

The constructor function of a derived class is free to use any and all parameters that it is declared as taking, whether one or more are passed along to a base class. Put differently, just because an argument is passed along to a base class does not preclude its use by the derived class as well. For example, this fragment is perfectly valid:

An access declaration restores the access level of an inherited member to what it was in its base class.

```
class derived: public base {
  int j;
public:
  // derived uses both x and y and then passes them to base.
  derived(int x, int y): base(x, y)
    {j = x*y; cout << "Constructing derived\n";}
// ...
```

One final point to keep in mind when passing arguments to base class constructors: An argument being passed can consist of any expression valid at the time, including function calls and variables. This is in keeping with the fact that C++ allows dynamic initialization.

Granting Access

When a base class is inherited as private, all members of that class (public, protected, or private) become private members of the derived class. However, in certain circumstances, you may want to restore one or more inherited members to their original access specification. For example, you might want to grant certain public members of the base class public status in the derived class even though the base class is inherited as private. To do this, you must use an *access declaration* within the derived class. An access declaration takes this general form:

base-class::member;

The access declaration is put under the appropriate access heading in the derived class. Notice that no type declaration is required (or allowed) in an access declaration.

To see how an access declaration works, let's begin with this short fragment:

```
class base {
public:
  int j;  // public in base
};

// Inherit base as private.
class derived: private base {
public:

  // here is access declaration
  base::j; // make j public again
  // ...
};
```

As you know, because **base** is inherited as private by **derived**, the public variable **j** is made a private variable of **derived** by default. However, the inclusion of this access declaration

```
base::j;
```

14

under **derived**'s public heading restores **j** to its public status.

You can use an access declaration to restore the access rights of public and protected members. However, you cannot use an access declaration to raise or lower a member's access status. For example, a member declared as private within a base class cannot be made public by a derived class. (Allowing this would destroy encapsulation!)

The following program illustrates the use of access declarations.

```
#include <iostream.h>

class base {
  int i;  // private to base
public:
  int j, k;
  void seti(int x) {i = x;}
  int geti() {return i;}
```

```
};

// Inherit base as private.
class derived: private base {
public:
  /* The next three statements override
     base's inheritance as private
     and restore j, seti() and geti() to
     public access. */
  base::j; // make j public again - but not k
  base::seti; // make seti() public
  base::geti; // make geti() public

// base::i;  // illegal, you cannot elevate access

  int a; // public
};

main()
{
  derived ob;

//ob.i = 10;  // illegal because i is private in derived

  ob.j = 20;  // legal because j is made public in derived
//ob.k = 30;  // illegal because k is private in derived

  ob.a = 40;  // legal because a is public in derived
  ob.seti(10);

  cout << ob.geti() << " " << ob.j << " " << ob.a;

  return 0;
}
```

Notice how this program uses access declarations to restore **j**, **seti( )** and **geti( )** to public status. The comments describe various other access restrictions.

Access declarations are supported in C++ to accommodate those situations in which most of an inherited class is intended to be made private, but a few members are to retain their public or protected status.

Reading C++ Inheritance Graphs

Sometimes C++ class hierarchies are depicted graphically to make them more easily understood. However, due to a quirk in the way they are usually drawn by C++ programmers, class inheritance graphs are sometimes misleading to newcomers. For example, consider a situation in which class A is inherited by class B, which in turn is inherited by C. Using standard C++ graphic notation, this situation is drawn as shown here:

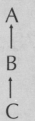

As you can see, the arrows point up, not down. While most people initially find the direction of the arrows to be counterintuitive, this is the style that most C++ programmers have adopted. In C++-style graphs, the arrow points to the base class. Thus, the arrow means "derived from", and not "deriving". Here is another example. Can you say, in words, what it means?

14

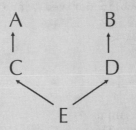

This graph states that class E is derived from both C and D. (That is, that E has multiple base classes, called C and D.) Further, C is derived from A, and D is derived from B.

While the direction of the arrows may be confusing at first, it is best that you become familiar with this style of graphic notation, since it is commonly used in books, magazines, and user's manuals.

Virtual Base Classes

An element of ambiguity can be introduced into a C++ program when multiple base classes are inherited. Consider this incorrect program:

```
// This program contains an error and will not compile.
#include <iostream.h>

class base {
public:
  int i;
};

// derived1 inherits base.
class derived1 :  public base {
public:
  int j;
};

// derived2 inherits base.
class derived2 : public base {
public:
  int k;
};

/* derived3 inherits both derived1 and derived2.
   This means that there are two copies of base
   in derived3! */
class derived3 : public derived1, public derived2 {
public:
  int sum;
};

main(void)
{
  derived3 ob;

  ob.i = 10;   // this is ambiguous; which i???
  ob.j = 20;
  ob.k = 30;

  // i ambiguous here, too
  ob.sum = ob.i + ob.j + ob.k;

  // also ambiguous, which i?
```

```
  cout << ob.i << " ";

  cout << ob.j << " " << ob.k << " ";
  cout << ob.sum;

  return 0;
}
```

As the comments in this program indicate, both **derived1** and **derived2** inherit **base**. However, **derived3** inherits both **derived1** and **derived2**. As a result, there are two copies of **base** present in an object of type **derived3**. Therefore, in an expression like

```
ob.i = 20;
```

which **i** is being referred to? The one in **derived1** or the one in **derived2**? Since there are two copies of **base** present in object **ob**, there are two **ob.i**s! As you can see, the statement is inherently ambiguous.

There are two ways to remedy the preceding program. The first is to apply the scope resolution operator to **i** and manually select one **i**. For example, the following version of the program will compile and run as expected.

```
// This program uses explicit scope resolution to select i.
#include <iostream.h>

class base {
public:
  int i;
};

// derived1 inherits base.
class derived1 :  public base {
public:
  int j;
};

// derived2 inherits base.
class derived2 : public base {
public:
  int k;
};

/* derived3 inherits both derived1 and derived2.
   This means that there are two copies of base
   in derived3! */
class derived3 : public derived1, public derived2 {
public:
```

14

```
    int sum;
};

main(void)
{
  derived3 ob;

  ob.derived1::i = 10;   // scope resolved, use derived1's i
  ob.j = 20;
  ob.k = 30;

  // scope resolved
  ob.sum = ob.derived1::i + ob.j + ob.k;

  // also resolved here
  cout << ob.derived1::i << " ";

  cout << ob.j << " " << ob.k << " ";
  cout << ob.sum;

  return 0;
}
```

The inheritance of a base class as *virtual* ensures that only one copy of it will be present in any derived class.

As you can see, by applying the ::, the program manually selects **derived1**'s version of **base**. However, this solution raises a deeper issue: What if only one copy of **base** is actually required? Is there some way to prevent two copies from being included in **derived3**? The answer, as you probably have guessed, is yes. And the solution is achieved with *virtual base classes*.

When two or more objects are derived from a common base class, you can prevent multiple copies of the base class from being present in an object derived from those objects by declaring the base class as virtual when it is inherited. To do this, you precede the name of the base class with the keyword **virtual** when it is inherited.

To illustrate this process, here is another version of the sample program in which **derived3** contains only one copy of **base**.

```
// This program uses virtual base classes.
#include <iostream.h>

class base {
public:
  int i;
};
```

```
// derived1 inherits base as virtual.
class derived1 : virtual public base {
public:
  int j;
};

// derived2 inherits base as virtual.
class derived2 : virtual public base {
public:
  int k;
};

/* derived3 inherits both derived1 and derived2.
   This time, there is only one copy of base class. */
class derived3 : public derived1, public derived2 {
public:
  int sum;
};

main(void)
{
  derived3 ob;

  ob.i = 10;   // now unambiguous
  ob.j = 20;
  ob.k = 30;

  // unambiguous
  ob.sum = ob.i + ob.j + ob.k;

  // unambiguous
  cout << ob.i << " ";

  cout << ob.j << " " << ob.k << " ";
  cout << ob.sum;

  return 0;
}
```

14

As you can see, the keyword **virtual** precedes the rest of the inherited class's specification. Now that both **derived1** and **derived2** have inherited **base** as virtual, any multiple inheritance involving them will cause only one copy of **base** to be present. Therefore, in **derived3** there is only one copy of **base**, and **ob.i = 10** is perfectly valid and unambiguous.

One further point to keep in mind: Even though both **derived1** and **derived2** specify **base** as virtual, **base** is still present in any object of either type. For example, the following sequence is perfectly valid.

```
// Define a class of type derived1.
derived1 myclass;

myclass.i = 88;
```

The only difference between a normal base class and a virtual one becomes evident when an object inherits the base class more than once. If the base class has been declared as virtual, then only one instance of it will be present in the inheriting object. Otherwise, multiple copies will be found.

Chapter

15

Virtual Functions and Polymorphism

As you know, one of the three major facets of object-oriented programming is polymorphism. As applied to C++, polymorphism is the term used to describe the process by which different implementations of a function can be accessed via the same name. For this reason, polymorphism is sometimes characterized by the phrase "one interface, multiple methods." This means that every member of a general class of operations can be accessed in the same fashion even though the specific actions associated with each operation may differ.

In C++, polymorphism is supported both at run time and at compile time. Operator and function overloading are examples of compile-time polymorphism. However, as powerful as operator and function overloading are, they cannot perform all the tasks required by a true, object-oriented language. Therefore, C++ also allows run-time polymorphism through the use of derived classes and *virtual functions*, and these are the major topics of this chapter.

This chapter begins with a short discussion of pointers to derived types, because they provide support for run-time polymorphism.

Pointers to Derived Types

The foundation of run-time polymorphism is the base class pointer. Pointers to base classes and derived classes are related in ways that other types of pointers are not. As you learned earlier in this book, a pointer of one type generally cannot point to an object of another type. However, base class pointers and derived objects are the exceptions to this rule. In C++, a base class pointer may also be used to point to an object of any class derived from that base. For example, assume that you have a base class called **B_class** and a class called **D_class**, which is derived from **B_class**. In C++, any pointer declared as a pointer to **B_class** can also be a pointer to **D_class**. Therefore, given

A base class pointer can point to any object derived from that base.

```
B_class *p; // pointer to object of type B_class
B_class B_ob; // object of type B_class
D_class D_ob; // object of type D_class
```

both of the following statements are perfectly valid:

```
p = &B_ob; // p points to object of type B_class
p = &D_ob; /* p points to object of type D_class,
               which is an object derived from B_class. */
```

In this example, **p** can be used to access all elements of **D_ob** inherited from **B_ob**. However, elements specific to **D_ob** cannot be referenced with **p** (unless a type cast is employed).

For a more concrete example, consider the following short program, which defines a base class called **B_class** and a derived class called **D_class**. This program uses a simple class hierarchy to store authors and titles.

```
// Using base pointers on derived class objects.

#include <iostream.h>
#include <string.h>

class B_class {
  char author[80];
public:
  void put_author(char *s) {strcpy(author, s); }
  void show_author() {cout << author << "\n";}
} ;
```

```
class D_class : public B_class {
  char title[80];
public:
  void put_title(char *num) {
    strcpy(title, num);
  }
  void show_title() {
    cout << "Title: ";
    cout <<  title << "\n";
  }
};

main()
{
  B_class *p;
  B_class B_ob;

  D_class *dp;
  D_class D_ob;

  p = &B_ob;   // address of base

  // Access B_class via pointer.
  p->put_author("Tom Clancy");

  // Access D_class via base pointer.
  p = &D_ob;
  p->put_author("William Shakespeare");

  // Show that each author went into proper object.
  B_ob.show_author();
  D_ob.show_author();
  cout << "\n";

  /* Since put_title() and show_title() are not part
     of the base class, they are not accessible via
     the base pointer p and must be accessed either
     directly, or, as shown here, through a pointer to the
     derived type.
  */
  dp = &D_ob;
  dp->put_title("The Tempest");
  p->show_author(); // either p or dp can be used here.
  dp->show_title( );

  return 0;
}
```

15

This program displays the following:

Tom Clancy
William Shakespeare

William Shakespeare
Title: The Tempest

In this example, the pointer **p** is defined as a pointer to **B_class**. However, it can point to an object of the derived class **D_class** and can be used to access those elements of the derived class that are inherited from the base class. However, remember that a base pointer cannot access those elements specific to the derived class (without the use of a type cast). This is why **show_title( )** is accessed with the **dp** pointer, which is a pointer to the derived class.

If you want to access elements defined by a derived class using a base class pointer, you must cast it into a pointer of the derived type. For example, this line of code will properly call the **show_title( )** function of **D_ob**.

```
((D_class *)p)->show_title();
```

The outer set of parentheses is necessary for associating the cast with **p** and not with the return type of **show_title( )**. While there is technically nothing wrong with casting a pointer in this manner, it is probably best avoided, because it simply adds confusion to your code. (Actually, most C++ programmers would consider this to be bad form.)

Another point to understand is that while a base pointer can be used to point to any type of derived object, the reverse is not true. That is, you cannot access an object of the base type by using a pointer to a derived class.

One final point: a pointer is incremented and decremented relative to its base type. Therefore, when a pointer to a base class is pointing at a derived object, incrementing or decrementing it will *not* make it point to the next object of the derived class. Instead, it will point to (what it thinks is) the next object of the base class. Therefore, you should consider it invalid to increment or decrement a pointer when it is pointing to a derived object.

The fact that a pointer to a base type can be used to point to any object derived from that base is extremely important, and fundamental to C++. As you will soon learn, this flexibility is crucial to the way C++ implements run-time polymorphism.

Virtual Functions

Run-time polymorphism is achieved through a combination of two features: inheritance and virtual functions. You learned about inheritance in the preceding chapter. Here, you will learn about the virtual function.

A *virtual function* is a function that is declared as **virtual** in a base class and redefined in one or more derived classes. Thus, each derived class can have its own version of a virtual function. What makes virtual functions interesting is what happens when a base class pointer is used to call one. When a virtual function is called through a base class pointer, C++ determines which version of that function to call based upon the *type* of the object *pointed to* by the pointer. And, this determination is made *at run time*. Thus, when different objects are pointed to, different versions of the virtual function are executed. In other words, it is the type of the object pointed to that determines which version of the virtual function will be executed. Therefore, if a base class contains a virtual function and if two or more different classes are derived from that base class, then when different types of objects are pointed to through a base class pointer, different versions of the virtual function are executed.

You declare a virtual function by preceding its declaration with the keyword **virtual**.

You declare a virtual function as virtual inside the base class by preceding its declaration with the keyword **virtual**. However, when a virtual function is redefined by a derived class, the keyword **virtual** need not be repeated (although it is not an error to do so).

A class that includes a virtual function is called a polymorphic class.

A class that includes a virtual function is called a *polymorphic class*. This term also applies to a class that inherits a base class containing a virtual function.

15

Examine this short program, which demonstrates the use of virtual functions:

```
// A short example that uses virtual functions.
#include <iostream.h>

class base {
public:
  virtual void who() { // specify a virtual
    cout << "Base\n";
  }
};

class first_d : public base {
public:
  void who() { // redefine who() relative to first_d
    cout << "First derivation\n";
  }
};
```

```
class second_d : public base {
public:
  void who() { // redefine who() relative to second_d
    cout << "Second derivation\n";
  }
};

main()
{
  base base_obj;
  base *p;
  first_d first_obj;
  second_d second_obj;

  p = &base_obj;
  p->who();  // access base's who

  p = &first_obj;
  p->who(); // access first_d's who

  p = &second_obj;
  p->who();  // access second_d's who

  return 0;
}
```

This program produces the following output.

> Base
> First derivation
> Second derivation

Let's examine the program in detail to understand how it works.

As you can see, in **base**, the function **who( )** is declared as virtual. This means that the function can be redefined by a derived class. Inside both **first_d** and **second_d**, **who( )** is redefined relative to each class. Inside **main( )**, four variables are declared: **base_obj**, which is an object of type **base**; **p**, which is a pointer to **base** objects; and **first_obj** and **second_obj**, which are objects of the two derived classes. Next, **p** is assigned the address of **base_obj**, and the **who( )** function is called. Since **who( )** is declared as virtual, C++ determines, at run time, which version of **who( )** is referred to by the type of object pointed to by **p**. In this case, **p** points to an object of type **base**, so it is the version of **who( )** declared in **base** that is executed. Next, **p** is assigned the address of **first_obj**. Recall that a base class pointer can be used to reference any derived class. Now, when **who( )** is called, C++

again checks to see what type of object is pointed to by **p** and, based on that type, determines which version of **who( )** to call. Since **p** points to an object of type **first_d**, that version of **who( )** is used. Likewise, when **p** is assigned the address of **second_obj**, the version of **who( )** declared inside **second_d** is executed.

Remember: It is determined at run time which version of a virtual function actually gets called. Further, this determination is based solely upon the type of the object that is being pointed to by a base class pointer.

A virtual function can be called normally, with the standard object/dot operator syntax. This means that in the preceding example, it would not be syntactically incorrect to access **who( )** using this statement:

```
first_obj.who();
```

However, calling a virtual function in this manner ignores its polymorphic attributes. It is only when a virtual function is accessed through a base class pointer that run-time polymorphism is achieved.

When a virtual function is redefined in a derived class, it is said to be overridden.

At first, the redefinition of a virtual function in a derived class seems to be a special form of function overloading. However, this is not the case. In fact, the two processes are fundamentally different. First, an overloaded function must differ in its type and/or number of parameters, while a redefined virtual function must have exactly the same type and number of parameters. In fact, the prototypes for a virtual function and its redefinitions must be exactly the same. If the prototypes differ, then the function is simply considered to be overloaded, and its virtual nature is lost. Another restriction is that a virtual function must be a member, not a friend, of the class for which it is defined. However, a virtual function can be a friend of another class. Also, it is permissible for destructor functions to be virtual, but not so for constructors.

15

Because of the restrictions and differences between overloading normal functions and redefining virtual functions, the term *overriding* is used to describe the redefinition of a virtual function.

Virtual Functions Are Inherited

Once a function is declared as virtual, it stays virtual no matter how many layers of derived classes it may pass through. For example, if **second_d** is derived from **first_d** instead of **base**, as shown in the next example, then **who( )** is still virtual and the proper version is still correctly selected.

```
// Derive from first_d, not base.
class second_d : public first_d {
public:
  void who() { // define who() relative to second_d
    cout << "Second derivation\n";
  }
};
```

The virtual attribute is inherited.

When a derived class does not override a virtual function, then the function as defined in the base class is used. For example, try this version of the preceding program.

```
#include <iostream.h>

class base {
public:
  virtual void who() {
    cout << "Base\n";
  }
};

class first_d : public base {
public:
  void who() {
    cout << "First derivation\n";
  }
};

class second_d : public base {
// who() not defined
};

main()
{
  base base_obj;
  base *p;
  first_d first_obj;
  second_d second_obj;

  p = &base_obj;
  p->who();  // access base's who()

  p = &first_obj;
  p->who(); // access first_d's who()

  p = &second_obj;
  p->who(); /* access base's who() because
```

```
                    second_d does not redefine it */

   return 0;
}
```

The program now outputs the following:

```
Base
First derivation
Base
```

Keep in mind that inherited characteristics of **virtual** are hierarchical. Therefore if, in the preceding example, **second_d** is derived from **first_d** instead of **base**, then when **who( )** is referenced relative to an object of type **second_d**, it is the version of **who( )** declared inside **first_d** that is called since it is the class closest to **second_d**, not the **who( )** inside **base**. The following program demonstrates this hierarchy.

```
#include <iostream.h>

class base {
public:
  virtual void who() {
    cout << "Base\n";
  }
};

class first_d : public base {
public:
  void who() {
    cout << "First derivation\n";
  }
};

// second_d now inherited first_d -- not base.
class second_d : public first_d {
// who() not defined
};

main()
{
  base base_obj;
  base *p;
  first_d first_obj;
  second_d second_obj;

  p = &base_obj;
```

15

```
    p->who();   // access base's who()

    p = &first_obj;
    p->who(); // access first_d's who()

    p = &second_obj;
    p->who(); /* access first_d's who() because
                 second_d does not redefine it */

    return 0;
}
```

This program produces the following output:

Base
First derivation
First derivation

As you can see, **second_d** now uses **first_d**'s version of **who( )** because that version is closest in the inheritance chain.

Why Virtual Functions?

As stated at the beginning of this chapter, virtual functions in combination with derived types allow C++ to support run-time polymorphism. And polymorphism is essential to object-oriented programming for one reason: It allows a generalized class to specify those functions that will be common to all derivatives of that class, while allowing a derived class to define the specific implementation of some or all of those functions. Sometimes this idea is expressed as follows: the base class dictates the general *interface* that any object derived from that class will have, but lets the derived class define the actual *method* itself. This is why the phrase "one interface, multiple methods" is often used to describe polymorphism.

Part of the key to successfully applying polymorphism is understanding that the base and derived classes form a hierarchy, which moves from greater to lesser generalization (base to derived). Hence, when used correctly, the base class provides all of the elements that a derived class can use directly. It also defines those functions that the derived class must implement on its own. This allows the derived class the flexibility to define its own methods, and yet still enforces a consistent interface. That is, since the form of the interface is defined by the base class, any derived class will share that common interface. Thus, the use of virtual functions makes it possible for the base class to define the generic interface that will be used by all derived classes.

At this point you might be asking yourself why a consistent interface with multiple implementations is important. The answer, again, goes back to the central driving force behind object-oriented programming: It helps the programmer handle increasingly complex programs. For example, if you develop your program correctly, then you know that all objects you derive from a base class are accessed in the same general way, even if the specific actions vary from one derived class to the next. This means that you need to remember only one interface, rather than several. Further, the separation of interface and implementation allows the creation of *class libraries*, which can be provided by a third party. If these libraries are implemented correctly, they will provide a common interface that you can use to derive classes of your own, which meet your specific needs.

A Simple Application of Virtual Functions

To get an idea of the power of the "one interface, multiple methods" concept, examine the following short program. It creates a base class called **figure**. This class is used to store the dimensions of various two-dimensional objects and to compute their areas. The function **set_dim( )** is a standard member function because this operation will be common to all derived classes. However, **show_area( )** is declared as virtual because the method of computing the area of each object will vary. The program uses **figure** to derive two specific classes called **square** and **triangle**.

```
#include <iostream.h>

class figure {
protected:
  double x, y;
public:
  void set_dim(double i, double j) {
    x = i;
    y = j;
  }
  virtual void show_area() {
    cout << "No area computation defined ";
    cout << "for this class.\n";
  }
} ;

class triangle : public figure {
  public:
    void show_area() {
      cout << "Triangle with height ";
      cout << x << " and base " << y;
      cout << " has an area of ";
```

15

```
      cout << x * 0.5 * y << ".\n";
    }
};

class square : public figure {
  public:
    void show_area() {
      cout << "Square with dimensions ";
      cout << x << "x" << y;
      cout << " has an area of ";
      cout << x *  y << ".\n";
    }
};

main()
{
  figure *p; // create a pointer to base type

  triangle t; // create objects of derived types
  square s;

  p = &t;
  p->set_dim(10.0, 5.0);
  p->show_area();

  p = &s;
  p->set_dim(10.0, 5.0);
  p->show_area();

  return 0;
}
```

As you can see, the interface to both **square** and **triangle** is the same even though both provide their own methods for computing the area of each of their objects.

Given the declaration for **figure**, is it possible to derive a class called **circle** that will compute the area of a circle, given its radius? The answer is yes. All that you need to do is to create a new derived type that computes the area of a circle. The power of virtual functions is based in the fact that you can easily derive a new type that will still share a common interface with other related objects. For example, here is one way to do it:

```
class circle : public figure {
  public:
    void show_area() {
      cout << "Circle with radius ";
```

```
          cout << x;
          cout << " has an area of ";
          cout <<   3.14 * x * x;
       }
};
```

Before trying to use **circle**, look closely at the definition for **show_area( )**. Notice that it uses only the value of **x**, which is assumed to hold the radius. (Remember, the area of a circle is computed using the formula πR^2.) However, the function **set_dim( )** as defined in **figure** assumes that it will be passed two values, not just one. Since **circle** does not require this second value, what course of action can we take?

There are two ways to resolve this problem. First and worst, you could simply call **set_dim( )** using a dummy value as the second parameter when using a **circle** object. This has the disadvantage of being sloppy, along with requiring that you remember a special exception, which violates the "one interface, many methods" philosophy.

A better way to resolve the problem is to give the **y** parameter inside **set_dim( )** a default value. Then, when calling **set_dim( )** for a circle, you need specify only the radius. When calling **set_dim( )** for a triangle or a square, you specify both values. The expanded program, which uses this method, is shown here:

15

```
#include <iostream.h>

class figure {
protected:
  double x, y;
public:
  void set_dim(double i, double j=0) {
    x = i;
    y = j;
  }
  virtual void show_area() {
    cout << "No area computation defined ";
    cout << "for this class.\n";
  }
} ;

class triangle : public figure {
  public:
    void show_area() {
      cout << "Triangle with height ";
      cout << x << " and base " << y;
      cout << " has an area of ";
```

```
        cout << x * 0.5 * y << ".\n";
    }
};

class square : public figure {
  public:
    void show_area() {
      cout << "Square with dimensions ";
      cout << x << "x" << y;
      cout << " has an area of ";
      cout << x *  y << ".\n";
    }
};

class circle : public figure {
  public:
    void show_area() {
      cout << "Circle with radius ";
      cout << x;
      cout << " has an area of ";
      cout << 3.14 * x * x << ".\n";
    }
} ;

main()
{
  figure *p; // create a pointer to base type

  triangle t; // create objects of derived types
  square s;
  circle c;

  p = &t;
  p->set_dim(10.0, 5.0);
  p->show_area();

  p = &s;
  p->set_dim(10.0, 5.0);
  p->show_area();

  p = &c;
  p->set_dim(9.0);
  p->show_area();

  return 0;
}
```

Tip: While virtual functions are syntactically easy to understand, their true power cannot be demonstrated in short examples. In general, polymorphism finds its greatest strength in large, complex systems. As you continue to use C++, opportunities to apply virtual functions will present themselves.

Pure Virtual Functions and Abstract Classes

As you have seen, when a virtual function that is not overridden in a derived class is called by an object of that derived class, the version of the function as defined in the base class is used. However, in many circumstances there will be no meaningful definition of a virtual function inside the base class. For example, in the base class **figure** used in the preceding example, the definition of **show_area( )** is simply a place holder. It will not compute and display the area of any type of object. As you will see when you create your own class libraries, it is not uncommon for a virtual function to have no meaningful definition in the context of its base class.

When this situation occurs, there are two ways you can handle it. One way, as shown in the example, is to simply have the function report a warning message. While this approach can be useful in certain situations, it will not be appropriate for all circumstances. For example, there may be virtual functions which simply must be defined by the derived class in order for the derived class to have any meaning. Consider the class **triangle**. It has no meaning if **show_area( )** is not defined. In this case, you want some method to ensure that a derived class does, indeed, define all necessary functions. In C++, the solution to this problem is the *pure virtual function*.

A pure virtual function is a virtual function that has no definition in its base class.

A pure virtual function is a function declared in a base class that has no definition relative to the base. As a result, any derived type must define its own version—it cannot simply use the version defined in the base. To declare a pure virtual function, use this general form:

virtual *type func-name(parameter-list)* = 0;

Here, *type* is the return type of the function, and *func-name* is the name of the function. For example, in the following version of **figure**, **show_area( )** is a pure virtual function.

15

```
class figure {
  double x, y;
public:
  void set_dim(double i, double j=0) {
    x = i;
    y = j;
  }
  virtual void show_area() = 0; // pure
};
```

By declaring a virtual function as pure, you force any derived class to define its own implementation. If a class fails to do so, the compiler will report an error. For example, try to compile this modified version of the figures program, in which the definition for **show_area( )** has been removed from the **circle** class.

```
/*
   This program will not compile because the class
   circle does not override show_area().
*/
#include <iostream.h>

class figure {
protected:
  double x, y;
public:
  void set_dim(double i, double j) {
    x = i;
    y = j;
  }
  virtual void show_area() = 0; // pure
} ;

class triangle : public figure {
  public:
    void show_area() {
      cout << "Triangle with height ";
      cout << x << " and base " << y;
      cout << " has an area of ";
      cout << x * 0.5 * y << ".\n";
    }
};

class square : public figure {
```

```
        public:
          void show_area() {
            cout << "Square with dimensions ";
            cout << x << "x" << y;
            cout << " has an area of ";
            cout << x *  y << ".\n";
          }
      };

      class circle : public figure {
      // no definition of show_area() will cause an error
      };

      main()
      {
        figure *p; // create a pointer to base type

        triangle t; // create objects of derived types
        square s;

        circle c; // Illegal -- can't create!

        p = &t;
        p->set_dim(10.0, 5.0);
        p->show_area();

        p = &s;
        p->set_dim(10.0, 5.0);
        p->show_area();

        return 0;
      }
```

15

A class that contains at least one pure virtual function is called an abstract class.

If a class has at least one pure virtual function, then that class is said to be *abstract*. An abstract class has one important feature: There can be no objects of that class. Instead, an abstract class must be used only as a base which other classes will inherit. The reason that an abstract class cannot be used to declare an object is, of course, that one or more of its functions have no definition. However, even if the base class is abstract, you still can use it to declare pointers, which are needed for supporting run-time polymorphism.

Polymorphism and the Purist

Throughout this book, and in this chapter, specifically, a distinction has been made between run-time and compile-time polymorphism. Compile-time polymorphic features are operator and function overloading. Run-time polymorphism is achieved with virtual functions. The most common definition of polymorphism is "one interface, multiple methods", and all of these features fit this meaning. However, some controversy does exist over the use of the term *polymorphism*.

Some OOP purists have insisted that the term refer only to events that occur at run time. Thus, they would say that only virtual functions support polymorphism. Part of this view is founded in the fact that the earliest polymorphic computer languages were interpreters (in which all events occur at run time). The advent of compiled polymorphic languages expanded the concept of polymorphism. However, some still argue that the term *polymorphism* should refer only to run-time events. Most C++ programmers disagree with this view and hold that the term applies both to run-time and to compile-time features. However, don't be surprised if some day, someone strikes up an argument with you over the use of this term!

Early Versus Late Binding

There are two terms that are commonly used when object-oriented programming languages are discussed: *early binding* and *late binding*. Relative to C++, these terms refer to events that occur at compile time and events that occur at run time, respectively.

Early binding binds a function call at compile time. Late binding binds a function call at run time.

Early binding means that a function call is resolved at compile time. That is, all information necessary for determining which function will be called is known when the program is compiled. Examples of early binding include standard function calls, overloaded function calls, and overloaded operator function calls. The principal advantage to early binding is efficiency—it is faster, and it often requires less memory. Its disadvantage is lack of flexibility.

Late binding means that a function call is resolved at run time. Thus, precisely which function will be called is determined "on the fly" as the program executes. As you now know, late binding is achieved in C++ through the use of virtual functions and derived types. The advantage to late binding is that it allows greater flexibility. It can be used to support a common interface, while allowing various objects that utilize that interface to define their own implementations. Further, it can be used to help you create class libraries, which can be reused and extended. Its disadvantage, however, is a slight loss of execution speed.

Whether your program uses early or late binding depends upon what the program is designed to do. (Actually, most large programs will use a combination of both.) Late binding is one of the most powerful features of C++. However, the price you pay for this power is that your program will run slightly slower. Therefore, it is best to use late binding only when it meaningfully adds to the structure and manageability of your program. (In essence, use—but don't abuse—the power.) Keep in mind, however, that the loss of performance caused by late binding is very slight, so when the situation calls for late binding, you should most definitely use it.

15

Chapter 16

The C++ I/O System

Since the beginning of this book, you have been using the C++ I/O system. However, you have been doing so without much formal explanation. The reason for this is easy to understand: C++'s approach to I/O is based upon an I/O class library and hierarchy. Therefore, it was not possible to present the theory and details of C++ I/O without first discussing classes and inheritance. Now it is time to examine the C++ I/O system in detail.

This chapter discusses several features of the C++ I/O system. C++'s I/O system is quite large, and it won't be possible to discuss every function, feature, or nuance, but this chapter will introduce you to those that are most important and commonly used. Specifically, the chapter discusses how to overload the << and >> operators so that you can input or output objects of classes that you design. It describes how to format output and how to use C++ I/O manipulators. The chapter ends by discussing file I/O.

415

C++ Streams

The most fundamental point to understand about the C++ I/O system is that it operates on *streams*. A stream is a common, logical interface to the various devices that comprise the computer. A stream either produces or consumes information. A stream is linked to a physical device by the C++ I/O system. All streams behave in the same manner, even if the actual physical devices they are linked to differ. Because all streams act the same, the same I/O functions and operators can operate on virtually any type of device. For example, the same method that you use to write to the screen can be used to write to a disk file or to the printer.

A stream is a consistent, logical interface that is linked to a physical file.

In its most common form, a stream is a logical interface to a file. As C++ defines the term "file," it can refer to a disk file, the screen, the keyboard, a port, a file on tape, and so on. Although files differ in form and capabilities, all streams are the same. The advantage to this approach is that to you, the programmer, one hardware device will look much like any other. The stream provides a consistent interface.

A stream is linked to a file through an open operation. A stream is disassociated from a file through a close operation.

There are two types of streams: text and binary. A text stream is used with ASCII characters. When a text stream is being used, some character translations may take place. For example, when the newline character is output, it may be converted into a carriage-return/linefeed sequence. For this reason, there might not be a one-to-one correspondence between what is sent to the stream and what is written to the file. A binary stream can be used with any type of data. No character translations will occur, and there is a one-to-one correspondence between what is sent to the stream and what is actually contained in the file.

The current location is the place within a file at which the next file access will occur.

One more concept to understand is that of the *current location*. The current location (also referred to as the *current position*) is the location in a file where the next file access will occur. For example, if a file is 100 bytes long and half the file has been read, the next read operation will occur at byte 50, which is the current location.

To summarize: In C++, I/O is performed through a logical interface called a stream. All streams have similar properties, and every stream is operated upon by the same I/O functions, no matter what type of file it is associated with. A file is the actual physical entity that contains the data. Even though files differ, streams do not. (Of course, some devices may not support all operations, such as random-access operations, so their associated streams will not support these operations either.)

The C++ Predefined Streams

C++ contains several predefined streams that are automatically opened when your C++ program begins execution. They are **cin**, **cout**, **cerr**, and **clog**. As you know, **cin** is the stream associated with standard input, and **cout** is the stream associated with standard output. The **cerr** stream is linked to standard output, and so is **clog**. The difference between these two streams is that **clog** is buffered, but **cerr** is not. This means that any output sent to **cerr** is immediately output, but output to **clog** is written only when a buffer is full. Typically, **cerr** and **clog** are streams to which program debugging or error information is written.

By default, the C++ standard streams are linked to the console, but they can be redirected to other devices or files by your program. They can also be redirected by the operating system.

The C++ Stream Classes

The C++ I/O system is defined by two related class hierarchies. These definitions are found in the header file **iostream.h**. The lowest-level class is called **streambuf**, and it contains the basic stream input and output operations. It provides the underlying support for the entire C++ I/O system. Unless you are doing advanced I/O programming, you will not need to use **streambuf** directly. The second class hierarchy begins with **ios**. The **ios** class provides support for formatted I/O. It is also used to derive three classes, **istream**, **ostream**, and **iostream**, that you can use to create streams. Using **istream** you can create an input stream; using **ostream** you can create an output stream; and using **iostream**, you can create a stream capable of both input and output.

16

Overloading the I/O Operators

In the preceding chapters, when a program needed to output or input the data associated with a class, special member functions were created whose only purpose was to output or input the class's data. While there is nothing, in itself, wrong with this approach, C++ allows a much better way of performing I/O operations on classes: by overloading the **<<** and the **>>** I/O operators.

In the language of C++, the **<<** operator is referred to as the *insertion* operator because it inserts characters into a stream. Likewise, the **>>** operator is called the *extraction* operator because it extracts characters from a stream. The operator functions that overload the insertion and extraction operators are generally called *inserters* and *extractors,* respectively.

An inserter
outputs
information
to a stream.
An extractor
inputs
information
from a
stream.

As you know, the insertion and extraction operators are already overloaded (in **iostream.h**) so that they are capable of performing stream I/O on any of C++'s built-in types. However, as mentioned earlier, it is possible to define these operators relative to classes that you define. In this section you will see how this is done.

Creating Inserters

As a simple first example, let's create an inserter for the version of the **three_d** class shown here:

```
class three_d {
public:
  int x, y, z; // 3-D coordinates
  three_d(int a, int b, int c) {x=a; y=b; z=c;}
};
```

To create an inserter function for an object of type **three_d**, you must define what an insertion operation is relative to it. To do this, you must overload the **<<** operator, as shown here:

```
// Display X, Y, Z coordinates (three_d's inserter).
ostream &operator<<(ostream &stream, three_d obj)
{
  stream << obj.x << ", ";
  stream << obj.y << ", ";
  stream << obj.z << "\n";
  return stream;  // return the stream
}
```

Let's look closely at this function, because many of its features are common to all inserter functions. First, notice that it is declared as returning a reference to an object of type **ostream**. This declaration is necessary so that several inserters of this type can be combined in a compound I/O expression. Next, the function has two parameters. The first is the reference to the stream which occurs on the left side of the **<<** operator. The second parameter is the object that occurs on the right side. (This parameter can also be a reference to the object, if you like.) Inside the function, the three values contained in an object of type **three_d** are output, and **stream** is returned.

Here is a short program that demonstrates the inserter.

```
#include <iostream.h>

class three_d {
public:
```

```
  int x, y, z; // 3-D coordinates
  three_d(int a, int b, int c) {x=a; y=b; z=c;}
} ;

// Display X, Y, Z coordinates - three_d inserter
ostream &operator<<(ostream &stream, three_d obj)
{
  stream << obj.x << ", ";
  stream << obj.y << ", ";
  stream << obj.z << "\n";
  return stream;   // return the stream
}

main()
{
  three_d a(1, 2, 3), b(3, 4, 5), c(5, 6, 7);

  cout << a << b << c;

  return 0;
}
```

This program displays the following output:

    1, 2, 3
    3, 4, 5
    5, 6, 7

If you eliminate the code that is specific to the **three_d** class you are left with the skeleton for an inserter function, as shown here:

16

```
ostream &operator<<(ostream &stream, class_type obj)
{
  // class specific code goes here
  return stream;   // return the stream
}
```

Within wide boundaries, what an inserter function actually does is up to you. However, good programming practice dictates that your inserter should produce reasonable output. Just make sure that you return **stream**.

You might be wondering why the **three_d** inserter was not coded as shown here:

```
// Limited version - don't use.
ostream &operator<<(ostream &stream, three_d obj)
{
```

```
    cout << obj.x << ", ";
    cout << obj.y << ", ";
    cout << obj.z << "\n";
    return stream;  // return the stream
}
```

In this version, the **cout** stream is hard-coded into the function. This limits the situations where it can be applied. Remember that the << operator can be applied to any stream and that the stream used in the << expression is passed to *stream*. Therefore, you must use the stream passed to the function if it is to work correctly in all cases. Only in this way can you create an inserter that can be used in any I/O expression.

Using Friend Functions to Overload Inserters

In the preceding program, the overloaded inserter function is not a member of **three_d**. In fact, neither inserter nor extractor functions can be members of a class. The reason for this is that when an **operator** function is a member of a class, the left operand (implicitly passed using the **this** pointer) is assumed to be an object of the class that has generated the call to the **operator** function. There is no way to change this. However, when inserters are overloaded, the left argument is a stream and the right argument is an object of the class. Therefore, overloaded inserters must be non-member functions.

The fact that inserters must not be members of the class they are defined to operate on raises a serious question: How can an overloaded inserter access the private elements of a class? In the preceding program, the variables **x**, **y**, and **z** were made **public** so that the inserter could access them. But hiding data is an important part of OOP, and forcing all data to be public is a serious inconsistency. However, there is a solution: an inserter can be a friend of a class. As a friend of the class for which it is defined, it has access to private data. To show you an example of this, the **three_d** class and sample program are reworked here, with the overloaded inserter declared as a friend.

```
#include <iostream.h>

class three_d {
    int x, y, z; // 3-D coordinates - - now private
public:
    three_d(int a, int b, int c) {x=a; y=b; z=c;}
    friend ostream &operator<<(ostream &stream, three_d obj);
} ;

// Display X, Y, Z coordinates - three_d inserter
```

```
ostream &operator<<(ostream &stream, three_d obj)
{
  stream << obj.x << ", ";
  stream << obj.y << ", ";
  stream << obj.z << "\n";
  return stream;  // return the stream
}

main()
{
  three_d a(1, 2, 3), b(3, 4, 5), c(5, 6, 7);

  cout << a << b << c;

  return 0;
}
```

Notice that the variables **x**, **y**, and **z** are now private to **three_d**, but can still be directly accessed by the inserter. Making inserters (and extractors) friends of the classes for which they are defined preserves the encapsulation principle of OOP.

Overloading Extractors

To overload an extractor, use the same general approach that you use when overloading an inserter. For example, the following extractor inputs 3-D coordinates. Notice that it also prompts the user.

```
// Get three-dimensional values - extractor.
istream &operator>>(istream &stream, three_d &obj)
{
  cout << "Enter X,Y,Z values: ";
  stream >> obj.x >> obj.y >> obj.z;
  return stream;
}
```

16

An extractor must return a reference to an object of type **istream**. Also, the first parameter must be a reference to an object of type **istream**. This is the stream that occurs on the left side of the **>>**. The second parameter is a reference to the variable that will be receiving input. Because it is a reference, the second parameter can be modified when information is input.

The skeleton of an extractor is shown here:

```
istream &operator>>(istream &stream, object_type &obj)
{
  // put your extractor code here
```

```
    return stream;
}
```

The following program demonstrates the extractor for objects of type
three_d.

```
#include <iostream.h>

class three_d {
  int x, y, z; // 3-D coordinates
public:
  three_d(int a, int b, int c) {x=a; y=b; z=c;}
  friend ostream &operator<<(ostream &stream, three_d obj);
  friend istream &operator>>(istream &stream, three_d &obj);
} ;

// Display X, Y, Z coordinates - inserter.
ostream &operator<<(ostream &stream, three_d obj)
{
  stream << obj.x << ", ";
  stream << obj.y << ", ";
  stream << obj.z << "\n";
  return stream; // return the stream
}

// Get three dimensional values - extractor
istream &operator>>(istream &stream, three_d &obj)
{
  cout << "Enter X,Y,Z values: ";
  stream >> obj.x >> obj.y >> obj.z;
  return stream;
}

main()
{
  three_d a(1, 2, 3);

  cout << a;

  cin >> a;
  cout << a;

  return 0;
}
```

Like inserters, extractor functions cannot be members of the class they are designed to operate upon. They can be friends or simply independent functions.

Except for the fact that you must return a reference to an object of type **istream**, you can do anything you like inside an extractor function. However, for the sake of structure and clarity, it is best to use extractors only for input operations.

C I/O Versus C++ I/O

As you may know, C++'s predecessor, C, has one of the most flexible yet powerful I/O systems of any of the structured languages. (In fact, it may be safe to say that among the world's structured programming languages, C's I/O system is unparalleled.) Given the power of C's I/O functions, you might be asking yourself why C++ defines its own I/O functions, since for the most part they duplicate those already contained in C. The answer is that the C I/O system provides no support for user-defined objects. For example, if you create the following structure in C,

```
struct my_struct {
  int count;
  char s[80];
  double balance;
} cust;
```

there is no way to customize or extend C's I/O system so that it knows about, and can perform I/O operations directly on, an object of type **my_struct**. However, since objects are at the core of object-oriented programming, it makes sense that C++ have an I/O system that can be made aware of objects that you create. Thus, a new, object-oriented I/O system was invented for C++. As you have seen, C++'s approach to I/O allows you to overload the << and >> operators so that they know about classes that you create.

One other point: Because C++ is a superset of C, all of C's I/O support is included in C++. (See Appendix A for an overview of C-based I/O.) Therefore, if you are migrating C programs to C++, you won't have to change all the I/O statements immediately. The C-based statements will still compile and run. It is just that C-based I/O has no object-oriented component.

Formatted I/O

Up to this point, the format for inputting or outputting information has been left to the defaults provided by the C++ I/O system. However, you can precisely control the format of your data in either of two ways. The first uses member functions of the **ios** class. The second uses a special type of function called a *manipulator*. We will begin by looking at formatting using the **ios** member functions.

Formatting with the ios Member Functions

Each C++ stream has associated with it a number of format flags that determine how data is displayed. They are encoded into a long integer. The format flags are named and given values within the **ios** class, typically using an enumeration, as shown here:

```
// ios formatting flags
enum {
  skipws = 0x0001,
  left = 0x0002,
  right = 0x0004,
  internal = 0x0008,
  dec = 0x0010,
  oct = 0x0020,
  hex = 0x0040,
  showbase = 0x0080,
  showpoint = 0x0100,
  uppercase = 0x0200,
  showpos = 0x0400,
  scientific = 0x0800,
  fixed = 0x1000,
  unitbuf = 0x2000,
  stdio = 0x4000
};
```

The values defined by this enumeration are used to set or clear flags that control some of the ways information is formatted by a stream. Generally, when a flag is set, its corresponding feature is turned on. When a flag is cleared, its feature is turned off, and the default formatting is used. The flags are described here.

When the **skipws** flag is set, leading whitespace characters (spaces, tabs, and newlines) are discarded when input is performed on a stream. When **skipws** is cleared, these whitespace characters are not discarded.

When the **left** flag is set, output is left-justified. When **right** is set, output is right-justified. When the **internal** flag is set, then a numeric value is padded to fill a field by inserting spaces between any sign or base character. (You will learn how to specify a field width shortly.)

By default, integer values are output in decimal. However, you can override this default. Setting the **oct** flag causes output to be displayed in octal. Setting the **hex** flag causes output to be displayed in hexadecimal. To return to decimal, set the **dec** flag.

Setting **showbase** causes the base of numeric values to be shown. For example, if the conversion base is hexadecimal, then the value AB will be displayed as **0xAB**.

By default, when scientific notation is displayed, the "e" is in lowercase. Also, when a hexadecimal value is displayed, the "x" is in lowercase. When **uppercase** is set, these characters are displayed in uppercase.

Setting **showpos** causes a leading plus sign to be displayed before positive integer values.

Setting **showpoint** causes a decimal point and trailing zeros to be displayed for all floating point output—whether needed or not.

When the **scientific** flag is set, floating point numeric values are displayed using scientific notation. When **fixed** is set, floating point values are displayed using normal notation. By default, when **fixed** is set, six decimal places are displayed. When neither flag is set, the compiler chooses an appropriate method.

When **unitbuf** is set, the C++ I/O system flushes output streams after each output operation. (You will need to check your compiler's user manual for additional, implementation-dependent details regarding **unitbuf**.)

16

stdio is not defined by the proposed ANSI C++ standard. This flag is typically used to provide compatibility with the C-based I/O system. Check your compiler's manual for details.

Tip: As you have learned, the format flags are held in a long integer. However, the proposed ANSI C++ standard defines a type name called **fmtflags** that is used to hold format information. At the time of this writing, no commonly available C++ compilers support this type. (You should check your compiler's user manual.) From a practical point of view, it is almost certain that **fmtflags** will used as a **typedef**ed name for a long integer, so no compatibility problems should arise.

To set a flag, use the **setf( )** function, whose most common form is shown here:

> long setf(long *flags*);

This function returns the previous settings of the format flags and turns on those flags specified by *flags*. For example, to turn on the **showbase** flag, you can use this statement:

> *stream*.setf(ios::showbase);

Here, *stream* is the stream you wish to affect. Notice the use of **ios::** to qualify **showbase**. Because **showbase** is an enumerated constant defined within the **ios** class, it must be qualified by **ios** when it is referred to. This principle applies to all of the format flags.

The following program uses **setf( )** to turn on both the **showpos** and **scientific** flags.

```
#include <iostream.h>

main()
{
  cout.setf(ios::showpos);
  cout.setf(ios::scientific);
  cout << 123 << " " << 123.23 << " ";

  return 0;
}
```

The output produced by this program is shown here:

> +123 +1.232300e+02

You may OR together as many flags as you like in a single call. For example, by ORing together **scientific** and **showpos**, as shown next, you can change the program so that only one call is made to **setf( )**.

```
cout.setf(ios::scientific | ios::showpos);
```

To turn off a flag, use the **unsetf( )** function, whose prototype is shown here:

> long unsetf(long *flags*);

The function returns the previous flag settings and turns off those flags specified by *flags*.

Sometimes it is useful to know the current flag settings. You can retrieve the current flag values using the **flags( )** function, whose prototype is shown here:

unsetf( ) clears format flags. *flags( )* obtains the current format flag settings.

```
long flags( );
```

This function returns the current value of the flags relative to the associated stream.

The following form of **flags( )** sets the flag values to those specified by *flags* and returns the previous flag values:

```
long flags(long flags);
```

To see how **flags( )** and **unsetf( )** work, examine this program. It includes a function called **showflags( )** that displays the state of the flags.

```
#include <iostream.h>

void showflags(long f);

main()
{
  long f;

  f = cout.flags();

  showflags(f);
  cout.setf(ios::showpos);
  cout.setf(ios::scientific);

  f = cout.flags();
  showflags(f);

  cout.unsetf(ios::scientific);

  f = cout.flags();
  showflags(f);

  return 0;
}

void showflags(long f)
{
```

16

```
   long i;

   for(i=0x4000; i; i = i >> 1)
     if(i & f) cout << "1 ";
     else cout << "0 ";

   cout << "\n";
}
```

When run, the program produces this output:

```
0 1 0 0 0 0 0 0 0 0 0 0 0 0 0 1
0 1 0 1 1 0 0 0 0 0 0 0 0 0 0 1
0 1 0 0 1 0 0 0 0 0 0 0 0 0 0 1
```

In addition to the formatting flags, you can also set the field width, the fill character, and the number of digits of precision, using these functions:

int width(int *len*);

char fill(char *ch*);

int precision(int *num*);

The **width( )** function returns the current field width and sets the field width to *len*. By default, the field width varies, depending upon the number of characters it takes to hold the data. The **fill( )** function returns the current fill character, which is a space by default, and makes the current fill character the same as *ch*. The fill character is the character used to pad output to fill a specified field width. The **precision( )** function returns the number of digits displayed after a decimal point and sets that value to *num*. (By default, there are six digits of precision.) Here is a program that demonstrates these three functions.

```
#include <iostream.h>

main()
{
  cout.setf(ios::showpos);
  cout.setf(ios::scientific);
  cout << 123 << " " << 123.23 << "\n";

  cout.precision(2); // two digits after decimal point
  cout.width(10);    // in a field of ten characters
  cout << 123 << " ";
  cout.width(10);
  cout << 123.23 << "\n";
```

```
cout.fill('#');  // fill using #
cout.width(10);  // in a field of ten characters
cout << 123 << " ";
cout.width(10);
cout << 123.23;

return 0;
}
```

The program displays this output:

```
+123    +1.232300e+02
        +123    +1.23e+02
######+123   #+1.23e+02
```

In some implementations it is necessary to reset the field width before each output operation. This is why **width( )** is called repeatedly in the preceding program.

Using I/O Manipulators

The C++ I/O system includes a second way in which you can alter the format parameters of a stream. This method uses special functions, called *manipulators*, that can be included in an I/O expression. The standard manipulators are shown in Table 16-1.

To use those manipulators that take arguments, you must include **iomanip.h** in your program.

You can use a manipulator to embed formatting instructions in an I/O expression.

A manipulator is used as part of a larger I/O expression. Here is a sample program that uses manipulators to control the format of its output.

16

```
#include <iostream.h>
#include <iomanip.h>

main()
{
  cout << setprecision(2) << 1000.243 << endl;
  cout << setw(20) << "Hello there.";

  return 0;
}
```

Manipulator	Purpose	Input/Output
dec	Format numeric data in decimal	Input and output
endl	Output a newline character and flush the stream	Output
ends	Output a null	Output
flush	Flush a stream	Output
hex	Format numeric data in hexadecimal	Input and output
oct	Format numeric data in octal	Input and output
resetiosflags (long f)	Turn off the flags specified in f	Input and output
setbase (int *base*)	Set the number base to *base*	Output
setfill (int *ch*)	Set the fill character to *ch*	Output
setiosflags (long f)	Turn on the flags specified in f	Input and output
setprecision (int p)	Set the number of digits of precision	Output
setw (int w)	Set the field width to w	Output
ws	Skip leading whitespace	Input

The C++ I/O
Manipulators
Table 16-1.

It produces this output:

```
1e+03
          Hello there.
```

Notice how the manipulators occur in the chain of I/O operations. Also, notice that when a manipulator does not take an argument, such as **endl** in the example, it is not followed by parentheses.

The following program uses **setiosflags( )** to set the **scientific** and **showpos** flags.

```cpp
#include <iostream.h>
#include <iomanip.h>

main()
{
  cout << setiosflags(ios::showpos);
  cout << setiosflags(ios::scientific);
  cout << 123 << " " << 123.23;

  return 0;
}
```

The program shown next uses **ws** to skip any leading whitespace when inputting a string into **s**.

```
#include <iostream.h>

main()
{
  char s[80];

  cin >> ws >> s;
  cout << s;

  return 0;
}
```

Creating Your Own Manipulator Functions

You can create your own manipulator functions. There are two types of manipulator functions: those that take arguments and those that don't. The creation of parameterized manipulators requires the use of techniques beyond the scope of this book. However, the creation of parameterless manipulators is described here.

All parameterless manipulator output functions have this skeleton:

```
ostream &manip_name(ostream &stream)
{
  // your code here

  return stream;
}
```

Here, **manip_name** is the name of the manipulator. It is important to understand that even though the manipulator has as its single argument a pointer to the stream upon which it is operating, no argument is specified when the manipulator is used in an output expression.

The following program creates a manipulator called **setup( )** that turns on left justification, sets the field width to 10, and specifies that the dollar sign will be the fill character.

```
#include <iostream.h>
#include <iomanip.h>

ostream &setup(ostream &stream)
{
```

16

```
    stream.setf(ios::left);
    stream << setw(10) << setfill('$');
    return stream;
}

main()
{
  cout << 10 << " " << setup << 10;

  return 0;
}
```

Custom manipulators are useful for two reasons. First, you might need to perform an I/O operation on a device for which none of the predefined manipulators applies—a plotter, for example. In this case, creating your own manipulators will make it more convenient when outputting to the device. Second, you may find that you are repeating the same sequence of operations many times. You can consolidate these operations into a single manipulator, as the foregoing program illustrates.

All parameterless input manipulator functions have this skeleton:

```
istream &manip_name(istream &stream)
{
  // your code here

  return stream;
}
```

For example, the following program creates the **prompt( )** manipulator. It displays a prompting message and then configures input to accept hexadecimal.

```
#include <iostream.h>
#include <iomanip.h>

istream &prompt(istream &stream)
{
  cin >> hex;
  cout << "Enter number using hex format: ";

  return stream;
```

```
}

main()
{
  int i;

  cin >> prompt >> i;
  cout << i;

  return 0;
}
```

Remember that it is crucial that your manipulator return *stream*. If this is not done, then your manipulator cannot be used in a compound input or output expression.

File I/O

You can use the C++ I/O system to perform file I/O. In order to perform file I/O, you must include the header file **fstream.h** in your program. It defines several important classes and values.

Opening and Closing a File

In C++, a file is opened by linking it to a stream. As you know, there are three types of streams: input, output, and input/output. To open an input stream you must declare the stream to be of class **ifstream**. To open an output stream, it must be declared as class **ofstream**. A stream that will be performing both input and output operations must be declared as class **fstream**. For example, this fragment creates one input stream, one output stream, and one stream capable of both input and output.

16

```
ifstream in;   // input
ofstream out;  // output
fstream both;  // input and output
```

Once you have created a stream, one way to associate it with a file is by using **open( )**. This function is a member of each of the three stream classes. Its prototype is shown here:

void open(const char *filename*, int *mode*, int *access*);

Here, *filename* is the name of the file; it can include a path specifier. The value of *mode* determines how the file is opened. It must be one (or more) of the following values (which are defined in **fstream.h**):

ios::app
ios::ate
ios::binary
ios::in
ios::nocreate
ios::noreplace
ios::out
ios::trunc

You can combine two or more of these values by ORing them together. Let's see what each of these values means.

Including **ios::app** causes all output to the file to be appended to the end. This value can only be used with files capable of output. Including **ios::ate** causes a seek to the end of the file to occur when the file is opened.

The **ios::in** value specifies that the file is capable of input. **ios::out** specifies that the file is capable of output. However, using **ifstream** to create a stream implies input, and using **ofstream** implies output, so in these cases, it is unnecessary to supply these values.

By default, files are opened in text mode. The **ios::binary** value causes a file to be opened in binary mode. As mentioned near the beginning of this chapter, in text mode, various character translations can take place, such as the conversion of carriage-return/linefeed sequences into newlines. However, when a file is opened in binary mode, no such character translations will occur. Any file, whether it contains formatted text or raw data, can be opened in either binary or text mode. The only difference is whether character translations take place.

Including **ios::nocreate** causes the **open( )** function to fail if the file does not already exist. The **ios::noreplace** value causes the **open( )** function to fail if the file does already exist.

The **ios::trunc** value causes the contents of a preexisting file by the same name to be destroyed, and truncates the file to zero length.

The value of *access* determines how the file can be accessed. In DOS/Windows environments, this value generally corresponds to the DOS/Windows file attribute codes, listed here:

Attribute	Meaning
0	Normal file; open access
1	Read-only file
2	Hidden file
4	System file
8	Archive bit set

You can OR two or more of these together. For DOS/Windows, a normal file has an *access* value of 0.

The following fragment opens a normal output file.

```
ofstream out;
out.open("test", ios::out, 0);
```

However, you will seldom (if ever) see **open( )** called as shown here, because both the *mode* and *access* parameters have default values. For **ifstream**, *mode* is **ios::in**, and for **ofstream** it is **ios::out**. The *access* parameter has a default value of 0 (normal file). Therefore, the preceding statement will usually look like this:

```
out.open("test"); // defaults to output and normal file
```

To open a stream for input and output, you must specify both the **ios::in** and the **ios::out** *mode* values, as shown in this example:

```
fstream mystream;
mystream.open("test", ios::in | ios::out);
```

If **open( )** fails, **mystream** will be 0.

Although it is entirely proper to use the **open( )** function for opening a file, most of the time you will not do so because the **ifstream**, **ofstream** and **fstream** classes have constructor functions that automatically open the file. The constructor functions have the same parameters and defaults as the **open( )** function. Therefore, the most common way you will see a file opened is shown in this example:

```
ifstream mystream("myfile"); // open file for input
```

*open( ) opens
a file, and
close( ) closes
a file.*

If, for some reason, the file cannot be opened, the value of the associated stream variable will be zero. Therefore, to confirm that the file has actually been opened, you will use code like that shown here:

```
ifstream  mystream("myfile"); // open file for input
if(!mystream) {
  cout << "Cannot open file.";
  //  process error
}
```

To close a file, use the member function **close( )**. For example, to close the file linked to a stream called **mystream**, you would use this statement:

```
mystream.close();
```

The **close( )** function takes no parameters and returns no value.

Reading and Writing Text Files

The easiest way to read from or write to a text file is to use the **<<** and **>>** operators. For example, this program writes an integer, a floating point value, and a string to a file called **test**.

```
#include <iostream.h>
#include <fstream.h>

main()
{
  ofstream out("test");
  if(!out) {
    cout << "Cannot open file.";
    return 1;
   }

  out << 10 << " " << 123.23 << "\n";
  out << "This is a short text file.";

  out.close();

  return 0;
}
```

The following program reads an integer, a **float**, a character, and a string from the file created by the previous program.

```
#include <iostream.h>
#include <fstream.h>

main()
{
  char ch;
  int i;
  float f;
  char str[80];

  ifstream in("test");
  if(!in) {
    cout << "Cannot open file.";
    return 1;
  }

  in >> i;
  in >> f;
  in >> ch;
  in >> str;

  cout << i << " " << f << " " << ch << "\n";
  cout << str;

  in.close();
  return 0;
}
```

Keep in mind that when the **>>** operator is used for reading text files, certain character translations occur. For example, whitespace characters are omitted. If you want to prevent any character translations, you must open a file for binary access. Also remember that when **>>** is used to read a string, input stops when the first whitespace character is encountered.

Unformatted Binary I/O

Formatted text files (like those used in the preceding examples) are useful for a variety of situations, but they do not have the flexibility of unformatted binary files. For this reason, C++ supports a number of binary (sometimes called "raw") file I/O functions.

There are two ways to write and read unformatted binary data to or from a file. First, you can write a byte using the member function **put( )**, and read a byte using the member function **get( )**.

The **get( )** function has many forms, but the most commonly used version is shown next, along with that of **put( )**:

16

get( ) reads a character from a file, and *put( )* writes a character to a file.

```
istream &get(char &ch);

ostream &put(char ch);
```

The **get( )** function reads a single character from the associated stream and puts that value in *ch*. It returns a reference to the stream. This value will be null if the end of the file is reached. The **put( )** function writes *ch* to the stream and returns a reference to the stream.

Remember: If you will be performing binary operations on a file, be sure to open it using the **ios::binary** mode specifier. Although the binary file functions will work on files opened for text mode, some character translations may occur. Character translations negate the purpose of binary file operations.

The following program will display the contents of any file on the screen. It uses the **get( )** function.

```
#include <iostream.h>
#include <fstream.h>

main(int argc, char *argv[])
{
  char ch;

  if(argc!=2) {
    cout << "Usage: PR <filename>\n";
    return 1;
  }

  ifstream in(argv[1], ios::in | ios::binary);
  if(!in) {
    cout << "Cannot open file.";
    return 1;
  }

  while(in) { // in will be 0 when eof is reached
    in.get(ch);
    cout << ch;
  }

  in.close();

  return 0;
}
```

When **in** reaches the end of the file it will be zero, causing the **while** loop to stop.

There is actually a more compact way to code the loop that reads and displays a file, as shown here:

```
while(in.get(ch))
  cout << ch;
```

This form works because **get( )** returns the stream **in**, and **in** will be zero when the end of the file is encountered.

This program uses **put( )** to write a string to a file.

```
#include <iostream.h>
#include <fstream.h>

main()
{
  char *p = "hello there";

  ofstream out("test", ios::out | ios::binary);
  if(!out) {
    cout << "Cannot open file.";
    return 1;
   }

  while(*p) out.put(*p++);

  out.close();

  return 0;
}
```

16

Reading and Writing Blocks of Data

To read and write blocks of binary data, use the **read( )** and **write( )** member functions. Their prototypes are shown here:

istream &read(unsigned char *buf*, int *num*);

ostream &write(const unsigned char *buf*, int *num*);

The **read( )** function reads *num* bytes from the associated stream and puts them in the buffer pointed to by *buf*. The **write( )** function writes *num* bytes to the associated stream from the buffer pointed to by *buf*.

The following program writes and then reads an array of integers.

read( ) inputs a block of data, and *write( )* outputs a block of data.

```cpp
#include <iostream.h>
#include <fstream.h>

main()
{
  int n[5] = {1, 2, 3, 4, 5};
  register int i;

  ofstream out("test", ios::out | ios::binary);
  if(!out) {
    cout << "Cannot open file.";
    return 1;
   }

  out.write((unsigned char *) &n, sizeof n);

  out.close();

  for(i=0; i<5; i++) // clear array
    n[i] = 0;

  ifstream in("test", ios::in | ios::binary);
  in.read((unsigned char *) &n, sizeof n);

  for(i=0; i<5; i++) // show values read from file
    cout << n[i] << " ";

  in.close();

  return 0;
}
```

Note that the type casts inside the calls to **read( )** and **write( )** are
necessary when operating on a buffer that is not defined as a character array.

gcount( ) returns the number of characters read by the last input operation.

If the end of the file is reached before *num* characters have been read, then **read( )** simply stops, and the buffer will contain as many characters as were available. You can find out how many characters have been read using another member function, called **gcount( )**, which has this prototype:

> int gcount( );

gcount( ) returns the number of characters read by the last input operation.

Detecting EOF

You can detect when the end of the file is reached using the member
function **eof( )**, which has this prototype:

   int eof( );

It returns non-zero when the end of the file has been reached; otherwise it
returns zero.

The following program uses **eof( )** to display the contents of a file on
the screen.

*eof( ) returns
true when
the end of
the file is
encountered.*

```cpp
// Detect end-of-file using eof().
#include <iostream.h>
#include <fstream.h>

main(int argc, char *argv[])
{
  char ch;

  if(argc!=2) {
    cout << "Usage: PR <filename>\n";
    return 1;
  }

  ifstream in(argv[1], ios::in | ios::binary);
  if(!in) {
    cout << "Cannot open file.";
    return 1;
  }

  while(!in.eof()) { // use eof()
    in.get(ch);
    cout << ch;
  }

  in.close();

  return 0;
}
```

16

A File Comparison Example

To sample the power and simplicity of the C++ file system, examine the
following program. It compares two files for equality. It does so by using the
binary file functions **read( )**, **eof( )**, and **gcount( )**. The program first

opens the files for binary operations. (This is necessary to prevent character translations from being performed.) Next, it reads one buffer at a time from each of the files and compares the contents. Since less than a full buffer may be read, it uses the **gcount( )** function to determine precisely how many characters are in the buffers. As you can see, when using the C++ file functions, very little code is needed to perform this (and other) file manipulations.

```cpp
// Compare files.
#include <iostream.h>
#include <fstream.h>

main(int argc, char *argv[])
{
  register int i;
  int numread;

  unsigned char buf1[1024], buf2[1024];

  if(argc!=3) {
    cout << "Usage: compare <file1> <file2>\n";
    return 1;
  }

  ifstream f1(argv[1], ios::in | ios::binary);
  if(!f1) {
    cout << "Cannot open file";
    return 1;
  }
  ifstream f2(argv[2], ios::in | ios::binary);
  if(!f2) {
    cout << "Cannot open file";
    return 1;
  }

  cout << "Comparing files...\n";

  do {
    f1.read((unsigned char *) buf1, sizeof buf1);
    f2.read((unsigned char *) buf2, sizeof buf2);

    // compare contents of buffers
    for(i=0; i<f1.gcount(); i++)
      if(buf1[i] != buf2[i]) {
        cout << "Files differ.\n";
        f1.close();
        f2.close();
```

```
        return 0;
      }

  } while(!f1.eof() && !f2.eof());

  /* If both files are not at eof, then one is longer
     than the other. */
  if(!f1.eof() || !f2.eof())
    cout << "Files are of differing sizes.\n";
  else
    cout << "Files are the same.\n";

  f1.close();
  f2.close();

  return 0;
}
```

Here is an experiment: The buffer size is hard-coded at 1024. As an exercise, change this value to a **const** variable, and try different buffer sizes. Find the optimal buffer size for your operating environment.

More Binary I/O Functions

In addition to the form shown earlier, the **get( )** function can be overloaded in several different ways. The prototypes for the two most commonly used overloaded forms are shown here:

> istream &get(char *buf, int num, char delim='\n');

> int get( );

16

The first overloaded form reads characters into the array pointed to by buf until either num characters have been read or the character specified by delim has been encountered. The array pointed to by buf will be null-terminated by **get( )**. If no delim parameter is specified, then by default a newline character acts as a delimiter. If the delimiter character is encountered in the input stream, it is *not* extracted. Instead, it remains in the stream until the next input operation.

The second overloaded form of **get( )** returns the next character from the stream. It returns EOF if the end of the file is encountered.

Another member function that performs input is **getline( )**. Its prototype is shown here:

> istream &getline(char *buf, int num, char delim='\n');

As you can see, this function is virtually identical to the **get(buf, num, delim)** version of **get( )**. It reads characters from input and puts them into the array pointed to by *buf* until either *num* characters have been read or until the character specified by *delim* is encountered. If not specified, *delim* defaults to the newline character. The array pointed to by *buf* is null-terminated. The difference between **get(buf, num, delim)** and **getline( )** is that **getline( )** reads and removes the delimiter from the input stream.

getline( ) is another C++ input function.

One good use for **getline( )** is to read a string that contains spaces. As you know, when you use **>>** to read a string, it stops reading when the first whitespace character is encountered. This makes **>>** useless for reading a string containing spaces. However, you can overcome this problem by using **getline( )**, as illustrated in this program:

```
// Use getline() to read a string that contains spaces.
#include <iostream.h>
#include <fstream.h>

main()
{
    char str[80];

    cout << "Enter your name: ";
    cin.getline(str, 79);

    cout << str << '\n';

    return 0;
}
```

Here, the final parameter to **getline( )** is allowed to default to a newline. This makes **getline( )** act much like the standard **gets( )** function.

You can obtain the next character in the input stream without removing it from that stream by using **peek( )**. It has this prototype:

peek( ) obtains the next character in the input stream.

int peek( );

peek( ) returns the next character in the stream, or EOF if the end of the file is encountered.

You can return the last character read from a stream to that stream by using **putback( )**. Its prototype is shown here:

putback( ) returns a character to the input stream.

istream &putback(char *c*);

where *c* is the last character read.

flush( )
flushes
an output
stream.

When output is performed, data is not immediately written to the physical device linked to the stream. Instead, information is stored in an internal buffer until the buffer is full. Only then are the contents of that buffer written to disk. However, you can force the information to be physically written to disk before the buffer is full by calling **flush( )**. Its prototype is shown here:

        ostream &flush( );

Calls to **flush( )** might be warranted when a program is going to be used in adverse environments (in situations where power outages occur frequently, for example).

Random Access

seekg( )
moves the
get pointer.
seekp( )
moves the
put pointer.

So far in this book, files have always been read or written sequentially. But you can also access a file in random order. In C++'s I/O system, you perform random access using the **seekg( )** and **seekp( )** functions. Their most common forms are shown here:

        istream &seekg(streamoff *offset*, seek_dir *origin*);

        ostream &seekp(streamoff *offset*, seek_dir *origin*);

Here, **streamoff** is a type defined in **iostream.h** that is capable of containing the largest valid value that *offset* can have. **seek_dir** is an enumeration that has these values:

Value	Meaning
ios::beg	Beginning of file
ios::cur	Current location
ios::end	End of file

16

The C++ I/O system manages two pointers associated with a file. One is the *get pointer*, which specifies where in the file the next input operation will occur. The other is the *put pointer* which specifies where in the file the next output operation will occur. Each time an input or an output operation takes place, the appropriate pointer is automatically advanced. However, using the **seekg( )** and **seekp( )** functions, it is possible to access the file in a non-sequential fashion.

The **seekg( )** function moves the associated file's current get pointer *offset* number of bytes from the specified *origin*. The **seekp( )** function moves the associated file's current put pointer *offset* number of bytes from the specified *origin*.

Generally, random access I/O should be performed only on those files opened for binary operations. The character translations that may occur on text files could cause a position request to be out of synch with the actual contents of the file.

The following program demonstrates the **seekp( )** function. It allows you to specify a file name on the command line, followed by the specific byte that you want to change in the file. The program then writes an **X** at the specified location. Notice that the file must be opened for read/write operations.

```
#include <iostream.h>
#include <fstream.h>
#include <stdlib.h>

main(int argc, char *argv[])
{
  if(argc!=3) {
    cout << "Usage: CHANGE <filename> <byte>\n";
    return 1;
  }

  fstream out(argv[1], ios::in | ios::out | ios::binary);
  if(!out) {
    cout << "Cannot open file.";
    return 1;
  }

  out.seekp(atoi(argv[2]), ios::beg);

  out.put('X');
  out.close();

  return 0;
}
```

The next program uses **seekg( )**. It displays the contents of a file, beginning with the location you specify on the command line.

```
#include <iostream.h>
#include <fstream.h>
#include <stdlib.h>

main(int argc, char *argv[])
{
  char ch;

  if(argc!=3) {
```

```
      cout << "Usage: NAME <filename> <starting location>\n";
      return 1;
  }

  ifstream in(argv[1], ios::in | ios::binary);
  if(!in) {
    cout << "Cannot open file.";
    return 1;
  }

  in.seekg(atoi(argv[2]), ios::beg);

  while(in.get(ch))
    cout << ch;

  return 0;
}
```

You can determine the current position of each file pointer using these functions:

> streampos tellg( );

> streampos tellp( );

tellg( ) returns the current get location, and tellp( ) returns the current put position.

Here, **streampos** is a type defined in **iostream.h** that is capable of holding the largest value that either function can return.

As you have seen, C++'s I/O system is both powerful and flexible. Although this chapter has discussed the most important and commonly used functions, C++ includes several other I/O functions that help you handle special situations. To learn more about these, you should consult the user's manual for your compiler.

16

Customized I/O and Files

Earlier in this chapter you learned how to overload the insertion and extraction operators relative to your own classes. You also learned how to create your own manipulators. In the examples, only console I/O was performed. However, because all C++ streams are the same, the same overloaded inserter function, for example, can be used to output to the screen or to a file with no changes whatsoever. This is one of the most important and useful features of C++'s approach to I/O.

The following program uses the overloaded **three_d** inserter to write coordinate information to a file called **threed**.

```
/* Use overloaded inserter to write three_d objects
   to a file. */
#include <iostream.h>
#include <fstream.h>

class three_d {
  int x, y, z; // 3-D coordinates - - now private
public:
  three_d(int a, int b, int c) {x=a; y=b; z=c;}
  friend ostream &operator<<(ostream &stream, three_d obj);
};

// Display X, Y, Z coordinates - three_d inserter
ostream &operator<<(ostream &stream, three_d obj)
{
  stream << obj.x << ", ";
  stream << obj.y << ", ";
  stream << obj.z << "\n";
  return stream;  // return the stream
}

main()
{
  three_d a(1, 2, 3), b(3, 4, 5), c(5, 6, 7);
  ofstream out("threed");

  if(!out) {
    cout << "Cannot open file.";
    return 1;
  }

  out << a << b << c;

  out.close();

  return 0;
}
```

If you compare this version of the **three_d** inserter to the one shown earlier in this chapter, you will find that no changes have been made to make it accommodate disk files. Once you correctly define an inserter or extractor, it will work with any stream.

Tip: Before moving on to the next chapter, take some time to experiment with the C++ I/O system. Specifically, try creating your own class and then defining an inserter and extractor for it. Also, try creating your own manipulators.

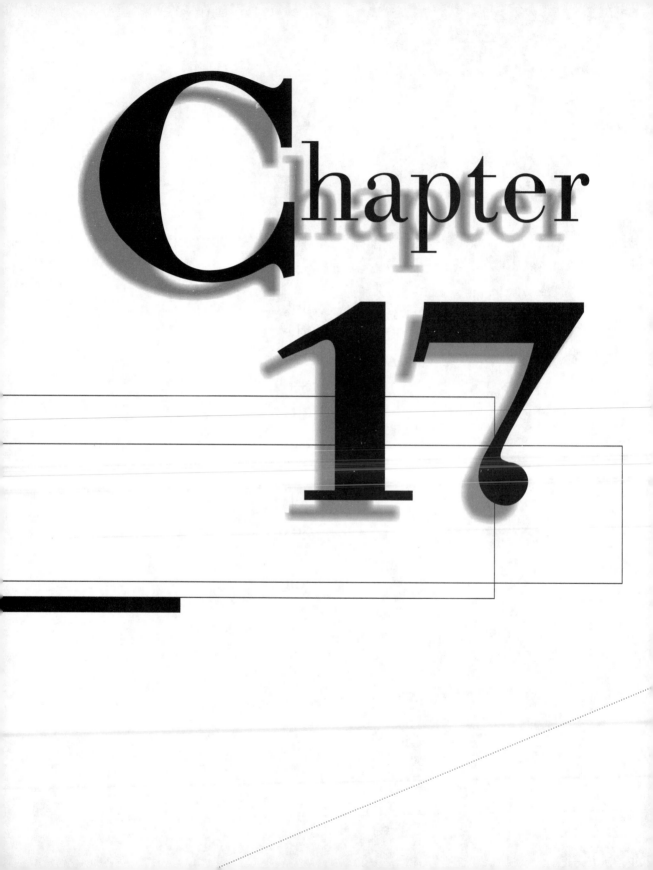

Chapter

17

Templates and Exception Handling

There are two important features that have recently been added to C++: templates and exception handling. While neither of these enhancements is technically necessary, both expand the scope of C++ and help you get the most from your programming efforts.

Using templates, it is possible to create generic functions and classes. In a generic function or class, the type of data upon which the function or class operates is specified as a parameter. Thus, you can use one function or class with several different types of data without having to explicitly recode specific versions for different data types. Both generic functions and generic classes are discussed in this chapter.

Exception handling is the subsystem of C++ that allows you, in a structured and controlled manner, to handle errors that occur at run time. Using C++ exception handling, your program can automatically invoke an error-handling routine when an error occurs. The principal advantage of exception handling is that it automates much of the error-handling code that previously had to be entered "by hand" into any large program.

Note: Neither templates nor exception handling were part of the original specification for C++, but both are defined by the proposed ANSI C++ standard and are supported by most C++ compilers available today. However, if you have an older compiler, it may not support one or both of these features. You will need to check your user's manual.

Generic Functions

A generic function defines a general set of operations that will be applied to various types of data. The type of data that the function will operate upon is passed to it as a parameter. Through a generic function, a single general procedure can be applied to a wide range of data. As you probably know, many algorithms are logically the same no matter what type of data is being operated upon. For example, the Quicksort sorting algorithm is the same whether it is applied to an array of integers or an array of floats. It is just that the type of the data being sorted is different. By creating a generic function, you can define the nature of the algorithm, independent of any data. Once you have done this, the compiler will automatically generate the correct code for the type of data that is actually used when you execute the function. In essence, when you create a generic function you are creating a function that can automatically overload itself.

A generic function is capable of overloading itself.

A generic function is created using the keyword **template**. The normal meaning of the word "template" accurately reflects its use in C++. It is used to create a template (or framework) which describes what a function will do, leaving it to the compiler to fill in the details as needed. The general form of a template function definition is shown here:

```
template <class Ttype> ret-type func-name(parameter list)
{
    // body of function
}
```

template is
the keyword
that begins
a generic
function
definition.

Here, *Ttype* is a placeholder name for a data type used by the function. This name may be used within the function definition. However, it is only a placeholder which the compiler will automatically replace with an actual data type when it creates a specific version of the function.

The following short example creates a generic function that swaps the values of the two variables with which it is called. Because the general process of exchanging two values is independent of the type of the variables, it is a good candidate for being made into a generic function.

```cpp
// Function template example.
#include <iostream.h>

// This is a function template.
template <class X> void swap(X &a, X &b)
{
  X temp;

  temp = a;
  a = b;
  b = temp;
}

main()
{
  int i=10, j=20;
  float x=10.1, y=23.3;
  char a='x', b='z';

  cout << "Original i, j: " << i << ' ' << j << endl;
  cout << "Original x, y: " << x << ' ' << y << endl;
  cout << "Original a, b: " << a << ' ' << b << endl;

  swap(i, j); // swap integers
  swap(x, y); // swap floats
  swap(a, b); // swap chars

  cout << "Swapped i, j: " << i << ' ' << j << endl;
  cout << "Swapped x, y: " << x << ' ' << y << endl;
  cout << "Swapped a, b: " << a << ' ' << b << endl;

  return 0;
}
```

17

Let's look closely at this program.

The line:

```
template <class X> void swap(X &a, X &b)
```

tells the compiler two things: that a template is being created and that a generic definition is beginning. Here, **X** is a generic type that is used as a placeholder. After the **template** portion, the function **swap( )** is declared, using **X** as the data type of the values that will be swapped. In **main( )**, the **swap( )** function is called using three different types of data: integers, **float**s, and **char**s. Because **swap( )** is a generic function, the compiler automatically creates three versions of **swap( )**: one that will exchange integer values, one that will exchange floating point values, and one that will swap characters. You should compile and try this program now. Also, try swapping other types of data.

As you read other C++ literature, you may encounter some alternate terms used in the discussion of templates. First, a generic function (that is, a function definition preceded by a **template** statement) is also called a *template function*. When the compiler creates a specific version of this function, it is said to have created a *generated function*. The act of generating a function is referred to as *instantiating* it. Put differently, a generated function is a specific instance of a template function.

Technically, the **template** portion of a generic function definition does not have to be on the same line as the function's name. The following example shows another common way to format the **swap( )** function.

```
template <class X>
void swap(X &a, X &b)
{
  X temp;

  temp = a;
  a = b;
  b = temp;
}
```

If you use this form, it is important to understand that no other statements can occur between the **template** statement and the start of the generic function definition. For example, the fragment shown next will not compile.

```
// This will not compile.
template <class X>
int i; // this is an error
```

```
void swap(X &a, X &b)
{
  X temp;

  temp = a;
  a = b;
  b = temp;
}
```

As the comments imply, the **template** specification must directly precede the function definition.

A Function with Two Generic Types

You can define more than one generic data type in the **template** statement by using a comma-separated list. For example, this program creates a generic function that has two generic types.

```
#include <iostream.h>

template <class type1, class type2>
void myfunc(type1 x, type2 y)
{
  cout << x << ' ' << y << endl;
}

main()
{
  myfunc(10, "hi");

  myfunc(0.23, 10L);

  return 0;
}
```

In this example, the placeholder types **type1** and **type2** are replaced by the compiler with the data types **int** and **char ***, and **double** and **long**, respectively, when the compiler generates the specific instances of **myfunc( )** within **main( )**.

Remember: When you create a generic function, you are, in essence, allowing the compiler to generate as many different versions of that function as are necessary for handling the various ways that your program calls the function.

17

Explicitly Overloading a Generic Function

Even though a template function overloads itself as needed, you can
explicitly overload one, too. If you overload a generic function, then that
overloaded function overrides (or "hides") the generic function relative to
that specific version. For example, consider the following, revised version of
the first example in this chapter.

```cpp
// Overriding a template function.
#include <iostream.h>

template <class X> void swap(X &a, X &b)
{
  X temp;

  temp = a;
  a = b;
  b = temp;
}

// This overrides the generic version of swap().
void swap(int &a, int &b)
{
  int temp;

  temp = a;
  a = b;
  b = temp;
  cout << "Inside swap(int &, int &).\n";
}

main()
{
  int i=10, j=20;
  float x=10.1, y=23.3;
  char a='x', b='z';

  cout << "Original i, j: " << i << ' ' << j << endl;
  cout << "Original x, y: " << x << ' ' << y << endl;
  cout << "Original a, b: " << a << ' ' << b << endl;

  swap(i, j); // this calls the explicitly overloaded swap()
```

```
swap(x, y); // swap floats
swap(a, b); // swap chars

cout << "Swapped i, j: " << i << ' ' << j << endl;
cout << "Swapped x, y: " << x << ' ' << y << endl;
cout << "Swapped a, b: " << a << ' ' << b << endl;

return 0;
}
```

As the comments indicate, when **swap(i, j)** is called, it invokes the explicitly overloaded version of **swap( )** defined in the program. Thus, the compiler does not generate this version of the generic **swap( )** function, because the generic function is overridden by the explicit overloading.

Manual overloading of a template, as shown in this example, allows you to tailor a version of a generic function to accommodate a special situation. However, in general, if you need to have different versions of a function for different data types, you should use overloaded functions rather than templates.

Generic Function Restrictions

Generic functions are similar to overloaded functions except that they are more restrictive. When functions are overloaded, you may have different actions performed within the body of each function. But a generic function must perform the same general action for all versions—only the type of data can differ. Consider the overloaded functions in the following example. These functions could *not* be replaced by a generic function, because they do not do the same thing.

```
void outdata(int i)
{
  cout << i;
}

void outdata(double d)
{
  cout << setprecision(10) << setfill('#');
  cout << d;
  cout << setprecision(6) << setfill(' ');
}
```

17

Creating a Generic abs( ) Function

Let's return to the **abs( )** function one last time. Recall that in Chapter 8, the standard library functions **abs( )**, **labs( )**, and **fabs( )** were consolidated into three overloaded functions called **abs( )**. Each of the overloaded versions of **abs( )** was designed to return the absolute value of a different type of data. While the manual overloading of **abs( )** in Chapter 8 was an improvement over the use of three different library functions (each having different names), it is still not the best way to create an absolute value function. Since the procedure that returns the absolute value of a number is the same for all types of numeric values, **abs( )** is an excellent choice for a generic function. Once a generic version of **abs( )** exists, the compiler can automatically create whatever version of the function it needs. You, the programmer, do not need to anticipate each application. (You also won't be cluttering your source code with multiple, manually overloaded versions.)

The following program contains the generic version of **abs( )**. You might want to compare it to the overloaded versions in Chapter 8. As you will see, the generic version has shorter source code and is more flexible.

```cpp
// A generic version of abs().
#include <iostream.h>

template <class X> X abs(X val)
{
  return val < 0 ? -val : val;
}

main()
{
  cout << abs(-10) << '\n'; // integer abs

  cout << abs(-10.0) << '\n'; // double abs

  cout << abs(-10L) << '\n'; // long abs

  cout << abs(-10.0F) << '\n'; // float abs

  return 0;
}
```

On your own, you should try to find other library functions that are good candidates for being made into generic functions. Remember, the key is that the same algorithm be applicable to a wide range of data.

Generic Classes

In addition to generic functions, you can also define a generic class. When you do this, you create a class that defines all the algorithms used by that class; however, the actual type of the data being manipulated will be specified as a parameter when objects of that class are created.

Generic classes are useful when a class uses logic that can be generalized. For example, the same algorithm that maintains a queue of integers will also work for a queue of characters, and the same mechanism that maintains a linked list of mailing addresses will also maintain a linked list of auto part information. When you create a generic class, it can perform the operation you define, such as maintaining a queue or a linked list, for any type of data. The compiler will automatically generate the correct type of object, based upon the type you specify when the object is created.

The general form of a generic class declaration is shown here:

```
template <class Ttype> class class-name {
    .
    .
    .
}
```

Here, *Ttype* is the placeholder type name, which will be specified when a class is instantiated. If necessary, you can define more than one generic data type using a comma-separated list.

Once you have created a generic class, you create a specific instance of that class using the following general form:

```
class-name <type> ob;
```

Here, *type* is the type name of the data that the class will be operating upon.

Member functions of a generic class are, themselves, automatically generic. You need not use **template** to explicitly specify them as such.

In the following program, the **queue** class (first introduced in Chapter 11) is reworked into a generic class. Thus, it can be used to queue objects of any type. In this example, a character queue and a floating point queue are created, but any data type can be used.

17

```
// Demonstrate a generic queue class.
#include <iostream.h>

const int SIZE=100;
```

```
// This creates the generic class queue.
template <class QType> class queue {
  QType q[SIZE];
  int sloc, rloc;
public:
  queue() {sloc = rloc = 0; }
  void qput(QType i);
  QType qget();
};

// Put an object into the queue.
template <class QType> void queue<QType>::qput(QType i)
{
  if(sloc==SIZE) {
    cout << "Queue is full";
    return;
  }
  sloc++;
  q[sloc] = i;
}

// Get an object from the queue.
template <class QType> QType queue<QType>::qget()
{
  if(rloc == sloc) {
    cout << "Queue Underflow";
    return 0;
  }
  rloc++;
  return q[rloc];
}

main()
{
  queue<int> a, b;   // create two integer queues

  a.qput(10);
  b.qput(19);

  a.qput(20);
  b.qput(1);

  cout << a.qget() << " ";
  cout << a.qget() << " ";
  cout << b.qget() << " ";
  cout << b.qget() << "\n";

  queue<double> c, d;   // create two double queues
```

```
    c.qput(10.12);
    d.qput(19.99);

    c.qput(-20.0);
    d.qput(0.986);

    cout << c.qget() << " ";
    cout << c.qget() << " ";
    cout << d.qget() << " ";
    cout << d.qget() << "\n";

    return 0;
}
```

As you can see, the declaration of a generic class is similar to that of a generic function. The actual type of data stored by the queue is generic in the class declaration. It is not until an object of the queue is declared that the actual data type is determined. When a specific instance of **queue** is declared, the compiler automatically generates all the functions and variables necessary for handling the actual data. In this example, two different types of queues are declared. Two are integer queues. Two are queues of **double**s. Pay special attention to these declarations:

```
queue<int> a, b;
```

```
queue<double> c, d;
```

Notice how the desired data type is passed inside the angle brackets. By changing the type of data specified when **queue** objects are created, you can change the type of data stored in that queue. For example, by using the following declaration, you can create another queue that stores character pointers.

```
queue<char *> chrptrQ;
```

You can also create queues to store data types that you create. For example, if you want to use the following structure to store address information,

```
struct addr {
  char name[40];
  char street[40];
  char city[30];
  char state[3];
  char zip[12];
}
```

17

then to use **queue** to generate a queue that will store objects of type **addr**, use a declaration like this:

```
queue<addr> obj;
```

As the **queue** class illustrates, generic functions and classes are powerful tools that you can use to maximize your programming efforts, because they allow you to define the general form of an object which can then be used with any type of data. You are saved from the tedium of creating separate implementations for each data type that you want the algorithm to work with. The compiler automatically creates the specific versions of the class for you.

An Example with Two Generic Data Types

A template class can have more than one generic data type. Simply declare all the data types required by the class in a comma-separated list within the **template** specification. For example, the following short example creates a class that uses two generic data types.

```
/* This example uses two generic data types in a
   class definition.
*/
#include <iostream.h>

template <class Type1, class Type2> class myclass
{
  Type1 i;
  Type2 j;
public:
  myclass(Type1 a, Type2 b) { i = a; j = b; }
  void show() { cout << i << ' ' << j << '\n'; }
};

main()
{
  myclass<int, double> ob1(10, 0.23);
  myclass<char, char *> ob2('X', "This is a test");

  ob1.show(); // show int, double
  ob2.show(); // show char, char *

  return 0;
}
```

This program produces the following output:

```
10 0.23
X This is a test
```

The program declares two types of objects. **ob1** uses integer and **double** data. **ob2** uses a character and a character pointer. For both cases, the compiler automatically generates the appropriate data and functions to accommodate the way the objects are created.

Creating a Generic Array Class

Before moving on to exception handling, let's look at another generic class application. As you saw in Chapter 13, you can overload the **[ ]** operator. Doing so allows you to create your own array implementations, including "safe arrays" that provide run-time boundary checking. As you know, in C++, it is possible to overrun (or underrun) an array boundary at run time without generating a run-time error message. However, if you create a class that contains the array, and allow access to that array only through the overloaded [ ] subscripting operator, then you can intercept an out-of-range index.

By combining operator overloading with a generic class, it is possible to create a generic safe array type that can be used for creating safe arrays of any data type. This type of array is created in the following program:

```
// A generic safe array example.
#include <iostream.h>
#include "stdlib.h"

const int SIZE = 10;

template <class AType> class atype {
  AType a[SIZE];
public:
  atype() {
    register int i;
    for(i=0; i<SIZE; i++) a[i] = i;
  }
  AType &operator[](int i);
};

// Provide range checking for atype.
template <class AType> AType &atype<AType>::operator[](int i)
```

17

```
   {
     if(i<0 || i> SIZE-1) {
       cout << "\nIndex value of ";
       cout << i << " is out-of-bounds.\n";
       exit(1);
     }
     return a[i];
   }

main()
{
   atype<int> intob; // integer array
   atype<double> doubleob; // double array

   int i;

   cout << "Integer array: ";
   for(i=0; i<SIZE; i++) intob[i] = i;
   for(i=0; i<SIZE; i++) cout << intob[i] << "   ";
   cout << '\n';

   cout << "Double array: ";
   cout.precision(2);
   for(i=0; i<SIZE; i++) doubleob[i] = (double) i/3;
   for(i=0; i<SIZE; i++) cout << doubleob[i] << "   ";
   cout << '\n';

   intob[12] = 100; // generates runtime error

   return 0;
}
```

This program implements a generic safe array type and then demonstrates its use by creating an array of integers and an array of **double**s. You should try creating other types of arrays. As this example shows, part of the power of generic classes is that they allow you to write the code once, debug it, and then apply it to any type of data without having to re-engineer it for each specific application.

Challenge: For simplicity, the preceding program uses fixed-size arrays. However, you can change the **atype** class so that arrays of varying dimensions can be declared. To accomplish this, specify the array dimension as a parameter to the **atype** constructor function, and dynamically allocate the array. Try to make this improvement on your own.

Exception Handling

Exception handling is a structured means by which your program can manage run-time errors.

C++ provides a built-in error-handling mechanism that is called *exception handling*. Using exception handling, you can more easily manage and respond to run-time errors. C++ exception handling is built upon three keywords: **try**, **catch**, and **throw**. In the most general terms, program statements that you want to monitor for exceptions are contained in a **try** block. If an exception (i.e., an error) occurs within the **try** block, it is thrown (using **throw**). The exception is caught, using **catch**, and processed. The following discussion elaborates upon this general description.

Any statement that throws an exception must have been executed from within a **try** block. (A function called from within a **try** block may also throw an exception.) Any exception must be caught by a **catch** statement which immediately follows the **try** statement that has thrown the exception. The general form of **try** and **catch** are shown here:

```
try {
  // try block
}
catch (type1 arg) {
  // catch block
}
catch (type2 arg) {
  // catch block
}
catch (type3 arg) {
  // catch block
}
    .
    .
    .
catch (typeN arg) {
  // catch block
}
```

throw throws an exception, which is caught by a *catch* statement.

The **try** block must contain the portion of your program that you want to monitor for errors. This section can be as short as a few statements within one function, or as all-encompassing as a **try** block that encloses the **main( )** function code (which would, in effect, cause the entire program to be monitored).

When an exception is thrown, it is caught by its corresponding **catch** statement, which then processes the exception. There can be more than one **catch** statement associated with a **try**. The type of the exception determines which **catch** statement is used. That is, if the data type specified by a **catch**

17

statement matches that of the exception, then that **catch** statement is executed (and all others are bypassed). When an exception is caught, *arg* will receive its value. Any type of data can be caught, including classes that you create.

The general form of the **throw** statement is shown here:

Exceptions must be thrown from within a ***try*** block.

    throw *exception*;

throw must be executed either from within the **try** block itself, or from any function called from within the **try** block (directly or indirectly). *exception* is the value thrown.

 Note: If you throw an exception for which there is no applicable **catch** statement, an abnormal program termination may occur. If your compiler complies with the proposed ANSI C++ standard, then throwing an unhandled exception will cause the **terminate( )** function to be invoked. By default, **terminate( )** calls **abort( )** to stop your program, but you can specify your own termination handler, if you like. You will need to refer to your compiler's library reference for details.

Here is a very simple example that shows how C++ exception handling operates.

```
// A simple exception handling example.
#include <iostream.h>

main()
{
  cout << "start\n";

  try { // start a try block
    cout << "Inside try block\n";
    throw 99; // throw an error
    cout << "This will not execute";
  }
  catch (int i) { // catch an error
    cout << "Caught an exception -- value is: ";
    cout << i << "\n";
  }

  cout << "end";

  return 0;
}
```

This program displays the following output:

```
start
Inside try block
Caught an exception — value is: 99
end
```

Look carefully at this program. As you can see, there is a **try** block containing three statements and a **catch(int i)** statement that processes an integer exception. Within the **try** block, only two of the three statements will execute: the first **cout** statement and the **throw**. Once an exception has been thrown, control passes to the **catch** expression, and the **try** block is terminated. That is, **catch** is *not* called. Rather, program execution is transferred to it. (The program's stack is automatically reset, as necessary, to accomplish this.) Thus, the **cout** statement following the **throw** will never execute.

After the **catch** statement executes, program control continues with the statements following the **catch**. However, a **catch** block commonly will end with a call to **exit( )**, **abort( )**, etc., because exception handling is often used to handle catastrophic errors.

abort( )

abort( ) is another of C++'s standard library functions. It has this prototype:

   void abort( );

abort( ) is somewhat similar to **exit( )** (with ehich you are already familiar) in that it causes immediate program termination. However, unlike **exit( )**, it does not return status information to the operating system, nor does it close any open files or flush any pending streams.

In practical terms, **abort( )** is a C++ program's "emergency stop" function. It should only be used after a catastrophic error has occurred.

17

As mentioned earlier, the type of the exception must match the type specified in a **catch** statement. For example, in the preceding program, if you change the type in the **catch** statement to **double**, then the exception will not be caught and abnormal termination will occur. This change is shown here:

```
// This example will not work.
#include <iostream.h>

main()
{
  cout << "start\n";

  try { // start a try block
    cout << "Inside try block\n";
    throw 99; // throw an error
    cout << "This will not execute";
  }
  catch (double i) { // Won't work for an int exception
    cout << "Caught an exception -- value is: ";
    cout << i << "\n";
  }

  cout << "end";

  return 0;
}
```

This program produces the following output because the integer exception will not be caught by the **catch(double i)** statement.

```
start
Inside try block
Abnormal program termination
```

An exception can be thrown from a statement that is outside the **try** block as long as it is within a function that is called from within **try** block. For example, this is a valid program:

```
/* Throwing an exception from a function outside the
   try block.
*/
#include <iostream.h>

void Xtest(int test)
{
  cout << "Inside Xtest, test is: " << test << "\n";
  if(test) throw test;
}

main()
{
  cout << "start\n";
```

```
try { // start a try block
  cout << "Inside try block\n";
  Xtest(0);
  Xtest(1);
  Xtest(2);
}
catch (int i) { // catch an error
  cout << "Caught an exception -- value is: ";
  cout << i << "\n";
}

cout << "end";

return 0;
}
```

This program produces the following output:

```
start
Inside try block
Inside Xtest, test is: 0
Inside Xtest, test is: 1
Caught an exception — value is: 1
end
```

A **try** block can be localized to a function. When this is the case, each time the function is entered, the exception handling relative to that function is reset. Examine this sample program:

```
#include <iostream.h>

// A try/catch can be inside a function other than main().
void Xhandler(int test)
{
  try{
    if(test) throw test;
  }
  catch(int i) {
    cout << "Caught One!  Ex. #: " << i << '\n';
  }
}

main()
{
  cout << "start\n";
```

17

```
    Xhandler(1);
    Xhandler(2);
    Xhandler(0);
    Xhandler(3);

    cout << "end";

    return 0;
}
```

This program displays the following output:

```
start
Caught One!  Ex. #: 1
Caught One!  Ex. #: 2
Caught One!  Ex. #: 3
end
```

As you can see, three exceptions are thrown. After each exception, the function returns. When the function is called again, the exception handling is reset.

Using Multiple catch Statements

As stated earlier, you can associate more than one **catch** statement with a **try**. In fact, it is common to do so. However, each **catch** must catch a different type of exception. For example, the program shown here catches both integers and strings.

```
#include <iostream.h>

// Different types of exceptions can be caught.
void Xhandler(int test)
{
  try{
    if(test) throw test;
    else throw "Value is zero";
  }
  catch(int i) {
    cout << "Caught One!  Ex. #: " << i << '\n';
  }
  catch(char *str) {
    cout << "Caught a string: ";
    cout << str << '\n';
  }
}
```

```
main()
{
  cout << "start\n";

  Xhandler(1);
  Xhandler(2);
  Xhandler(0);
  Xhandler(3);

  cout << "end";

  return 0;
}
```

This program produces the following output:

```
start
Caught One!  Ex. #: 1
Caught One!  Ex. #: 2
Caught a string: Value is zero
Caught One!  Ex. #: 3
end
```

As you can see, each **catch** statement responds only to its own type.

In general, **catch** expressions are checked in the order in which they occur in a program. Only a matching statement is executed. All other **catch** blocks are ignored.

Options for Exception Handling

There are several additional features and nuances to C++ exception handling that make it easier and more convenient to use. These attributes are discussed here.

Catching All Exceptions

In some circumstances you will want an exception handler to catch all exceptions instead of just a certain type. This is easy to accomplish. Simply use this form of **catch**:

```
catch(...) {
  // process all exceptions
}
```

17

Here, the ellipsis matches any type of data.

The following program illustrates **catch(...)**.

```cpp
// This example catches all exceptions.
#include <iostream.h>

void Xhandler(int test)
{
  try{
    if(test==0) throw test; // throw int
    if(test==1) throw 'a'; // throw char
    if(test==2) throw 123.23; // throw double
  }
  catch(...) { // catch all exceptions
    cout << "Caught One!\n";
  }
}

main()
{
  cout << "start\n";

  Xhandler(0);
  Xhandler(1);
  Xhandler(2);

  cout << "end";

  return 0;
}
```

This program displays the following output.

```
start
Caught One!
Caught One!
Caught One!
end
```

As you can see, all three **throw**s were caught using the one **catch** statement.

One very good use for **catch(...)** is as the last **catch** of a cluster of catches. In this capacity, it provides a useful default or "catch all" statement. For example, this slightly different version of the preceding program explicitly catches integer exceptions, but relies upon **catch(...)** to catch all others.

```
// This example uses catch(...) as a default.
#include <iostream.h>

void Xhandler(int test)
{
  try{
    if(test==0) throw test; // throw int
    if(test==1) throw 'a'; // throw char
    if(test==2) throw 123.23; // throw double
  }
  catch(int i) { // catch an int exception
    cout << "Caught " << i << '\n';
  }
  catch(...) { // catch all other exceptions
    cout << "Caught One!\n";
  }
}

main()
{
  cout << "start\n";

  Xhandler(0);
  Xhandler(1);
  Xhandler(2);

  cout << "end";

  return 0;
}
```

The output produced by this program is shown here:

```
start
Caught 0
Caught One!
Caught One!
end
```

As this example suggests, using **catch(...)** as a default is a good way to catch all exceptions that you don't want to handle explicitly. Also, by catching all exceptions, you prevent an unhandled exception from causing an abnormal program termination.

17

Restricting Exceptions

When a function is called from within a **try** block, you can restrict what type of exceptions that function can throw. In fact, you can also prevent that function from throwing any exceptions whatsoever. To accomplish these restrictions, you must add a **throw** clause to a function definition. The general form of this clause is:

```
ret-type func-name(arg-list) throw(type-list)
{
   // ...
}
```

Here, only those data types contained in the comma-separated *type-list* can be thrown by the function. Throwing any other type of expression will cause abnormal program termination. If you don't want a function to be able to throw *any* exceptions, then use an empty list.

Note: If your compiler complies with the draft ANSI C++ standard, then attempting to throw an exception that is not supported by a function will cause the **unexpected( )** function to be called. By default, this causes **abort( )** to be called, which causes abnormal program termination. However, you can specify your own termination handler, if you like. You will need to refer to your compiler's library reference for details.

The following program shows how to restrict the types of exceptions that can be thrown from a function.

```
// Restricting function throw types.
#include <iostream.h>

// This function can only throw ints, chars, and doubles.
void Xhandler(int test) throw(int, char, double)
{
  if(test==0) throw test; // throw int
  if(test==1) throw 'a'; // throw char
  if(test==2) throw 123.23; // throw double
}

main()
{
  cout << "start\n";

  try{
    Xhandler(0); // also, try passing 1 and 2 to Xhandler()
```

```
  }
  catch(int i) {
    cout << "Caught int\n";
  }
  catch(char c) {
    cout << "Caught char\n";
  }
  catch(double d) {
    cout << "Caught double\n";
  }

  cout << "end";

  return 0;
}
```

In this program, the function **Xhandler( )** can only throw integer, character, and **double** exceptions. If it attempts to throw any other type of exception, then an abnormal program termination will occur. (That is, **unexpected( )** will be called.) To see an example of this, remove **int** from the list and retry the program.

It is important to understand that a function can only be restricted in what types of exceptions it throws back to the **try** block that has called it. That is, a **try** block *within* a function can throw any type of exception, as long as the exception is caught *within* that function. The restriction applies only when throwing an exception outside of the function.

The following change to **Xhandler( )** prevents it from throwing any exceptions.

```
// This function can throw NO exceptions!
void Xhandler(int test) throw()
{
  /* The following statements no longer work.  Instead,
     they will cause an abnormal program termination. */
  if(test==0) throw test;
  if(test==1) throw 'a';
  if(test==2) throw 123.23;
}
```

Rethrowing an Exception

17

If you wish to rethrow an exception from within an exception handler, you can do so by calling **throw** by itself, with no exception. This causes the current exception to be passed on to an outer **try/catch** sequence. The most likely reason for calling **throw** this way is to allow multiple handlers access to the exception. For example, perhaps one exception handler manages one aspect of an exception and a second handler copes with another aspect. An exception can only be rethrown from within a **catch** block (or from any function called from within that block). When you rethrow an exception, it will not be recaught by the same **catch** statement. It will propagate to the next **catch** statement. The following program illustrates rethrowing an exception. It rethrows a **char *** exception.

```cpp
// Example of "rethrowing" an exception.
#include <iostream.h>

void Xhandler()
{
  try {
    throw "hello"; // throw a char *
  }
  catch(char *) { // catch a char *
    cout << "Caught char * inside Xhandler\n";
    throw ; // rethrow char * out of function
  }
}

main()
{
  cout << "start\n";

  try{
    Xhandler();
  }
  catch(char *) {
    cout << "Caught char * inside main\n";
  }

  cout << "end";

  return 0;
}
```

This program displays the following output:

```
start
Caught char * inside Xhandler
Caught char * inside main
end
```

Chapter

18

Miscellaneous
C++ Issues

This is the last chapter in this book that discusses elements of the C++ language. (The following chapter describes the C++ preprocessor directives, which technically are not part of the language.) In this chapter, several features of C++ not covered in the previous chapters are described, and a few loose ends are tied together. Specifically, the chapter covers function pointers, static members, the pointer-to-member operators, the **asm** keyword, linkage specification, and conversion functions. It begins with a discussion of C++'s array-based I/O.

Array-Based I/O

In addition to console and file I/O, C++'s stream-based I/O system allows *array-based I/O*. Array-based I/O uses RAM as either the input device, the output device, or both. Array-based I/O is performed through normal C++ streams. In fact, everything you already know about C++ I/O is applicable to array-based I/O. The only thing that makes array-based I/O unique is that the device linked to the stream is memory.

Array-based I/O uses an array for an input and/or output device.

In some C++ literature, array-based I/O is referred to as *in-RAM I/O*. Also, because the streams are, like all C++ streams, capable of handling formatted information, sometimes array-based I/O is called *in-RAM formatting*. (Also, the archaic term *incore formatting* is occasionally used. However, since core memory is largely a thing of the past, this book will use the terms in-RAM and array-based.)

To use array-based I/O in your programs, you must include **strstream.h**.

The Array-Based Classes

The array-based I/O classes are **istrstream**, **ostrstream**, and **strstream**. These classes are used to create input, output, and input/output streams, respectively. All of these classes are supported by the **strstreambuf** class, which defines several low-level details that are used by the array-based I/O classes. Further, the **istrstream** class is derived from **istream**, the **ostrstream** class is derived from **ostream**, and **strstream** has **iostream** as a base class. Therefore, all array-based classes are indirectly derived from **ios**, and have access to the same member functions that the "normal" I/O classes do.

Creating an Array-Based Output Stream

To perform output to an array, you must link that array to a stream using this **ostrstream** constructor:

ostrstream *ostr*(char **buf*, int *size*, int *mode*=ios::out);

Here, *buf* is a pointer to the array that will be used to collect characters written to the stream *ostr*. The size of the array is passed in the *size* parameter. By default, the stream is opened for normal output, but you can OR various other options with it to create the mode that you need. (These options are discussed in Chapter 16.) For example, you might include **ios::app** to cause output to be written at the end of any information already contained in the array. For most purposes, *mode* will be allowed to default.

Once you have opened an array-based output stream, all output to that stream is put into the array. However, no output will be written outside the bounds of the array. An attempt to do so will result in an error.

Here is a simple program that demonstrates an array-based output stream.

```
#include <strstream.h>
#include <iostream.h>

main()
{
  char str[80];

  ostrstream outs(str, sizeof(str));

  outs << "C++ array-based I/O. ";
  outs << 1024 << hex << " ";
  outs.setf(ios::showbase);
  outs << 100 << ' ' << 99.789 << ends;

  cout << str;  // display string on console

  return 0;
}
```

This program displays the following:

C++ array-based I/O. 1024 0x64 99.789

Keep in mind that **outs** is a stream like any other stream; it has the same capabilities as any other type of stream that you have seen earlier. The only difference is that the device that it is linked to is memory. Because **outs** is a stream, manipulators like **hex** and **ends** are perfectly valid. **ostream** member functions, such as **setf( )**, are also available for use.

This program manually null-terminates the array by using the **ends** manipulator. Whether the array will be automatically null-terminated or not depends on the implementation, so it is best to perform null termination manually if it is important to your application. In the preceding program, the **ends** manipulator is used to null-terminate the string, but you could also use '**\0**'.

You can determine how many characters are in the output array by calling the **pcount( )** member function. It has this prototype:

```
int pcount( );
```

pcount( )
returns the
number of
characters
currently in
an output
array.

The number returned by **pcount( )** also includes the null terminator, if it exists.

The following program demonstrates **pcount( )**. It reports that **outs** contains 18 characters: 17 characters plus the null terminator.

```
#include <strstream.h>
#include <iostream.h>

main()
{
  char str[80];

  ostrstream outs(str, sizeof(str));

  outs << "abcdefg ";
  outs << 27 << " "  << 890.23;
  outs << ends;  // null terminate

  cout << outs.pcount(); // display how many chars in outs

  cout << " " << str;

  return 0;
}
```

Using an Array as Input

To link an input stream to an array, use this **istrstream** constructor:

```
istrstream istr(const char *buf);
```

Here, *buf* is a pointer to the array that will be used as a source of characters each time input is performed on the stream *istr*. The contents of the array pointed to by *buf* must be null-terminated. However, the null terminator is never read from the array.

Here is a sample program that uses a string as input.

```cpp
#include <iostream.h>
#include <strstream.h>

main()
{
  char s[] = "10 Hello 0x75 42.73 OK";

  istrstream ins(s);

  int i;
  char str[80];
  float f;

  // reading: 10 Hello
  ins >> i;
  ins >> str;
  cout << i << " " << str << endl;

  // reading 0x75 42.73 OK
  ins >> i;
  ins >> f;
  ins >> str;

  cout << hex << i << " " << f << " " << str;

  return 0;
}
```

If you wish only part of a string to be used for input, use this form of the **istrstream** constructor:

istrstream *istr*(const char **buf*, int *size*);

Here, only the first *size* elements of the array pointed to by *buf* will be used. This string need not be null-terminated, since it is the value of *size* that determines the size of the string.

Streams linked to memory behave just like those linked to other devices. For example, the following program demonstrates how the contents of any text array can be read. When the end of the array (same as end-of-file) is reached, **ins** will be zero.

```
/* This program shows how to read the contents of any
      array that contains text. */
#include <iostream.h>
#include <strstream.h>

main()
{
  char s[] = "10.23 this is a test <<>><<?!\n";

  istrstream ins(s);

  char ch;

  /* This will read and display the contents
      of any text array. */

  ins.unsetf(ios::skipws); // don't skip spaces
  while (ins) {   // 0 when end of array is reached
    ins >> ch;
    cout << ch;
  }

  return 0;
}
```

Using Binary I/O

Remember that array-based I/O has all of the function and capability of "normal" I/O. Therefore, arrays linked to array-based streams can also contain binary information. When reading binary information you may need to use the **eof( )** function to determine when the end of the array has been reached. For example, the following program shows how to read the contents of any array—binary or text—using the binary input function **get( )**.

```cpp
#include <iostream.h>
#include <strstream.h>

main()
{
  char *p = "this is a test\1\2\3\4\5\6\7";

  istrstream ins(p);

  char ch;

  // read and display binary info
  while (!ins.eof()) {
    ins.get(ch);
    cout << hex << (int) ch << ' ';

  }
  return 0;
}
```

In this example, the values formed by \1\2\3, etc. are non-printing values.

To output binary characters, use the **put( )** function. If you need to read buffers of binary data, you can use the **read( )** member function. To write buffers of binary data, use the **write( )** function.

Input/Output Array-Based Streams

To create an array-based stream that can perform both input and output use this **strstream** constructor function:

strstream *iostr*(char **buf*, int *size*, int *mode*);

Here, *buf* points to the string that will be used for I/O operations. The value of *size* specifies the size of the array. The value of *mode* determines how the stream *iostr* operates. For normal input/output operations, *mode* will be **ios::in | ios::out**. For input, the array must be null-terminated.

Here is a program that uses an array to perform both input and output.

```
// Perform both input and output.
#include <iostream.h>
#include <strstream.h>

main()
{
  char iostr[80];

  strstream ios(iostr, sizeof(iostr), ios::in | ios::out);

  int a, b;
  char str[80];

  ios << "10 20 testing";
  ios >> a >> b >> str;
  cout << a << " " << b << " " << str << endl;

  return 0;
}
```

This program first writes **10 20 testing** to the array and then reads it back in again.

Using Dynamic Arrays

In the first part of this chapter, when you linked a stream to an output array, the array and its size were passed to the **ostrstream** constructor. This approach is fine as long as you know the maximum number of characters that you will be outputting to the array. However, what if you don't know how large the output array needs to be? The solution to this problem is to use a second form of the **ostrstream** constructor, shown here:

```
ostrstream( );
```

When this constructor is used, **ostrstream** creates and maintains a dynamically allocated array, which automatically grows in length to accommodate the output that it must store.

To access the dynamically allocated array, you must use a second function, called **str( )**, which has this prototype:

```
char *str( );
```

str( ) freezes an output array and returns a pointer to it. This function "freezes" the array and returns a pointer to it. You use the pointer returned by **str( )** to access the dynamic array as a string. Once a dynamic array is frozen, it cannot be used for output again. Therefore, you will not want to freeze the array until you are through outputting characters to it.

Here is a program that uses a dynamic output array.

```
#include <strstream.h>
#include <iostream.h>

main()
{
  char *p;

  ostrstream outs;   // dynamically allocate array

  outs << "C++ array-based I/O ";
  outs << -10 << hex << " ";
  outs.setf(ios::showbase);
  outs << 100 << ends;

  p = outs.str(); // Freeze dynamic buffer and return
                  // pointer to it.

  cout << p;

  delete p;   // Free dynamic buffer created by ostrstream().
  return 0;
}
```

As this program illustrates, once a dynamic array has been frozen, it is your responsibility to release its memory back to the system when you are through with it. However, if you never freeze the array, then the memory is automatically freed when the stream is destroyed.

18

You can also use dynamic I/O arrays with the **strstream** class, which can perform both input and output on an array.

It is possible to freeze or unfreeze a dynamic array by calling the **freeze( )** function. Its prototype is shown here:

freeze( ) freezes or unfreezes an output array.

    void freeze(int *action* = 1);

This function can be used to freeze or unfreeze a dynamic array. If *action* is non-zero, the array is frozen. If *action* is zero, the array is unfrozen.

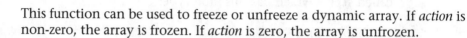

Tip: Array-based I/O is a powerful tool because it allows you to construct output in advance, prior to actually sending it to an external device. Array-based I/O is especially useful for working with graphical operating systems. For example, in Windows programming, you often need to construct output in advance.

Pointers to Functions

A particularly confusing yet powerful feature of C++ is the *function pointer*. Even though a function is not a variable, it still has a physical location in memory that can be assigned to a pointer. The address assigned to the pointer is the entry point of the function. This pointer can then be used in place of the function's name. Function pointers also allows functions to be passed as arguments to other functions.

To understand how function pointers work, you must understand a little about how a function is compiled and called in C++. First, as each function is compiled, source code is transformed into object code, and an entry point is established. When a call is made to a function while your program is running, a machine language "call" is made to this entry point. Therefore, a pointer to a function actually contains the memory address of the entry point of the function.

A pointer to a function points to the entry point of that function.

The address of a function is obtained by using the function's name, without any parentheses or arguments. (This is similar to the way an array's address is obtained when only the array name, without indices, is used.) If you assign the address of a function to a pointer, then you can call that function using the pointer. For example, study the following program. It contains two functions, **vline( )** and **hline( )**, which draw vertical and horizontal lines of a specified length on the screen.

```
#include <iostream.h>

void vline(int i), hline(int i);

main()
{
  void (*p)(int i);

  p = vline; // point to vline()

  (*p)(4); // call vline()

  p = hline; // point to hline()

  (*p)(3); // call hline()

  return 0;
}
void vline(int i)
{
    for( ;i; i--) cout << "-";
    cout << "\n";
}

void hline(int i)
{
    for( ; i; i--) cout << "|\n";
}
```

Let's examine this program in detail. The first line after **main( )** declares a pointer to a function that takes one integer argument and returns no value. It does not in any way specify what that function is. All it does is create a pointer that can be used to point to a function of that type. Because of the C++ precedence rules, the parentheses around the ***p** are necessary.

The next line assigns to **p** the address of **vline( )**. The line after that actually calls **vline( )** with an argument of 4.

The program then assigns the address of **hline( )** to **p** and calls **hline( )** using the pointer.

Although the preceding example uses a function pointer in a trivial manner for the sake of illustration, function pointers have very important uses. One of these is to allow a function to be passed the address of another function. An important example of this is the **qsort( )** function, which is found in C++'s standard library. The **qsort( )** function is a sorting function based upon the Quicksort algorithm and it sorts the contents of an array. Its prototype is shown here:

$$\text{void qsort(void *} start, \text{ size\_t } length, \text{ size\_t } size,$$
$$\text{int (*} compare) \text{ (const void *, const void *));}$$

qsort( ) is the C++ standard library sorting function.

The prototype for **qsort( )** is in **stdlib.h**, which also defines the type **size_t**, which is essentially an **unsigned int**. To use **qsort( )** you must pass it a pointer to the start of the array of objects you wish sorted in *start*, the length of the array in *length*, the width of each element (in bytes) in *size*, and a pointer to a comparison function.

The comparison function used by **qsort( )** compares two elements. It must return less than zero if the first argument points to a value that is less than the second, zero if they are equal, and greater than zero if the second argument points to a value less than the first.

To see how **qsort( )** can be used, try this program:

```cpp
#include <iostream.h>
#include <stdlib.h>
#include <string.h>

int comp(const void *a, const void *b);

main()
{
  char str[] = "Function pointers provide flexibility.";

  qsort(str, strlen(str), 1, comp);
  cout << "sorted string: " << str;

  return 0;
}

int comp(const void *a, const void *b)
{
  return * (char *) a - * (char *) b;
}
```

This program sorts the string **str** into ascending order. Since **qsort( )** is generic, it can be used to sort any type of data. For example, the following program sorts an array of integers. To ensure portability, it uses **sizeof** to find the width of an integer.

```
#include <iostream.h>
#include <stdlib.h>

int comp(const void *a, const void *b);

main()
{
  int num[] = {10, 4, 3, 6, 5 ,7 ,8};
  int i;

  qsort(num, 7, sizeof(int), comp);

  for(i=0; i<7; i++)
    cout << num[i] << ' ';

  return 0;
}

int comp(const void *a, const void *b)
{
  return * (int *) a - * (int *) b;
}
```

Although function pointers may still be somewhat confusing to you, with a little practice and thought, you should have no trouble using them. There is one more aspect to function pointers, however, that you need to know about; it concerns overloaded functions.

Finding the Address of an Overloaded Function

Finding the address of an overloaded function is a bit more complex than obtaining the address of a single function. Since there are two or more versions of an overloaded function, there must be some mechanism that determines which specific version's address is obtained. The solution is both elegant and effective. When obtaining the address of an overloaded function, it is *the way the pointer is declared* that determines which overloaded function's address will be obtained. In essence, the pointer's declaration is compared to those of the overloaded functions. The function whose declaration matches is the one whose address is obtained.

The following sample program contains two versions of a function called **space( )**. The first version outputs **count** number of spaces to the screen. The second version outputs **count** number of whatever type of character is passed to **ch**. In **main( )**, two function pointers are declared. The first one is specified as a pointer to a function having only one integer parameter. The second is declared as a pointer to a function taking two parameters.

18

```
/* Illustrate assigning function pointers to
   overloaded functions. */
#include <iostream.h>

// Output count number of spaces.
void space(int count)
{
  for( ; count; count--) cout << ' ';
}

// Output count number of chs.
void space(int count, char ch)
{
  for( ; count; count--) cout << ch;
}

main()
{
  /* Create a pointer to void function with
     one int parameter. */
  void (*fp1)(int);

  /* Create a pointer to void function with
     one int parameter and one character parameter. */
  void (*fp2)(int, char);

  fp1 = space; // gets address of space(int)

  fp2 = space; // gets address of space(int, char)

  fp1(22);   // output 22 spaces
  cout << "|\n";

  fp2(30, 'x'); // output 30 xs
  cout << "|\n";

  return 0;
}
```

As the comments illustrate, the compiler is able to determine which overloaded function to obtain the address of, based upon how **fp1** and **fp2** are declared.

To review: When you assign the address of an overloaded function to a function pointer, it is the declaration of the pointer that determines which function's address is assigned. Further, the declaration of the function pointer must exactly match one and only one of the overloaded functions. If it does not, ambiguity will be introduced, causing a compile-time error.

Static Class Members

The keyword **static** can be applied to members of a class. Its meaning in this context is similar to its meaning when applied to "normal" variables. When you declare a member of a class as **static**, you are telling the compiler that no matter how many objects of the class are created, there is only one copy of the **static** member. That is, a **static** member is *shared* by all objects of the class. All **static** data is initialized to 0 if no other initialization is specified.

A single ***static*** *class member is shared by all objects of that class.*

When you declare a **static** data member within a class, you are *not* defining it. Instead, you must provide a global definition for it elsewhere, outside the class. This is done by redeclaring the **static** variable using the scope resolution operator to identify which class it belongs to. This causes storage to be allocated for the **static** variable.

Here is an example that uses a **static** member. Examine the program and try to understand how it works.

```
#include <iostream.h>

class counter {
  static int count;
public:
  void setcount(int i) {count = i;};
  void showcount() {cout << count << " ";}
};

int counter::count; // define count

main()
{
  counter a, b;

  a.showcount(); // prints 0
  b.showcount(); // prints 0

  a.setcount(10); // set static count to 10

  a.showcount(); // prints 10
  b.showcount(); // also prints 10

  return 0;
}
```

Notice that the static integer **count** is both declared inside the **counter** class and defined as a global variable. As stated earlier, this is necessary because the declaration of **count** inside **counter** does *not* allocate storage for the variable. C++ initializes **count** to 0 since no other initialization is

18

given. This is why the first calls to **showcount( )** both display 0. Next, object **a** sets **count** to 10. Next, both **a** and **b** use **showcount( )** to display its value. Because there is only one copy of **count** shared by **a** and **b**, both cause the value 10 to be displayed.

Remember: When you declare a member of a class as **static**, you are causing only one copy of that member to be created; it will then be shared by all objects of the class.

Although you may not see an immediate need for **static** members, as you continue to write programs in C++, you will find them very useful in certain situations because they allow you to avoid the use of global variables.

You can also declare **static** member functions. **static** member functions only have access to other **static** members. They cannot access non-**static** data; nor can they call non-**static** functions. Frankly, the use of **static** member functions is somewhat limited.

Using the asm Keyword

While C++ is a comprehensive and powerful programming language, there are a few highly specialized situations which it cannot handle. (For example, there is no C++ statement that disables interrupts.) To accommodate special situations, C++ provides a "trap door" that allows you to drop into assembly code at any time, bypassing the C++ compiler entirely. This "trap door" is the **asm** statement. Using **asm**, you can embed assembly language directly into your C++ program. This assembly code is compiled without any modification, and it becomes part of your program's code at the point at which the **asm** statement occurs.

*Assembly code is embedded directly into a C++ program using the **asm** keyword.*

The general form of the **asm** keyword is shown here,

   asm ("*op-code*");

where *op-code* is the assembly language instruction that will be embedded in your program. However, several compilers also allow the following forms of **asm**:

```
asm instruction ;

asm instruction newline

asm {
   instruction sequence
}
```

Here, *instruction* is any valid assembly language instruction. Because of the implementation-specific nature of **asm** you must check the user's manual that came with your compiler for details.

Caution: A thorough working knowledge of assembly language programming is required for using the **asm** statement. If you are not proficient with assembly language, it is best to avoid using **asm**, because very nasty errors may result.

Linkage Specification

In C++ you can specify how a function is linked into your program. By default, functions are linked as C++ functions. However, by using a *linkage specification* you can cause a function to be linked as a different type of language function. The general form of a linkage specifier is shown here,

extern *"language" function-prototype*

The linkage specifier allows you to determine how a function is linked.

where *language* denotes the desired language. All C++ compilers support both C and C++ linkage. Some will also allow linkage specifiers for FORTRAN, Pascal, or BASIC. (You will need to check the user's manual for your compiler.)

This program causes **myCfunc( )** to be linked as a C function.

```
#include <iostream.h>

extern "C" void myCfunc();

main()
```

```
{
  myCfunc();

  return 0;
}

// This will link as a C function.
void myCfunc()
{
  cout << "This links as a C function.\n";
}
```

Note: The **extern** keyword is a necessary part of the linkage specification. Further, the linkage specification must be global; it cannot be used inside of a function.

You can specify more than one function at a time using this form of the linkage specification:

```
extern "language" {
  prototypes
}
```

The use of a linkage specification is rare, and you will probably not need to use one. Its main use is to allow third-party routines written in another language to be used by a C++ program.

The .* and –>* Pointer-to-Member Operators

The pointer-to-member operators allow you to access a class member through a pointer to that member.

The .* and –>* are called *pointer-to-member* operators. Their job is to allow you to access a member of a class given a pointer to that member. Neither of these operators was part of the first specification of C++. The reason for their creation is to allow some rather specialized situations to be handled. These two operators are needed because a pointer to a member does not fully define an address. Instead, it provides an offset into an object of the member's class at which that member can be found. Therefore, to access a member of a class given a pointer to it requires that both the class and the member be used. Since the * operator cannot link a class with a pointer to a member, the .* and –>* operators were created.

If the preceding paragraph seems a bit confusing, the following example should help clear things up. This program displays the summation of the number 7. It accesses the function **sum_it( )** and the variable **sum** using member pointers.

```
// Pointer-to-member example.
#include <iostream.h>

class myclass {
public:
  int sum;
  void myclass::sum_it(int x);
};

void myclass::sum_it(int x) {
  int i;

  sum = 0;
  for(i=x; i; i--) sum += i;
}

main()
{
  int myclass::*dp;   // pointer to an integer class member
  void (myclass::*fp)(int x); // pointer to member function
  myclass c;

  dp = &myclass::sum;   // get address of data
  fp = &myclass::sum_it; // get address of function

  (c.*fp)(7);   // compute summation of 7
  cout << "summation of 7 is " << c.*dp;

  return 0;
}
```

Inside **main( )**, this program creates two member pointers: **dp**, which will point to the variable **sum** and **fp**, which will point to the function **sum_it( )**. Note carefully the syntax of each declaration. The scope resolution operator is used to specify which class is being referred to. The program also creates an object of **myclass** called **c**.

Next, the program obtains the addresses of **sum** and **sum_it( )** and assigns them to **dp** and **fp**, respectively. As stated earlier, these addresses are really just offsets into an object of **myclass**, at which point **sum** and **sum_it( )** will be found. Next, the program uses the function pointer **fp** to call the **sum_it( )** function of **c**. The extra parentheses are necessary in order to correctly associate the **.*** operator. Finally, the program displays the summed value by accessing **c**'s **sum** through **dp**.

When you are accessing a member of an object using an object or a reference, you must use the **.*** operator. However, if you are using a pointer to the

18

object, you need to use the –>* operator, as illustrated in this version of the preceding program.

```cpp
#include <iostream.h>

class myclass {
public:
  int sum;
  void myclass::sum_it(int x);
};

void myclass::sum_it(int x) {
  int i;

  sum = 0;
  for(i=x; i; i--) sum += i;
}

main()
{
  int myclass::*dp;   // pointer to an integer class member
  void (myclass::*fp)(int x); // pointer to member function
  myclass *c, d; // c is now a pointer to an object

  c = &d; // give c the address of an object

  dp = &myclass::sum;   // get address of data
  fp = &myclass::sum_it; // get address of function

  (c->*fp)(7);   // now, use ->* to call function
  cout << "summation of 7 is " << c->*dp; // use ->*

  return 0;
}
```

In this version **c** is now a pointer to an object of type **myclass**, and the –>* operator is used to access **sum** and **sum_it( )**.

Remember that the pointer-to-member operators are designed for special-case applications. You will not need them in your normal, day-to-day programming tasks.

Creating Conversion Functions

Sometimes you will create a class that you will want to be able to freely mix with other types of data in an expression. While overloaded operator functions can provide a means of mixing types, sometimes a simple type conversion is all that is needed. In this case, you can use a type conversion function to convert your class into a type compatible with that of the rest of the expression. The general format of a type conversion function is:

A conversion function automatically converts a class type into another type.

operator (*type*)( ) {return *value*;}

Here, *type* is the target type that you are converting your class to and *value* is the value of the class after conversion. A conversion function must be a member of the class for which it is defined.

To illustrate how to create a conversion function, let's use the **three_d** class once again. Suppose that you want to be able convert an object of type **three_d** into an integer so that it can be used in an integer expression. Further, the conversion will take place by using the product of the three dimensions. To accomplish this, you will use a conversion function that looks like this:

```
operator int() { return x * y * z; }
```

Here is a program that illustrates how the conversion function works.

```
#include <iostream.h>

class three_d {
  int x, y, z; // 3-D coordinates
public:
  three_d(int a, int b, int c) {x=a; y=b; z=c;}

  three_d operator+(three_d op2) ;
  friend ostream &operator<<(ostream &stream, three_d &obj);

  operator int() {return x*y*z;}
} ;

// Display X, Y, Z coordinates - three_d inserter.
```

```
ostream &operator<<(ostream &stream, three_d &obj)
{
  stream << obj.x << ", ";
  stream << obj.y << ", ";
  stream << obj.z << "\n";
  return stream;  // return the stream
}

three_d three_d::operator+(three_d op2)
{
  three_d temp(0, 0, 0);

  temp.x = x+op2.x;
  temp.y = y+op2.y;
  temp.z = z+op2.z;
  return temp;
}

main()
{
  three_d a(1, 2, 3), b(2, 3, 4);

  cout << a << b;

  cout << b+100;  // displays 124 because of conversion to int
  cout << "\n";
  cout << a+b;  // displays 3, 5, 7 - no conversion

  return 0;
}
```

The program displays this output:

    1, 2, 3
    2, 3, 4
    124
    3, 5, 7

As the program illustrates, when a **three_d** object is used in an integer expression, such as **cout << b+100**, the conversion function is applied to the object. In this specific case, the conversion function returns the value 24, which is then added to 100. However, when no conversion is needed, as in **cout << a+b**, the conversion function is not called.

Once you have created a conversion function, it will be called whenever that conversion is required, including when an object is passed as a parameter to a function. For example, the **three_d**-to-**int** conversion function is also called if a **three_d** object is passed to the standard **abs( )** function, because **abs( )** requires an integer argument.

Remember: You can create different conversion functions to meet different needs. You could define one that converts to **double** or **long**, for example. Each will be applied automatically. Conversion functions further help you integrate new class types that you create into your C++ programming environment.

C++ Keyword Extensions

As mentioned earlier in this book, there are several keywords that the ANSI C++ committee is considering for inclusion in the C++ standard. However, at the time of this writing there are no commonly available compilers that support these keywords; nor is there any guarantee that all (or some) of them will actually be included in the final C++ standard. None of these extended keywords were part of the original specification for C++, nor were they part of any common, preexisting implementation of C++, and they are not necessary for programming in C++ or fully taking advantage of it. For these reasons, the extended keywords are not discussed in detail. However, a list of these keywords, along with a brief explanation of each, is provided here. You will want to check the user's manual for your compiler to see if any of these keywords are supported.

bool
bool is a type specifier. There are only two values of type **bool**: **true** and **false**.

const_cast
const_cast can be used to override **const** and/or **volatile** when a type conversion is performed.

dynamic_cast
dynamic_cast performs a run-time cast for polymorphic class types.

false
See **bool**.

mutable

mutable allows a member of an object to override **const**ness. That is, a **mutable** member of a **const** object is not **const**, and can be modified.

namespace

namespace declares a block in which other identifiers can be declared. Thus, an identifier declared within a **namespace** becomes a "sub-identifier" linked to the surrounding **namespace** identifier. (In essence, **namespace** creates a named scope.)

reinterpret_cast

reinterpret_cast casts one type of value into another. For example, it converts a pointer into an integer type.

static_cast

static_cast is a non-polymorphic cast. For example, a base class pointer can be cast into a derived class pointer.

true

See **bool**.

typeid

typeid obtains the type of an expression.

using

using specifies a default scope resolution qualifier.

wchar_t

wchar_t supports wide characters (i.e., 16-bit characters). **wchar_t** allows C++ to accommodate the large character sets required by some human languages.

Chapter

19

The C++ Preprocessor

This final chapter concludes our examination of C++ by discussing the C++ *preprocessor*. The preprocessor is that part of the compiler that performs various text manipulations on your program prior to the actual translation of your source code into object code. You can give text manipulation commands to the preprocessor. These commands are called *preprocessor directives* and, although not technically part of the C++ language, they expand the scope of its programming environment.

The C++ preprocessor contains the following directives:

```
#define
#error
#include
#if
#else
#elif
#endif
#ifdef
#ifndef
#undef
#line
#pragma
```

As is apparent, all preprocessor directives begin with a **#** sign. Each will be examined here in turn.

Note: The C++ preprocessor is a holdover from C. Some of its features have been rendered redundant by newer and better C++ language elements. However, since many programmers still use the preprocessor, and because it is still part of the C++ language environment, you must be familiar with its capabilities.

#define

#define is used to define an identifier and a character sequence that will be substituted for the identifier each time it is encountered in the source file. The identifier is called a *macro name* and the replacement process is called *macro substitution*. The general form of the directive is:

#define
defines a
macro name.

#define *macro-name character-sequence*

Notice that there is no semicolon in this statement. There can be any number of spaces between the identifier and the character sequence, but once the sequence begins, it is only terminated by a newline.

For example, if you wanted to use the word UP for the value 1 and the word DOWN for the value 0, you would declare these two macro **#define**s:

```
#define UP 1
#define DOWN 0
```

These statements will cause the compiler to substitute a 1 or a 0 each time the name UP or DOWN is encountered in your source file. For example, the following will print **1 0 2** on the screen.

```
cout << UP << ' ' << DOWN << ' ' << UP + UP;
```

Once a macro name has been defined, it can be used as part of the definition of other macro names. For example, the following code defines the names **ONE**, **TWO**, and **THREE** to their respective values.

```
#define ONE    1
#define TWO    ONE+ONE
#define THREE ONE+TWO
```

It is important to understand that the macro substitution is simply the replacing of an identifier with its associated string. Therefore, if you wish to define a standard message, you might write something like this:

```
#define GETFILE "Enter File Name"


   .
   .
   .


cout << GETFILE;
```

C++ will substitute the string "Enter File Name" when the identifier **GETFILE** is encountered. To the compiler, the **cout** statement will actually appear to be

```
cout << "Enter File Name";
```

No text substitutions will occur if the identifier occurs within a string. For example,

```
#define GETFILE "Enter File Name"
   .
   .
   .
cout << "GETFILE is a macro name\n";
```

will not print

Enter File Name is a macro name

but rather

GETFILE is a macro name

If the string is longer than one line, you can continue it on the next by placing a backslash at the end of the line, as shown in this example.

```
#define LONG_STRING "this is a very long \
string that is used as an example"
```

It is common practice among C++ programmers to use capital letters for macro names. This convention helps anyone reading the program know at a glance that a macro substitution will take place. Also, it is best to put all **#define**s at the start of the file, or perhaps, in a separate include file, rather than sprinkling them out in the program.

One use of macro substitutions that you will commonly find is to define "magic numbers" that occur in a program. For example, you may have a program that defines an array and has several routines that access that array. Instead of "hard-coding" the array's size with a constant, it is better to define a name that represents the size, and then use that name whenever the size of the array is needed. Therefore, if the size of the array changes, then you only have to change it in one place in the file and recompile. For example,

```
#define MAX_SIZE 100

float balance[MAX_SIZE];
```

Tip: It is important to remember that C++ provides a better way of defining constants. This is to use the **const** specifier to define a constant. However, many C++ programmers have migrated from C, where **#define** is commonly used for this purpose. Thus, you will likely see it frequently in C++ code, too.

The **#define** directive has another feature: The macro name can have arguments. Each time the macro name is encountered the arguments associated with it are replaced by the actual arguments found in the program. This creates a *function-like* macro. Here is an example,

A function-like macro is a macro that takes arguments.

```
// Use a function-like macro.
#include <iostream.h>

#define MIN(a,b)  (((a)<(b)) ? a : b)

main()
{
  int x, y;
```

```
   x = 10;
   y = 20;
   cout << "The minimum is " << MIN(x, y);

   return 0;
}
```

When this program is compiled, the expression defined by **MIN(a,b)** will be substituted, except that **x** and **y** will be used as the operands. That is, the **cout** statement will be substituted to look like this.

```
cout << "The minimum is: " << ((x)<(y)) ? x : y);
```

In essence, the function-like macro is a way to define a function that has its code expanded inline rather than called.

The apparently redundant parentheses surrounding the **MIN** macro are necessary to ensure proper evaluation of the substituted expression because of the relative precedence of the operators. In fact the extra parentheses should be applied in virtually all function-like macros. In general, you must be very careful how you define function-like macros; otherwise, there can be surprising results. For example, consider this short program, which uses a macro to determine whether a value is even or odd.

```
// This program will give the wrong answer.

#include <iostream.h>

#define EVEN(a) a%2==0 ? 1 : 0

main()
{
  if(EVEN(9+1)) cout << "is even";
  else cout << "is odd";

  return 0;
}
```

This program will not work correctly because of the way the macro substitution is made. When compiled, the **EVEN(9+1)** is expanded to

```
9+1%2==0 ? 1 : 0
```

As you should recall, the **%** (modulus) operator has higher precedence than the plus operator. This means that the **%** operation is first performed on the 1 and that the result is added to 9, which (of course) does not equal 0. To fix the problem, there must be parentheses around **a** in the macro definition of **EVEN**, as is shown in this corrected version of the program.

```
// This program is now fixed.

#include <iostream.h>

#define EVEN(a) (a)%2==0 ? 1 : 0

main()
{
  if(EVEN(9+1)) cout << "is even";
  else cout << "is odd";

  return 0;
}
```

Now, the **9+1** is evaluated prior to the modulus operation. In general, it is a good idea to surround macro parameters with parentheses to avoid unforeseen troubles like the one just described.

The use of macro substitutions in place of real functions has one major benefit: because macro substitution code is expanded inline, no overhead for a function call is incurred, so the speed of your program increases. However, this increased speed might be paid for with an increase in the size of the program, due to duplicated code.

Tip: Although still commonly seen in C++ code, the use of function-like macros has been rendered completely redundant by the **inline** specifier, which accomplishes the same goal better and more safely. (Remember, **inline** causes a function to be expanded in line rather than called.) Also, **inline** functions do not require the extra parentheses needed by most function-like macros. However, function-like macros will almost certainly continue to be a part of C++ programs for some time to come, because many longtime C/C++ programmers continue to use them out of habit.

#error

When the **#error** directive is encountered, it forces the compiler to stop compilation. This directive is used primarily for debugging. The general form of the directive is

#error *error-message*

#error
displays
an error
message.

Notice that the *error-message* is not between double quotes. When the compiler encounters this directive, it displays the error message and other information and terminates compilation. Your implementation determines what information will actually be displayed. (You might want to experiment with your compiler to see what is displayed.)

#include

The **#include** preprocessor directive instructs the compiler to include another source file with the one that has the **#include** directive in it. The source file to be read in must be enclosed between double quotes or angle brackets. For example, the following two directives both instruct C++ to read and compile the header for the I/O system.

#include
includes
another
source file.

```
#include <iostream.h>
#include "iostream.h"
```

Typically, **#include** is used to include a header file.

Whether the filename is enclosed by quotes or angle brackets determines how the search for the specified file is conducted. If the filename is enclosed between angle brackets, the compiler searches for it in one or more implementation-defined directories. If the filename is enclosed between quotes, then the compiler searches for it in some other implementation-defined directory, which is typically the current working directory. If the file is not found in this directory, the search is restarted as if the filename had been enclosed between angle brackets. Since the search path is implementation defined, you will need to check your compiler's user manual for details.

Conditional Compilation Directives

There are several directives that allow you to selectively compile portions of your program's source code. This process, called *conditional compilation*, is widely used by commercial software houses that provide and maintain many customized versions of one program.

#if, #else, #elif, and #endif

The general idea behind the **#if** directive is that if the constant expression following the **#if** is true, then the code between it and an **#endif** will be compiled; otherwise the code will be skipped over. **#endif** is used to mark the end of an **#if** block.

The general form of **#if** is

```
#if constant-expression
    statement sequence
#endif
```

If the constant expression is true, the block of code will be compiled; otherwise it will be skipped. For example,

```
// A simple #if example
#include <iostream.h>

#define MAX 100
main()
{
#if MAX>10
  cout << "Extra memory required.\n";
#endif

  // ...
  return 0;
}
```

#if, #ifdef, #ifndef, #elif, and #else are the C++ conditional compilation directives.

This program will display the message on the screen because, as defined in the program, **MAX** is greater than 10. This example illustrates an important point. The expression that follows the **#if** is *evaluated at compile time*. Therefore, it must contain only identifiers that have been previously defined and constants. No variables can be used.

The **#else** directive works in much the same way as the **else** statement that forms part of the C++ language: it establishes an alternative if the **#if** directive fails. The previous example can be expanded to include the **#else** directive, as shown here:

```
// A simple #if/#else example
#include <iostream.h>

#define MAX 6
main()
{
#if MAX>10
```

```
  cout << "Extra memory required.\n");
#else
  cout << "Current memory OK.\n";
#endif

  // ...

  return 0;
}
```

In this program, **MAX** is defined to be less than 10, so the **#if** portion of the code is not compiled, but the **#else** alternative is. Therefore, the message **Current memory OK** is displayed.

Notice that the **#else** is used to mark both the end of the **#if** block and the beginning of the **#else** block. This is necessary because there can only be one **#endif** associated with any **#if**.

The **#elif** means "else if" and is used to establish an if-else-if ladder for multiple compilation options. The **#elif** is followed by a constant expression. If the expression is true, then that block of code is compiled, and no other **#elif** expressions are tested or compiled. Otherwise, the next in the series is checked. The general form is:

```
#if expression
    statement sequence
#elif expression 1
    statement sequence
#elif expression 2
    statement sequence
#elif expression 3
    statement sequence
#elif expression 4

    .
    .
    .

#elif expression N
    statement sequence
#endif
```

For example, this fragment uses the value of **COMPILED_BY** to define who compiled the program.

```
#define JOHN 0
#define BOB 1
#define TOM 2

#define COMPILED_BY JOHN

#if COMPILED_BY == JOHN
  char who[] = "John";
#elif COMPILED_BY == BOB
  char who[] = "Bob";
#else
  char who[] = "Tom";
#endif
```

#ifs and **#elif**s can be nested. In this case, the **#endif**, **#else** or **#elif** associate with the nearest **#if** or **#elif**. For example, the following is perfectly valid:

```
#if COMPILED_BY == BOB
   #if DEBUG == FULL
      int port = 198;
   #elif DEBUG == PARTIAL
      int port = 200;
   #endif
#else
   cout << "Bob must compile for debug output.\n";
#endif
```

#ifdef and #ifndef

Another method of conditional compilation uses the directives **#ifdef** and **#ifndef**, which mean "if defined" and "if not defined", respectively, and refer to macro names.

The general form of **#ifdef** is:

> #ifdef *macro-name*
>   *statement sequence*
> #endif

If the *macro-name* has been previously defined in a **#define** statement, the statement sequence between the **#ifdef** and **#endif** will be compiled.

The general form of **#ifndef** is:

```
#ifndef macro-name
   statement sequence
#endif
```

If *macro-name* is currently undefined by a **#define** statement, then the block of code is compiled.

Both the **#ifdef** and **#ifndef** can use an **#else** statement, but not an **#elif**. For example,

```
#include <iostream.h>

#define TOM

main()
{
#ifdef TOM
  cout << "Programmer is Tom.\n";
#else
  cout << "Programmer is unknown.\n";
#endif
#ifndef RALPH
  cout << "RALPH not defined.\n";
#endif
  return 0;
}
```

will print **Programmer is Tom** and **RALPH not defined**. However, if **TOM** were not defined then **Programmer is unknown** would be displayed, followed by **RALPH not defined**.

You can nest **#ifdef**s and **#ifndef**s in the same way as **#if**s.

#undef

The **#undef** directive is used to remove a previously defined definition of a macro name. The general form is:

```
#undef macro-name
```

Consider this example:

```
#define TIMEOUT 100
#define WAIT 0

// ...

#undef TIMEOUT
#undef WAIT
```

Here, both **TIMEOUT** and **WAIT** are defined until the **#undef** statements are encountered.

The principal use of **#undef** is to allow macro names to be localized to only those sections of code that need them.

Using defined

In addition to **#ifdef**, there is a second way to determine if a macro name is defined. You can use the **#if** directive in conjunction with the **defined** compile-time operator. For example, to determine if the macro **MYFILE** is defined, you can use either of these two preprocessing commands:

```
#if defined MYFILE
```

or

```
#ifdef MYFILE
```

You can also precede **defined** with the **!** to reverse the condition. For example, the following fragment is compiled only if **DEBUG** is not defined.

```
#if !defined DEBUG
  cout << "Final version!\n";
#endif
```

Tip: One reason for using **defined** is that it allows the existence of a macro name to be determined by an **#elif** statement.

19

The Diminishing Role of the Preprocessor

The C++ preprocessor is directly derived from the C preprocessor, and it offers no enhancements over its C counterpart. In fact, the role of the preprocessor in C++ is much smaller than it is in C. One reason for this is that many of the chores that are performed by the preprocessor in C are performed by language elements in C++. Stroustrup has stated that one of his goals when creating C++ was to render the preprocessor completely redundant so that, ultimately, it could be removed from the language entirely.

At this time, the preprocessor is already partially redundant. For example, two of the most common uses for **#define** have been replaced by C++ statements. Specifically, its abilities to create a constant value and to define a function-like macro are now redundant. In C++ there are better ways of doing both these jobs. To create a constant, simply define a **const** variable. To create an inline function, use the **inline** specifier. Both of these procedures are better ways of accomplishing what has been done using **#define**.

Another example of the replacement of preprocessor elements with language elements is the single-line comment. One of the reasons this element was created was to allow comments to be commented-out. As you know, the /* ... */ style comment cannot be nested. This means that you cannot comment-out a fragment of code that includes /*...*/ comments. However, you can comment-out // comments by surrounding them with a /* ... */ comment. The ability to comment-out code renders the conditional compilation directives, such as **#ifdef**, at least partially redundant.

In the future development of C++, watch for new features to be added that further diminish the role of, and the need for, the preprocessor. Remember, the elimination of the preprocessor is one of the long-range goals of C++.

#line

The **#line** directive is used to change the contents of _ _LINE_ _ and _ _FILE_ _, which are predefined macro names. _ _LINE_ _ contains the line number of the line currently being compiled, and _ _FILE_ _ contains the name of the file being compiled. The basic form of the **#line** command is:

#line *number "filename"*

#line changes
the contents
of the
_ _LINE_ _
and _ _FILE_ _
macros.

Here *number* is any positive integer, and the optional *filename* is any valid
file identifier. The line number becomes the number of the current source
line and the filename becomes the name of the source file. **#line** is primarily
used for debugging purposes and for special applications.

For example, the following program specifies that the line count will begin
with 200. The **cout** statement displays the number 202 because it is the
third line in the program after the **#line 200** statement.

```
#include <iostream.h>

#line 200 // set line counter to 200
main()    // now this is line 200
{         // this is line 201
  cout <<  _ _LINE_ _;  // prints 202

  return 0;
}
```

#pragma

The **#pragma** directive is an implementation-defined directive that allows
various instructions, defined by the compiler's creator, to be given to the
compiler. The general form of the **#pragma** directive is:

#pragma
is an
implementation-
defined
preprocessing
directive.

    #pragma *name*

Here, *name* is the name of the **#pragma** you want. If the *name* is
unrecognized by the compiler, then the **#pragma** directive is simply
ignored and no error results.

Tip: Check the user's manual that came with your compiler to see what
types of pragmas it supports. You might find some that are valuable to your
programming efforts. Typical **#pragma**s include those that determine what
compiler warning messages are issued, how code is generated, and what
library is linked.

The # and ## Preprocessor Operators

C++ supports two preprocessor operators: # and ##. These operators are used
in conjunction with **#define**.

The **#** operator causes the argument it precedes to become a quoted string. For example, consider this program.

```
#include <iostream.h>

#define mkstr(s)   # s

main()
{
  cout << mkstr(I like C++);

  return 0;
}
```

The C++ preprocessor turns the line

```
cout << mkstr(I like C++);
```

into

```
cout << "I like C++";
```

The **##** operator is used to concatenate two tokens. Here is an example:

```
#include <iostream.h>

#define concat(a, b)   a ## b

main()
{
  int xy = 10;

  cout << concat(x, y);

  return 0;
}
```

The preprocessor transforms

```
cout << concat(x, y);
```

into

```
cout << xy;
```

If these operators seem strange to you, keep in mind that they are not needed or used in most programs. They exist primarily to allow some special cases to be handled by the preprocessor.

Predefined Macro Names

C++ specifies six built-in predefined macro names. They are

    _ _LINE_ _
    _ _FILE_ _
    _ _DATE_ _
    _ _TIME_ _
    _ _STDC_ _
    _ _cplusplus

Each will be described here, in turn.

The _ _**LINE**_ _ and _ _**FILE**_ _ macros were introduced in the discussion of **#line**. Briefly, they contain the current line number and filename of the program when it is being compiled.

The _ _**DATE**_ _ macro contains a string of the form *month/day/year* that is the date of the translation of the source file into object code.

The _ _**TIME**_ _ macro contains the time at which the program was compiled. The time is represented in a string having the form *hour:minute:second*.

The meaning of _ _**STDC**_ _ is implementation-defined. Generally, if _ _**STDC**_ _ is defined, then the compiler will accept only standard C/C++ code that does not contain any non-standard extensions.

If your program is compiled as a C++ program, then _ _**cplusplus** is defined. Otherwise, it is not defined.

Final Thoughts

You have come a long way since Chapter 1. If you have read and worked through all the examples in this book, then you can call yourself a C++ programmer. Like many things, programming is best learned by doing, so the best way to reinforce what you have learned is to write many programs. Also, look at examples of C++ programs written by other people. If possible, study the C++ code written by several different programmers, paying attention to how the program is designed and implemented. Look for shortcomings as well as strong points. This will broaden the way you think about programming. Finally, experiment. Push your limits. You will be surprised at how quickly you become an expert C++ programmer!

Appendix

A

C-Based I/O

This appendix presents a brief overview of the C I/O system. Even though you will normally use the C++ I/O system, there are several reasons why you will need to understand the fundamentals of C-based I/O. First, if you will be working on C code (especially if you are converting it to C++) then you will need to understand how the C I/O system works. Second, it is common to find both C and C++ I/O within the same program. This is especially true when the program is very large and has been written by multiple programmers over a long period of time. Third, a great number of existing C programs continue to be used and maintained. Finally, many books and periodicals contain programs written in C. To understand them, you need to understand the basics of the C I/O system.

Remember: For C++ programs you should use the C++ object-oriented I/O system.

The C I/O system and the C++ object-oriented I/O system are fundamentally different. First, the C I/O system is function-based, while the C++ approach is operator-based. Second, the C I/O system is not object-oriented and cannot operate directly on data types that you create. Finally, the C I/O system is defined by the ANSI C standard.

This appendix covers the most common C-based I/O functions. However, the C standard library contains a very rich and diverse assortment of I/O functions—more than can be covered here. If you will be doing extensive work in C, you will want to explore your compiler's user manual for details on other C-based I/O functions. Also, the C I/O system is discussed at length in my book *C: The Complete Reference* (Osborne/McGraw-Hill, 1990). This book also provides an in-depth discussion of all aspects of ANSI standard C, including all library functions.

To use the C-based I/O you must include the header file **stdio.h**. **stdio.h** is more or less the C equivalent of **iostream.h**.

Note: The code examples in this appendix are in C, not C++. Therefore, if you want to try the examples, you must compile the programs as C, not C++, programs.

C I/O Uses Streams

Like the C++ I/O system, the C-based I/O system operates on streams. At the beginning of a program's execution, three predefined text streams are opened. They are **stdin**, **stdout**, and **stderr**. (Some compilers also open other, implementation-dependent streams.) These streams are the C versions of **cin**, **cout**, and **cerr**. They each refer to a standard I/O device connected to the system, as shown here:

Stream	Device
stdin	keyboard
stdout	screen
stderr	screen

Remember that most operating systems, including DOS, Windows and Unix, allow I/O redirection, so routines that read or write to these streams may be redirected to other devices. (Redirection of I/O is the process whereby information that would normally go to one device is rerouted to another device by the operating system.) You should never try to explicitly open or close these streams.

Each stream that is associated with a file has a file control structure of type **FILE**. This structure is defined in the header **stdio.h**. You must not make modifications to this file control block.

A

Understanding printf( ) and scanf( )

The two most commonly used C-based I/O functions are **printf( )** and **scanf( )**. The **printf( )** function is used to write data to the console; **scanf( )**, its complement, reads data from the keyboard. Both **printf( )** and **scanf( )** can operate on any of the built-in data types, including characters, strings, and numbers. However, since these functions are not object-oriented, they cannot operate directly upon class types that you create. Both **printf( )** and **scanf( )** are examined here.

printf( )

The **printf( )** function has this prototype:

   int printf(const char *fmt_string*, ...);

The first argument, *fmt_string*, defines the way any subsequent arguments are displayed. This argument is often called the *format string*. It contains two things: text and format specifiers. Text is printed on the screen and has no other effect. The format specifiers define the way arguments that follow the format string are displayed. A format specifier begins with a percent sign, and is followed by the format code. The format specifiers are shown in Table A-1. There must be exactly the same number of arguments as there are format specifiers, and the format specifiers and the arguments are matched in order. For example, this **printf( )** call

```
printf("Hi %c %d %s", 'c', 10, "there!");
```

displays: **Hi c 10 there!**.

The **printf( )** function returns the number of characters output. It returns a negative value if an error occurs.

Format Specifier	Meaning
%c	A single character
%d	Decimal
%i	Decimal
%e	Scientific notation
%f	Decimal floating point
%g	Use %e or %f, whichever is shorter
%n	The associated argument must point to an integer which will receive the number of characters output so far.
%o	Octal
%p	Displays a pointer
%s	Character string
%u	Unsigned decimal
%x	Hexadecimal
%%	A % sign

The **printf( )**
Format
Specifiers
Table A-1.

The format specifiers may have modifiers that specify the field width, the number of decimal places, and a left-justification flag. An integer placed between the % sign and the format specifier acts as a minimum-field-width specifier. This pads the output with spaces to ensure that it is at least a certain minimum length. If the string or number is greater than that minimum, it will be printed in full, even if it overruns the minimum. If you wish to pad with 0s, place a 0 before the field-width specifier. For example, %05d will pad a number of less than five digits with 0s so that its total length is five.

To specify the number of decimal places printed for a floating point number, place a decimal point after the field-width specifier, followed by the number of decimal places you wish to display. For example, %10.4f will display a number at least ten characters wide with four decimal places. When this is applied to strings or integers, the number following the period specifies the maximum field length. For example, %5.7s will display a string that is at least five characters long but does not exceed seven. If the string is longer than the maximum field width, the characters will be truncated from the end.

By default, all output is right-justified: if the field width is larger than the data printed, the data will be placed on the right edge of the field. You can force the information to be left-justified by placing a minus sign directly after the %. For example, %–10.2f will left-justify a floating-point number with two decimal places in a ten-character field. Here is a program that demonstrates field-width specifiers and left-justification.

```c
#include <stdio.h>
main(void)
{
  printf("|%10.5f|\n", 123.23);
  printf("|%-10.5f|\n", 123.23);
  printf("|%10.5s|\n", "Hello there");
  printf("|%-10.5s|\n", "Hello there");
  return 0;
}
```

This program displays the following output.

```
|   123.23000|
| 123.23000  |
|       Hello|
| Hello      |
```

There are two format specifier modifiers that allow **printf( )** to display **short** and **long** integers. These modifiers can be applied to the **d**, **i**, **o**, **u**, and **x** type specifiers. The **l** modifier tells **printf( )** that a **long** data type follows. For example, **%ld** means that a **long int** is to be displayed. The **h** modifier instructs **printf( )** to display a **short int**. Therefore, **%hu** indicates that the data is of the short unsigned integer type.

The **l** modifier can also prefix the floating point commands **e**, **f**, and **g**. In this context, it indicates that a **double** follows.

scanf( )

C's general-purpose console input routine is **scanf( )**. It can read all the built-in data types and automatically convert numbers into the proper internal format. It is much like the reverse of **printf( )**. The general form of **scanf( )** is:

int scanf(const char *fmt_string,...);

The control string consists of three classifications of characters:

Format specifiers
Whitespace characters
Non-whitespace characters

The **scanf( )** function returns the number of fields that are input. It returns **EOF** (defined in **stdio.h**) if a premature end-of-file is reached.

The input format specifiers are preceded by a % sign. They tell **scanf( )** what type of data is to be read next. For example, **%s** reads a string while **%d** reads an integer. These codes are listed in Table A-2.

A whitespace character in the control string causes **scanf( )** to skip over one or more whitespace characters in the input stream. A whitespace character is either a space, a tab, or a newline. In essence, one whitespace character in the control string will cause **scanf( )** to read, but not store, any number (including zero) of whitespace characters up to the first non-whitespace character.

A non-whitespace character causes **scanf( )** to read and discard a matching character. For example, **"%d,%d"** causes **scanf( )** to first read an integer, then read and discard a comma, and finally read another integer. If the specified character is not found, **scanf( )** will terminate.

All the variables used to receive values through **scanf( )** must be passed by their addresses. This means that all arguments must be pointers to the variables used as arguments. This allows **scanf( )** to alter the contents of an argument. (C does not support the reference parameter.) For example, if you wish to read an integer into the variable **count**, you would use the following **scanf( )** call:

```
scanf("%d", &count);
```

Format Specifier	Meaning
%c	Read a single character
%d	Read a decimal integer
%i	Read a decimal integer
%e	Read a floating point number
%f	Read a floating point number
%g	Read a floating point number
%n	Corresponding argument receives an integer value equal to the number of characters read so far.
%o	Read an octal integer
%p	Read a pointer
%s	Read a string
%u	Read an unsigned integer
%x	Read a hexadecimal integer

The **scanf( )** Format Specifiers

Table A-2.

Strings will be read into character arrays, and the array name, without any index, is the address of the first element in an array. So, to read a string into the character array **address**, you would use

```
char address[80];
scanf("%s", address);
```

In this case, **address** is already a pointer, and need not be preceded by the **&** operator.

The data items read by **scanf( )** must be separated by spaces, tabs, or newlines. Punctuation such as commas, semicolons, and the like do not count as separators. This means that

```
scanf("%d%d", &r, &c);
```

will accept an input of **10 20**, but fail with **10,20**. As in **printf( )**, the **scanf( )** format codes are matched, in order, with the variables receiving input in the argument list.

An ***** placed after the **%** and before the format code will read data of the specified type but will not assign it to any variable. Thus,

```
scanf("%d%*c%d", &x, &y);
```

given the input **10/20** will place the value 10 into **x**, discard the division sign, and give **y** the value 20.

The format specifiers can specify a maximum-field-length modifier. This is an integer number placed between the % and the format-specifier code that limits the number of characters read for any field. For example, if you wish to read no more than 20 characters into **str**, then you would write

```
scanf("%20s", str);
```

If the input stream is greater than 20 characters, then a subsequent call to input begins where this call leaves off. For example, if

ABCDEFGHIJKLMNOPQRSTUVWXYZ

is entered as the response to the **scanf( )** call in this example, then only the first 20 characters, or up to the 'T,' are placed into **str**, because of the maximum-size specifier. This means that the remaining characters, "UVWXYZ" have not yet been used. If another **scanf( )** call is made, such as

```
scanf("%s", str);
```

then the characters "UVWXYZ" are placed into **str**. If a whitespace is encountered, input for a field may terminate before the maximum field length is reached. In this case, **scanf( )** will move on to the next field.

Although spaces, tabs, and newlines are used as field separators, they are read like any other characters when single characters are being read. For example, with an input stream of "x y",

```
scanf("%c%c%c", &a, &b, &c);
```

will return with the character 'x' in **a**, a space in **b**, and the character 'y' in **c**.

Be careful: if you have any other characters in the control string, including spaces, tabs, and newlines, those characters will be used to match and discard characters from the input stream. Any character that matches is discarded. For example, given the input stream **10t20**

```
scanf("%st%s", &x, &y);
```

will place 10 into **x** and 20 into **y**. The 't' is discarded because of the 't' in the control string. For another example,

```
scanf("%s ", name);
```

will *not* return until you type a character *after* you type a whitespace character. This is because the space after the **%s** has instructed **scanf( )** to read and discard spaces, tabs, and newline characters until a non-whitespace character is entered.

Another feature of **scanf( )** is the *scanset*. A scanset defines a list of characters that will be matched by **scanf( )** and stored in a character array variable. The **scanf( )** function inputs characters, putting them into the corresponding character array, as long as they are members of the scanset. When a character is entered that does not match any in the scanset, **scanf( )** null-terminates the corresponding array and moves on to the next (if any) field.

You define a scanset by putting a list of the characters you want to scan for inside square brackets. The beginning square bracket must be prefixed by a percent sign. For example, this scanset tells **scanf( )** to read only the letters X, Y, and Z.

```
%[XYZ]
```

The argument corresponding to the scanset must be a pointer to a character array. Upon return from **scanf( )**, the array will contain a null-terminated string composed of the characters read. For example, the following program uses a scanset to read digits into **s1**. As soon as a non-digit is entered, **s1** is null-terminated, and characters are read into **s2** until the next whitespace character is entered.

```
/* A simple scanset example. */
#include <stdio.h>

main(void)
{
  char s1[80], s2[80];

  printf("Enter numbers, then some letters\n");
  scanf("%[0123456789]%s", s1, s2);
  printf("%s %s", s1, s2);
  return 0;
}
```

You can specify a range inside a scanset using a hyphen. For example, the following scanset tells **scanf( )** to accept the characters A through Z.

```
%[A-Z]
```

You can specify more than one range within a scanset. For example, this program reads digits and then letters.

```
/* A scanset example using ranges. */
#include <stdio.h>

main(void)
{
  char s1[80], s2[80];

  printf("Enter numbers, then some letters\n");
  scanf("%[0-9]%[a-zA-Z]", s1, s2);
  printf("%s %s", s1, s2);
  return 0;
}
```

You can specify an inverted set if the first character in the set is a ^. When the ^ is present, it instructs **scanf( )** to accept any character that *is not* defined by the scanset. The following modification of the preceding example uses the ^ to invert the type of characters the scanset will read.

```
/* A scanset example using inverted ranges. */
#include <stdio.h>
```

```
main(void)
{
  char s1[80], s2[80];

  printf("Enter non-numbers, then some non-letters\n");
  scanf("%[^0-9]%[^a-zA-Z]", s1, s2);
  printf("%s %s", s1, s2);
  return 0;
}
```

One important point to remember is that the scanset is case sensitive. Therefore, if you want scan for both uppercase and lowercase letters, they must be specified individually.

The C File System

While the C file system differs from that used by C++, it largely parallels it. The C file system is composed of several interrelated functions. The most common are listed in Table A-3.

These functions require that the header file **stdio.h** be included in any program in which they are used.

The common thread that ties the C I/O system together is the file pointer. A file pointer is a pointer to information that defines various things about the file, including its name, status, and current position. In essence, the file pointer identifies a specific disk file, and is used by the stream associated with it to tell each of the C I/O functions where to perform operations. A file pointer is a pointer variable of type **FILE**, which is defined in **stdio.h**.

Function	Purpose
fopen( )	Opens a stream
fclose( )	Closes a stream
fputc( )	Writes a character to a stream
fgetc( )	Reads a character from a stream
fseek( )	Seeks to specified byte in a stream
fprintf( )	Is to a stream what printf( ) is to the console
fscanf( )	Is to a stream what scanf( ) is to the console
feof( )	Returns true if end-of-file is reached
ferror( )	Returns true if an error has occurred
rewind( )	Resets the file position indicator to the beginning of the file
remove( )	Erases a file

The Most Common C File System Functions

Table A-3.

A

The remainder of this appendix discusses the basic file functions.

fopen( )

fopen( ) serves three functions:

1. It opens a stream for use
2. It links a file with that stream
3. It returns a **FILE** pointer to that stream

Most often, and for the rest of this discussion, the file is a disk file. The **fopen( )** function has this prototype

FILE *fopen(const char *filename*, const char *mode*);

where *filename* points to the name of the file that is being opened, and *mode* points to a string containing the desired open status. The legal values for *mode* are shown in Table A-4. The filename must be a string of characters which comprise a filename valid in the operating system; it may also include a path specification.

The **fopen( )** function returns a pointer of type **FILE**. This pointer identifies the file, and is used by most other file system functions. It should never be altered by your code.

As Table A-4 shows, a file can be opened in either text mode or binary mode. In text mode, carriage-return/linefeed sequences are translated into newline characters on input. On output, the reverse occurs: newlines are translated into carriage-return/linefeeds. No such translations occur on binary files.

Mode	Meaning
"r"	Open a text file for reading
"w"	Create a text file for writing
"a"	Append to a text file
"rb"	Open a binary file for reading
"wb"	Create a binary file for writing
"ab"	Append to a binary file
"r+"	Open a text file for read/write
"w+"	Create a text file for read/write
"a+"	Open or create a text file for read/write
"r+b"	Open a binary file for read/write
"w+b"	Create a binary file for read/write
"a+b"	Open a binary file for read/write

The Legal
Values for
mode
Table A-4.

If you wished to open a file for writing with the name **test**, then you would write:

```
fp = fopen("test", "w");
```

where **fp** is a variable of type **FILE ***. However, you will usually see it written like this:

```
if((fp = fopen("test", "w"))==NULL) {
  printf("Cannot open file.");
  exit(1);
}
```

This method detects any error in opening a file, such as a write-protected or a full disk, before attempting to write to it. A null, which is 0, is used because no file pointer will ever have that value. **NULL** is a macro defined in **stdio.h**.

If you use **fopen( )** to open a file for output, then any preexisting file by that name will be erased and a new file started. If no file by that name exists, then one will be created. If you want to add to the end of an existing file, then you must use mode "a". (In this case, if the file does not exist it will be created.) Opening a file for read operations requires that the file exists. If it does not, an error will be returned. Finally, if a file is opened for read/write operations it will not be erased if it exists; however, if it does not exist it will be created.

fputc( )

The **fputc( )** function is used to write characters to a stream that was previously opened for writing using the **fopen( )** function. Its prototype is:

```
int fputc(int ch, FILE *fp);
```

Here, *fp* is the file pointer returned by **fopen( )**, and *ch* is the character to be output. The file pointer tells **fputc( )** which disk file to write to. For historical reasons, *ch* is an **int** but only the low-order byte is used.

If an **fputc( )** operation is a success, then it will return the character written. Upon failure an **EOF** is returned.

fgetc( )

The **fgetc( )** function is used to read characters from a stream opened in read mode by **fopen( )**. Its prototype is:

```
int fgetc(FILE *fp);
```

Here, *fp* is a file pointer of type **FILE** returned by **fopen( )**. For historical reasons **fgetc( )** returns an integer, but the high-order byte is 0.

The **fgetc( )** function will return **EOF** when the end of the file has been reached. Therefore, to read a text file until the end-of-file mark is read, you could use the following code:

```
ch = fgetc(fp);

while(ch!=EOF) {
  ch = fgetc(fp);
}
```

feof( )

As stated earlier, the C file system can also operate on binary data. When a file is opened for binary input, it is possible that an integer value equal to **EOF** may be read. This would cause the routine given above to indicate an end-of-file condition even though the physical end of the file had not been reached. To solve this problem, C includes the function **feof( )**, which is used to determine end-of-file when reading binary data. It has this prototype

```
int feof(FILE *fp);
```

where, *fp* identifies the file. The **feof( )** function returns non-zero if the end of the file has been reached; otherwise zero is returned. Therefore, the following routine reads a binary file until end-of-file is encountered.

```
while(!feof(fp)) ch = fgetc(fp);
```

Of course, this same method can be applied to text files, as well.

fclose( )

The **fclose( )** function closes a stream that was opened by a call to **fopen( )**. It writes any data still remaining in the disk buffer to the file and does a formal operating-system-level close on the file. A call to **fclose( )** frees the file control block associated with the stream and makes it available for reuse. As you probably know, there is an operating system limit to the number of open files you can have at any one time, so it may be necessary to close one file before opening another.

The **fclose( )** function has the following prototype:

```
int fclose(FILE *fp);
```

where *fp* is the file pointer returned by the call to **fopen( )**. A return value of
zero signifies a successful close operation; **EOF** is returned if an error occurs.
Generally, the only time **fclose( )** will fail is when a diskette has been
prematurely removed from the drive or if there is no more space on the disk.

Using fopen( ), fgetc( ), fputc( ) and fclose( )

The functions **fopen( )**, **fget( )**, **fputc( )**, and **fclose( )** comprise a
minimal set of file routines. The following program demonstrates these
functions by using them to copy a file. Notice that the files are opened in
binary mode, and that **feof( )** is used to check for end of file.

```c
/* This program will copy one file to another. */
#include <stdio.h>

main(int argc, char *argv[])
{
  FILE *in, *out;
  char ch;

  if(argc!=3) {
    printf("You forgot to enter a filename\n");
    return 1;
  }

  if((in=fopen(argv[1], "rb")) == NULL) {
    printf("Cannot open source file.\n");
    return 1;
  }
  if((out=fopen(argv[2], "wb")) == NULL) {
    printf("Cannot open destination file.\n");
    return 1;
  }

  /* This code actually copies the file. */
  while(!feof(in)) {
    ch = fgetc(in);
    if(!feof(in)) fputc(ch, out);
  }

  fclose(in);
  fclose(out);
  return 0;
}
```

ferror( ) and rewind( )

The **ferror( )** function is used to determine if a file operation has produced an error. It has this prototype

    int ferror(FILE *fp)

where *fp* is a valid file pointer. **ferror( )** returns true if an error has occurred during the last file operation; it returns false otherwise. Because each file operation sets the error condition, **ferror( )** should be called immediately after each file operation; otherwise an error may be lost.

The **rewind( )** function will reset the file position indicator to the beginning of the file specified as its argument. The prototype is

    void rewind(FILE *fp)

where *fp* is a valid file pointer.

fread( ) and fwrite( )

The C file system provides two functions, **fread( )** and **fwrite( )**, that allow the reading and writing of blocks of data. These functions are similar to C++'s **read( )** and **write( )** functions. Their prototypes are

    size_t fread(void *buffer, size_t num_bytes,
            size_t count, FILE *fp)

    size_t fwrite(const void *buffer, size_t num_bytes,
            size_t count, FILE *fp);

In the case of **fread( )**, *buffer* is a pointer to a region of memory that will receive the data read from the file. The function reads *count* number of objects, each object being *num_bytes* in length, from the stream pointed to by *fp*. **fread( )** returns the number of objects read, which may be less than *count* if an error or the end of the file is encountered.

For **fwrite( )**, *buffer* is a pointer to the information that will be written to the file. The function writes *count* number of objects, each object being *num_bytes* in length, to the stream pointed to by *fp*. **fwrite( )** returns the number of objects written, which will be equal to *count* unless an error occurs.

As long as the file has been opened for binary data, **fread( )** and **fwrite( )** can read and write any type of information. For example, this program writes a **float** to a disk file.

```
/* Write a floating point number to a disk file. */
#include <stdio.h>

main(void)
{
  FILE *fp;
  float f=12.23;

  if((fp=fopen("test","wb"))==NULL) {
    printf("Cannot open file.\n");
    return 1;
  }

  fwrite(&f, sizeof(float), 1, fp);

  fclose(fp);
  return 0;
}
```

As this program illustrates, the buffer can be, and often is, simply a variable.

One of the most useful applications of **fread( )** and **fwrite( )** involves the reading and writing of arrays or structures. For example, the following fragment writes the contents of the floating point array **balance** to the file "balance" using a single **fwrite( )** statement. Next, it reads the array, using a single **fread( )** statement, and displays its contents.

```
#include <stdio.h>

main(void)
{
  register int i;
  FILE *fp;
  float balance[100];

  /* open for write */
  if((fp=fopen("balance","w"))==NULL) {
    printf("Cannot open file.\n");
    return 1;
  }

  for(i=0; i<100; i++) balance[i] = (float) i;

  /* This saves the entire balance array in one step. */
  fwrite(balance, sizeof balance, 1, fp);
  fclose(fp);
```

```
    /* zero array */
    for(i=0; i<100; i++) balance[i] = 0.0;

    /* open for read */
    if((fp=fopen("balance","r"))==NULL) {
      printf("Cannot open file.\n");
      return 1;
    }

    /* This reads the entire balance array in one step. */
    fread(balance, sizeof balance, 1, fp);

    /* display contents of array */
    for(i=0; i<100; i++) printf("%f ", balance[i]);

    fclose(fp);
    return 0;
}
```

Using **fread( )** and **fwrite( )** to read or write complex data is more efficient than using repeated calls to **getc( )** and **putc( )**.

fseek( ) and Random-Access I/O

You can perform random read and write operations using the C I/O system with the help of **fseek( )**, which sets the file position indicator. Its prototype is

   int fseek(FILE *fp, long numbytes, int origin);

where fp is a file pointer returned by a call to **fopen( )**; numbytes is the number of bytes from origin to seek to, and origin is one of the following macros (defined in **stdio.h**):

Origin	Macro name
Beginning of file	SEEK_SET
Current position	SEEK_CUR
End of file	SEEK_END

Therefore, to seek numbytes from the start of the file, origin should be **SEEK_SET**. To seek from the current position use **SEEK_CUR**, and from the end of the file use **SEEK_END**.

The **fseek( )** function returns zero on success, and non-zero if a failure occurs.

The use of **fseek( )** on text files is not recommended, because the character translations will cause position errors to result. Therefore, its use is suggested only for binary files. For example, if you wanted to read the 234th byte in a file called **test**, you could use the following code:

```
func1(void)
{
  FILE *fp;

  if((fp=fopen("test", "rb")) == NULL) {
    printf("cannot open file\n");
    exit(1);
  }

  fseek(fp, 234L, SEEK_SET);
  return getc(fp);    /* read one character */
                      /* at 234th position */

  }
}
```

A return value of zero means that **fseek( )** succeeded. A non-zero value indicates failure.

fprintf( ) and fscanf( )

In addition to the basic I/O functions discussed above, the C I/O system includes **fprintf( )** and **fscanf( )**. These functions behave exactly like **printf( )** and **scanf( )** except that they operate on files. For this reason, these functions are commonly found in C programs. The prototypes of **fprintf( )** and **fscanf( )** are

   int fprintf(FILE *fp, const char *fmt_string, ...);

   int fscanf(FILE *fp, const char *fmt_string, ...);

where *fp* is a file pointer returned by a call to **fopen( )**. Except for directing their focus to the file defined by *fp*, they operate exactly like **printf( )** and **scanf( )**, respectively.

Erasing Files

The **remove( )** function erases the specified file. Its prototype is:

   int remove(const char *filename);

It returns zero upon success, and non-zero if it fails.

INDEX

B

C

J

K

L

M

N

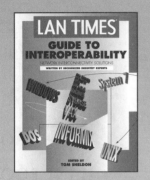

The NEW CLASSICS

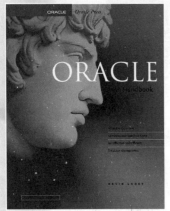

ORACLE DBA HANDBOOK

by Kevin Loney

Every DBA can learn to manage a networked Oracle database efficiently and effectively with this comprehensive guide.

Price: $34.95 U.S.A.
Available Now
ISBN: 0-07-881182-1
Pages: 704, paperback

TUNING ORACLE

by Michael J. Corey, Michael Abbey and Daniel J. Dechichio, Jr.

Learn to customize Oracle for optimal performance and productivity with this focused guide.

Price: $29.95 U.S.A.
Available Now
ISBN: 0-07-881181-3
Pages: 336, paperback

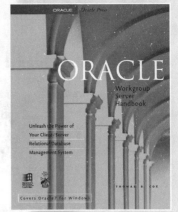

ORACLE WORKGROUP SERVER HANDBOOK

by Thomas B. Cox

Take full advantage of the power and flexibility of the new Oracle Workgroup Server and Oracle7 for Windows with this comprehensive handbook.

Covers Oracle7 for Windows

Price: $27.95 U.S.A.
Available Now
ISBN: 0-07-881186-4
Pages: 320, paperback

ORACLE: A BEGINNER'S GUIDE

by Michael Abbey and Michael J. Corey

For easy-to-understand, comprehensive information about Oracle RDBMS products, this is the one book every user needs.

Price: $29.95 U.S.A.
Available Now
ISBN: 0-07-882122-3
Pages: 560, paperback

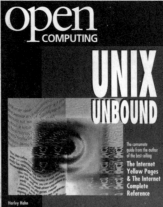

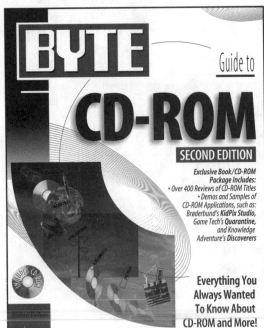

ORDER BOOKS DIRECTLY FROM OSBORNE/McGRAW-HILL

For a complete catalog of Osborne's books, call 510-549-6600 or write to us at 2600 Tenth Street, Berkeley, CA 94710

☎ Call Toll-Free: 1-800-822-8158
24 hours a day, 7 days a week in U.S. and Canada

✉ Mail this order form to:
McGraw-Hill, Inc.
Customer Service Dept.
P.O. Box 547
Blacklick, OH 43004

Fax this order form to:
1-614-759-3644

EMAIL
7007.1531@COMPUSERVE.COM
COMPUSERVE GO MH

Ship to:

Name _____

Company _____

Address _____

City / State / Zip _____

Daytime Telephone: _____
(We'll contact you if there's a question about your order.)

ISBN #	BOOK TITLE	Quantity	Price	Total
0-07-88				
0-07-88				
0-07-88				
0-07-88				
0-07-88				
0-07088				
0-07-88				
0-07-88				
0-07-88				
0-07-88				
0-07-88				
0-07-88				
0-07-88				
0-07-88				

	Shipping & Handling Charge from Chart Below	
	Subtotal	
	Please Add Applicable State & Local Sales Tax	
	TOTAL	

Shipping & Handling Charges

Order Amount	U.S.	Outside U.S.
Less than $15	$3.50	$5.50
$15.00 - $24.99	$4.00	$6.00
$25.00 - $49.99	$5.00	$7.00
$50.00 - $74.99	$6.00	$8.00
$75.00 - and up	$7.00	$9.00

Occasionally we allow other selected companies to use our mailing list. If you would prefer that we not include you in these extra mailings, please check here: ☐

METHOD OF PAYMENT

☐ Check or money order enclosed (payable to Osborne/McGraw-Hill)

☐ AMERICAN EXPRESS   ☐ DISCOVER   ☐ MasterCard   ☐ VISA

Account No. [ ][ ][ ][ ][ ][ ][ ][ ][ ][ ][ ][ ][ ][ ][ ][ ]

Expiration Date _____

Signature _____

In a hurry? Call 1-800-822-8158 anytime, day or night, or visit your local bookstore.

Thank you for your order

Code BC640SL

About the Author...

Herbert Schildt is the world's leading C/C++
author. His programming books have sold more
than one-and-a-half million copies worldwide
and have been translated into all major foreign
languages. He is author of the best-sellers,
Teach Yourself C and **Teach Yourself C++**.
He has also written **The Annotated ANSI C
Standard**, **C: The Complete Reference**,
C++: The Complete Reference, and
numerous other books on C and C++. Schildt
is the president of Universal Computing
Laboratories, a software consulting firm in
Mahomet, Illinois. He holds a master's degree
in computer science from the University of
Illinois.

C++ from the
Ground Up